MECI

MECHANICAL MOVEMENTS

A TREATISE ON DIFFERENT TYPES
OF MECHANISMS AND VARIOUS
METHODS OF TRANSMITTING, CON-
TROLLING AND MODIFYING MOTION,
TO SECURE CHANGES OF VELOCITY,
DIRECTION, AND DURATION OR TIME
OF ACTION

BY

FRANKLIN D. JONES

ASSOCIATE EDITOR OF MACHINERY
AUTHOR OF "TURNING AND BORING," "PLANING AND MILLING,"
"GAGING TOOLS AND METHODS," ETC.

FIRST EDITION

NEW YORK
THE INDUSTRIAL PRESS
LONDON: THE MACHINERY PUBLISHING CO., LTD.
1919

COPYRIGHT, 1918,
BY
THE INDUSTRIAL PRESS
NEW YORK

COMPOSITION AND ELECTROTYPING BY F. H. GILSON COMPANY, BOSTON, U. S. A.

This scarce antiquarian book is included in our special *Legacy Reprint Series*. In the interest of creating a more extensive selection of rare historical book reprints, we have chosen to reproduce this title even though it may possibly have occasional imperfections such as missing and blurred pages, missing text, poor pictures, markings, dark backgrounds and other reproduction issues beyond our control. Because this work is culturally important, we have made it available as a part of our commitment to protecting, preserving and promoting the world's literature. Thank you for your understanding.

MECHANISMS
AND
MECHANICAL MOVEMENTS

PREFACE

THIS treatise on mechanisms and mechanical movements is intended for designers of machinery and for all interested in originating new mechanical devices or in developing and perfecting those now in use. In view of the fact that there is an almost endless variety of mechanisms, it might seem impracticable to deal with such a broad subject in a single volume of this size. As the classes of mechanisms, however, which differ radically in principle, are few in comparison with those which simply vary in form, it was considered not only practicable, but very desirable, to present in one volume a variety of mechanical devices representing different types of mechanisms and selected especially to illustrate important fundamental principles.

The designers of machines or mechanisms in general are constantly engaged in the solution of problems pertaining to motion and its transmission. The motion derived from some source of power must be modified to produce certain effects, and various changes in regard to velocity, direction, and time of action may be necessary. Frequently, the same result may be obtained by forms of mechanisms which differ entirely in principle and effectiveness, and it is essential to employ an approved method. The purpose of this treatise is not only to explain how various mechanical motions may be produced and controlled, but to show the relation between the theoretical and practical sides of the subject. The examples include many ingenious mechanical combinations and are practical designs which not only illustrate the principles involved, but indicate exactly how those principles are applied. An understanding of these concrete examples will prove much more beneficial than a study of abstract theories, which only give an inadequate conception of their application in the design of mechanisms of various types.

Many technical graduates and draftsmen understand the proportioning of parts to safely withstand certain stresses more thoroughly than they do the use of different combinations of parts either for transmitting, reversing, or otherwise modifying motion to secure whatever action or effect may be required. Frequently, the stress involved or the strength of the parts is of little importance, and the principal problem is one pertaining to motion, especially in the development of new forms of mechanisms. While a general knowledge of mechanisms and their possibilities could be obtained by studying miscellaneous designs, this would involve considerable duplication of effort, because so many mechanical devices which vary as to form and purpose are identical in principle. The different forms of mechanisms described in this volume represent many distinct types, and they have been classified and arranged so that various modifications of the same general type may readily be compared.

The columns of MACHINERY were of valuable assistance in supplying information and illustrations regarding various types of mechanisms, especially of the classes common to the machine-building and machine-tool fields. Special mention should be made of the excellent examples of mechanisms obtained from the contributions of G. W. Armstrong and G. M. Meyncke. The study of mechanical movements is of especial importance at the present time, owing to the increasing use of automatic machines in almost every branch of manufacture, and this treatise is published in the belief that it will be of practical value to many designers, draftsmen, mechanical engineers, and inventors engaged in originating and planning new developments.

THE AUTHOR.

NEW YORK, *January*, 1918.

CONTENTS

Chapter I

MOTIONS AND GENERAL METHODS OF TRANSMISSION IN MACHINES

PAGES

Classes of Motion — Velocity and Acceleration — Velocity Ratio — Angular Velocity — Link Mechanisms — Universal Joint — Straight-line Motions — Toggle Joint — Pantograph Mechanisms — Transmission by Frictional and Toothed Gearing — Transmission by Flexible Bands, Ropes, and Chains — Trains of Mechanism — Analyzing Action of Epicyclic Gearing.   1–38

Chapter II

SPEED-CHANGING AND CONTROLLING MECHANISMS

Types of Mechanical Speed-changing Mechanisms — Arrangement of Cone-pulley Drives — Combination of Cone-pulley and Gearing — Geared Speed-changing Mechanisms — Frictional Speed-changing Devices — Multiple-disk Type of Speed-changing Mechanism — Friction Disk and Epicyclic Gear Combination — Governors of Centrifugal and Inertia Types.. 39–59

Chapter III

CONVERSION OF ROTARY AND RECTILINEAR MOTIONS

Crank and Connecting-rod — Relative Motions of Crank-pin and Cross-head — the Eccentric — the Crank and Slotted Cross-head or Scotch Yoke — Cylinders which Revolve about a Stationary Crank — Cylinders which Revolve within an Eccentric Track — Rack and Gear Combination — Methods of

Doubling Stroke — Single- and Double-stroke Toggle Mechanisms — Press-bed Motions for Flat or Cylinder Presses — the Napier Motion — Reciprocating Motion from Epicyclic Gearing.. 60–96

CHAPTER IV

REVERSING MECHANISMS

Intermediate Spur Gears for Reversing Motion — Bevel Gear Type of Reversing Mechanism — Reversal of Motion with Friction Disks — Operation of Reversing Clutches — Controlling Point of Reversal by Special or Auxiliary Mechanism — Planer Reversing Mechanism — Reversal of Motion through Epicyclic Gearing — Automatic Ratchet Reversing Mechanism — Automatic Control of Spindle Reversal — Automatic Variation in Point of Reversal — Reversal of Motion after Predetermined Number of Revolutions........ 97–123

CHAPTER V

QUICK-RETURN MOTIONS

Quick-return Motion from Crank and Oscillating Link — Whitworth Quick-return Motion — Modification of Whitworth Motion — Quick-return Motion from Elliptical Gearing — Eccentric Pinion and Elliptical Gearing for Quick-return Motion.. 124–133

CHAPTER VI

INTERMITTENT MOVEMENTS

Ratchet Gearing — Ratchet Mechanisms for Releasing Sprockets — Automatic Disengagement of Ratchet Gearing — Escapements — Automatic Reduction of Intermittent Movement — Gearing for Uniform and Variable Intermittent Motion — High-speed Intermittent Gearing of Moving Picture Projector — the Geneva Type of Intermittent Gearing — Intermittent Gears for Shafts at Right Angles — Adjustable Intermittent Motion — Automatic Variation of Intermittent Motion — Automatic Indexing Mechanism — Action of an Adding Mechanism.. 134–183

CONTENTS

Chapter VII

IRREGULAR MOTIONS

Plate Cams — Positive Motion Cams — Return Cam for Follower to Secure Positive Motion — Yoke Type of Cam Follower — Inverse Cams — Wiper and Involute Cams — Cylinder or Barrel Cam — Automatic Variation of Cam Motion — Varying Dwell of Cam Follower — Automatic Variation of Cam Rise and Drop — Sectional Interchangeable Cams for Varying Motion — Mechanism for Engaging Cams in a Group Successively — Obtaining Resultant Motion of Several Cams — Double-shifting Cam..........................184-201

Chapter VIII

DIFFERENTIAL MOTIONS

Differential Screw — Chinese Windlass — Differential Motions from Epicyclic Gearing — Compound Differential Gears for Varying Speeds — Differential Motion between Revolving Screw and Nut — Differential Feeding Mechanism for Revolving Spindle — Application of Floating Lever Principle — Controlling Mechanisms for Steam Steering Gears — Substitute for Floating Lever — Differential Governors for Water Turbines — Differential Gearing of Automobiles — Speed Regulation through Differential Gearing — Differential Action through a Cam-controlled Gear — Differential Mechanism of a Gear-cutting Machine — Differential Hoisting Mechanism — Differential Speed Indicator...............202-229

Chapter IX

CLUTCHES AND TRIPPING MECHANISMS

Controlling Motion by Means of Clutches — Positive and Friction Clutches — Multiple-disk Friction Clutches — Rapid-acting Multiple-disk Clutch equipped with Brake — Magnetic and Induction Clutches — Clutches that Automatically Disengage — Automatic Tripping Mechanisms for Stopping a Machine or some Moving Part — Breakable Pins to Prevent Overload — Automatic Clutch Control to Prevent Overload —

Pressure of Frictional Gearing varied according to Load — Automatic Relief Mechanisms for Forging Machines — Automatic Speed-limiting Devices — Electromagnetic Tripping Devices..230–280

Chapter X

AUTOMATIC FEEDING MECHANISMS

Automatic Feeding Attachments having Inclined Chutes — Attachment for Automatically Feeding Pinion Staffs — Magazine Attachment for Narrow Bushings — Revolving Magazine Attachment — Hopper Feeding Mechanism for Screw Blanks — Simple Arrangement for Feeding Shells with Closed Ends Foremost — Feeding Bullets with Pointed Ends Foremost — Feeding Shells Successively and in any Position — Feeding Shells Successively and Gaging the Diameters..............281–297

MECHANISMS AND MECHANICAL MOVEMENTS

CHAPTER I

MOTIONS AND GENERAL METHODS OF TRANSMISSION IN MACHINES

MACHINES of various classes are designed to modify energy and adapt it to useful work. The energy is derived from some natural source and is transmitted through the members composing the mechanical device to the place where work is to be performed. The construction of any machine or mechanism involves, first, a combination of parts which will produce the necessary motion, and, second, the formation and proportioning of these parts so that the required amount of energy may be transmitted. In the design of any machine, then, there are two distinct branches of work. One branch pertains to motion and the other to the magnitude of the forces involved and the mechanical means for transmitting them without breakage or excessive distortion of the different machine members. Evidently, the means for obtaining the right kind of motion and of modifying it to suit specific purposes may be studied without considering the forces which are to act upon the machine parts or the proportioning of these parts with reference to stresses, etc. This volume deals principally with various well-known mechanical movements and contains illustrated descriptions of mechanisms which have been applied to many different types of machinery.

Classes of Motion. — When motion of a machine part does not vary in direction, it is said to be *continuous;* when the direction of motion reverses, it is *reciprocating*, and when there are periods of rest, it is *intermittent*. A body in motion may be free or constrained. The motion is said to be free when the body may move in any direction in accordance with the forces acting upon it, whereas the term *constrained motion* means that the direction of movement is confined to a restricted path. The planets in their flight through space are examples of free motion, the path or orbit of a planet being determined by the resultant of all the forces acting upon it. The moving parts of every machine represent examples of constrained motion. For instance, the cross-head of an engine is constrained and caused to move in a straight path by a guide or guides. Owing to the angular positions of the connecting-rod, the cross-head is subjected to thrusts which would cause it to move laterally were it not for the straight guiding surfaces that are strong enough to resist the opposing force. A shaft which revolves in fixed bearings is another simple example of constrained motion. The characteristic feature of constrained motion is that all points in a body having such motion follow definite paths when the action of any force produces motion. In ordinary machine construction, the forces tending to move a constrained part from the desired path are not absolutely counteracted, because the fixed members are deformed somewhat under stress; the degree of such deflection may readily be reduced to practicable limits, as it depends upon the dimensions, form, and physical characteristics of the parts which oppose the stresses.

Plane Motion. — Practically all of the movable parts of machines have either a plane motion, a helical motion, or a spherical motion. A body has a plane motion when all points in that body move in parallel planes. Nearly all movable machine parts have plane motion. For instance, any point in the rim of a flywheel, as at a (diagram A, Fig. 1), moves in a plane xx perpendicular to the axis of rotation, and any other point, as at b, moves in a plane yy parallel to xx. A part which moves along a straight path also has plane motion. The piston, piston-rod, or cross-head of a steam engine are simple examples. Referring to diagram B, Fig. 1, it will be seen that all points, as at c and d, move in parallel straight lines. Plane motion may be either rotation, translation, or a combination of these movements. When all points of a body move in concentric circles about a fixed axis or at constant distances from a line perpendicular to the planes in which the various points move, the body has a plane motion of rotation, as illustrated by diagram *A*, Fig. 1. Revolving pulleys, shafts, gears, cranks, etc., all have a plane motion of rotation; the motion may be either continuous or intermittent. When all points move with equal velocities along parallel paths, the motion is known as *rectilinear translation*. The piston or cross-head of an engine, the carriage of a lathe, and the table of a planer are all examples of this motion. The side rod of a locomotive represents an example of *cur-*

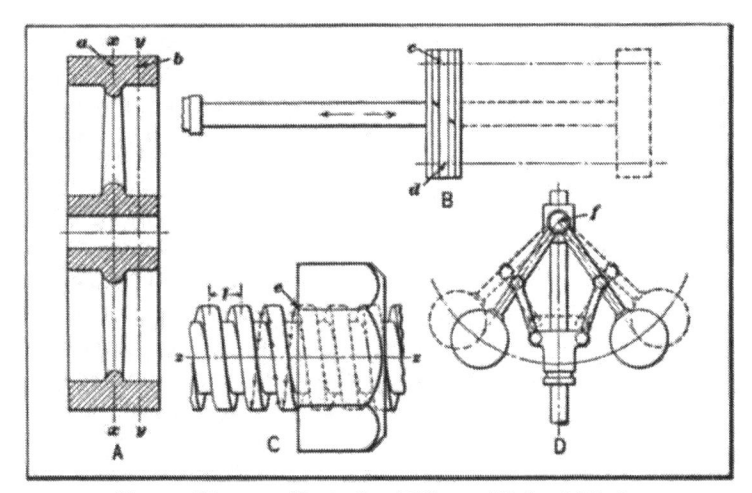

Fig. 1. Diagrams illustrating Different Kinds of Motion

vilinear translation, as various points in the body of the rod follow curved paths which lie in parallel planes. The word "translation," when used alone, is generally understood to mean rectilinear translation. In plane motion, the motion of any two points of a body determine the motion of the entire body. For instance, if the motions of any two points of a connecting-rod are known for any period, the motion of the entire rod for the period is also known.

Helical Motion. — When all points in a body have a motion of rotation about a fixed axis, combined with a translation parallel to the axis, this is known as "helical motion." The movement of a nut along a screw is a common example of helical motion. As a nut is screwed onto a bolt, any point, as at e (see diagram C, Fig. 1), moves around the axis zz and at the same time advances, thus following a helical path, as indicated by the arrows. The relation between the rotation about axis zz and the translation parallel to this axis is constant in nearly all applications of helical motion to machines; the lead l or pitch of the helix, which corresponds to the translation for one complete rotation, is constant in a regular helical motion.

Spherical Motion. — When all points in a body move in the surfaces of imaginary spheres and at constant distances from a fixed point or common center, the motion is "spherical." There are comparatively few examples of spherical motion in machine construction. The "fly-ball" steam engine governor, illustrated by diagram D, Fig. 1, is an example of spherical motion. Variations in the speed of the engine cause the balls to swing about the fixed point or center f as they revolve, so that the movements coincide with a spherical surface. The ball-and-socket joint is another illustration of spherical motion.

Velocity and Acceleration. — Velocity is the rate at which a moving part changes its position, and numerically it represents the units of distance traversed in a unit of time. Thus the rate of motion or the distance traversed divided by the time required may be expressed in feet per second or minute, miles per hour, etc. When the distance traversed by a point along its path in a given time is expressed in linear measure, the rate of motion is referred to as *linear velocity*.

When velocity is variable, the rate at which it changes is known as *acceleration*. If the speed of a wheel having a peripheral velocity of 20 feet per second is increased to 30 feet per second, within a period of two seconds, the acceleration will be 5 feet per second. If the change of velocity were at a uniform rate, the acceleration would be constant, but, if the change of velocity were not uniform, the mean acceleration in the preceding example would be 5 feet per second; however, this does not necessarily represent the actual rate of increase during any one second. In the design of various classes of machines, the problem may relate either to actual velocity, the rate of change or acceleration, or to the ratio of the velocities of different parts.

Velocity Ratio. — The term "velocity ratio" relates to the comparative velocities of driving and driven members. For instance, if two gear wheels are so proportioned that one rotates twice as fast as the other, the velocity ratio would be either 2 or ½, depending upon whether the gear having the higher speed were mentioned first. If the driving gear had a velocity of 50 revolutions per minute and the driven gear 25 revolutions per minute, the velocity ratio of the driving to the driven gear would equal $\frac{50}{25} = 2$. The actual velocity of these gears might be changed, but the velocity ratio would be the same. Thus, if the speed of the driving gear were doubled, the driven gear would also rotate twice as fast and the ratio would still be 2 or 2 to 1, as commonly expressed. The velocity ratio is of especial importance in the design of various classes of mechanisms, owing to the necessity of obtaining the proper relative motions between movable parts.

Angular Velocity. — The angular velocity of a rotating body is equivalent to the angle through which any radius of the body turns in one second, and it is generally expressed in radians. The angular velocity in radians is equal to the linear velocity in feet per second, divided by the radius in feet, of the point on the revolving body, the angular velocity of which is required. If D equals the velocity of a point on the periphery of a body in feet per second, and R equals the radius of the revolving body in feet, then the angular velocity in radians equals $\frac{D}{R}$. For instance, if a flywheel 12 feet in diameter revolves at 60 revolutions per minute, the angular velocity will equal $\frac{2 \times 3.1416 \times 60}{60}$ = 6.2832 radians. A radian is the angle subtended by an arc equal to the radius of the circle forming the path of the point in motion. One radian equals $\frac{180}{3.1416}$ = 57.296 degrees.

Cycle of Motions. — Machines and mechanisms of practically all classes have moving parts which, after passing through a series of motions, all occupy the same relative positions as at the beginning of the movements. The completion of the entire series of movements constitutes a *cycle*. The cycle of a planer or shaper corresponds to a forward and return stroke; in the case of a steam engine, one revolution of the crank represents a cycle. While gas and gasoline engines are commonly classified as two-cycle and four-cycle, this use of the word "cycle" is erroneous. The terms "two-stroke cycle" and "four-stroke cycle" are preferable and accurate, since two strokes complete a single cycle in one case and four strokes, a single cycle in the other. The *period* of a cycle is the time elapsing while the motions constituting the cycle take place.

Positive Driving. — Motion is said to be transmitted *positively* when the mechanical construction is such that the velocity ratio of a driving and driven member remains constant. If two cylindrical parts having parallel axes are in contact, one can only transmit motion to the other through frictional resistance at the line of contact. With this arrangement, the resistance against which motion could be transmitted would depend upon the amount of friction, and there would be no positive assurance that slippage between the driver and follower would not occur. If it were possible to produce surfaces that were perfectly smooth, a very small resistance would prevent the driver and follower from rotating in unison. If instead of smooth cylinders, however, teeth were provided, as in gearing, the drive would be positive or compulsory, because slipping could not occur unless the teeth were broken. A positive drive has been defined as one so arranged that there is an increasing contact radius of the driver, although this is not invariably the case. When the operation of a mechanism depends upon the action of a spring or a weight (gravity), it is a non-positive or force-closed mechanism, and is generally considered inferior, mechanically, to the positive type, although, in many cases, the non-positive method of transmitting motion is entirely satisfactory and comparatively inexpensive.

General Methods of Transmitting Motion. — The method of transmitting motion from one movable member of a machine or mechanism to another part or combination of parts depends upon the motion of the driving member and the kind of motion required for the driven member, the relation of one part to the other as to the distance and position, the amount of energy or power to be transmitted, and other factors. Ordinarily, motion is transmitted by an actual contact of parts forming the mechanism, although this is not invariably the case, as the transmission may be electrical and not mechanical or by physical connection. The general methods of transmitting motion from one part to another, which are commonly employed in different kinds of mechanisms, will first be illustrated by simple diagrams which merely show the principles involved. These diagrams represent methods of transmitting motion from some form of driving member or "driver" to a driven member or follower. The practical application of these principles to various designs in actual use will be considered in chapters to follow.

Direct Transmission by Shafting. — A plain shaft which is used as a connecting link between the shaft of one machine or mechanism and the shaft of another represents an efficient method of transmission, although, in this case, the shafting rotates as a unit, and, therefore, it is not possible by this direct form of transmission to change the velocity ratio of the driving and driven members, as it is merely a rigid shaft and not a form of transmission which, by varying the proportions or design, will give a different relation between the speed of the driver and follower. While the flexible shaft is also used extensively to transmit motion, especially when the driven part must have a free or universal movement, the driving shaft and follower also rotate as a unit, and this method of transmission does not afford means of changing the velocity ratio, as may be done with the different forms of transmission to be described.

Link Mechanisms. — A link is a rigid body for connecting parts of a mechanism, and it may be used for holding or guiding some other member or combination of parts, or for transmitting motion. There are many parts of machines which belong to the general class of links but which have special names. For instance, when a link has an oscillating movement about some axis or fulcrum, the names *lever* and *rocker* are commonly applied, whereas, if the link makes complete revolutions, it may be classified as a *crank*. When a link is used to transmit motion from a rotating crank to a part having a reciprocating movement, it is usually called a *connecting-rod* or *pitman*. On a steam engine, the connecting-rod joins the cross-head with the crank on the main shaft. The motion of the eccentric is transmitted to the valve by the *eccentric rod*, which is another example of the special names applied to links. If a slotted member is used to connect the ends of forward- and reverse-motion eccentric rods, this is known as a "link," as in the case of the well-known Stephenson link motion for steam engines.

Applications of Levers. — Levers, as applied to different kinds of mechanisms, are commonly used to transmit motion from one line or plane to another, and for guiding movable parts, as, for example, the end of a rod having a reciprocating motion. Levers which have an oscillating movement about a pin or fulcrum may have parallel lines of motion, or lines of motion which intersect. Diagram *A*, Fig. 2, shows a lever which transmits motion from one line *aa* to another parallel line *bb*. As the lever oscillates about pin *c*, the pins by which the two rods are connected to the lever have a circular motion, as indicated by the arcs. A line *aa* or *bb*, representing the general direction of the motion, is called the *center-line of motion*. In the case of a steam engine of the reciprocating type, the center-line of motion is a line passing through the center of the cylinder and the center of the crankshaft. When the engine is running, the connecting-rod oscillates an equal distance each side of this center-line of motion.

Diagram *B* shows a lever having lines of motion *aa* and *bb*, which are not parallel. When the lines of motion intersect, as in this case, the lever is known as a *bellcrank lever*. A lever for reversing the direction of motion is shown at *C*, the fulcrum, in this case, being between the driving and driven connecting links; thus, when one rod moves to the right, the other rod moves to the left, and *vice versa*. A lever for reversing the

TRANSMISSION OF MOTION 9

motion and changing its direction is shown at *D*. The form of lever shown at *E* is used for transmitting motion from one line to another that is not in the same plane. Such a lever or " rocker arm," as it is called, is used on locomotives equipped with the Stephenson link motion to transmit motion from the eccentric rods inside the frame to the valve rod on the outside. Diagram *F* illustrates one of the many ways in which levers may be ap-

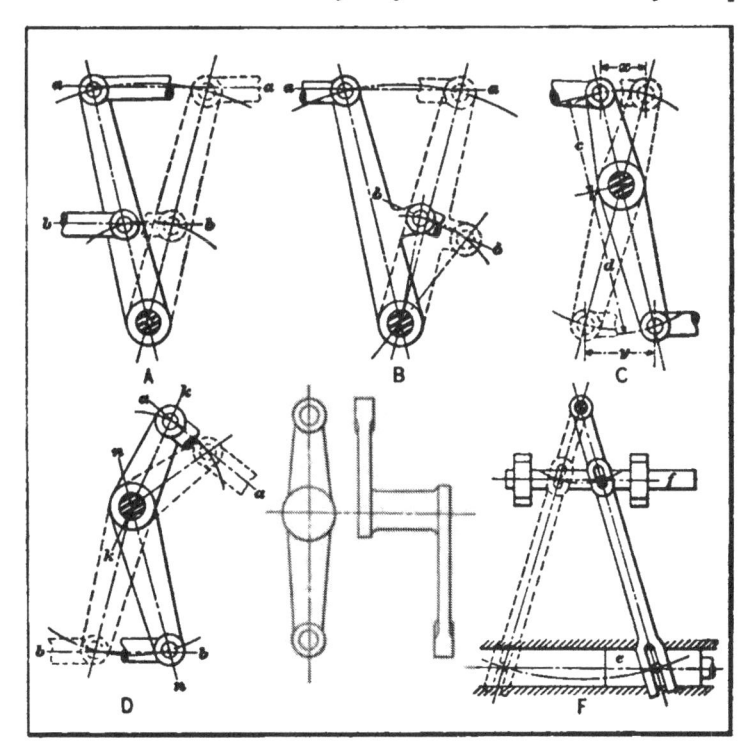

Fig. 2. Various Applications of Levers

plied to obtain different results. In this case, the lever transmits the motion of part *e* to *f* on a reduced scale. These two parts are mounted in guides and move in straight parallel lines, and the lever has elongated slots in which the pins slide. This arrangement is shown as a reducing motion, and is sometimes applied to steam engines when taking indicator cards. The part *e* represents the cross-head and *f* a sliding bar which is connected by a cord to the indicator drum, the motion of which must correspond to that of the cross-head, but on a reduced scale. Levers may be arranged in other ways for reducing motion. The lever method of reducing motion, however, has been replaced quite extensively by more compact and accurate forms of mechanisms, such as the "reducing wheel." Motion is transmitted from the cross-head to the indicator by cords that wind about drums which vary in diameter and give the required reduction of motion.

Position of Levers Relative to Lines of Motion. — In the design of levers, there are certain points that should be observed:

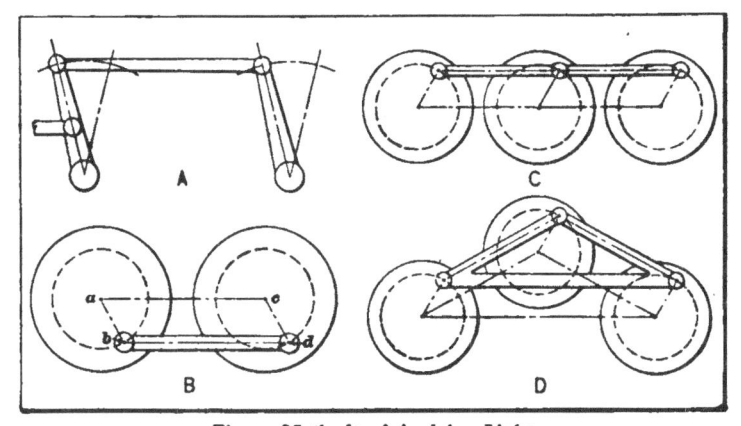

Fig. 3. Methods of Applying Links

First, a line passing through the center of the fulcrum and the center of the connecting pin should be at right angles to the center-line of motion when the lever or lever arm is in its central position. For instance, when center-line *kk* (see diagram *D*, Fig. 2) is in mid-position, it should be perpendicular to the center-line of motion *aa* so that the upper lever arm will move an equal distance each way from this central position. Similarly, line *nn* should be perpendicular to *bb* when the lower lever arm is in mid-position.

A second point of importance is to so locate the connecting pin that its center moves an equal distance each side of the center-line of motion; that is, the center of this pin should be as far from the center-line of motion when at the end of its movement as when in mid-position. The third point to consider is the relative lengths of the lever arms or the distance from the fulcrum to each connecting pin. The lengths of these arms must be proportional to the extent of their motion. For instance, the horizontal distance x (see diagram C) traversed by the upper connecting pin for a given movement y depends upon the relative lengths of arms c and d; thus $x : c :: y : d$, or, if $c = 6$ inches, $d = 12$ inches, and $y = 5$ inches, $x = \dfrac{6 \times 5}{12} = 2.5$ inches.

Link Connection between Oscillating or Rotating Parts. — A rigid link may be used to transmit motion from one oscillating or rotating part to another. Diagram A, Fig. 3, illustrates how two oscillating levers are connected by a link which simply ties both levers together. The driving wheels of a locomotive are connected by side rods or links, as shown at B, so that the wheels rotate in unison. With a transmission of this kind, dimensions ab and cd must be equal and also ac and bd so that the four center-lines form a parallelogram. This method of transmitting motion may also be employed for a series of rotating parts. At C, three wheels are shown connected, and at D, three wheels which are not arranged in a straight line. In the latter case, the link is of triangular form and its bearings must be spaced to correspond with the distance between the fixed centers. When the axes of the driver and follower are not parallel, links may also be used to transmit motion, although such an arrangement is not common except in universal joints.

Universal Joint or Hooke's Coupling. — A form of link work for transmitting motion between two shafts which are at an angle to each other is shown at A, Fig. 4. This is known as a *universal joint* or *Hooke's coupling*. The axes of each shaft are in the same plane and, with the design of joint shown, they have forked ends which are pivoted to some form of connecting link b. The axes of the two shafts and of the pivots intersect, as the illustration shows. As the shafts revolve, the connecting link b between them receives a spherical motion, and, if the driving shaft rotates at a uniform speed, a variable speed will be imparted to the driven shaft, although it will make the same number of revolutions in a given time. In order to simplify the construction, the connecting pins of many universal joints are offset as shown at *B*; when the axes of the pins do not intersect, the variation in the angular velocity of the driven shaft is somewhat increased. The speed of the driven shaft is alternately less and greater than the speed of the driving shaft. The variations in angular velocity between the driver and follower can be eliminated by using a double joint, as at *C*, and an intermediate shaft between the two main shafts which has the same inclination relative to each shaft. Uni-

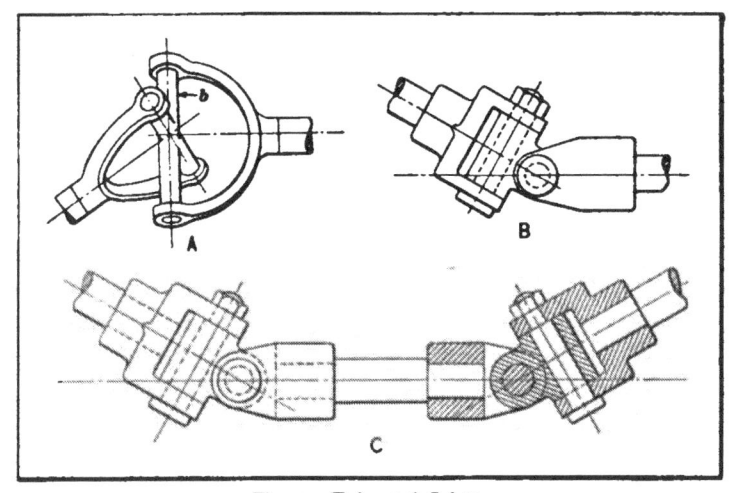

Fig. 4. Universal Joints

versal joints which operate on the same general principle as the designs illustrated in Fig. 4 are made in many different forms.

Straight-line Motions. — A combination of links arranged to impart a rectilinear motion to a rod or other part independently of guides or ways is known either as a *straight-line* motion or a *parallel* motion, the former term being more appropriate. Mechanisms of this type were used on steam engines and pumps of early designs to guide the piston-rods, because machine tools had not been developed for planing accurate guides. The principal application of straight-line motions at the present time is on steam engine indicators for imparting a rectilinear movement to the pencil or tracing point. The principle of the well-known parallel motion, invented by James Watt in 1784, is illustrated by the diagram, Fig. 5. Links A and B are free to oscillate about fixed pins at their outer ends, and are connected by link C. A point D may be located on the center-line of link C, which follows approximately a straight line when links A and B are given an oscillating movement, because, when A moves from its central position, the center of pin E moves to the left along its circular path while the center of

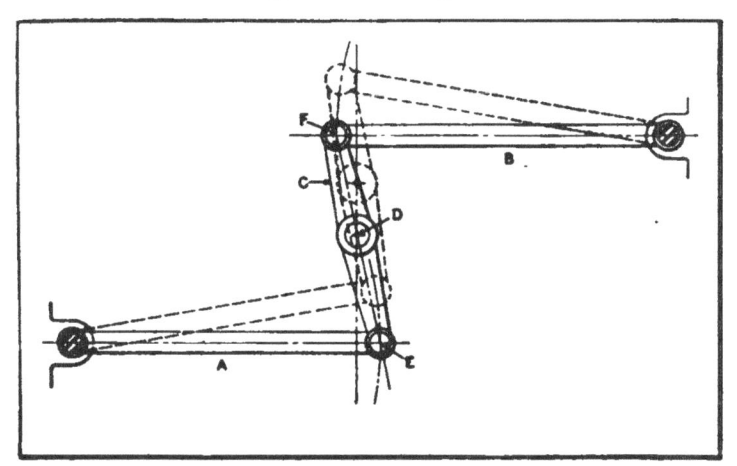

Fig. 5. The Watt Straight-line Motion

pin F moves to the right. As the motion of point D is affected by both links A and B, it moves very nearly in a straight line, provided D is correctly located and the angular motion of the links does not exceed about 20 degrees. Very few straight-line mechanisms produce a motion which is absolutely straight, and the general practice is to so design them that the guided part will be on the line when at the center and extreme ends of the stroke.

Scott Russell Straight-line Motion. — The mechanism illustrated in Fig. 6 will give an exact straight-line motion, but it is necessary to have an accurate plane surface upon which block C can slide. In addition to this sliding block, there are two links AC and DB. The link DB is one-half the length of AC and the shorter link is connected at a point B midway between A and C. The shorter link oscillates about a stationary pivot at D as end A is moved up or down along the straight line AD. Since AB, DB, and BC are equal, a circle with B as the center will intersect points A, D, C for any angle DCA; consequently, the line AD, traced by point A is perpendicular to DC, since ADC is always a right angle.

Instead of having guides or a plane surface for the sliding block C, the mechanism is sometimes modified by attaching the block end of link AC to another link which is free to oscillate about a fixed pivot so located that the link will be perpen-

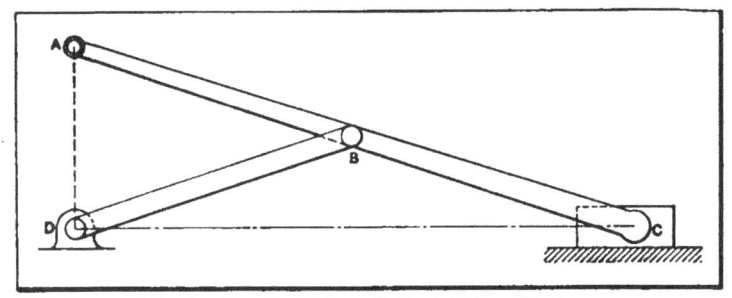

Fig. 6. The Scott Russell Straight-line Motion

dicular to the line CD, when in its mid-position. The longer this link and the greater the radius of the arc described by the connecting point at C, the more nearly will C move in a straight line; hence, the longer this link, the less point A deviates from a straight line. This modification of the Scott Russell straight-line motion is sometimes called the *grasshopper motion*.

Straight-line Motions for Indicators. — Some form of straight-line motion is necessary on a steam engine indicator in order that the motion of the indicator piston will produce a parallel movement of the tracer point or pencil, which draws a diagram on the paper or indicator card. The cylinder of the indicator is open at the bottom and is connected by suitable pipes with each end of the steam engine cylinder, so that the under side of the indicator piston is subjected to the varying pressure acting upon the engine piston. The upward movement of the indicator piston resulting from the steam pressure is resisted by a spiral spring of known resilience, and a rod extending above the piston connects with some form of link work designed to give a straight-line motion to the tracer point. When the engine is running and the indicator is in communication with the steam cylinder, variations of pressure will be recorded by the vertical movement of the pencil or tracer which is brought into contact with paper wound about a cylindrical drum that is rotated by the reciprocating motion of the engine cross-head.

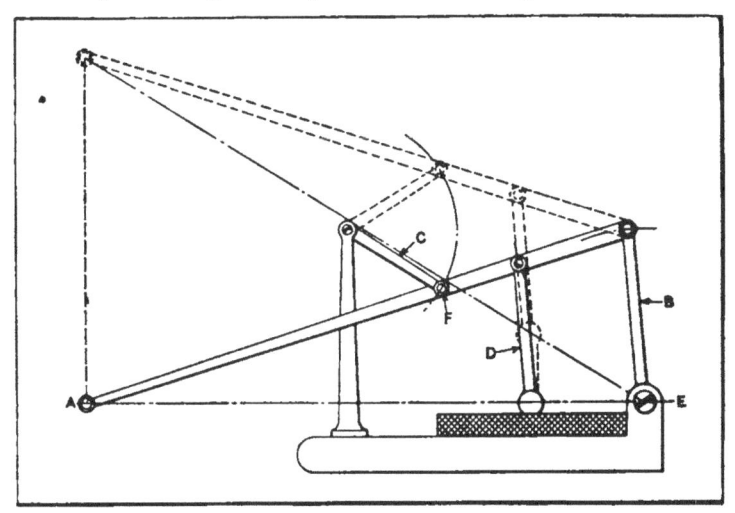

Fig. 7. Straight-line Motion of Thompson Indicator

The straight-line or parallel motion of one indicator is shown in Fig. 7. The arm A which carries the pencil at its outer end is pivoted to link B which, in turn, is pivoted to the top of the indicator. As arm A moves upward, the outer end is guided along a straight line by link C, which oscillates about a fixed pivot and is connected to arm A at F. This mechanism is so proportioned that a line from A to E intersects the point at which link D is attached to the piston.

The straight-line motion of another steam engine indicator is shown in Fig. 8. This mechanism, like the one previously described, is so arranged that the fulcrum A of the entire mechanism, the connection *B*, and the pencil point *C* are always in a straight line. The fundamental principle of this mechanism is that of the pantograph. If link *D* were removed and replaced by another link at *E*, both parallel and equal in length to *FG*, this would result in a well-known form of pantograph mechanism. The length of link *D* to replace *E* may be determined as follows: The procedure is to first ascertain, by trial, a convenient location for the point at which link *D* is to connect with link *BG*. The path followed by point *H* as end *C* is moved along a straight line is plotted on a large scale for all positions

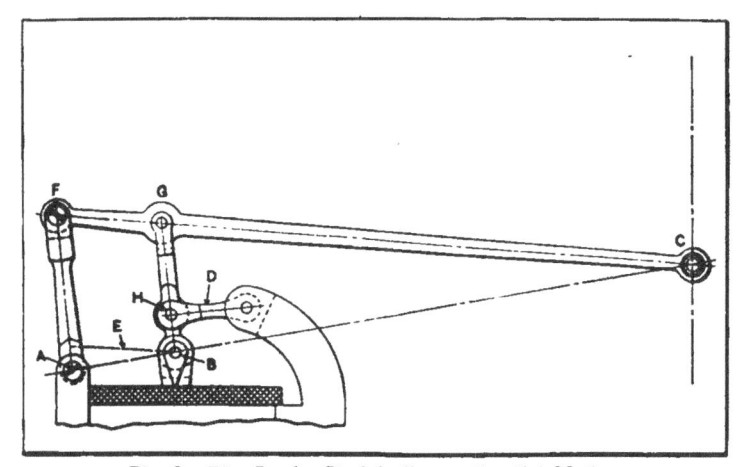

Fig. 8. The Crosby Straight-line or Parallel Motion

of the linkage within the required range of movement. This path will be approximately the arc of some circle, and the fixed pivot for link *D* is located at the center of this circle. If a link at *E* were actually used in place of link *D*, a straight-line motion at *C* could be obtained, providing the pivot *B* had a straight-line motion. Any form of guide intended to insure a straight movement at *B* would be objectionable, since it is desirable to reduce the friction of mechanisms of this type to a minimum. It is also essential to have the parts as light as possible in order to minimize the inertia and the effect of momentum, which is especially troublesome when taking cards from engines operating at high speed.

With the parallel motion of another indicator, a pin on the pencil arm corresponding to the one shown at F in Fig. 8 engages a curved slot in a stationary plate which is secured to the indicator in a vertical position. This curved slot takes the place of a link, and its curvature is such as to compensate for the tendency of the pencil to move in an arc.

Peaucellier Straight-line Motion. — The link mechanism shown in Fig. 9 will give an exact straight-line motion. This

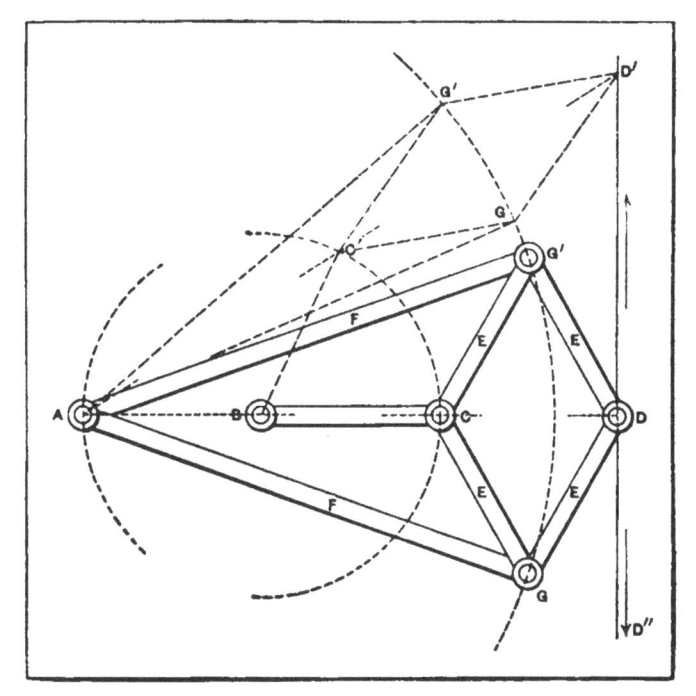

Fig. 9. Arrangement of Peaucellier Linkage for Straight-line Motion

mechanism was invented by Peaucellier, a French army officer. It is composed of seven links moving about two fixed centers of motion, A and B. The four equal links E form a rhombus; the links F are equal, and the center B is midway between A and C. If the point D be moved in the direction of the arrows, it will be constrained to move in the straight path $D'D''$, which is perpendicular to the line of centers $ABCD$. This may be tested experimentally. The path of the point C is the circumference $AC'C$; and the path of GG' is the arc described with the radius F. If the center-line of the links E and F be assumed in any position such as $AC'D'$, it will be found that the rhombus the sides of which represent the length of the links E takes the position shown in the drawing.

In Fig. 9, the centers A and B are external to the links E. A variation of the linkage is shown in Fig. 10, in which the centers A and B are within the rhombus. The links F are equal, and center B is midway between A and C, as in Fig. 9. The corresponding links and points in the figures are labeled

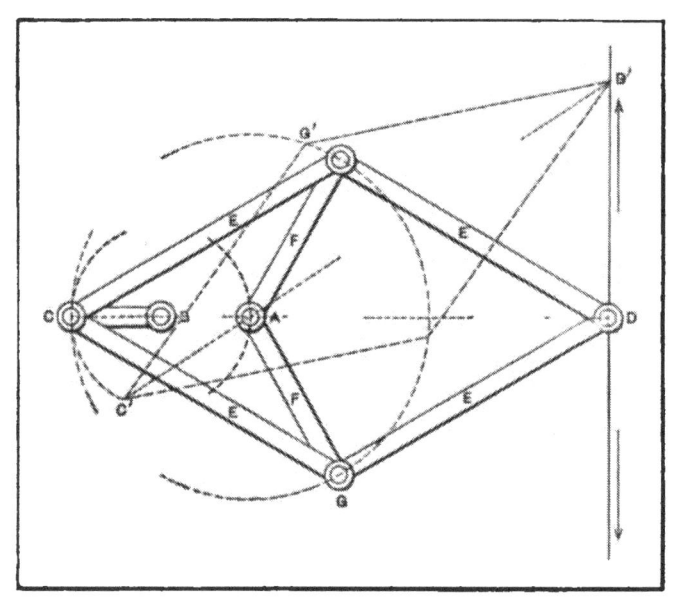

Fig. 10. Modification of Peaucellier Straight-line Mechanism

with the same letters; it may be shown experimentally that the point D is compelled to move in a straight line perpendicular to the line of centers $CBAD$.

Toggle Joint. — A link mechanism commonly known as a *toggle joint* is applied to machines of different types, such as drawing and embossing presses, stone crushers, etc., for securing great pressure. The principle of the toggle joint is shown by the diagrams *A* and *B*, Fig. 11. There are two links, *b* and *c*, which are connected at the center. Link *b* is free to swivel about a fixed pin or bearing at *d*, and link *c* is connected to a sliding member *e*. Rod *f* joins links *b* and *c* at the central connection. When force is applied to rod *f* in a direction at right angles to center-line *xx*, along which the driven member *e* moves, this force is greatly multiplied at *e*, because a movement at the joint *g* produces a relatively slight movement at *e*. As the angle α becomes less, motion at *e* decreases and the force increases until the links are in line, as at *B*. If $R =$ the

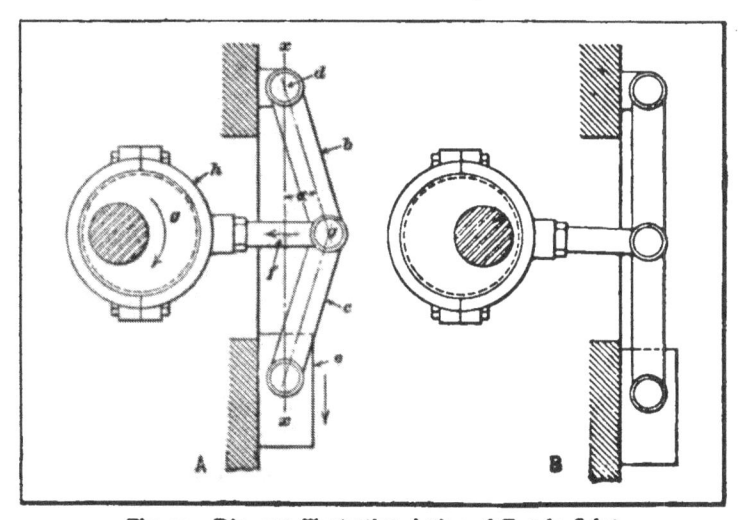

Fig. 11. Diagram Illustrating Action of Toggle Joint

resistance at *e*; $P =$ the applied power or force; and $\alpha =$ the angle between each link and a line *xx* passing through the axes of the pins, then:

$$2 R \sin \alpha = P \cos \alpha.$$

Pantograph Mechanisms. — A pantograph is a combination of links which are so connected and proportioned as to length that any motion of one point in a plane parallel to that of the link mechanism will cause another point to follow a similar path either on an enlarged or a reduced scale. Such a mechanism may be used as a reducing motion for operating a steam engine indicator, or to control the movements of a metal cutting tool. For instance, most engraving machines have a pantograph mechanism interposed between the tool and a tracing point which is guided along lines or grooves of a model or pattern. As the tracing point moves, the tool follows a similar path, but to a reduced scale, and cuts the required pattern or design on the work.

A simple form of pantograph is shown by the diagram, Fig. 12. There are four links, *a*, *b*, *c*, and *d*. Links *a* and *b* are equal in length, as are links *c* and *d*, thus forming a parallelogram. A fifth connecting link *e* is parallel to links *c* and *d*. This mechanism is free to swivel about a fixed center *f*. Any

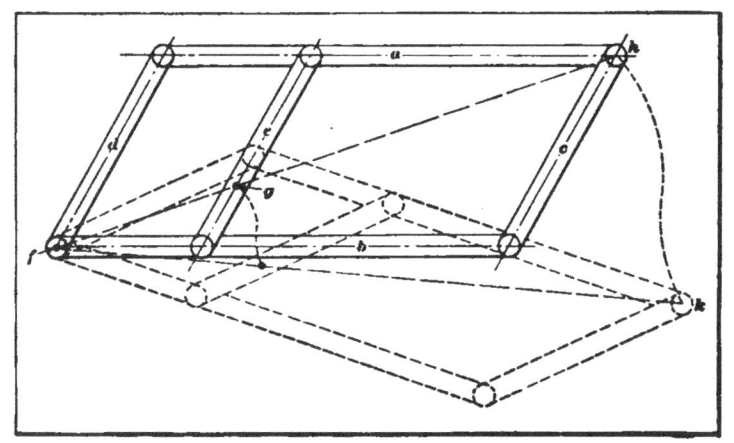

Fig. 12. Pantograph for Reproducing Motion on a Reduced or Enlarged Scale

movement of *h* about *f* will cause a point *g* (which coincides with a straight line passing through *f* and *h*) to describe a path similar to that followed by *h*, but on a reduced scale. For instance, if *h* were moved to *k* following the path indicated by the dotted line, point *g* would also trace a similar path.

Another form of pantograph mechanism is shown at *A* in Fig. 13. This pantograph, which is sometimes called "lazy tongs," is used to some extent for obtaining the reduction of motion between an engine cross-head and the indicator drum when taking indicator cards. The pantograph is pivoted at *b* by a stud which may be secured to a block of wood or angle

TRANSMISSION OF MOTION 21

iron attached to a post or in any convenient place. The end *a* has a pin which is connected to the cross-head of the engine. The cord which transmits motion to the indicator drum is attached to the cord-pin *e* on a cross-bar. This cross-bar may be placed in different positions relative to the pivot *b*, by changing screws at *c* and *d*; the cord-pin *e*, however, must always be in line with the fixed pivot *b* and pin *a*. The position of the cross-bar in relation to pivot *b* determines the length of the travel of cord-pin *e* and, consequently, the rotary movement of the

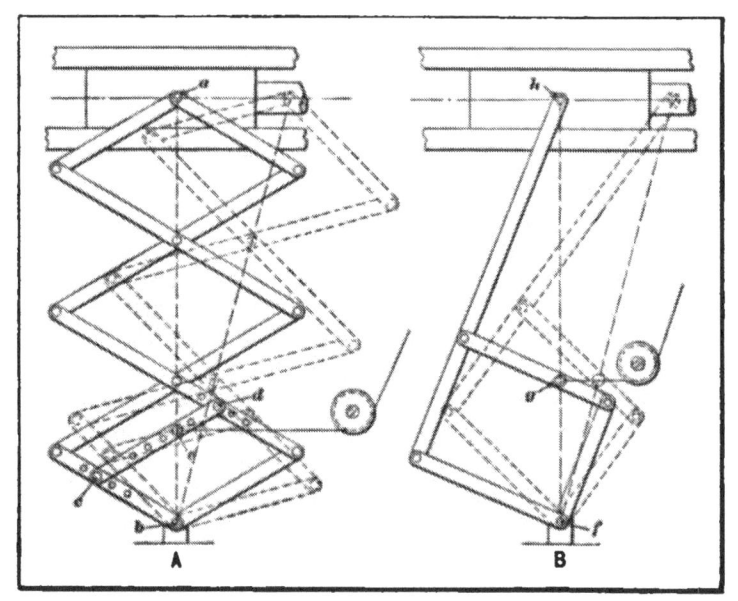

Fig. 13. Pantograph Mechanisms applied to Engine Cross-head to Reduce Motion when Taking Indicator Cards

indicator drum and the length of the diagram which the pencil traces upon the indicator card. The objection to this reducing mechanism is the liability of lost motion resulting from wear in the numerous joints.

Another form of pantograph reducing mechanism is shown at *B* in Fig. 13. In this case, there are four links joined together in the form of a parallelogram, and one of the links is extended and pivoted to the engine cross-head. The swiveling movement of the pantograph is about the fixed pivot f, and the cord which operates the indicator drum is attached at g. As the illustration indicates, this point of attachment g coincides with a line passing through the pivots f and h, the same as for the pantograph shown at A. If F = the length of the engine stroke and L, the length required for the indicator diagram,

$$F : L = fh : fg, \quad \text{or} \quad \frac{F}{L} = \frac{fh}{fg}.$$

Cams. — The name "cam" is applied to various forms of revolving, oscillating, or sliding machine members which have edges or grooves so shaped as to impart to a follower a motion which is usually variable and, in many cases, quite complex. Cams are generally used to obtain a motion which could not be derived from any other form of mechanism. Most cams revolve and the follower or driven member may have either a rectilinear or oscillating motion. The acting surface of the cam is in direct contact either with the follower or with a roller attached to the follower to reduce friction. Different types of cams are described in Chapter VII.

The Screw. — The screw, which is used in so many different ways in machine construction, may be considered as a type of cam having one or more grooves of helical form. One important difference between a cam and a screw is in the follower which encircles the screw and is in contact with the groove or thread throughout several turns. When a screw is used primarily to transmit rectilinear motion to a nut or follower, its rotation must, of necessity, be reversed, unless provision is made for disengaging the follower and returning it by other means, since the thread groove or grooves wind about the screw only in one direction. The lead-screw of a lathe may rotate continuously when cutting a thread, because a split nut on the carriage may be disengaged from the lead-screw when the carriage is to be returned to the starting position. The axial movement of the follower or nut for each revolution of the screw will equal the lead of the thread. The lead is equivalent to the pitch or distance between the centers of adjacent threads, if the screw has a single thread. The lead of a double-threaded screw equals twice the pitch, and for a triple-threaded screw, three times the pitch. The lead then equals the distance that any one of the threads of a multiple-threaded screw advances in one complete turn and also the distance that a nut would advance if given one complete turn. The object of using multiple-threaded screws is to increase the lead and resulting axial motion of the nut or screw per revolution, without weakening the screw by cutting a single thread of coarser pitch into it, and also to avoid using a single-threaded screw of larger diameter.

When a screw imparts motion to a follower, the latter does not always move parallel to the axis of the screw, as in the case of a nut. For instance, if a screw is in mesh with a wheel having teeth which successively engage the screw threads, the wheel may be given a rotary motion. This form of transmission will be referred to later in connection with gearing.

Transmission by Friction Gearing. — When rotary motion does not need to be transmitted positively, driving and driven members which are in contact and simply roll against each other are used for some classes of mechanisms. Transmissions of this kind are commonly classified as "friction gearing." The diagram A, Fig. 14, illustrates the principle of a friction drive for parallel shafts. The pinion a may consist of flanges between which paper, straw fiber, or some other material which will give a high coefficient of friction is compressed. This pinion may bear against a cast-iron wheel. The action is purely frictional as the pinion and wheel revolve together and the velocity ratio remains constant, unless the resistance to motion exceeds the frictional resistance.

Diagram B shows a form of friction gearing which has been used quite extensively for varying the feeding movements of metal-cutting tools, etc. The small "brush wheel" c in this case bears against the flat face of a cast-iron disk d, and the relative speeds are varied by changing the radial position of wheel c. If brush wheel c is cylindrical, there is the disadvantage that its surface (which has a uniform peripheral velocity) is in contact with plate d the surface velocity of which varies

24   MECHANICAL MOVEMENTS

according to the radius at any point. For instance, the velocity of d is greater at the outer corner of wheel c than at the inner corner of c; therefore, the wheel should be as narrow as is practicable, and the edge is sometimes rounded to reduce the contact area. Leather fiber wheels are recommended for friction gear-

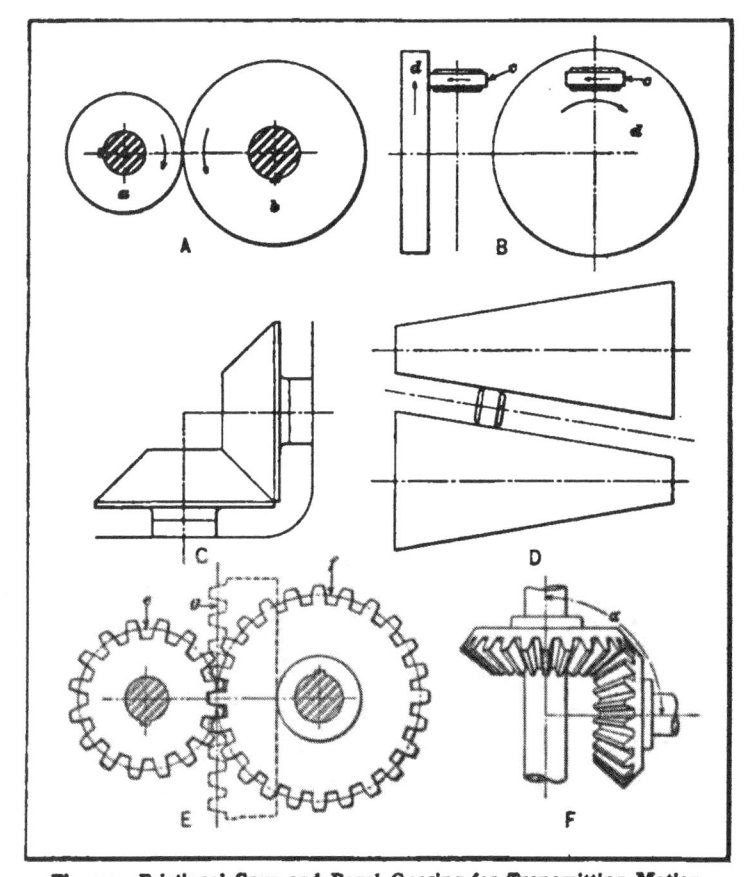

Fig. 14. Frictional Spur and Bevel Gearing for Transmitting Motion

ing when the face width is small and the contact pressure excessive. Friction gearing of the bevel type is illustrated at C. Diagram D illustrates in principle a type of friction gearing used for varying the speed of parallel shafts. The driving and driven members are conical and are separated somewhat so that motion is transmitted through an intermediate part which may be in the form of a wheel or band that may be shifted for varying the speed.

The power that can be transmitted through friction gearing depends upon the physical character of the materials forming the surfaces in contact and also upon the normal pressure between these two surfaces. For instance, if one wheel is formed of paper and the other of iron, the coefficient of friction of the paper wheel against the iron wheel in conjunction with the pressure with which they are held in contact will determine the driving value. This pressure must not be great enough to injure the paper, and the friction material should be of a very firm texture to enable it to endure high pressure without a reduction of the frictional coefficient, as a small reduction of the latter factor would offset the effect of a relatively large gain in pressure-enduring qualities. Friction materials are now available which combine the essential qualities of durability and driving power very satisfactorily. When a paper wheel is in contact with a cast-iron wheel, the former should preferably be the driving member, because it is made of softer material and its surface would be injured and eventually ruined by even occasional and momentary rotation of an iron wheel against it under pressure, as when starting from rest, especially with an excessive load. When the softer paper wheel is the driver, if the resistance to motion exceeds the frictional resistance so that slipping occurs, the tendency is to wear off the edge of the rotating driver evenly instead of forming a flat spot upon it, as would be the case if it were the driven member and remained stationary.

The method of applying contact pressure is adapted to conditions, but, in general, the lever-operated eccentric box or thrust box is commonly used; it is a simple method for giving hand or power control. In some cases, more elaborate devices are used. The pressure may be positively applied and it may be made to vary automatically as the load increases or decreases. As friction is essential to the operation of this type of gearing, care should be taken to prevent any great reduction of the driving power by the accumulation of grease or other foreign matter on the friction surfaces. Rigid support for the friction wheels and the maintenance of a good contact between the working surfaces are also of importance. Friction gearing is not a suitable form of transmission where it is essential to maintain a prescribed relation between driving and driven parts of a mechanism throughout an entire cycle of operations. In some cases, however, a transmission which is not positive is preferable in that it constitutes a safety device and prevents the transmission of shocks or an excessive amount of power to parts of a mechanism which might thereby be injured. Friction gearing is also very simple in design, and operates smoothly and quietly.

Transmission by Toothed Gearing. — The slipping that often occurs when motion is transmitted by cylinders or cones which roll in contact may be avoided by employing wheels or gearing having teeth or projections which intermesh and insure a positive drive and a constant velocity ratio. In designing the teeth of gearing, the object is to so shape the contact surfaces that the motion obtained will be equivalent to friction gearing when no slipping occurs. Toothed gears for transmitting motion between parallel shafts as shown at E, Fig. 14, are known as *spur gears*. This is the most common type of gearing, and it is found in all classes of mechanisms. The pitch circles e and f correspond to cylinders in contact, and the teeth, if correctly formed, will transmit a continuous and unvarying motion between the driving and driven gears. If one of the spur gears could be straightened out, as indicated by the dotted lines, until the pitch circle is changed to a straight line g, this would be known as a *rack*. A spur gear meshing with a rack will transmit to the latter a straight-line movement, when it is the driving member, and receive rotary motion when the rack is the driver. This form of gearing is applied in many different ways.

When toothed gearing has pitch surfaces which correspond to the frustums of rolling cones, as shown at F, it is known as *bevel gearing*. This type of gearing is usually employed to connect shafts which are at right angles, although the angle α may be greater or less than 90 degrees. When the shafts are at right angles and the pitch diameter of both gears is equal, they are

TRANSMISSION OF MOTION 27

known as *miter gears*. The axes of ordinary bevel gears lie in the same plane. The *skew bevel gear* is a special form for connecting shafts which are at an angle to each other and not in the same plane. This form of gearing has been used very little.

Another type of gearing for shafts which are not parallel and which do not lie in the same plane is shown at A, Fig. 15. This is called *spiral gearing* or, more properly, *helical gearing*. The pitch surfaces are cylindrical, the same as with spur gears, but the teeth, instead or being parallel to the axes, follow helical

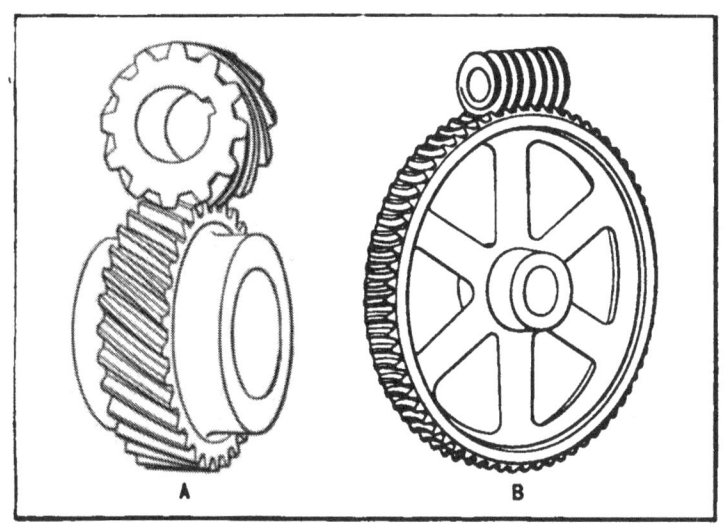

Fig. 15. Spiral and Worm Gearing for Transmitting Motion

curves like screw threads; for this reason, helical gears are sometimes called *screw gears*. The axes of the shafts may be at right angles, as shown in the illustration, or at some other angle. If the distance between the shafts is not great enough to permit using helical gears, it may be necessary to resort to skew bevel gears. Helical gearing is sometimes used for connecting parallel shafts instead of spur gears, especially when smoothness of action and high speed are essential. The general practice is to use a double helical or *herringbone gear* which corresponds to two helical gears placed together, having right- and left-hand teeth in order to eliminate end-thrust. A herringbone gear on one shaft meshes with a herringbone gear on another shaft and, as the teeth are of right- and left-hand obliquity, the end-thrust resulting from the angularity of the teeth is neutralized.

The *worm gearing* shown at B, Fig. 15, is similar in principle to spiral gearing; the worm usually has either a single or a double thread which meshes with the teeth of the worm-wheel. The worm is the driver and the velocity ratio depends upon the number of teeth in the worm-wheel and the number of threads on the worm. For instance, if the worm-wheel has 40 teeth, 40 revolutions of a single-threaded worm will be required for one

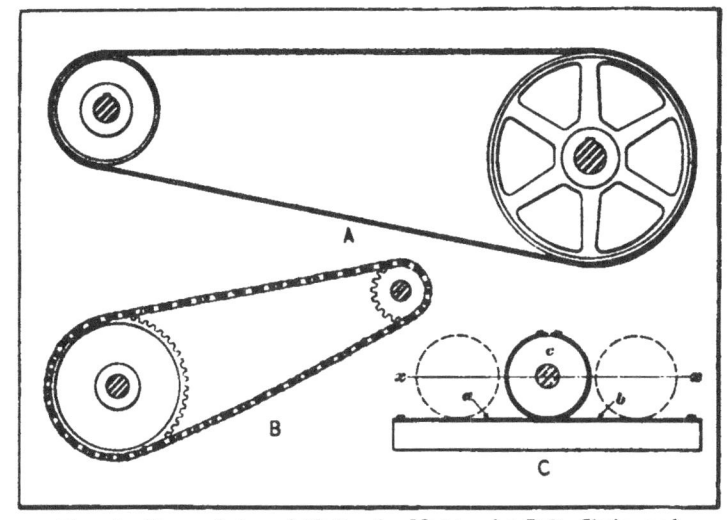

Fig. 16. Transmission of Motion by Means of a Belt, Chain, and Flexible Band

revolution of the worm-wheel, whereas a double-threaded worm would revolve 20 times for one revolution of the worm-wheel. A single-threaded worm is, in reality, a spiral gear having one continuous tooth. There are many special forms of gearing, some of which will be described later.

Transmission by Flexible Bands, Ropes, or Chains. — A very common method of transmitting motion from one shaft to another is shown at A, Fig. 16. A pulley or wheel is attached to each shaft and a continuous band or belt extends around both pulleys so that they rotate in unison, provided the frictional resistance between the belt and pulley rims is sufficient to transmit the required amount of energy or power. The connecting belt or band for pulleys of the form shown may be of leather, cotton, or cotton and rubber composition. Thin steel bands operating upon smooth rimmed pulleys have also been used to a limited extent. For drives of the type illustrated at A, leather belts are generally used, although belts made of cotton duck impregnated with rubber are extensively used, especially where the belts are exposed to the weather or to the action of steam, as they do not absorb moisture or stretch as readily as do leather belts. Canvas stitched belting saturated with oil is also frequently used in preference to either leather or rubber (cotton duck and rubber) belting. The shafts may be parallel or at an angle, and frequently the belt is guided by idler pulleys in its passage from one pulley to another. Belts are usually flat bands, although round belts operating upon grooved pulleys are often used, especially upon smaller classes of machinery. Cotton and Manila ropes have been used in many factories and mills for transmitting power from the power plant to different lines of shafting, although this type of transmission has been replaced to a considerable extent by electrical equipment. With the English or multiple system, a number of parallel ropes are used; each rope forms a continuous belt, and the required number are placed side by side in grooves formed in the rims of the driving and driven sheaves or pulleys. With the continuous or American system, one long rope winds around and fills all the grooves of the driving and driven pulleys, and is guided from the last groove back to the first one by an idler pulley.

Many classes of mechanisms to which the belt type of transmission is applicable require a positive drive, especially when it is necessary to transmit considerable power from one shaft to another and the distance between the shafts is comparatively small. Belts composed of chain links which engage teeth formed on the sprockets are extensively used. (See diagram B, Fig. 16.) The chain transmission is often applied where the center-to-center distance between shafts is too short for leather or similar belting and too long for transmitting motion by gearing.

The teeth of the sprockets engage the spaces between the link blocks or rollers, and a positive drive is thus obtained. As there is no initial tension on the chain, the pull on the shaft bearings and the resulting friction is reduced. The chains used for this purpose vary in regard to the form and accuracy of the links and sprockets. For either belt or chain drives, the velocity ratio or relative speed of the driving and driven pulleys or sprockets depends upon their respective diameters.

The belts, ropes, or chains previously referred to are for transmitting rotary motion continuously. Flexible bands are sometimes used to impart rotary motion to a reciprocating shaft. Diagram C, Fig. 16, illustrates one application. The steel bands or ribbons, a and b, are wrapped about drum c, and the ends of these bands are attached to the drum. The outer ends of the bands are also attached to some stationary member. When the shaft carrying drum c is given a reciprocating movement in a plane xx, as illustrated by the dotted lines, the drum is caused to revolve in conjunction with the traversing movement, first in one direction and then in the other. This particular form of mechanism is used for generating involute curves on the teeth of gear-cutters, by holding the hardened cutter on the arbor of drum c and rolling it in contact with the plane face of a grinding wheel, the wheel face representing the side of an involute rack tooth. Mechanisms operated in this way necessarily have a reciprocating motion, since the rotary movement reverses as the band is wrapped and unwrapped around the drum. A hoisting mechanism of the type which has a drum and an attached rope that is wound and unwound for raising and lowering a load is another example of transmission by a flexible connector. In many cases, the drum to which one end of the rope is attached is the driver while hoisting the load, whereas, in lowering, the drum is driven in a reverse direction by the action of gravity on the load.

Trains of Mechanisms. — While a single pair of pulleys and a connecting belt, or a single pair of meshing gears, may be employed for transmitting motion from one shaft to another, it is often desirable or necessary to use a series of pulleys or gears

TRANSMISSION OF MOTION 31

between the driving and driven shafts. Various combinations of links, cams, etc., may also be used to connect driving and driven members. In general, any series of pulleys, gears, links, cams, etc., regardless of their order or combination, is known as a *train of mechanism*. If motion is transmitted entirely through gearing, the combination of gears is called a *gear train*. Trains of gears, pulleys, etc., are common to all classes of mechanisms and may be necessary either for obtaining a required

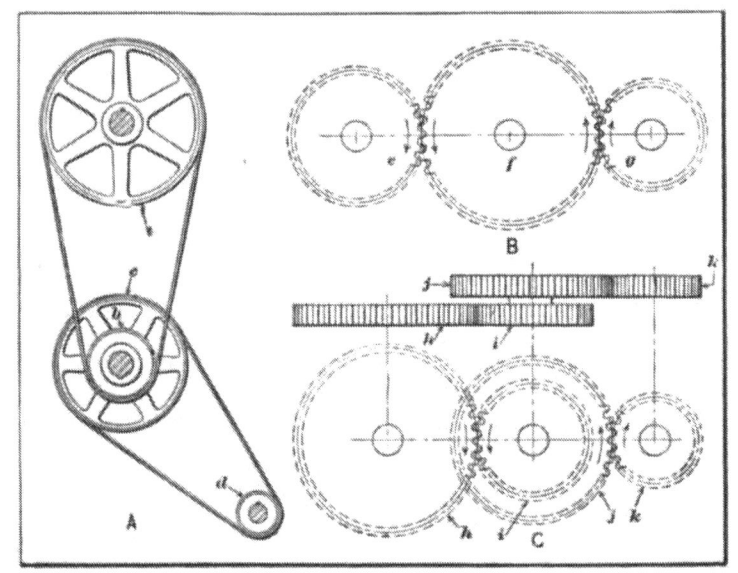

Fig. 17. Train of Pulleys and Trains of Gearing

velocity ratio or for transmitting motion when the driving and driven members are so located that a more direct method of transmission is not practicable. Motion is often transmitted through trains of gearing specially arranged so that speed changes may readily be obtained by manipulating suitable controlling levers.

The diagram A, Fig. 17, shows a train of pulleys for transmitting motion from pulley a to pulley d. Pulleys a and c are drivers and pulleys b and d, followers. If the speed of pulley a and the diameters of all the pulleys are known, the speed of pulley d may be found as follows: Find the product of the diameters of the driving pulleys; divide by the product of the diameters of the driven pulleys, and multiply the quotient by the revolutions per minute of the first driving pulley *a*. If the speeds for pulleys *a* and *d* are given and it is desired to find the diameters of all the pulleys, proceed as follows: Find the speed ratio by placing the number of revolutions of the driving pulley as the numerator and the number of revolutions of the driven pulley as the denominator of a fraction, and reduce this fraction to its lowest terms. Then divide both the numerator and denominator of the fraction, thus expressing the ratio as two factors, and multiply each " pair " of factors by the same number until pulleys with suitable diameters are found. (One factor in the numerator and one in the denominator are considered as " one pair.") Sometimes motion is transmitted through more than one pair of pulleys, especially when the required velocity ratio is high, to avoid using one very large pulley and one very small one.

Trains of Spur Gears. — A train of four spur gears is shown at *B*, Fig. 17. The number and arrangement of gears in a train vary considerably. The shafts may all lie in the same plane or be in different planes, and the train of gearing may serve other purposes than merely transmitting motion from one shaft to another. The driver *e* transmits motion to gear *g* through an intermediate gear *f* called an *idler gear*. While the " idler " affects the direction of rotation, it does not affect the velocity ratio. Idler gears are used on many engine lathes for connecting the " change-gears " of different sizes used for screw cutting. The idler stud is carried by an adjustable arm or plate, and its position is varied to suit the diameters of the driving and driven gears. The arrangement shown at *C* is known as *compound gearing;* this term is applied whenever there is one or more pairs of gearing in the train, attached to the same shaft or stud. Assuming that *h* is the driver, motion is transmitted to driven gear *i*, and by the second driver *j* of the train, to driven gear *k*.

The direction of rotation of the first and last gears in a train will be opposite if the number of axes be even, but, if there is an odd number of axes, the first and last gears will revolve in the same direction. The relative speeds of two gears running in mesh are inversely as their diameters or numbers of teeth. For instance, if a driving gear has 20 teeth and a driven gear, 60 teeth, three revolutions of the driver will be required for one revolution of the driven gear. To obtain the speed of the driven gear, multiply the number of teeth in the driver by its speed in revolutions per minute, and divide the product by the number of teeth in the driven gear. An idler gear placed between the driving and driven gears will not affect the result.

To determine the speed of the last gear of a compound train of gearing, find the product of the diameters or numbers of teeth of all the driving gears; divide by the corresponding product of all of the driven gears, and multiply the quotient by the revolutions per minute of the first driving gear. This rule may also be applied when belt pulleys and gears are combined in one train. With such combination, the diameters of the pulleys, and either the pitch diameters of the gears or the numbers of teeth, could be used in making the calculations.

Epicyclic Gear Trains. — If one of the gears in a train is fixed or stationary, and another gear (or gears) revolves about the stationary gear in addition to rotating relative to its own axis, the mechanism is known as an *epicyclic train of gearing*, because points on the revolving gears describe epicycloidal curves. The two gears a and b (see diagram A, Fig. 18) are held in mesh by a link c. If this link remains stationary and gear a makes one revolution, the number of revolutions made by gear b will equal the number of teeth in a divided by the number of teeth in b, or the pitch diameter of a divided by the pitch diameter of b. If a and b represent either the pitch diameters of the gears or numbers of teeth, the revolutions of b to one turn of a equal $\frac{a}{b}$. If gear a is held stationary and link c is given one turn about the axis of a, then the revolutions of gear b, relative to arm c, will also equal $\frac{a}{b}$, the same as when gear a was revolved once with the arm held stationary. Since a rotation of arm c will cause a rotation of gear b in the same direction about its axis, the total number of revolutions of gear b, relative to a fixed plane, for one turn of c, will equal 1 (the turn of c) plus the revolutions of b relative to c, or $1 + \frac{a}{b}$. For example, if gear a has 60 teeth and

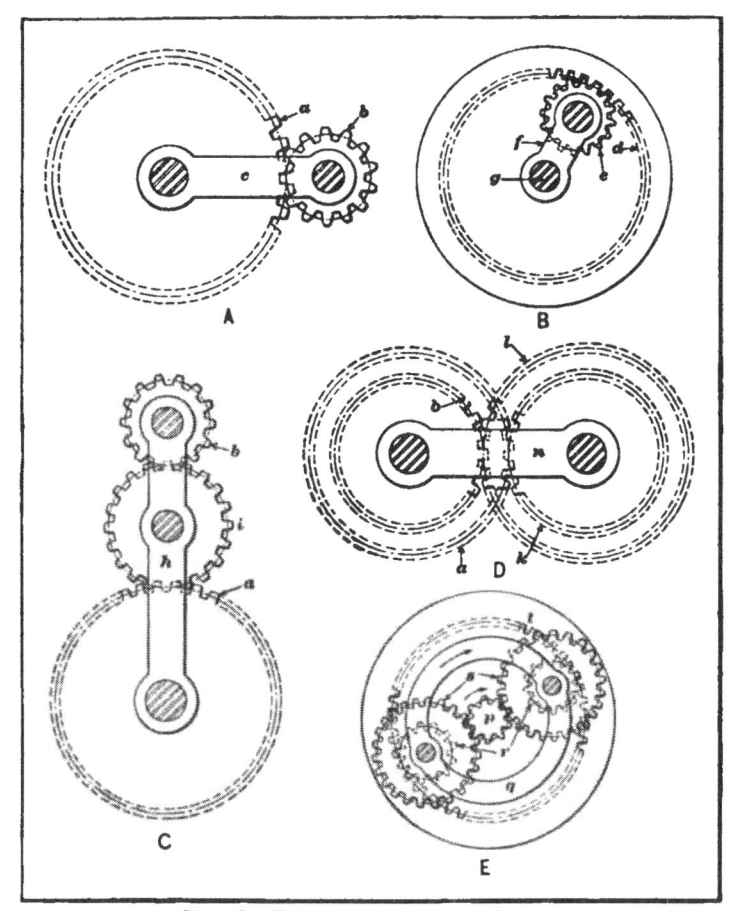

Fig. 18. Epicyclic or Planetary Gearing

gear b, 20 teeth, one turn of arm c would cause b to rotate $\frac{60}{20}$, or 3 times about its own axis; gear b, however, also makes one turn about the axis of gear a, so that the total number of revolutions relative to a fixed plane equals $1 + \frac{60}{20} = 4$ revolutions.

In order to illustrate the distinction between the rotation of b around its own axis and its rotation relative to a fixed plane, assume that b is in mesh with a fixed gear a and also with an outer internal gear that is free to revolve. If the speed of the internal gear is required, it will be necessary, in calculating this speed, to consider not only the rotation of b about its own axis, but also its motion around a, because the effect of this latter motion on the internal gear, for each turn of link c, is equivalent to an additional revolution of b.

Diagram B, Fig. 18, represents an internal gear d in mesh with gear e on arm f. If arm f is held stationary, the revolutions of e for one turn of d equal $\frac{d}{e}$, d and e representing the numbers of teeth or pitch diameters of the respective gears. If the internal gear is held stationary and arm f is turned about axis g, the rotation of e about its axis will be clockwise when f is turned counter-clockwise, and *vice versa;* hence, the revolutions of gear e, relative to a fixed plane, for one turn of f about g, will equal the difference between 1 (representing the turn of f) and the revolutions equal to $\frac{d}{e}$.

Method of Analyzing Epicyclic Gear Trains. — A simple method of analyzing epicyclic gearing is to consider the actions separately. For instance, with the gearing shown at A, Fig. 18, the results obtained when link c is fixed and the gear a (which normally would be fixed) is revolved are noted; if gear a is revolved in a clockwise direction, then, in order to reproduce the action of the gearing, the entire mechanism, locked together as a unit, is assumed to be given one turn counter-clockwise. The results are then tabulated, using plus and minus signs to indicate directions of rotation. Assume that gear a has 60 teeth and gear b, 20 teeth, and that + signs represent counter-clockwise movements and − signs clockwise movements. If link c is held stationary and gear a is turned clockwise (−) one revolution, gear b will revolve counter-clockwise (+) $\frac{60}{20}$ revolution. Next consider all of the gears locked together so that the entire combination is revolved one turn in a counter-clockwise (+) direction, thus returning gear *a* to its original position. The practical effect of these separate motions is the same as though link *c* were revolved once about the axis of a fixed gear *a* which is the way in which the gearing operates normally. By tabulating these results as follows, the motion of each part of the mechanism may readily be determined:

	Gear *a*	Link *c*	Gear *b*
Link Stationary	−1 turn	0 turn	+1⅔ turn
Gears Locked	+1 turn	+1 turn	+1 turn
Number of Turns	0	+1	+4

The algebraic sums in line headed "Number of Turns" indicate that, when gear *a* is held stationary and link *c* is given one turn about the axis of *a*, gear *b* will make 4 revolutions relative to a fixed plane in a counter-clockwise or + direction, when link *c* is turned in the same direction.

The application of this method to the arrangement of gearing shown at *B*, Fig. 18, will now be considered. Assume that gear *d* has 60 teeth and gear *e*, 20 teeth. Then, if gear *d* is turned clockwise with link *f* stationary, and the entire mechanism with the gears locked is turned counter-clockwise, an analysis of the separate motions previously referred to will give the following results:

	Gear *d*	Link *f*	Gear *e*
Link Stationary	−1 turn	0 turn	−1⅔ turn
Gears Locked	+1 turn	+1 turn	+1 turn
Number of Turns	0	+1	−2

Effect of Idler in Epicyclic Gear Train. — If an idler gear *i* is placed between gears *a* and *b* (diagram *C*, Fig. 18), the latter will rotate about its axis in a direction opposite to that of the link (the same as with the arrangement shown at *B*), and the revolutions of gear *b*, relative to a fixed plane, for one turn of link *h* about the axis of *a*, will equal the difference between 1 (representing the turn of *h*) and the revolutions equal to $\frac{a}{b}$.

Assume that gear *a* has 60 teeth, idler gear *i*, 30 teeth, and gear *b*, 20 teeth. Then the turns of *b*, relative to a fixed member for one turn of *h* about the axis of *a*, are shown by the following analysis:

	Gear a	Idler i	Link h	Gear b
Link Stationary	−1 turn	+$\frac{36}{35}$ turn	0 turn	−$\frac{36}{35}$ turn
Gears Locked	+1 turn	+1 turn	+1 turn	+1 turn
Number of Turns	0	+3	+1	−2

The direction of rotation of b, relative to a fixed member, may or may not be in the same direction as that of link h, depending upon the velocity ratio between gears a and b. If gears a and b are of the same size, one turn of link h will cause b to revolve once about its own axis, but, as this rotation is in a direction opposite to that of h, one motion neutralizes the other, so that b has a simple motion of circular translation relative to a fixed member. If gear b were twice as large as a, it would then revolve, for each complete turn of link h, one-half revolution about its own axis, in a direction opposite to the motion of h; this half turn subtracted from the complete turn of link h gives a half turn in the same direction as h, relative to a fixed member.

Compound Train of Epicyclic Gearing. — Diagram D, Fig. 18, illustrates a compound train of epicyclic gearing. This arrangement modified to suit different conditions is commonly employed. Gear a represents the fixed member and meshes with gear k, which is attached to the same shaft as gear l. Gear l meshes with gear b the axis of which coincides with that of fixed gear a. Assume that gear a has 36 teeth, gear k, 34 teeth, gear l, 35 teeth, and gear b, 35 teeth. Then one turn of link n about the axis of gear a would give the following results:

	Gear a	Link n	Gears k and l	Gear b
Link Stationary	−1 turn	0 turn	+$\frac{36}{34}$ turn	−($\frac{36}{34} \times \frac{35}{35}$) turn
Gears Locked	+1 turn	+1 turn	+1 turn	+1 turn
Number of Turns	0	+1	+2$\frac{1}{17}$	−$\frac{1}{17}$

From this analysis, it will be seen that, for each counter-clockwise turn of link n, the rotation of gear b equals $1 - \dfrac{a}{k} \times \dfrac{l}{b}$, in which the letters correspond either to the pitch diameters or numbers of teeth in the respective gears shown at D in Fig. 18. If the value of $\dfrac{a}{k} \times \dfrac{l}{b}$ is less than 1, gear b will revolve in the same direction as link *n*, whereas, if this value is greater than 1, gear *b* will revolve in the opposite direction.

Compound epicyclic gearing may be used for obtaining a very great reduction in velocity between the link *n* and the last gear *b* in the train. As an extreme example, suppose gear *a* has 99 teeth, gear *k*, 100 teeth, gear *l*, 101 teeth, and gear *b*, 100 teeth. The speed of gear *b* will equal $1 - \frac{99 \times 101}{100 \times 100} = \frac{1}{10,000}$ revolution; hence link *n* would have to make 10,000 revolutions for each revolution of gear *b*. The arrangement of epicyclic gearing shown at *D* is known as a *reverted train*.

Diagram *E* shows another arrangement of reverted train. An internal gear *t* forms part of the mechanism, and either this gear, frame *q*, or pinion *p* may be the stationary member, depending upon the application of the mechanism. In this case, instead of a single set of gears between *p* and *t*, there is a double set located diametrically opposite and connected by a suitable frame *q*. This arrangement is similar to the mechanism of a certain type of geared hoist. The central pinion *p* is the driving member, internal gear *t* is stationary, and the frame *q* is the driven member and imparts motion to the hoisting sheave.

Sun and Planet Motion. — A mechanism of the general type illustrated by diagram *A*, Fig. 18, was employed by Watt for transmitting motion from the connecting-rod to the engine shaft, because the crank motion had been patented previously. This mechanism is known as a " sun and planet " motion, the fixed gear *a* representing the sun and the revolving gear *b*, the planet. In applying this mechanism to an engine, one gear was keyed on the shaft and the other was fixed to the connecting-rod. The connecting link between the gears was loose on both shafts. A forward and return stroke of the piston caused the connecting-rod gear to pass once around the shaft gear, but without revolving on its own axis, as it was attached to the connecting-rod. With this arrangement, if both gears are of the same diameter, the shaft gear will make two revolutions for one turn of the connecting link between the gears or one revolution for each stroke.

CHAPTER II

SPEED-CHANGING AND CONTROLLING MECHANISMS

THE speed at which a machine or mechanism operates may be either uniform or variable, and be controlled either automatically or by some form of hand-manipulated device. If the motion is transmitted by a combination of gearing or other mechanical means, the rate of speed may be varied by changing the velocity ratio of the mechanism that transmits the motion. When the rate of speed depends upon the action of a fluid such as steam, the speed may be regulated by controlling the amount of steam that is used and the resulting pressure against the moving element. The object in regulating and controlling the speed of a machine depends upon the type of machine and its use. If it is utilized in manufacturing a certain product, the rate of speed may be limited by the nature of the operation it performs; moreover, the speed may need to be varied at times because of changes in operating conditions. This is frequently the case with machine tools. Another important use for speed-regulating mechanisms is to vary the motion of some operating tool-slide or other part which must move at a rate depending upon conditions that are subject to change. The speed regulation of a prime mover such as an engine or a steam turbine is to insure a uniform speed regardless of ordinary variations in the resistance to motion of the driven member or changes in the steam pressure.

When speed variations are essential to the operation of machines such, for example, as are used for some kinds of manufacturing work, the changes are usually obtained by hand-controlled speed-changing devices. If such variations are seldom required, it may be necessary to stop the machine and make an adjustment, or replace one or more gears with others of different diameters. When changes of speed are frequently needed, the machine is generally equipped with some mechanical device enabling one or more variations to be obtained rapidly, by simply moving a wheel, lever, or rod which controls the combination or velocity ratio of the mechanism through which the motion is transmitted. If the machine is of the automatic type, the speed may be regulated according to varying conditions, by the mechanism of the machine itself, which is constructed or adjusted beforehand to give the proper changes. The exact arrangement of the details depends, in any case, upon conditions such as the speed variation required, the importance of rapid changes, the relation of the speed-controlling mechanism to other parts of the machine, etc.

Mechanical devices for varying the speed are of special importance on machine tools. In fact, most machine tools are so constructed that the speed of the cutting tool or of the part being operated upon can be varied, the range or extent of the variation depending upon the type of machine. These changes are desirable in order to cut different kinds of metal at the most efficient speed; for example, soft brass may be turned, drilled, or planed at a much higher speed than cast iron or steel, and, by using the fastest speed that is practicable, obviously the rate of production is increased. Another important reason for speed variation is to secure the proper surface speed for revolving parts, regardless of the diameter, and the correct cutting speeds for rotating tools of different sizes. In the case of lathes or other turning machines, the speed of the work is increased as the diameter decreases, in order to maintain a cutting or surface speed which is considered suitable for the kind of metal being machined. Similarly, drilling or boring machines are so designed that the speed of the drill or boring bar can be varied in accordance with the diameter of the hole being drilled or bored. The design of this part of any machine tool involves determining the minimum and maximum speeds that would ordinarily be required, the total number of variations, the amount or increment by which each step or change varies, and the design of the mechanical device for securing speed changes and transmitting them to the work-spindle or tool. These speed-changing devices usually consist of different combinations of gearing, although belt-driven pulleys and friction gearing are often utilized.

Types of Mechanical Speed-changing Mechanisms. — When a variation of speed is obtained by changing the velocity ratio of two or more parts forming a train of mechanism, one of the following methods is generally employed: (1) By means of conical pulleys connected by a belt or cone-pulleys having " steps " of different diameters upon which a connecting belt may be shifted; (2) by the use of cone-pulleys in conjunction with one or more sets of gears; (3) by means of toothed gears exclusively, with an arrangement that enables the motion to be

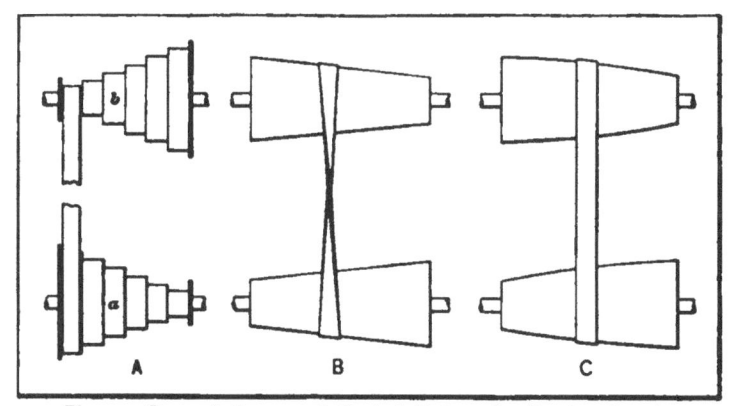

Fig. 1. Stepped Cones and Conical Pulleys for Varying Speeds

transmitted through different ratios or combinations of gearing; (4) by employing a friction transmission consisting of driving and driven disks, pulleys, or wheels, so arranged that one member (or an intermediate connecting device) can be shifted relative to the axis of the other for varying the speed. These different types or classes of speed-changing mechanisms are constructed in various ways.

Arrangement of Cone-pulley Drives. — Diagram A, Fig. 1, illustrates a very simple arrangement for varying speeds, and one which has been extensively employed in connection with machine tools and other classes of machinery. Two cone or stepped pulleys are so located that the large and small steps of one pulley are opposite the small and large steps of the other pulley; consequently, when a connecting belt is shifted from one step to another, the speed is varied. If pulley a is the driver and the belt is in the position shown, the driven pulley b will rotate at the fastest speed, and the speed will be gradually diminished as the belt is shifted toward the right. In designing cone-pulleys, it is important to proportion the different steps so that a belt of fixed length will have approximately the same tension for any position on the pulley.

In the operation of some machines, it is desirable to secure very gradual speed changes, without stopping the driving and driven members for shifting a connecting belt. One simple way of securing such changes is illustrated by the diagrams B and C, Fig. 1. The pulleys in this case are either frustums of cones, as shown at B, or of conoidal form, as at C. The form shown at B is suitable for a crossed-belt, since the crossing of the belt makes it equally tight at corresponding positions on the two cones, which would not be the case with an open belt. When the latter is required, it is preferable to use the curved cone as illustrated at C. While the conical or conoidal pulleys provide very gradual speed changes, the belt tends to shift toward the large end of these pulleys, although such action may be prevented by the guide used for moving the belt to obtain speed changes. Special means of compensating for the taper of the driving and driven cones have been devised. One form of patented cone-pulley drive consists of two conical pulleys of the form illustrated at B; these pulleys are connected by an open belt which, instead of bearing directly on the pulleys, passes over inner bands or belts beveled on the inner face to correspond with the taper of the pulleys. There is one of these compensating bands or auxiliary belts for each pulley; these belts are traversed with the main driving belt when the latter is shifted for varying the speed. Another patented method of compensating for the taper of cone-pulleys is arranged as follows: Instead of connecting the two pulleys directly by one belt, two belts are used, which transmit motion through an intermediate double cone-pulley, which is shifted with the driving belt for obtaining speed changes.

SPEED-CHANGING MECHANISMS 43

Combination of Cone-pulley and Gearing. — One method of using a cone-pulley in conjunction with gearing is illustrated by diagram A, Fig. 2. This particular arrangement is commonly employed on engine lathes and is known as "back-gearing." When the pulley is driving the spindle direct, it is usually locked to the spindle by means of a bolt which connects it with the "face gear" d, the latter being attached to the spindle. For the direct drive, the back-gears are disengaged and the main spindle and cone-pulley revolve together. By disengaging the cone-

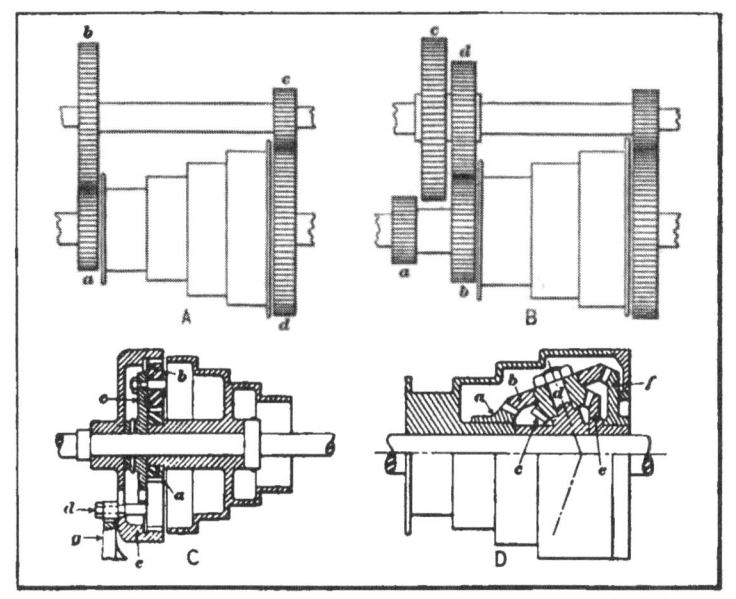

Fig. 2. Gear and Cone-pulley Combinations for Varying Speed

pulley from gear d so that it rotates freely about the spindle and engaging the back-gears, motion is transmitted from the "cone gear" a to gear b, and from c to d; in this way, the range of speeds obtained by the direct drive is doubled. With a four-step cone-pulley, there would be four direct speeds and four slower speeds with the back-gears engaged, the drive being so proportioned that a gradual increase of speeds from the minimum to the maximum, or *vice versa*, may be obtained. The sleeve which carries the two back-gears revolves about a shaft having eccentric bearings at the ends, so that, by turning this shaft with a lever, the back-gears are engaged or disengaged.

Many modern engine lathes have double back-gears, one arrangement being shown at B. There are two cone gears a and b and two mating gears c and d on the rear shaft, so that a double range of geared speeds may be obtained, in addition to variations secured with the direct drive; thus, with a three-step cone-pulley, there would be a total of nine speeds. The gears c and d are shifted along the rear shaft for changing their position relative to the cone gears. A modification of the double back-geared drive is so arranged that the two gears on the rear shaft are connected by a friction clutch controlled by a conveniently located lever. Another design of lathe headstock gearing is commonly known as "triple gearing," although this term is not always applied to the same form of drive by machine-tool builders. Ordinarily, however, a lathe is said to be triple-geared when there are two gear shafts. The cone-pulley speeds are doubled by driving through one combination of gears, and a third range of speeds is obtained by transmitting the motion through the other combination, the pinion of the second shaft being engaged directly with a large internal gear on the faceplate. Triple gearing is used on large lathes and the direct drive to the faceplate provides a very powerful turning movement, such as is required for taking heavy cuts on castings or forgings of large diameter.

Cone-pulley and Epicyclic Gearing. — The use of a cone-pulley and planetary or epicyclic gearing is shown at C, Fig. 2. The cone-pulley has a pinion a, which meshes with pinion b, mounted on a stud carried by plate c. Pinion b also meshes with an internal gear forming part of casting e. This casting and the cone-pulley are both loose upon the shaft, but plate c is keyed to it. When lock-pin d engages a notch in plate c, the gears are locked together and the shaft is driven directly by the cone, the entire mechanism revolving as a unit. When lock-pin d is engaged with a stationary arm g, the internal gear is prevented from rotating and motion is transmitted to the spindle of the machine from the cone-pulley, as pinion a causes pinion b to revolve about the stationary internal gear and carry with it plate c, which transmits a slower speed to the spindle than is obtained with the direct drive. This design, which has been applied to some upright drilling machines, is sometimes known as a "differential back-gear."

Another cone-pulley containing epicyclic gearing is shown by the diagram D, Fig. 2. Bevel gears are employed in this case, instead of spur gears, and the combination is known as "Humpage's gear." This gearing was designed originally to replace the back-gearing of a lathe, but it has been applied to various classes of machinery. When used in conjunction with a cone-pulley, the arrangement is as follows: The cone-pulley is loosely mounted on its shaft and carries a pinion a which meshes with gear b. This gear is locked to pinion c, thus forming a double gear that is free to turn about arm d, the hub of which is also loosely mounted on the spindle or shaft. Gear b meshes with gear f, whereas pinion c meshes with gear e. Diametrically opposite arm d, there is another arm which carries gears corresponding to b and c. This additional gearing is included because of its balancing effect and need not be considered in studying the action of the gearing. The gear e is keyed to the spindle, and, except when a direct drive is employed, gear f is stationary. With the fulcrum gear f stationary and gear a revolving, gear e and the spindle are rotated at a much slower speed, as the arm d and the intermediate connecting gears roll around gear f. The direction in which gear e rotates for a given movement of gear a depends upon the ratio of the gearing, and the direction may be reversed by changing the relative sizes of the gears. When the ratio $\dfrac{f \times c}{b \times e}$ is less than 1, gears a and e will revolve in the same direction, whereas, if this ratio is greater than 1, they will revolve in opposite directions. This is a very compact form of gearing and the velocity ratio may be varied considerably by a slight change in the relative sizes of the gears.

The velocity ratio when $\dfrac{f \times c}{b \times e}$ is less than 1 may be determined by the following formula, in which the letters represent the numbers of teeth in the gears marked with corresponding reference letters in the illustration:

$$\text{Ratio} = \frac{\frac{f}{a} + 1}{1 - \frac{f \times c}{b \times e}}.$$

If gear a has 12 teeth, b, 40 teeth, c, 16 teeth, e, 34 teeth, and f, 46 teeth, then,

$$\text{Ratio} = \frac{\frac{46}{12} + 1}{1 - \frac{46 \times 16}{40 \times 34}} = \frac{4\frac{5}{8}}{\frac{39}{85}} = 10.53$$

Therefore, gear a will revolve 10.53 times while gear e is making one revolution. If the expression $\frac{f \times c}{b \times e}$ is greater than 1, the formula may be changed as follows:

$$\text{Ratio} = \frac{\frac{f}{a} + 1}{\frac{f \times c}{b \times e} - 1}.$$

Geared Speed-changing Mechanisms. — When toothed gearing is used exclusively in a speed-changing mechanism, the most common arrangements may be defined as the (1) sliding-gear type; (2) the clutch-controlled type; (3) the gear-cone and sliding-key type; (4) the gear-cone and expanding-clutch type; (5) the gear-cone and tumbler-gear type; and (6) the multiple crown-gear and shifting-pinion type. Diagram A, Fig. 3, illustrates the principle of the sliding-gear design. One of the parallel shafts carries two fixed gears, a and c; the gears b and d on the other shaft are free to slide axially so that motion may be transmitted either through gears a and b or c and d. The first combination gives a faster speed than the latter, because driving gear a is larger than gear c. For obtaining a greater range of speeds, two or more sets of sliding gears are used in many cases.

Clutch Method of Control. — Diagram B, Fig. 3, illustrates the use of a clutch for controlling speed changes. This clutch is located between the two driven gears and it can be engaged

SPEED-CHANGING MECHANISMS 47

with either of these gears by a lengthwise movement effected usually by a lever. While this clutch is free to slide axially, it is prevented from revolving about the shaft by a spline or key. The driven gears, however, turn freely about the shaft unless engaged by the clutch. A positive clutch is shown in the diagram, or one having teeth which engage corresponding notches in the hubs of the gears; many of the clutches for speed-changing mechanisms, however, are of the friction type.

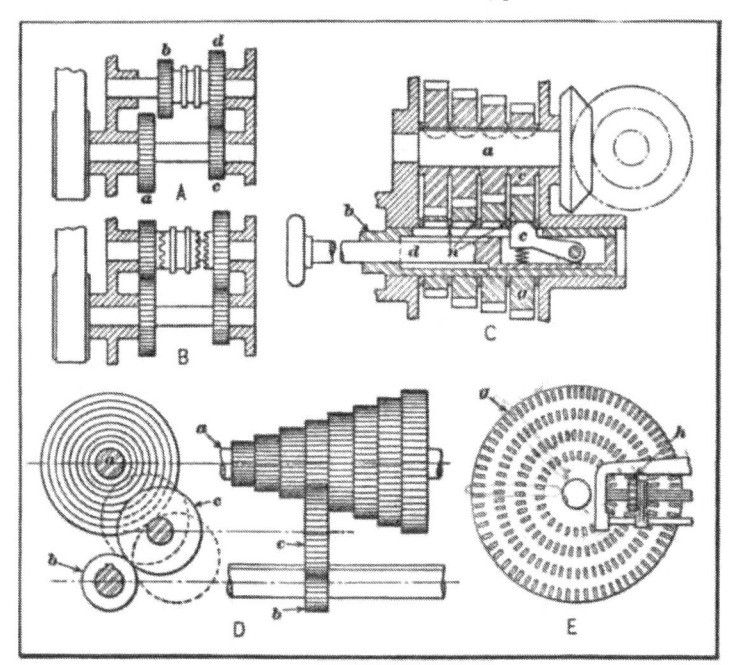

Fig. 3. Diagrams illustrating Different Types of All-geared Speed-changing Mechanisms

In the diagrams A and B, single-belt pulleys are shown upon the driving shafts. This is a common method of rotating the initial driving shaft of speed-changing mechanisms of the all-geared type, the shaft rotating at a constant speed and all of the changes being obtained by the shifting of gears or clutches. On many machines, however, the single constant-speed belt pulley is replaced either by a motor of the constant-speed type or one of the variable-speed type.

Intermeshing Gear Cones and Sliding Key. — The use of intermeshing gear cones and a sliding key for changing speeds is represented by diagram C, Fig. 3. Two cones of gears are mounted upon parallel shafts so that they intermesh, one shaft being the driver and the other, the driven member. All of the gears on shaft a are attached to it, whereas those on shaft b are free to revolve around the shaft, except when engaged by the key c, which can be shifted from one gear to another by moving rod d. If the key were in the position shown by the diagram, the drive would be through gears g and e; if a were the driving shaft, the speed of shaft b could be increased by engaging the key with gears to the left. Obviously, the number of speed changes corresponds to the number of gears in the cone.

The driving end of the key projects through a slot in the shaft and the edges are beveled to an angle of about 45 degrees, so that, as the key is moved in a lengthwise direction, it will be depressed by the action of the beveled edge against a steel washer or guard n placed between each pair of gears. With this arrangement, the key is completely disengaged from one gear before meshing with the next one, which is essential with a drive of this kind. The key is forced upward into engagement with the keyways of the different gears, by means of a spring beneath it. A modification of the mechanism just described is so arranged that, instead of locking the gears in the upper cone by means of a sliding key, each gear is fitted with a ring which may be expanded by means of a wedge, the action of which is controlled by suitable means. The gear-cone and sliding-key mechanism is applied to many different types of machine tools, although this form of mechanism is usually installed either for transmitting feeding motion or in connection with spindle drives which require a relatively small amount of power.

Gear-cone and Tumbler-gear Mechanism. — The arrangement of a gear-cone and tumbler-gear mechanism is represented by diagram D, Fig. 3. There is a cone of gears on shaft a and a pinion b which is free to slide on a splined shaft and is connected with cone gears of different diameters, by means of the tumbler gear c. The tumbler gear is carried by an arm which can be shifted parallel to the axis of the gear cone for aligning the tumbler gear with any one of the cone gears; this arm can also be moved at right angles to the axis of the gear cone for bringing the tumbler gear into mesh with the various sizes of gears composing the cone (as shown by the dotted circles), and provision is made for locking the arm in its different positions. Cone-and-tumbler gearing is not always arranged as shown by diagram D; for instance, the tumbler gear, instead of engaging with a pinion mounted upon a splined shaft, may mesh with a long pinion, or the tumbler gear may be carried by a frame which is adjusted to bring the tumbler gear into mesh with the different cone gears. Another modification consists of a cone of gears which are adjusted axially for alignment with the tumbler gear which is only moved in a radial direction.

Multiple Crown-gear and Shifting Pinion. — The multiple crown-gear type of speed-changing mechanism is represented by diagram E, Fig. 3. The crown gear g has several concentric rows of teeth, and the speed is varied by shifting the pinion h so that it engages a row of larger or smaller diameter. This mechanism has been applied to drilling machines for varying the feeding movements of the drill.

The design and application of the various kinds of speed-changing mechanisms previously described, and the exact arrangement of the gears or other parts are governed very largely by the type of machine and the general nature of the work which it does. Mechanisms of the same general type are often constructed along different lines, and in many cases various combinations are employed.

Frictional Speed-changing Devices. — Friction gearing of various forms is applied to some classes of machinery as a means of obtaining speed changes, although the other types of speed-changing mechanisms previously referred to are much more extensively employed. The frictional type is simple in design and has the further advantage of providing very gradual speed changes. If a definite relation, however, must be maintained between the driving and driven members, the frictional transmission is not suitable, but, in some cases, the fact that it is not positive and tends to slip when subjected to excessive loads is a good feature, as it serves to protect the driven mechanism against excessive stresses.

Fig. 4 shows a type of frictional speed-changing mechanism which has been quite generally used, the details of construction being modified somewhat, owing to variations in the amount of power to be transmitted and other factors affecting the design. The particular arrangement referred to is applied to a Norton running-balance indicating machine. The motor which drives the machine revolves the leather-faced driving disk A which is

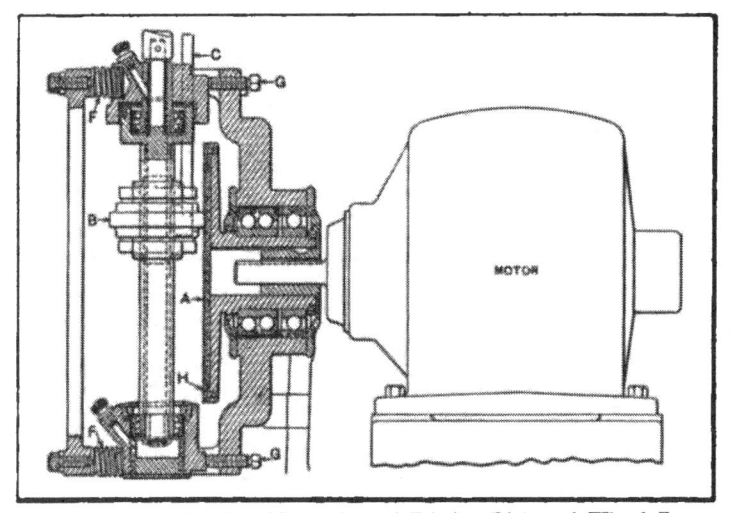

Fig. 4. Speed-changing Mechanism of Friction Disk and Wheel Type

in contact with a steel wheel B. The vertical shaft passing through the driven wheel transmits motion to a horizontal shaft (not shown) at the top of the machine, which, in turn, revolves whatever part is to be tested for running balance. Variations in the speed of the work are obtained by changing the position of wheel B relative to the axis of the driving disk A. The adjustments of wheel B are controlled by a hand lever provided with a notched quadrant for holding it in a given position. This hand lever is connected with the slide of wheel B by link C. A reversal of motion is obtained by simply shifting wheel B to the opposite side of the axis of the driving disk. The wheel is held against the leather-faced disk with sufficient pressure by means of springs *F* which are provided with screws for varying the compression. If the leather disk becomes flattened out or thin from wear, the wheel *B* may be adjusted inward by means of stop-screws *G*. The leather disk is held in place by a retaining ring *H*. With a mechanism of this kind, the adjustments for changing the speed should only be made when the driving disk is running.

Many speed-changing mechanisms of the friction type have opposing cones which are connected by some intermediate member that may be adjusted to vary the speed. The use of an ordinary belt has already been referred to. Fig. 5 shows an arrangement for regulating the speed of a driven shaft, by changing the position of a wheel *A* placed between the driving cone *B* and the driven cone *C*. These two cones are made of cast iron and the bearing surface of the intermediate wheel is formed of leather disks

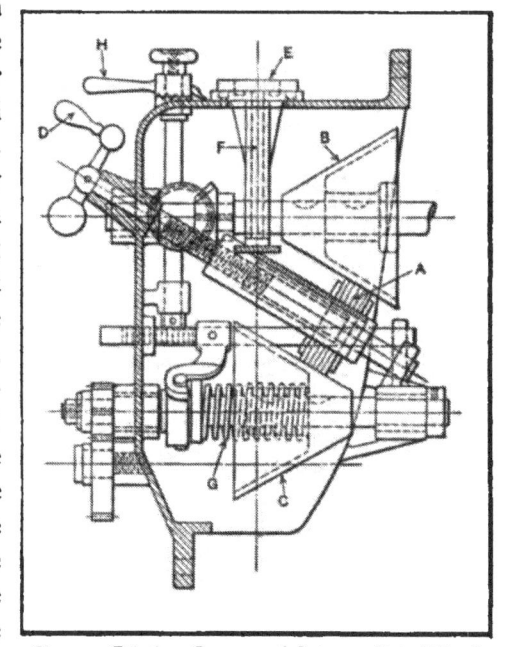

Fig. 5. Friction Cones and Intermediate Wheel for Varying Speeds

held in place between two flanges or collars. This particular mechanism is used for varying the feeding movement of a cold-metal saw. The handle *D* connecting with a screw is used for controlling the position of the intermediate wheel and the rate of speed. A dial at *E* shows the rate of feed per minute, this dial being connected through shaft *F* and a gear at the lower end with a rack on the adjustable member, so that any change in the position of the wheel is indicated by the dial. The lower friction cone is held in contact with the wheel by means of a spring *G*, the tension of which may be regulated by lever *H*. This lever is provided with graduations so that the same tension as well as the rate of feed per minute may be duplicated.

Another method of transmitting motion from a driving to a driven cone is shown in Fig. 6, which illustrates the Evans friction cones. The two cone-pulleys are not directly in contact with each other, but bear against a band or ring of leather which

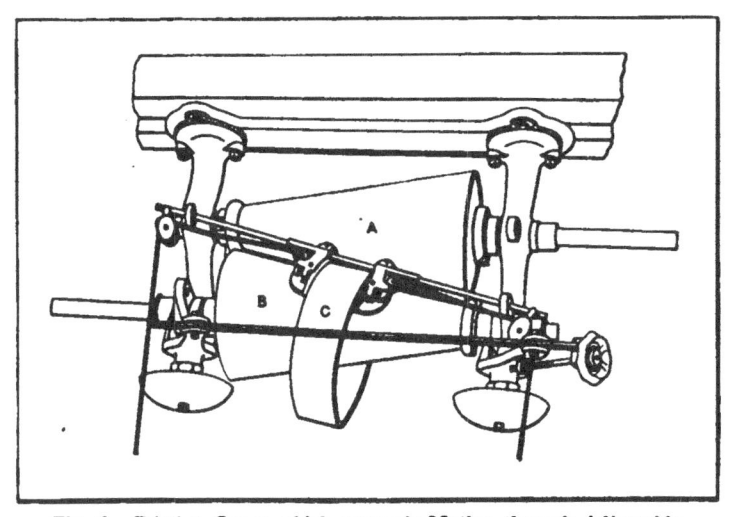

Fig. 6. Friction Cones which transmit Motion through Adjustable Leather Ring or Belt

serves to transmit the motion. The speed of the driven cone is varied by simply shifting this leather ring so that it bears against a larger or smaller part of the cones. If cone *A* is the driver, the speed of cone *B* would be gradually increased if belt *C* were shifted toward the right, since the practical effect of this shifting movement is to increase the diameter of the driving pulley. This mechanism is used ordinarily as a variable-speed countershaft. There are two general methods of starting or stopping the driven members. Some friction cones are so arranged that the leather ring is shifted to a parallel part of the cones for disengaging the drive, and others are so designed that one cone is raised and lowered by the shifting lever, thus starting and stopping at the same speed.

Multiple-disk Type of Speed-changing Mechanism. — The variable-speed mechanism shown in Fig. 7 is an ingenious design that is applied to some of the Brown & Sharpe cylindrical grinding machines for changing the rotary speed of the part being ground and also the rate of the table traverse. Three levers grouped around a dial at the front of the machine are used for

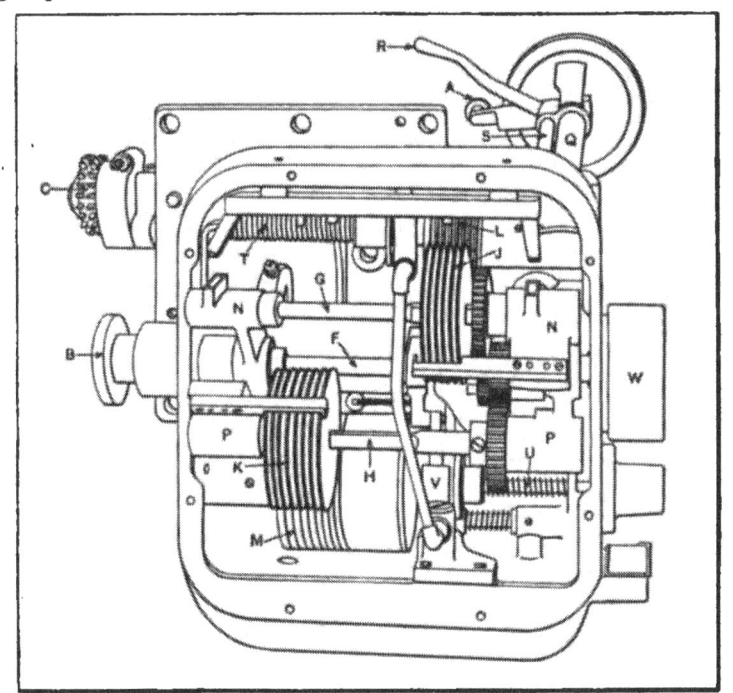

Fig. 7. Multiple Friction Disk Type of Speed-changing Mechanism

controlling the mechanism. The position of lever A governs the rotary speed of the work, and another lever in front of the circular dial (not shown in the illustration) serves to change the rate of the table traversing movement. These changes of work speed and table traverse are entirely independent. The long lever R is used for starting and stopping the rotation of the work and the traversing movement of the table simultaneously. The mechanism is driven from a driving shaft which runs at a constant speed and connects with coupling B. The sprocket C is connected to the reversing mechanism and drives the table traverse. Another sprocket (not shown) is connected by a pair of silent chains and a splined shaft, with a driving member for the headstock.

The mechanism operates as follows: The shaft F carrying coupling B drives shafts G and H at a constant speed through spur gearing. The shafts G and H carry a series of hardened steel disks mounted on square portions of the shafts. These disks J and K are ground slightly convex and each group of disks intermeshes with another group or series of hardened steel disks L and M. Each of these driven disks has a rim at the periphery so that the point of contact with the driving disk is always at the outer edge. The shafts G and H are mounted in swinging brackets N and P, both of which pivot on shaft F, thus allowing the position of disks J and K to be varied relative to the disks L and M. If the convex disks J are swung towards the recessed disks L, the surfaces of disks J, which actually do the driving, decrease in radius and, consequently, the speed of disks L and their shaft also decreases. The lever A controls the position of bracket P and the speed of the headstock, whereas the lever at the front of the dial (not shown) controls bracket N and the feeding movements of the table. Motion is transmitted to these brackets through bevel pinions meshing with segment gears on the brackets.

With this mechanism, slight variations in speed may be obtained while the machine is in motion. When lever R is shifted for stopping the machine, a cam at the end of shaft S operates a lever which relieves the pressure applied to disks L and M by the springs shown at T and U. This lever also applies brakes which quickly stop the table and headstock. When the lever is raised for starting the mechanism, the disks L and M grip the intermeshing disks J and K, and the driven members are started without shock, the action being very similar to the well-known multiple-disk friction clutch. A plunger pump at V pumps oil from the bottom of the case to a distributor at the top which lubricates the entire mechanism.

SPEED-CHANGING MECHANISMS

Concave Friction Disks and Inclined Wheel. — The frictional variable-speed transmission shown in Fig. 8 is an example of the type having annular concave frictional surfaces engaged by an intermediate wheel the inclination of which is varied for changing the speed. The principle upon which the device operates is illustrated by the diagram at the left. The two disks having annular concave surfaces are rotated from some source of power and run loose on shaft A which is driven at a variable speed. The intermediate wheel D is pivoted at O to arm B, so that it can be inclined as indicated by the dotted lines. The drive to shaft A is transmitted through arm B. When wheel

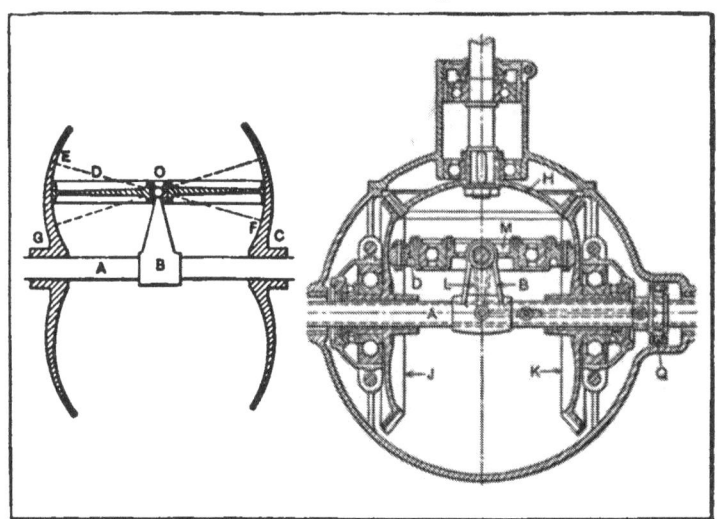

Fig. 8. Variable-speed Transmission having Annular Concave Surfaces and Inclinable Friction Wheel

D is parallel to shaft A, as shown in the illustration, and the two disks B and C are revolving in opposite directions at the same speed, wheel D will simply revolve about pivot O, and arm B and shaft A will remain stationary. If wheel D is inclined, however, as indicated by the dotted line EF, the contact surface at E will be revolving at a higher circumferential speed than the surface F on disk C; consequently, pivot O, arm B, and shaft A will be given a rotary motion, the rate of which depends upon the angularity of wheel D. The greater the angularity, the greater will be the difference in the diameter of the contact surfaces of disks G and C and the higher the speed of shaft A. By inclining wheel D in the opposite direction, the rotation of shaft A can be reversed.

A variable-speed mechanism designed on this principle is shown at the right of the diagram in Fig. 8. A bevel gear H mounted on the end of the driving shaft revolves the two bevel gears J and K mounted on shaft A, which is the driven member. These bevel gears J and K have annular concave surfaces which engage the cork surface of wheel D. This wheel revolves on an annular ball bearing, the inner race of which is attached to ring M pivoted on a stud carried by arm B. The angular position of wheel D is controlled by a lever L integral with the pivoted ring M. This lever is connected with ring Q which is engaged by a forked lever similar to the form used for shifting clutches.

An objection to variable-speed mechanisms based on this principle is that the variation of speed does not change the torque, so that, even though there is considerable speed reduction, the torque will not be proportionally greater, because the limiting factor for the torque is the frictional adherence between the driving and driven contact surfaces, and this frictional resistance is independent of the speed at which the shaft A is running; consequently, while variable-speed devices in general are of such construction that the torque increases when the speed decreases, in the present case the speed is variable, while the torque remains constant. As the main feature of variable-speed devices is often not the variation of speed as much as the increased torque obtained by a decrease in speed, the objection referred to is one of great importance.

Friction Disk and Epicyclic Gear Combination. — A very high velocity ratio or great reductions of speed, as well as extremely small variations of speed, may be obtained by the mechanism to be described. This mechanism (see Fig. 9) is a combination of friction disks and a train of epicyclic or differential gearing. The two disks D and E are free to revolve upon the vertical shaft C, and the hubs of these disks form the bevel gears F and G. Between these two bevel gears are the additional gears T and

J mounted on pin H, which is attached to shaft C. The disks D and E are in frictional contact with wheels N and O, and their position is regulated by screw K, which is rotated through disks L and R. If wheel N is revolved and disks D and E are equidistant from the axes of wheels N and O (as shown in the illustration), both disks will revolve at the same speed, but in opposite directions. As gears F and G also rotate at the same speed, the intermediate gears T and J merely revolve idly upon pin H, which remains in one position. Any change in the position of disks D and E relative to the wheels N and O will result in reducing the speed of one disk and increasing the speed of the other one; consequently, gears T and J begin to advance around whichever gear F or G has the slower motion, so that pin H and shaft C revolve in the same direction as the more rapidly revolving gear. If disks D and E

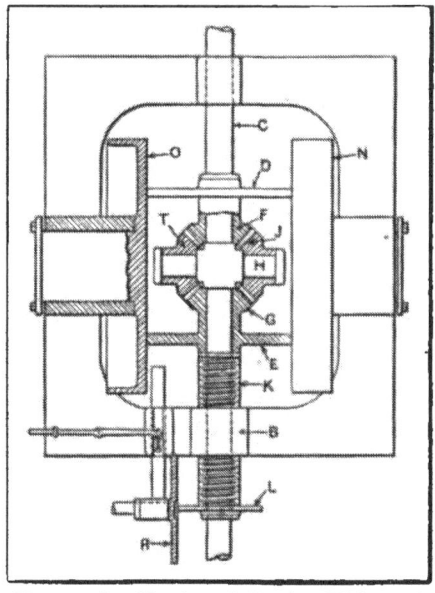

Fig. 9. Combination of Friction Disks and Epicyclic Gear Train for Obtaining Great Reduction of Speed

are only moved a small amount from the central position, the differential action in the gearing and the motion of shaft C will be at a very slow rate. The direction of rotation may be changed by moving the disks upward or downward.

Centrifugal and Inertia Governors. — When the regulation of speed is automatically controlled, some form of governing mechanism of the centrifugal type is commonly employed. Many of the governors used on steam engines depend for their action upon the effect of centrifugal force on a rotating element. In the case of a " fly-ball " governor (see diagram D, Fig. 1,

Chapter I) weights or balls attached to pivoted levers are revolved by the engine and if the speed increases above normal, the balls or weighted levers move outward from the axis of rotation, owing to the increase in centrifugal force. This change in the position of the revolving balls may be transmitted through suitable connecting levers and rods to a valve which partly closes, thus reducing the steam supply. When a governor of this type is applied to a Corliss engine, the release of the steam valves and the point of cut-off is controlled directly by the governor. Most governors of the fly-ball type are equipped with one or more springs which tend to resist the outward movement of the revolving balls.

The inertia or centrifugal-inertia governor, which is now used so extensively, is attached to the flywheel and regulates the speed by varying the position of the eccentric or crankpin that operates the valve. The general principle upon which this type of governor operates is illustrated by the design shown in Fig. 10. This particular governor has an inertia bar A with enlarged ends to increase the weight at the ends. This bar is pivoted at B where there is a roller bearing to reduce the frictional resistance. The eccentric C is attached to the inertia bar and it has an elongated hole or opening to permit movements relative to the crankshaft. Directly opposite the eccentric is a third weight D, which balances the effect of gravity on the eccentric. A heavy coil spring E is attached to the inertia bar. A rod F is pivoted to the bar on the opposite side of

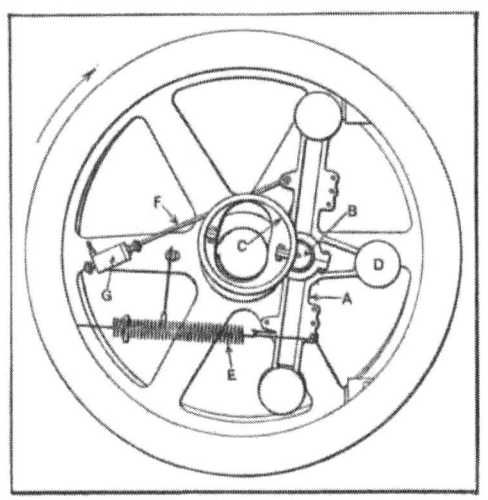

Fig. 10. Centrifugal-inertia Type of Engine Governor

bearing *B* and is connected to a loose-fitting piston in the oil dashpot *G*.

The flywheel revolves in the direction shown by the arrow and speed variations cause a slight movement of the inertia bar about its bearing in one direction or another, thus changing the position of the eccentric, which changes the point of cut-off. If the speed increases, the inertia bar lags behind momentarily and the steam is cut off earlier during the stroke because the eccentric swings inward and shortens the travel of the valve. If a sudden increase of load should cause the engine to run slower, lever *A*, as a result of its inertia, would tend to continue running at the faster speed, which would swing the lever forward about bearing *B* in the direction of rotation, thus increasing the valve travel and admitting more steam to the cylinder by delaying the point of cut-off. The spring end of the inertia bar is the heavier and the speed of rotation depends entirely upon the equilibrium between the centrifugal force acting upon the inertia bar and the tension of the spring, while the actual movement of the governor parts is effected by the inertia of the weighted end of the bar. The sensitiveness of the governor may be varied by adjusting a by-pass valve upon cylinder *G*. Other governors of this general type vary in regard to the form of the weighted lever and the arrangement of springs or other details. The inertia type is preferable to the purely centrifugal design for engines subjected to sudden and decided load changes.

CHAPTER III

CONVERSION OF ROTARY AND RECTILINEAR MOTIONS

MACHINES of many different types are equipped with some form of mechanism for changing a rotary motion to a rectilinear or straight-line motion, or *vice versa*. The design of such a mechanism may depend upon the kind of motion required, the amount of power to be transmitted, or other considerations. In this chapter, the common or standard methods are described, and also a number of special mechanisms.

Crank and Connecting-rod. — The crank and connecting-rod illustrated in Fig. 1 is a very simple and common arrangement which, when applied to a steam or gas engine, changes the rectilinear movement of the piston and cross-head to a rotary motion for revolving the crankshaft of the engine. This crank mechanism is also used frequently on machines of many different types, not only to transform rectilinear to rotary motion, but to secure a rectilinear movement from a driving member which revolves. The air compressor is an example of the latter application, the rotation of the crank, in this case, being changed to a rectilinear motion for the compressor piston, and there are many other examples to be found in practice. The distance traversed by the part moving in a straight line is equal to the diameter of the circle described by the center of the crankpin, and this distance is known as the *stroke*.

Dead-center Position. — When the center of the crankpin is at either A or B (Fig. 1), it is said to be on the "dead center," because the crank and connecting-rod are then in line, and a force or pressure applied to the piston or cross-head will not cause the crank to revolve, so long as it remains on the dead center or in line with the direction in which the force is applied. To avoid difficulty in starting engines of the duplex type, such as locomotives, for instance, the crankpins are located 90 degrees apart, so that, when one engine is on the dead center, the other crankpin is in position for transmitting the maximum amount of power; thus there is never any difficulty in starting.

Relative Motions of Crankpin and Cross-head. — In some cases, especially in connection with steam engine work, it is important to note the relative motions of the crankpin and cross-head, or whatever part has a straight-line movement. The crankpin has a practically uniform velocity, but the sliding

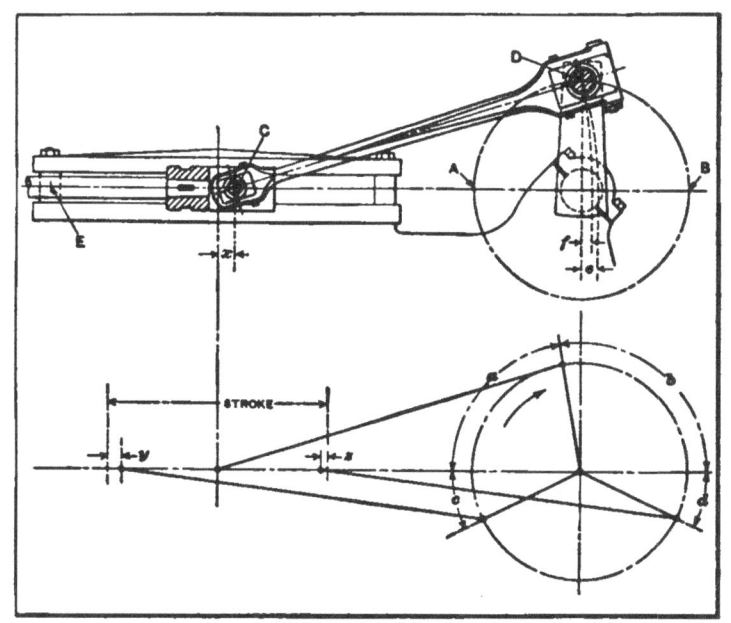

Fig. 1. Diagrams showing Relative Motions of Crankpin and Cross-head

member, which in the case of a steam engine consists of the cross-head and piston, has a variable velocity. Each time the cross-head reaches the end of its stroke, it starts from a state of rest and the velocity increases during approximately one-half of its stroke and then decreases until the cross-head again comes to a state of rest at the opposite end of the stroke. The relative positions of the crankpin and cross-head also vary at every point of the stroke; for instance, when the crankpin is in the mid-position (as shown in Fig. 1), the cross-head is a distance

x away from the center of its stroke. The position of the crank when the cross-head has traversed one-half its stroke is indicated by the lower diagram. If the crank were rotating in the direction indicated by the arrow, it would turn through some arc a less than 90 degrees, to bring the cross-head to its mid-position, and through a greater arc b for the remaining half of the stroke of the cross-head. It will thus be seen that the relative motion between the cross-head and crank during the first half of the stroke is different from that of the second half. This variation in movement is further illustrated by locating the distances that the cross-head moves for equal movements of the crank; for example, if the crank is moved through an arc c, from the dead-center position, the cross-head will move a distance y, but if the crank is placed on the opposite dead center and then moved through an arc d, which is equal to c, the cross-head will move a distance z, which is less than y. This is due to the fact that one-half of the crankpin circle curves toward the cross-head, whereas the other half curves away from it. This variation of motion has an important effect on the design of steam-engine valve-gears, and it is objectionable in some types of mechanisms. (The connecting-rod shown in Fig. 1 was drawn somewhat shorter than it should be, in order to magnify the effects of angularity. The length of the connecting-rod from the center of the cross-head wrist-pin to the center of the crankpin is usually equal to from $4\frac{1}{2}$ to $6\frac{1}{2}$ times the crank radius, on steam engines.)

The Eccentric. — The eccentric is a modified form of crank and produces a motion similar to that of an ordinary crank and connecting-rod. The eccentric may be considered as a crankpin which is so enlarged that it surrounds the main shaft. In reality, the eccentric g (see Fig. 11, Chapter I) is mounted on the shaft and is surrounded by an eccentric strap h to which the connecting-rod is attached. The eccentric is very useful when a relatively small movement is required, and it is not practicable to obtain it by a crank located at the end of the shaft. Eccentrics have been extensively used for operating steam engine valve-gears, and for many other purposes. The distance from the center of the eccentric to the center of the shaft upon which it is mounted is known as the *eccentricity*. The eccentricity corresponds to the radius of an equivalent crank. The terms " throw " and " eccentricity " are sometimes used interchangeably, but, according to general usage, the *throw* is equal to the diameter of the circle described by the eccentric center, and it is equivalent to twice the eccentricity.

Crank and Slotted Cross-head. — The irregularity in the motion of a cross-head relative to the crank with the form of crank mechanism illustrated in Fig. 1 depends upon the length of the connecting-rod. If an arc is struck from point D with C as a center, the distance e will represent the displacement of the cross-head from its mid-position when the crank has turned through 90 degrees. As the radius CD representing the length of the connecting-rod is increased, obviously there will be less irregularity in the motion. For instance, if E were taken as a center and ED represented the length of the connecting-rod, the displacement of the cross-head from mid-position would be less, as indicated by dimension f. Therefore, it will be seen that the greater the length of the connecting-rod, the less the irregularity of motion. If it were practicable to use a connecting-rod of very great length, an arc intersecting point D and the horizontal center-line would only be a very slight distance from the center of the main shaft. With such an arrangement, the horizontal movement of the cross-head would be practically the same as the movement of the crankpin measured horizontally. If the connecting-rod were of infinite length, theoretically the movement of the cross-head and crankpin in a horizontal direction would be alike.

A simple form of mechanism for eliminating the irregularity of motion previously referred to is illustrated at A in Fig. 2. This mechanism is known as a " crank and slotted cross-head " or the *Scotch yoke*. The cross-head a has a slot which is at right angles to the center-line xx representing the direction of rectilinear movement. The crankpin carries a block, which is a sliding fit in this slot, and is free to revolve about the pin. As the crank revolves, the distance which the crankpin moves, as measured in a horizontal direction, will be the same as the movement of the cross-head. This mechanism is sometimes called a *harmonic motion*, because if the crank rotates uniformly, the cross-head will be given a harmonic motion. When a point, as at *b*, moves with uniform velocity along a circular path, point *c* will have a harmonic motion along the center-line *xx*; hence, harmonic motion may be defined as the movement of a point along the diameter of a circle, which is projected from a point moving with uniform velocity along the circumference.

The crank and slotted cross-head has been applied to some types of steam pumps. One of the rods extending from the

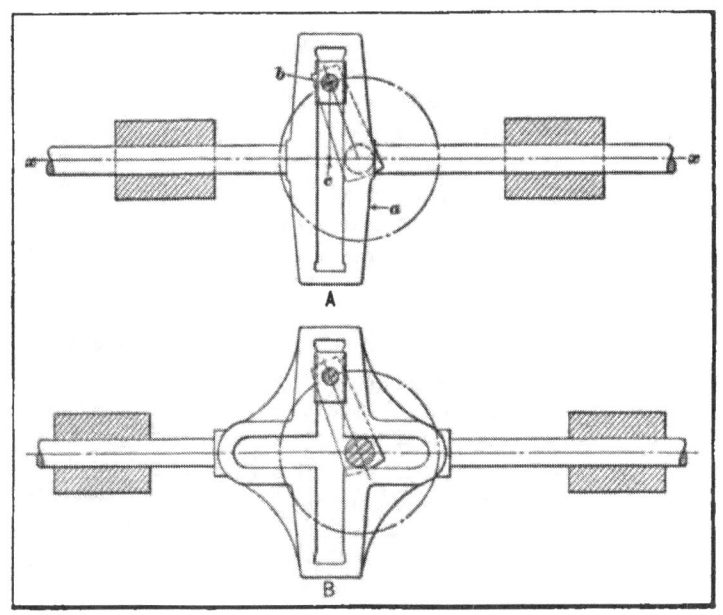

Fig. 2. Slotted Cross-head or Scotch Yoke

slotted cross-head carries the steam piston and the other, the water piston. The crank is a driven member, and its radius regulates the length of the stroke. By mounting a flywheel on the crankshaft, steam may be cut off before the end of the stroke and used expansively, because of the energy stored in the flywheel. The crank and slotted cross-head is a very compact form of mechanism, although the sliding motion of the block in the slotted member causes more friction and wear than the ordinary crank and connecting-rod of the type shown in Fig. 1. The latter is also simpler in construction and is, therefore, used almost exclusively as an engine connection, as well as for many other classes of machinery.

The diagram B, Fig. 2, shows a modification of the crank and slotted cross-head or Scotch yoke. This mechanism gives the same motion as the one illustrated at A, but the cross-head has two slots at right angles to each other, so that it can be placed

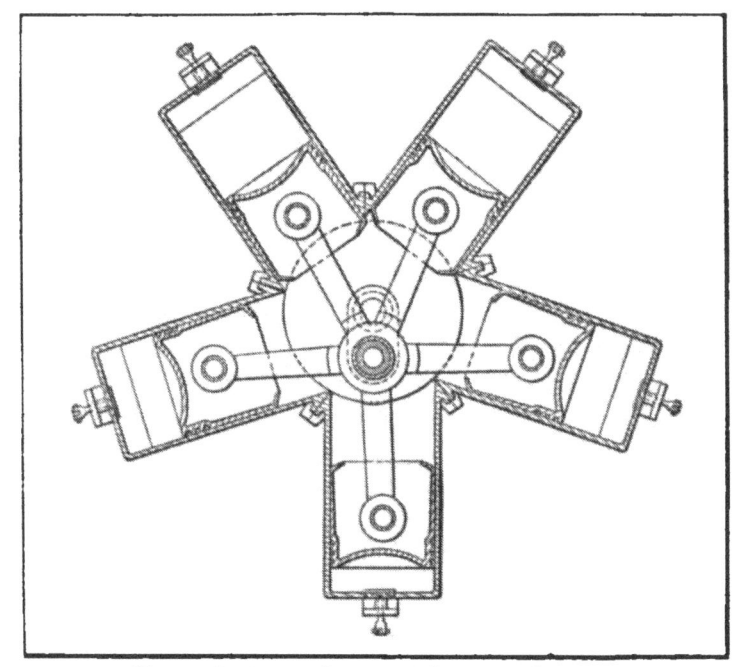

Fig. 3. Stationary Crank and Revolving Cylinders

anywhere on a continuous shaft. The vertical slot is for the sliding crank block, whereas the horizontal slot forms a clearance space for the shaft. With this design, the crank could be placed at any intermediate point on the shaft without using a center crank. It is not as compact, however, as form A, and the vertical slot is not continuous, which is an objectionable feature.

Cylinders which Revolve about a Stationary Crank. — A crank which is connected to a piston or other reciprocating part ordinarily revolves, but a piston may be given a rectilinear motion relative to a cylinder by holding the crank in a fixed position and revolving the cylinder, connecting-rod, and piston about the crank. An example illustrating this method of utilizing the crank is shown by the diagram, Fig. 3, which illustrates the general arrangement of a type of aeroplane motor that is extensively used. With this form of motor, as the cylinders revolve about the stationary crank, the pistons move in and out relative to the cylinders, the same as though the latter were stationary and the crank revolved. The cylinders form the flywheel and drive the propeller and, as they revolve rapidly, the temperature is reduced sufficiently by air cooling and without any auxiliary cooling device. The gyroscopic effect of the rotating cylinders also serves to steady the aeroplane in its flight. The valves for controlling the admission of the gas and the exhaust are actuated by a single cam and are closed by the outward movements resulting from centrifugal force. The higher the speed of the motor, the greater the centrifugal force and also the greater the necessity for a rapid closing of the valves.

Cylinders which Revolve Within an Eccentric Track. — The design of the aeroplane motor shown in Fig. 4 illustrates another method of obtaining a rectilinear motion of a piston relative to a cylinder. The six cylinders are formed in one solid casting and rotate within eccentric annular tracks A which extend around both side walls of the casing. The pistons are carried by trunnions supported by ball bearings B. There are two of these ball bearings for each piston, and they are free to run on the annular tracks A. When the cylinder casting revolves, it carries with it the pistons and the ball bearings; as the center of tracks A is offset relative to the axis about which the cylinder rotates, the pistons are given an inward and outward motion relative to the cylinders. The pins upon which the pistons are mounted carry guide shoes that reciprocate in slots formed in the cylinder walls for about half the length of the cylinder. These guide shoes are intended to steady the action of the piston and reduce wear on the cylinders.

The action of the motor will be more apparent by noting the

position of each piston relative to its cylinder. For instance, the piston shown at *C* is at the inner end of its stroke as it is opposite that part of the annular tracks which is nearest to the axis about which the cylinders revolve. When the motor is in operation, the charge of compressed gas is fired at approximately this position, and then, as the cylinders revolve in a clockwise direction, the piston moves outward from this point while the

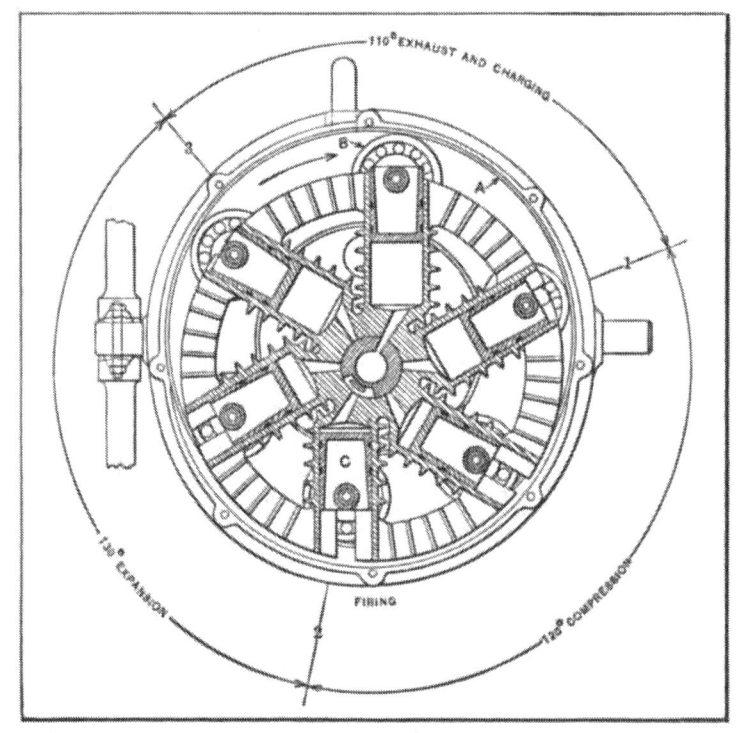

Fig. 4. Cylinders revolving within an Eccentric Track, which imparts a Reciprocating Motion to Pistons

ignited charge of gas is expanding, as indicated by the arrow extending between radial lines 2 and 3. This charge is then exhausted and a new charge is drawn in and compressed as the cylinder and piston pass between radial lines 1 and 2, as indicated in the illustration.

Rack and Gear Combination. — A rack connecting with a spur gear or pinion is commonly used to change rotary motion to rectilinear motion, or *vice versa*. Ordinarily, the spur gear is the driver, but this order is sometimes reversed and a rack is given a reciprocating movement for revolving a pinion. The driving mechanism of a planer, shown in Fig. 5, Chap. IV, represents a typical example of a rack and gear combination. The rack *L* is attached to the bed or platen of the planer, and meshing with this rack is a large gear *M*, known as a "bull-wheel," which receives its rotary motion through a train of gearing connecting with a shaft upon which the driving pulleys *B*

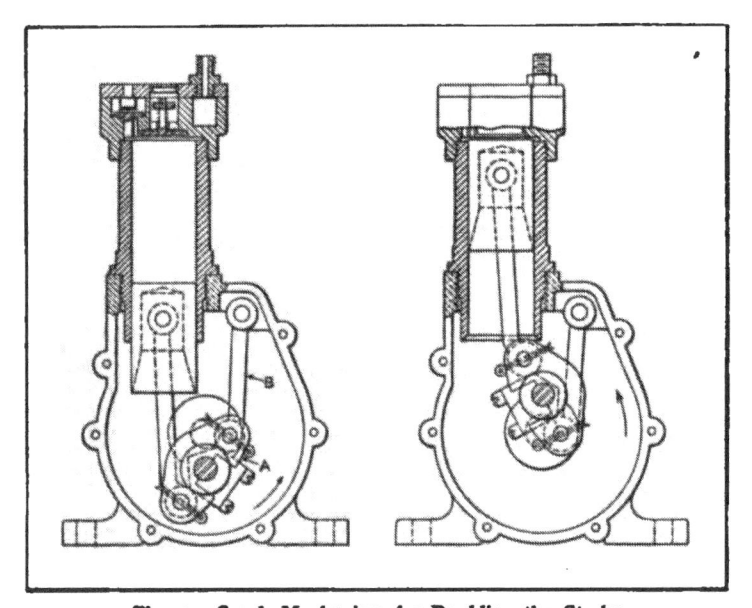

Fig. 5. Crank Mechanism for Doubling the Stroke

are mounted. These pulleys are driven by open and cross belts which are alternately shifted from loose pulleys to a central pulley which is keyed to the shaft. The point of reversal is controlled by dogs *K* which may be adjusted along the side of the table for varying the length of the stroke. The planer table rests in V-shaped ways or guiding surfaces which cause it to move in a straight line.

Crank Mechanism for Doubling the Stroke. — A crank and link mechanism is shown in Fig. 5 which makes it possible to obtain a rectilinear motion approximately equal to twice the throw of the driving crank. This mechanism is shown applied to an air pump for use on automobiles, either for the inflation of tires or in connection with engine starting apparatus requiring compressed air. The crank proper is of the center type with a bearing on each side. The connecting-rod is attached to the yoke A which is mounted on the main crankpin. The opposite end of this yoke is pivoted to link B which is suspended from a pin attached to the compressor casing. As the crankshaft rotates, this link oscillates and so controls the position of yoke A that the stroke of the piston is approximately doubled. The view to the left shows the piston at the lower end of its stroke. As the crank turns in a counter-clockwise direction, link B swings to the right so that the right-hand end of yoke A is forced downward and the left-hand end upward, as indicated by the right-hand illustration which shows the piston at the top of its stroke. The advantage of this crank mechanism is that it enables a comparatively large capacity to be obtained from a small compact pump.

Crank-driven Pinion Engaging Upper and Lower Racks. — Another method of doubling the stroke when a crank of relatively small size is necessary, owing to a limited space, or desirable, in order to obtain a compact design, is by means of a fixed and a movable rack having a crank-driven pinion interposed between them. The pinion is pivoted to the end of the crank connecting-rod so that it is free to roll along the stationary rack when the crank revolves. As the result of this rolling movement of the pinion, the movable rack is given a rectilinear motion equal to twice the stroke of the crank, or twice the diameter of the path described by the crankpin. This mechanism has been used for driving the beds of cylinder presses.

A modification of the plain gear-driven crank is shown in Fig. 6 which illustrates the bed motion of a two-revolution pony press. The driving and driven gears A and B are of the elliptical form in order to compensate for the motion derived from a crank rotating at uniform velocity. The driven gear B revolves the crank which, in turn, transmits motion to pinion C by means of the connecting-rod shown. This pinion is rolled in first one direction and then the other along the stationary rack D, and imparts a rectilinear motion to rack E and the press bed. The press bed moves a distance equal to twice the distance that the axis of gear C moves, or four times the radius of the driving crank. The elliptical gears are so proportioned and located relative to the crank as to give a more uniform motion to the press bed than could be obtained with a crank rotating at uniform velocity. With an ordinary crank, whatever part is given a rectilinear motion starts from a state of rest, and the velocity gradually increases toward the center of the stroke and then decreases until it again becomes zero at the opposite end of the stroke.

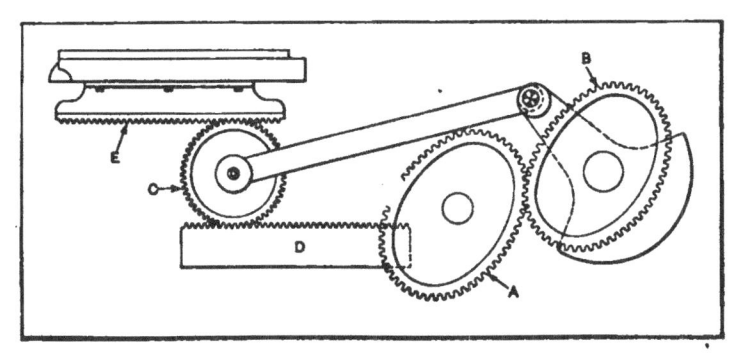

Fig. 6. Crank-driven Pinion engaging Stationary and Movable Rack for Doubling Stroke

With the elliptical gearing shown, as the pinion C approaches either end of its stroke and the crank advances toward the " dead-center " position, the long side or radius of the driving gear comes into engagement with the driven gear and increases its velocity, and also the velocity of the crank. As the return stroke begins, the velocity of the driven gear and crank gradually decreases, because the radius of the working side of the driving gear gradually diminishes; the result is that, when the crank is at right angles to the line along which the axis of pinion C moves and is in a position to impart the maximum velocity to pinion C, the speed of the crank is slowest, because it is then driven by the shortest radius of the driving gear. As the crank moves away from this central position at right angles to the center-line of motion, the speed is gradually accelerated again so that pinion C does not slow down as it would with a crank rotating at uniform speed. The reversal of the heavy press bed is assisted by means of "air springs" or cushions, the same as on cylinder presses in general. This mechanism is intended for small presses.

Single- and Double-stroke Toggle Mechanism. — The toggle mechanism previously described in connection with Fig. 11, Chapter I, is often utilized for changing a rotary to a rectilinear motion, especially when a powerful squeezing action is required.

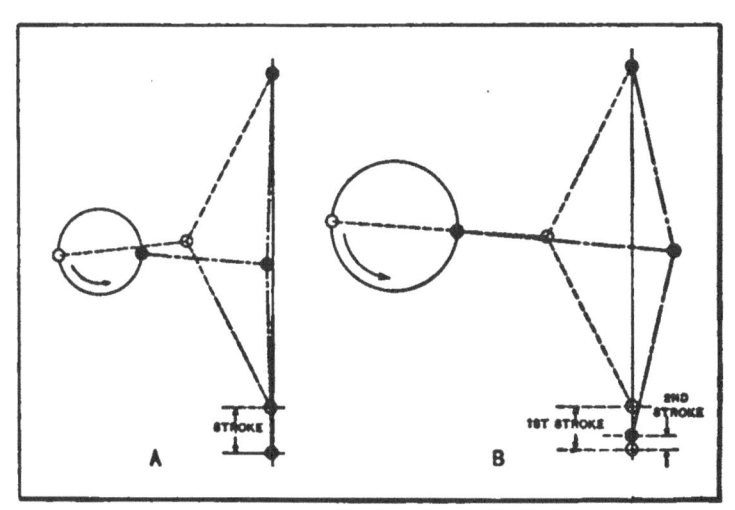

Fig. 7. Diagrams showing Action of Single- and Double-stroke Toggle Mechanism

An arrangement of this kind is used on some cold-heading machines, such as are employed for forming heads on bolts, rivets, etc. The diagram A, Fig. 7, illustrates a crank-driven toggle mechanism which gives a forward and return stroke for each revolution of the crank. When the links of the toggle are straightened, as indicated by the heavy lines, the punch which forms the head on the work is at the end of its stroke, and it is then withdrawn as the crank makes another half revolution. This form of drive as applied to a cold-header is known as the "two-cycle type," because two revolutions of the crankshaft are necessary to complete a rivet or bolt requiring two blows of the punch.

Many classes of work cannot be done satisfactorily with a single stroke, owing to the amount of metal that must be upset in order to form the head of a bolt or rivet. A design of toggle mechanism which is extensively used on double-stroke machines is illustrated by the diagram *B*, Fig. 7. With this arrangement, two blows are obtained for each revolution of the crank connecting with the toggle. The location of the crank is such that the links of the toggle are straightened before the crank has made one-half revolution; consequently, when the half revolution is completed, the links of the toggle are carried beyond the center-line, as indicated by the diagram, which causes the ram and die to be withdrawn preparatory to making a second stroke. As the crank continues to revolve and the toggle is again straightened, a second working stroke is made and then the ram and die are withdrawn; this cycle of operations is repeated for each revolution of the crank. The two strokes which are obtained for each revolution of the crank may be of unequal length, as shown by the diagram, or of equal length, depending upon the position of the crank relative to the line of the straightened toggle. A cold-header having this form of drive is known as a " one-cycle " machine, since it will impart two blows to the work for each revolution of the crankshaft.

Toggle Mechanism of Drawing Press. — One way of arranging the toggle mechanism of a drawing press is illustrated in Fig. 8. When a press of this kind is in operation, the sheet of metal to be drawn is pressed firmly down upon the die face by a blank-holder, while the drawing punch forces the metal into or through the die. The blank-holder prevents the sheet stock from buckling, and it should remain in the downward position while the drawing punch is at work. Toggle mechanisms are employed on large drawing presses to operate the blank-holder. The toggle mechanism illustrated in Fig. 8 is operated from crank *H* on the main crankshaft. This crank connects with link *A*, the lower end of which is attached to yoke *B*. The upper end of

ROTARY AND RECTILINEAR MOTIONS 73

yoke B is guided by link E, which is pivoted to the frame of the press, and the lower end is guided by another link C pivoted at D. These two links C and D compel the yoke to move in practically a vertical straight line when it is traversed by the action of crank H. Attached to the yoke are two other links connecting with bellcranks F and G which, in turn, are pivoted to the side of the press frame. The outer arms of these bellcranks are connected by long links or rods with cranks on the ends of two

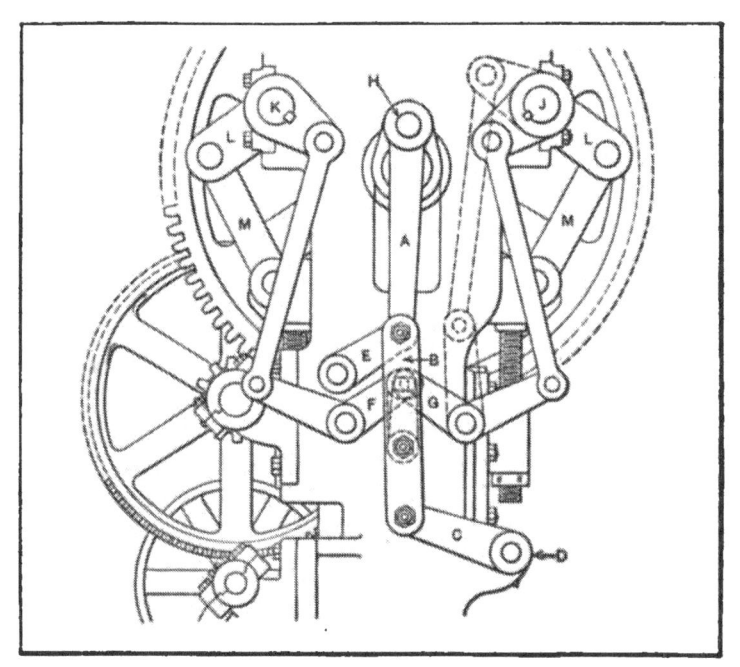

Fig. 8. Application of Toggle Mechanism to a Drawing Press

rockshafts J and K, at the front and rear of the press, respectively. From these rockshafts, motion is transmitted to the blankholder by means of arms L and links M. The dotted lines on one side indicate the action of the rockshaft and its connecting link when in the extreme upper position. The bellcrank levers F and G, together with the links connecting them with the rockshafts J and K, form a toggle mechanism which is straightened out at the same time that the driving crank H is passing its center and the arms *L* and links *M* are in line. This central or straight-line position for the toggles occurs while the blank is being held for the drawing operations; the blank-holder dwells or remains down long enough to enable the drawing punch to complete its work before the sheet metal stock is released by the blank-holder. The slide to which the drawing punch is attached receives its motion from the main crankshaft.

Reversing Screw. — When a relatively slow but powerful movement is required, a reversing screw may be employed for changing rotary motion to rectilinear motion. Broaching machines of the horizontal type, which operate by pulling long broaches through holes in castings and forgings, are equipped with the reversing screw type of drive. As the broaching is done by a series of cutting teeth which gradually increase in size in order to produce a hole of the required shape progressively, considerable power is required for pulling the broach through the work, especially when cutting hard tough metal. Therefore, the draw-head to which the broach is attached is given a rectilinear movement by means of a screw which does not revolve but is moved in a lengthwise direction by a nut. The screw passes through this nut which is held against endwise movement, and, with one design, is rotated from the driving shaft through suitable gearing. This gearing is so proportioned that a comparatively slow motion is imparted to the nut and screw for the cutting stroke and a faster movement for the return or idle stroke. The nut which engages the screw is alternately connected with these two combinations of gearing by means of a clutch that is shifted by adjustable tappets or dogs that control the length of the stroke. Some of the smaller broaching machines intended for lighter work have belt pulleys that revolve about the screw in opposite directions, and are alternately engaged with a central clutch which transmits motion to the draw nut on the screw.

Worm and Rack Drive. — A worm or short screw which meshes with a rack represents another form of reversing screw drive. This arrangement, which is often referred to as the " spiral gear," or " Sellers " drive, has been applied to a limited extent to planers for transmitting motion from the driving shaft to the planer table. Motion is transmitted from the driving shaft, through bevel gears to a shaft which extends under the bed diagonally and carries the spiral pinion or worm that meshes with a rack attached to the under side of the table. The diagonal position of the worm-shaft or its angle relative to the rack is such that the meshing or working side of the worm will be in alignment with the rack teeth. Smoothness of action is the principal advantage claimed for the worm and rack drive.

Double Rack and Shifting Gear. — If a gear rotating continuously in one direction is located between parallel racks, so that it can be engaged with first one rack and then the other, these racks will be moved in opposite directions. For instance, if the top side of the gear moves one rack to the right, the lower side will move the other rack toward the left. Some flat-bed printing presses are equipped with this double-rack and shifting-gear mechanism for driving the bed in first one direction and then the other. With mechanisms of this class, one rack is first traversed past the gear; when the gear and rack are entirely disengaged, the gear is shifted axially far enough to align it with the other rack. While this shifting movement takes place, the motion of the bed is arrested, and it is reversed by some auxiliary mechanism which moves it far enough to bring the other rack into engagement with the driving gear. Press bed motions of this general type differ principally in regard to the method of moving the press bed at the ends of the stroke, at the time when the driving gear and rack are disengaged.

Crank Type of Reversal for Press Bed Motion. — An ingenious mechanism of the double-rack and shifting-gear type is shown diagrammatically in Fig. 9. This design is applied to Miehle flat-bed or cylinder presses. In the operation of presses of this general type, the sheets to be printed are carried around by a revolving cylinder K so that contact is made with a flat form on the press bed which moves horizontally beneath the cylinder. This cylinder makes one revolution during the printing stroke and a second revolution while the press bed is being returned. In order to avoid contact between the cylinder and the bed or form during the return stroke, the cylinder is raised slightly by

76   MECHANICAL MOVEMENTS

a suitable mechanism. The rotation of the cylinder is continuous in one direction and it is imperative that the cylinder and press bed move exactly in unison. The circumferential velocity of the cylinder should equal the linear velocity of the bed, because any relative motion would cause slurring on the printed sheet and it would be impossible to obtain sharp clean-cut impressions. As the cylinder revolves at a uniform speed, obviously the mechanism for driving the bed must be designed to give a uniform motion while the impression is being made. In order to prop-

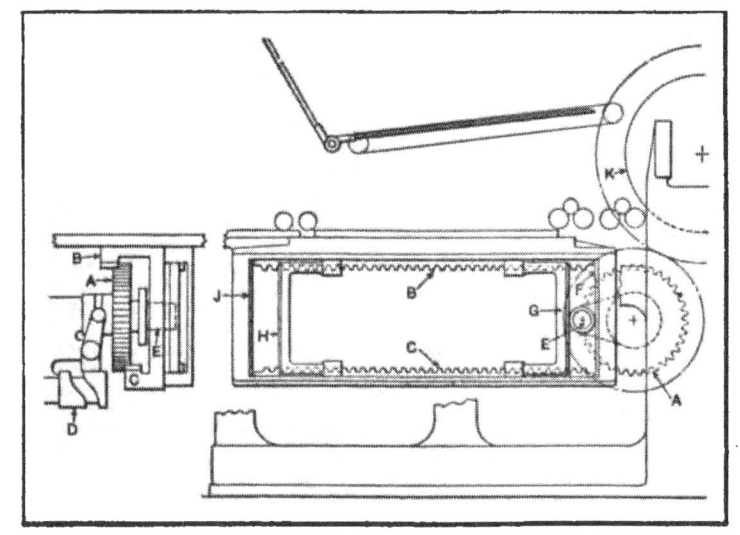

Fig. 9. Double-rack Shifting-gear and Crank Combination for Traversing Bed of a Printing Press

erly time the motion of the cylinder and bed, the cylinder is connected by gearing and suitable shafts with gear A, which transmits motion to the bed; therefore, the press bed motion must be designed to reverse the movement of the bed without reversing the motion of gear A, since this gear rotates in unison with the cylinder or continuously in one direction.

This driving gear A is mounted between parallel racks B and C, both of which are attached to and travel with the bed. The distance between the pitch lines of these racks corresponds to the pitch diameter of the driving gear A. The racks are not directly in line, but are offset as shown by the end view, so that, when the gear is in mesh with one rack, it will clear the other one. The lateral movement of gear A for aligning it alternately with racks B and C is derived from cam D, which transmits motion by means of a lever and yoke engaging the gear hub.

When the press is in operation, the bed is moved in one direction by the engagement of gear A with rack B and in the opposite direction by meshing gear A with rack C. If gear A is revolving in a clockwise direction while in mesh with rack C, the latter and the press bed (the motion of which is constrained by guides) will move toward the left. When the press is in motion, this movement toward the left continues until the rack is entirely out of mesh with gear A; just before the disengagement of gear A and rack C, the crankpin E, which is provided with rollers, comes around and enters between the parallel faces of a fixed reversing shoe F and a swinging or movable reversing shoe G. The fixed shoe is rigidly attached to the press bed and rack frame, whereas the movable shoe is pivoted and free to swivel. This swinging reversing shoe has a pin on its lower side (not shown) which engages a slot or cam that controls its swinging movements. As soon as rack C has moved far enough to the left for shoe G to clear the crankpin, the cam swings the shoe inward so that crankpin E is confined temporarily between the faces of shoes G and F, which form a vertical guide or slot. As the crankpin passes its lowest position and begins to move upward, the roller on it bears against the face of G and " picks up " the load as gear A moves out of mesh with rack C.

When crankpin E arrives at the position shown in the illustration, the motion of the press bed is reversed, because a roller on the crankpin then engages the face of shoe F thus moving the driven member toward the right. The motion continues to be derived from the crank independently of the disengaged gear and rack, until the crankpin has passed the top quarter or highest position; then gear A enters the upper rack B and the motion is transmitted entirely through the gear and rack until the crank again comes into action at the opposite end of the stroke. At this end, the crankpin is again confined between a

78 MECHANICAL MOVEMENTS

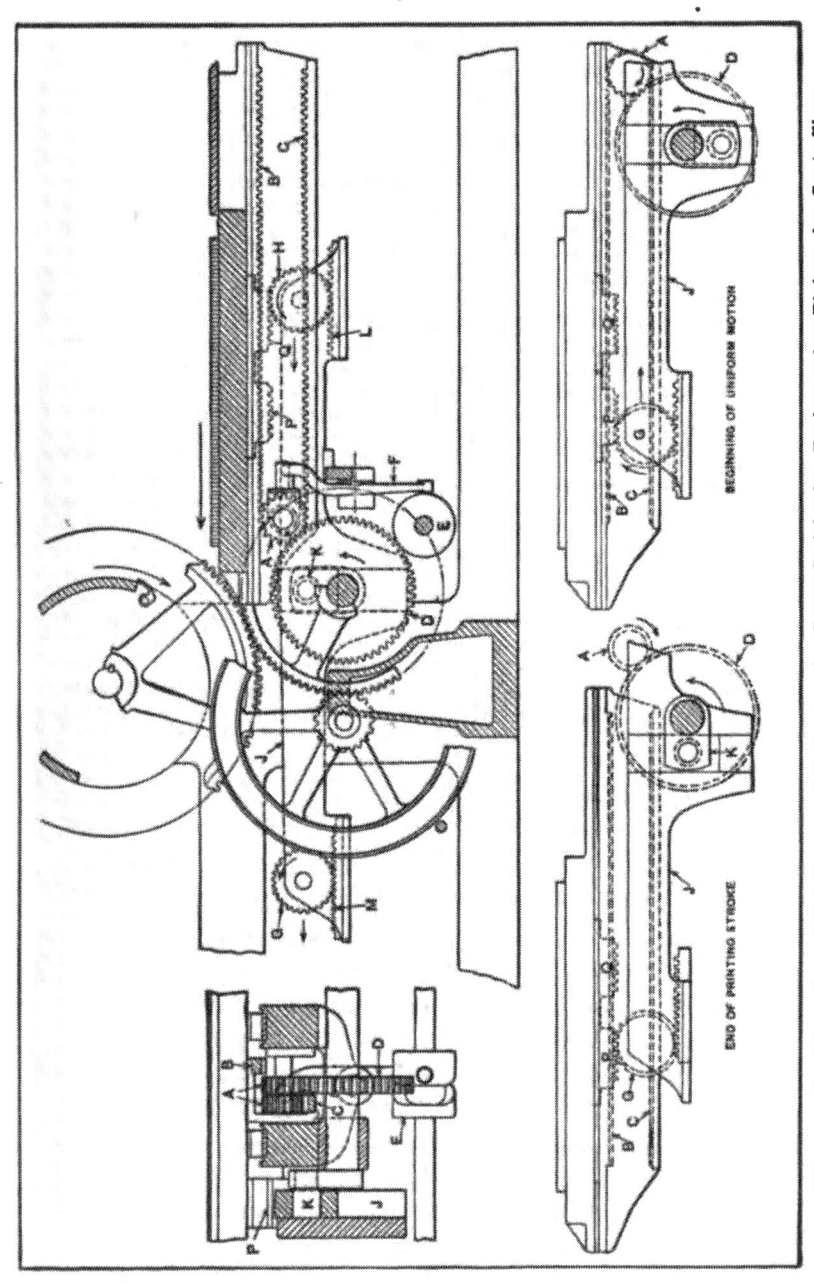

Fig. 10. Double-rack and Shifting-gear Mechanism for Press Bed having Reciprocating Pinions for Controlling Motion at Ends of Stroke

swinging shoe *H* and a fixed shoe *J*. After rack *B* has moved out of engagement with gear *A*, crankpin *E*, which is now in its highest position, comes into contact with shoe *H* and continues the movement toward the right while making a quarter turn, and then reverses the motion as it swings downward against the face of shoe *J*. While crankpin *E* is controlling the motion and gear *A* is entirely out of mesh, this gear is shifted by cam *D* out of line with the rack *B* which it just left, and into line with rack *C*.

An ingenious feature of this mechanism lies in the provision of two rollers for crankpin *E* and locating the fixed and swinging shoes in different vertical planes. With this arrangement, each roller is free to revolve in opposite directions as the crankpin moves along the vertical faces of the shoes. The momentum of the bed is gradually checked at the points of reversal, by air cushions or " air springs." A plunger enters a cylinder at each end of the stroke and air is compressed to arrest the movement, and, by expanding, this air assists in accelerating the heavy bed when its motion is reversed. Provision is made for regulating the air cushion or pressure according to the speed of the press. The air cushion is a feature common to flat-bed or cylinder presses in general.

Reversal of Motion by Reciprocating Pinions. — The mechanism illustrated in Fig. 10 is similar, in some respects, to the press bed motion just described, in that the parallel-rack and shifting-gear construction is employed. The method of operating the press bed at the ends of the stroke, however, is entirely different from that shown in Fig. 9, as reciprocating pinions are used to pick up the load and reverse the motion. The uniform motion of the bed is derived from pinion *A* which is constantly in mesh with gear *D* carried on the main driving shaft. Pinion *A* is located between parallel racks *B* and *C* which are attached to the press bed. These racks are offset, as in the design shown in Fig. 9, so that the pinion will clear one rack while in engagement with the other one. The shifting of the pinion is controlled by cam *E* which transmits motion to the pinion by means of lever *F*. The pinions for reversing the motion of the bed are located at G and H. The shafts upon which these pinions are mounted are connected to a heavy yoke J which has a vertical slot or groove in which a swiveling block attached to the crank K operates. This crank is rotated by the main driving shaft, and transmits to yoke J and pinions G and H a rectilinear motion equal to the throw of the crank. This is a harmonic motion, as yoke J and the sliding crank-block operate on the same principle as the well-known Scotch yoke. The outer ends of yoke J are supported by horizontal guides, and the pinions G and H are constantly in mesh with short racks M and L along which the pinions roll as the crank moves them to and fro.

The action of the mechanism will be apparent by considering the various movements which occur during a forward and return stroke. The side view of the assembled mechanism shows the press bed in the position where the driving pinion A has just come into engagement with the lower rack C. As this pinion rotates in a clockwise direction, the bed will be driven to the left with a uniform motion. (The relative positions of pinion A and racks B and C are clearly shown by the end view.) When the bed has moved so far to the left that pinion A is about to roll out of mesh at the right-hand end of rack C, pinion G, which, meanwhile, has been moving along its rack M, comes into engagement with another short rack P (see also end view) attached to the bed. To insure the proper engagement of pinion G with rack P, the action of crank K relative to the motion of the bed is so timed that pinion G is rolling to the left when rack P which is also moving to the left comes into engagement with it. As pinion A leaves rack C, pinion G, which is then in mesh with P, continues the movement of the bed toward the left until crank K is in the position shown by the diagram in the lower left-hand corner of the illustration, which represents the end of the printing stroke. Further rotation of crank K in the direction indicated by the arrow causes a reversal of the rolling motion of pinion G and starts the press bed toward the right, motion being transmitted from G to rack P. While this reversal of movement occurs, pinion A is being shifted by cam E into alignment with the upper rack B.

When crank K has moved a quarter revolution from the position it occupies at the extreme end of the stroke, pinion A comes into mesh with the upper rack B and the short rack P leaves pinion G. The view at the lower right-hand corner of Fig. 10 shows pinion A about to enter rack B and pinion G leaving rack P. As the rectilinear motion of yoke J is harmonic, the movement of the bed is uniformly retarded as it approaches the point of reversal and is then accelerated until pinion A engages its rack, when the motion is uniform. When pinion A enters at the end of either rack, the velocity of the movement derived from crank K and the reciprocating pinion corresponds to the velocity obtained from the driving pinion A, so that there is no abrupt change of motion as the load is being transferred from the reversing pinion to the driving pinion A. As the press bed approaches the opposite end of its stroke, pinion H comes into engagement with rack Q and continues the movement for a short distance each side of the point of reversal or while pinion A is out of mesh with either rack and is being shifted, the action being the same as previously described.

Napier Motion for Press Beds. — When a gear or pinion is in mesh with a single rack and rotates in one position, obviously both the gear and rack must reverse their direction of motion at the end of each stroke. The gear, however, may rotate continuously in one direction if it is arranged to engage the upper and lower sides of a rack designed especially to permit such engagement. A mechanism of this type, known as the Napier motion and also as " mangle gearing," has been extensively used for imparting a rectilinear motion to the tables of flat-bed printing presses. The principle of the Napier motion will be apparent by referring to Fig. 11. The rack A is attached to a frame B which is secured to the table of the printing press. The rack teeth are of such a form that the gear C may mesh with the rack on either the upper or lower sides. The shaft D, upon which the gear C is mounted, is rotated through a universal coupling, which permits it to swing in a vertical plane so that the gear may pass from the upper side of the rack to the lower side, and *vice versa*. The gear shaft is made to move in a vertical

82 MECHANICAL MOVEMENTS

plane by a stationary slotted guide E having a vertical slot that is engaged by a sliding block mounted on the shaft. Spherical-shaped rollers F are mounted at each end of the rack, and the gear has a socket or spherical depression formed in it for engaging the rollers, each time the gear moves around the end of the rack when passing from one side to the other. Opposite each end of the rack, there are guide plates G having curved surfaces which are concentric with the rollers at the ends of the rack.

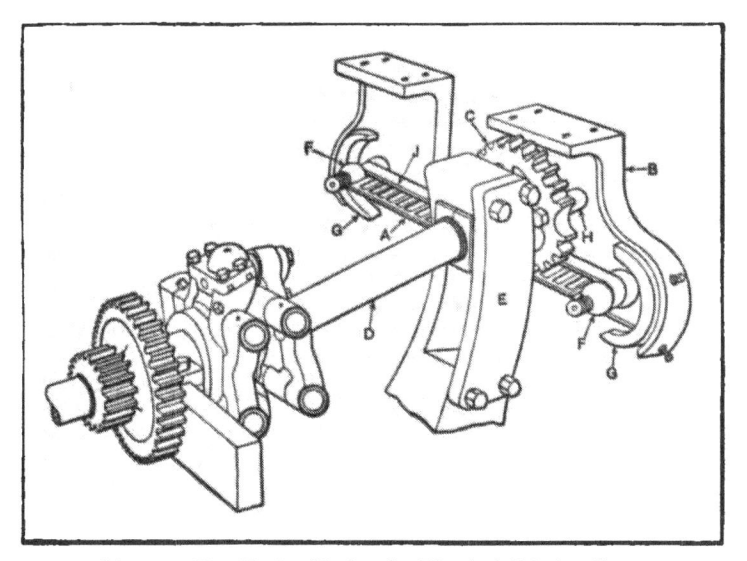

Fig. 11. The Napier Motion for Flat-bed Printing Press

The gear C also carries a roller H which engages these curved guides as the gear moves upward or downward at the points of reversal.

The action of the mechanism is as follows: If the gear is on the upper side of the rack, as shown in the illustration, and it is revolving to the left or counter-clockwise, the rack will be driven to the right with a velocity equal to the motion at the pitch circle of the gear. As soon as the gear engages the roller F on the end of the rack, it begins to move downward in a vertical plane, because its motion is constrained by guide E. When the gear is in mid-position so that its axis coincides with the center-line of the rack, it will have made a quarter turn, thus moving the center of roller F farther to the right, a distance equal to the radius of the pitch circle. Farther movement of the gear downward causes the rack to reverse and move toward the left; the gear then operates on the under side of the rack until the roller at the right-hand end of the rack is engaged, when the upward movement of the gear takes place and there is another reversal of motion.

The total length of the stroke is equal to the distance between the centers of the rollers on the rack, plus the pitch diameter of the gear. The length of the rack must equal the pitch circumference of the gear or some multiple of it, so that the rollers at the end will engage the socket or depression in the gear at the points of reversal. If a gear is used having two roller spaces located 180 degrees apart, the length of the rack or the center-to center distance between the rollers may be some multiple of half the pitch circumference. The teeth on each side of the rack incline from the horizontal at the same angle as the gear axis when in its upper and lower positions, to obtain a full contact of the gear teeth. The gear also has a plain cylindrical shoulder on the inner side, which rolls upon a plane surface J at the base of the rack, to give a smoother action than would be obtained from a gear supported entirely by tooth contact. This arrangement of gearing imparts a uniform motion to the press table, excepting any variable movement resulting from a universal joint, and gives a gradual reversal of motion at the ends of the stroke. The Napier motion may be designed for any length of stroke, although the stroke remains constant, as there is no way of making an adjustment.

Variable Reciprocating Motion. — The fly frames used in the manufacture of cotton goods are equipped with a mechanism for traversing the rovings or slightly twisted slivers of cotton as they pass between the rolls of the fly frame, which is used to make the rovings more slender and give them a twist. The reason for traversing the roving as it passes between a steel and a leather-covered roll is to prevent wearing the leather covering at one place. On some machines, this reciprocating or traversing motion is obtained from a crank or a cam. This simple arrangement distributes the wear but, if the length of traverse is uniform, the tendency is for the leather covering to wear the most at the points of reversal. In order to distribute the wear more evenly, the mechanism shown in Fig. 12 was designed. With this arrangement, the length of traverse gradually increases until it reaches a maximum and then decreases until the shortest length of traverse is obtained; the gradual increasing and decreasing of the stroke are then repeated.

The diagram A illustrates graphically the action obtained with a crank motion, and diagram B illustrates the variable stroke

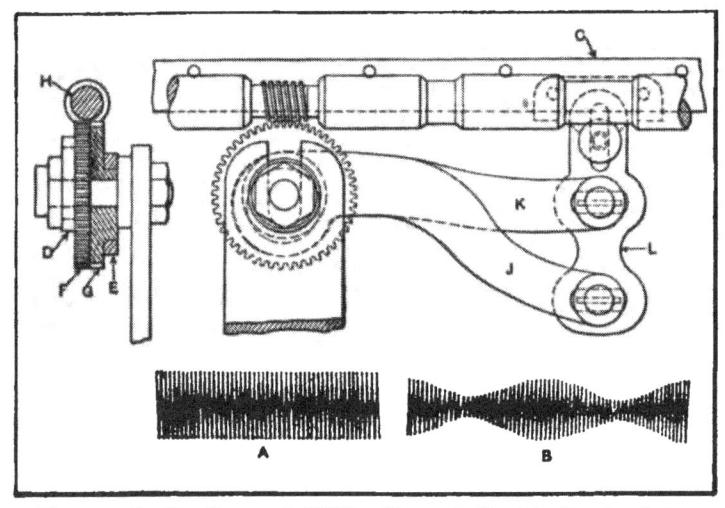

Fig. 12. Double Gear and Shifting Eccentric Combination for Automatically varying Traversing Movements

derived from the mechanism to be described. The guide-bar C, which extends the full length of the rolls, has small holes opposite each roll section through which the rovings pass, and it is this guide-bar which receives the reciprocating motion. The automatic variation of the traversing movement is derived from two eccentrics D and E, which revolve at different rates of speed. These eccentrics are formed on the hubs of gears F and G, which are adjacent to each other, and are both driven by one worm H as shown by the end view. The motion of the eccentrics is transmitted to guide-bar C through rods J and K and the bracket L. One of the gears meshing with worm H has one more tooth than the other, which causes the gears to rotate at a varying speed. The result is that the eccentrics formed on the two gear hubs are continually changing their position relative to each other, which automatically varies the length of traverse for guide-bar C. For instance, at one period during the cycle of movements, both eccentrics will move rods J and K in the same direction, and, at another period, one eccentric rod will be moving backward while the other is moving forward, thus reducing the stroke of the guide-bar. The connections between the eccentric rods and the bracket are adjustable; an adjustment is also provided where the bracket is attached to the guide-bar, so that the maximum traversing movement may be varied.

Reciprocating Motion from Epicyclic Gearing. — What is known as a "wabble" gear is used on mowing machines for imparting a rapid reciprocating motion to the cutter bar. The arrangement of this gearing and the other parts of the mechanism is shown in Fig. 13. The internal gear C is so mounted that it cannot rotate but is free to oscillate on a universal gimbal joint D. The gear B which meshes with one side of C is mounted on the main shaft which connects with the driving wheels. The frame J is rigidly connected to gear C and is pivoted in the revolving part H. By this means, gear C is given an oscillating or wabbling movement, so that the entire gear describes or follows a circular path. This circular motion causes the teeth of gear C to mesh with those of gear B all around the circumference for each rotation of the part H. This part H turns on a fixed shaft E and acts somewhat as a flywheel to maintain steadiness of action besides constraining gear C to follow a circular path.

In this case, gear C has forty-eight teeth and gear B, forty-six teeth; therefore, if gear B were free to turn on its shaft, it would be displaced two teeth for each rotation of part H or each time gear C completed a circular movement. Consequently, twenty-three revolutions of part H and a like number of oscillations of frame J would be required to turn B one revolution. Tracing the motion in the opposite direction, it will be noted that one rotation of gear B, which acts as the driver when the mechanism is in operation, will cause twenty-three oscillations or wabbling movements of gear C and a like number of rotations for part H. The frame J is connected to the cutter bar by the ball joint at K, so that one turn of the driving wheels which are mounted on shaft A will traverse the cutter bar twenty-three times. This combination of gearing makes it possible to use a gear B having only two teeth less than the number in gear C, which would be practically impossible with gears having teeth parallel to the axis of

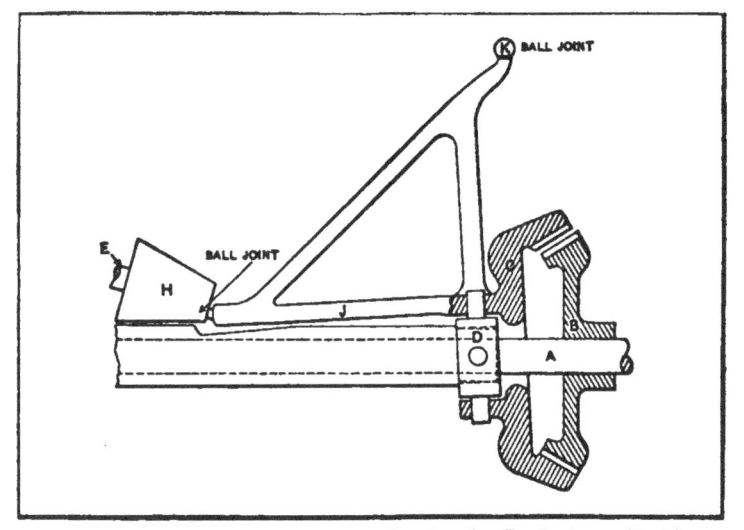

Fig. 13. Epicyclic or "Wabble" Gearing for Producing a Rapid Reciprocating Motion

the shaft. With the usual forms of epicyclic gearing, in which a high velocity ratio is obtained, the efficiency of transmission is low on account of the excessive tooth friction, but, in this case, the efficiency is said to be nearly as high as that obtained with a train of spur gears having the same velocity ratio.

Epicyclic Gear and Crank Combination. — The mechanism illustrated in Fig. 14 is applied to an electric coal-puncher. One of the difficulties encountered in designing coal-punchers, excepting the solenoid type, has been in changing the rotation of the motor into a reciprocating motion for the drill. If the blow is directly dependent upon the motor, the latter causes trouble, owing to the vibrations and strains incident to the blows of the pick, and if springs are utilized they are liable to break. Types having separate motors and flexible shaft connections have also been tried in order to avoid some of these difficulties, but complications were introduced which at least partially offset the benefits derived.

The coal-puncher of which the mechanism shown in Fig. 14 forms a part uses both compressed air and electricity. Power for operating the coal-puncher is obtained from a motor and the compressed air gives the blow. There is no direct connection between the motor and striking pick, so that the vibrations are cushioned. The illustration shows the mechanical means by which the rotation of the motor armature is changed to a reciprocating motion for driving the air-compressing piston. A small pinion attached to the armature shaft engages a large driving gear (not shown) which has a solid web carrying the stud d upon which the crank pinion e is mounted. This crank pinion has 33 teeth and meshes with internal gear f which is rigidly fastened to the frame of the machine and is concentric with the main driving gear which surrounds it. The pitch diameter of the crank pinion e is just one-half that of the internal gear f which has 66 teeth. The crankpin g is attached to the pinion e and engages cross-head h which is mounted in guides and receives a rectilinear motion as pinion e revolves around the internal gear. Attached to the cross-head, there is a piston-rod a which enters the air-compressing cylinder and has a piston secured to its forward end.

When the main driving gear is revolved by the motor, the crank pinion stud d describes a circular path, as indicated by the arrows, thus causing pinion e to revolve about the stud and around the internal gear. When the pin d has moved one-quarter of a revolution, it will be in the position shown by the illustration to the right, and pin g attached to cross-head h will be in the center of the internal gear. At the completion of one-half a revolution, pin g will have moved in a straight line a distance equal to the pitch diameter of the internal gear, and will be at the right-hand end of its stroke. Similarly, at three-quarters of a revolution, the pin will again be in mid-position, and at the completion of a full revolution, it will be at the starting point, as shown by the view to the left. In this way, the crank pinion, as it revolves around the internal gear, transmits to pin g and the attached cross-head h a rectilinear forward and backward movement. The cross-head is mounted in guides,

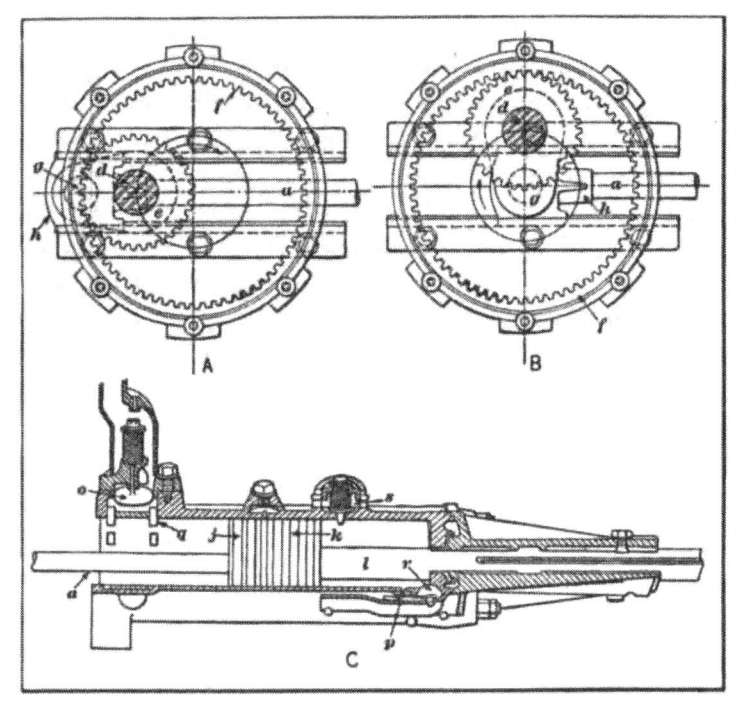

Fig. 14. Epicyclic Gear and Crank Combination from which Reciprocating Motion is derived

but pin g would follow a straight line even though guides were not used.

The way in which the air is compressed and utilized to impel the pick-carrying piston forward, all in one cylinder, will be described. A sectional view of the air cylinder is shown at C in Fig. 14. The air cylinder contains two pistons j and k. The rear piston j is attached to rod a connecting with the cross-head. The front piston k has no connection with j, but it is attached to the drill or pick socket by the rod l. The first stroke of the pick is purely mechanical. The rear piston j moves forward, pushing the front piston k. During this stroke, air is drawn into the cylinder behind the piston j, through the main inlet valve o. On the return stroke, this air is compressed and at the same time the front piston k is drawn back by the partial vacuum created by the piston j, air being admitted in front of k through a port p. When the return stroke is completed, the rear piston has passed the by-pass opening q in the cylinder, which opening is between the two pistons at the time. This allows the compressed air to force the front piston forward, exactly as in any compressed air drill. In this way, the first real stroke of the machine is made; that is, the mechanical stroke previously mentioned is made only once or when starting from rest. On the forward stroke of the piston k, the air in front escapes through the port p, but after the piston has passed and, therefore, closed this port, a sufficient amount of air remains to cushion the blow and prevent damage to the front cylinder head. This cushion of air may leak somewhat, and to prevent an insufficient supply remaining, which would have the effect of creating a partial vacuum in this space and holding the piston on the return stroke, a small inlet valve r is placed in the forward part of the cylinder. This allows air to flow in under these conditions before the open port is passed. When the front piston k has made its forward stroke, the rear piston follows, mechanically driven as before, and would compress the air which has just made the stroke of the front piston, were it not for the so-called vacuum valve s which allows all air between the pistons above a certain pressure to escape to the atmosphere. This action prevents the two piston faces from coming together.

A mechanism operating on the same general principle as the one shown in Fig. 14 has been applied to printing presses of the flat-bed type, for imparting a rectilinear motion to the bed. This mechanism has the advantage of giving a long, gradually increasing and decreasing motion with a short crank and without the use of a connecting-rod or a slotted cross-head; therefore, it can be applied to some classes of mechanisms when there would not be sufficient room for a connecting-rod or in preference to the slotted yoke, because of mechanical objections to the latter. In designing this mechanism, the center of pin g should exactly coincide with the pitch circle of the internal gear; then, if the internal gear has twice as many teeth as the revolving gear, the

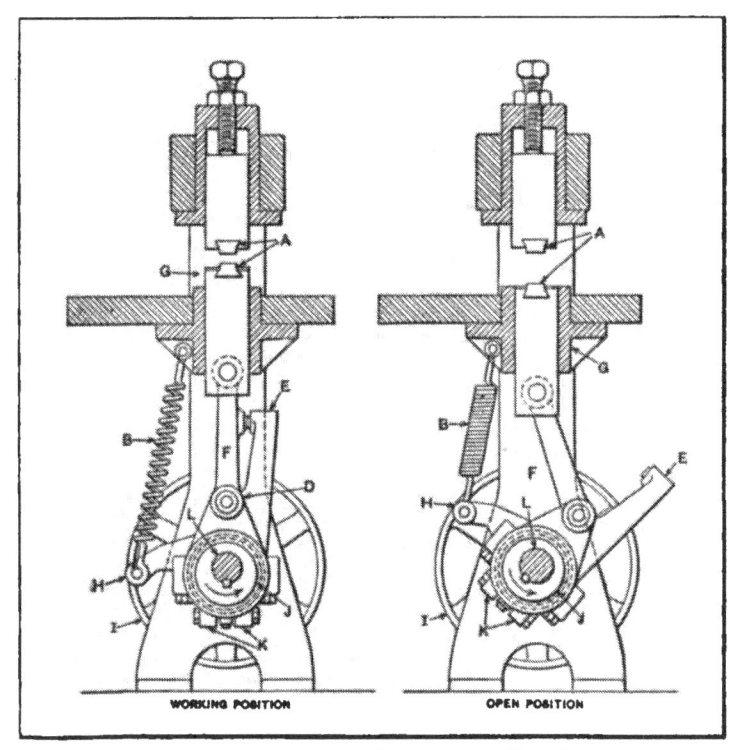

Fig. 15. Mechanism for Shifting Reciprocating Part from Working Position Automatically

center of g will move in a straight line, even though its motion is not constrained by means of guides.

Shifting Reciprocating Part from Working Position. — The machine shown in Fig. 15 is used in a certain branch of the leather business to press a leather product between a pair of dies A by a series of reciprocating motions given to the lower die, which is afterwards withdrawn to the " open position " shown at the right, to allow the removal and insertion of the work. The mechanism to be described serves to automatically locate the lower die in the open position when the driving belt is shifted to the loose pulley, and into the " working " position as eccentric *j*, which imparts motion to ram *G*, is rotated by shifting the belt to the tight pulley. The shaft to which this eccentric is keyed turns in the direction shown by the arrow. The upper half of the eccentric strap is pivoted to the connecting-rod at *D* and carries an arm *H* to which is attached the long spring *B*. If there were nothing to prevent it, the spring would evidently tend to pull the joint *D* over, as shown by the right-hand view. In this position, with the belt on the loose pulley, the machine is ready to receive the work. The lugs *K* are attached to a leather band friction, bearing on an extension of the eccentric surface, and shown in dotted lines behind the eccentric strap. A finger screwed to the lower half of the strap and projecting between the lugs serves to keep the brake in position. If the machine is started by throwing the belt onto the tight pulley, the brake grips the eccentric with sufficient force to overcome the slight tension of spring *B*, and joint *D* is moved back to the central working position, where buffer *E* has reached its seat on the connecting-rod. As the shaft continues to turn, the brake slips on its seat and the eccentric gives the desired movement to the ram. When the operation is completed, the belt is shifted to the loose pulley, and spring *B* turns the shaft, eccentric, and strap backward until the machine is again in the open position with the ram lowered to allow a change of work.

Rectilinear Motion from Revolving Pawls. — The mechanism for driving a conveyor is shown in Fig. 16. This conveyor consists of a pair of endless chains between which the conveyor buckets are carried. These buckets are hung on pivots, so that they are kept in an upright position by gravity. The chains are equipped with wheels which run on tracks. The chains and buckets are propelled along the tracks as indicated by the arrow, by a system of rotating pawls which receive their motion from a large gear *D*. Each pawl, in turn, engages one of a series of pins on the chain and, after having pushed the conveyor ahead, the pawl is raised by cam *C* and the next pawl repeats the oper-

92   MECHANICAL MOVEMENTS

ation. When a pawl, as at *A*, is passing through the lowest arc of its travel, the conveyor is propelled forward. The pawl shown at *B* has passed the lowest point, and it gradually lags behind the conveyor, so that the end of the pawl is readily lifted out of engagement without interference. As will be seen, the inner end of pawl *B* is in contact with the cam surface which controls its position.

Adjustable Rectilinear Motion. — The mechanism shown in Fig. 17 is for traversing the table of a grinding machine along the

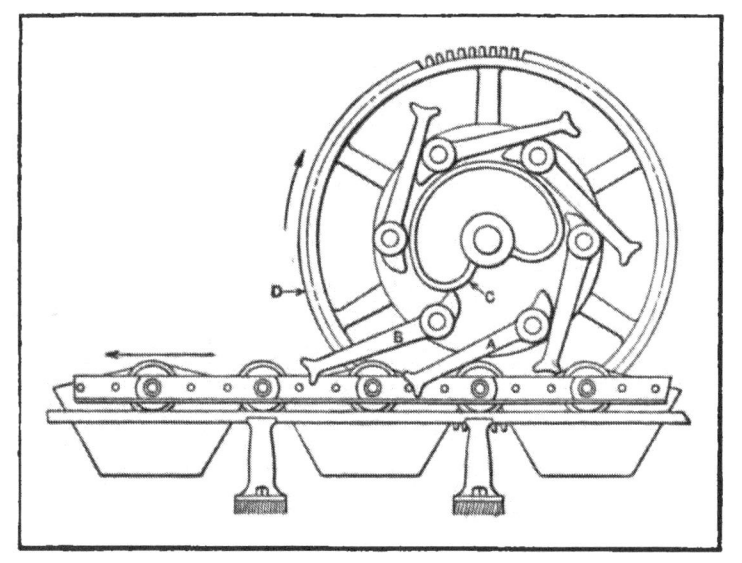

Fig. 16. Arrangement for Obtaining Rectilinear Motion from Revolving Pawls

bed. This machine, which is of a comparatively small size, is intended for internal and external grinding operations; thus it is necessary to provide means for readily changing the stroke of the table. With the mechanism illustrated, any variation in stroke can be obtained from zero to the maximum while the machine is operating. The motion for the table is derived from a heart-shaped cam *C* mounted on a vertical shaft which is driven through a speed-changing mechanism. This cam engages a roll attached to the lower side of an oscillating arm *A* having on its upper side another roll *B* which can be adjusted relative to the pivot P about which the arm oscillates. This upper roll operates between the parallel faces of yoke D, and the latter is attached to a rod E located beneath the table of the machine. On the under side of the table and extending throughout its entire length is a dovetailed slide-way in which is fitted a block that is attached to and moves with the reciprocating rod E. By means of a suitable lever, this block which fits into the dovetailed slide-way, can be clamped in various positions for changing the location of the table. The action of the mechanism is as follows: When the cam C is rotating, arm A oscillates about pivot P and, through

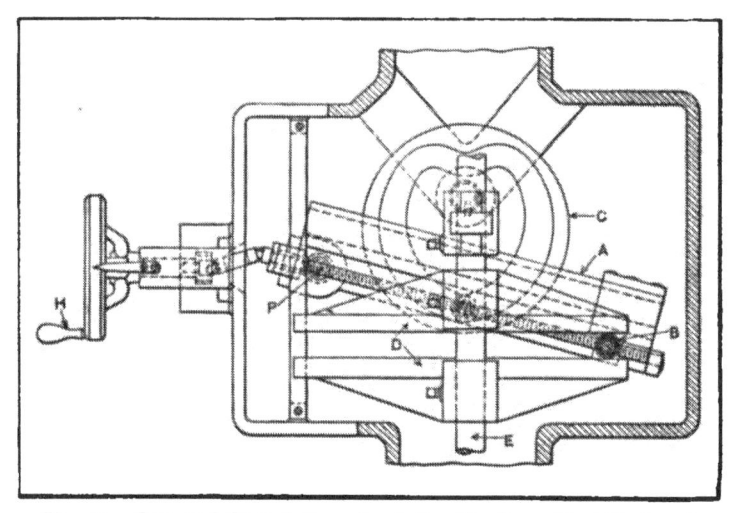

Fig. 17. Cam and Slotted Cross-head Combination with Adjustment for Varying Stroke

roller B, transmits a rectilinear motion to yoke D, rod E, and the table. The length of this movement or stroke is governed by the position of roll B relative to pivot P, which may be varied by means of a screw that is connected through a universal joint with a shaft upon which handwheel H is mounted. When roll B is moved inward until it is directly over pivot P, no movement will be imparted to yoke D or the table.

Motion of Drop-hammer Lifting Mechanism. — The drop-hammers used for making drop-forgings are so designed that the hammer head is raised by rolls which run in opposite directions and bear against opposite sides of a board attached to the hammer head. Front and side elevations of a drop-hammer lifting mechanism are shown in Fig. 18. The board A passes between the rolls B and C. One roll rotates in a fixed position and the other one is alternately pressed against the board and then withdrawn from it, when the hammer is in operation. The pressure of the movable roll is applied for raising the hammer head and released for allowing it to drop upon the work. The roll that is withdrawn is usually the front one which has an eccentric bearing so that a slight rotary movement will cause the roll to release

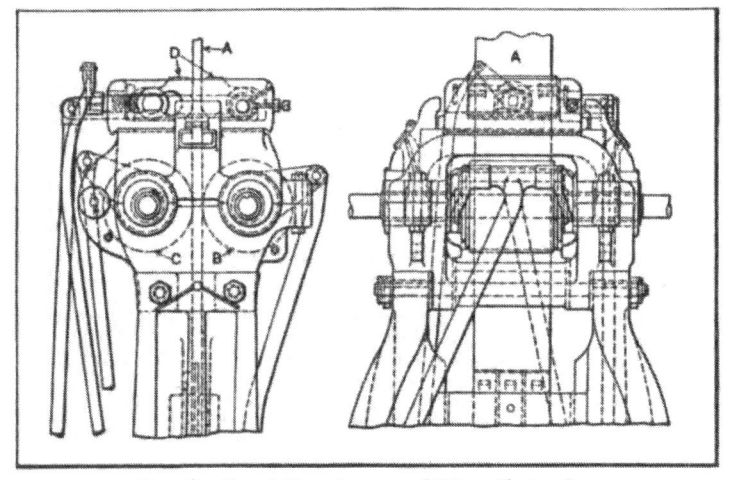

Fig. 18. Board Drop-hammer Lifting Mechanism

the board. As the hammer drops and approaches the bottom of its stroke, it engages some form of trip or latch which holds the eccentric roll in the outward position so that the roll moves in against the board; the hammer is then immediately elevated preparatory to striking another blow. As the hammer approaches the top of its stroke, the eccentric roll is again automatically withdrawn, thus stopping any further upward movement. The hammer will then fall and repeat the cycle of movements and will continue to run automatically, provided the board clamps at D are not allowed to grip the board. The position of these clamps is controlled by a foot-treadle. When this treadle is released, the clamps grip the board as it reaches the top of its stroke and starts to move downward, so that the hammering action discontinues until the foot-treadle is again depressed. This mechanism for transmitting the rotary motion of the rolls to board *A*, which has a rectilinear movement, is similar in principle to the rack and pinion, except that motion is transmitted entirely by frictional contact instead of by means of teeth which give a positive drive.

Combined Rectilinear and Rotary Movements. — The piston of the pump shown in Fig. 19 has, in addition to a rectilinear movement, a rotary motion. This pump was designed for pumping water or other liquids containing foreign materials, such as weeds, pieces of rope, paper, etc., which might enter the

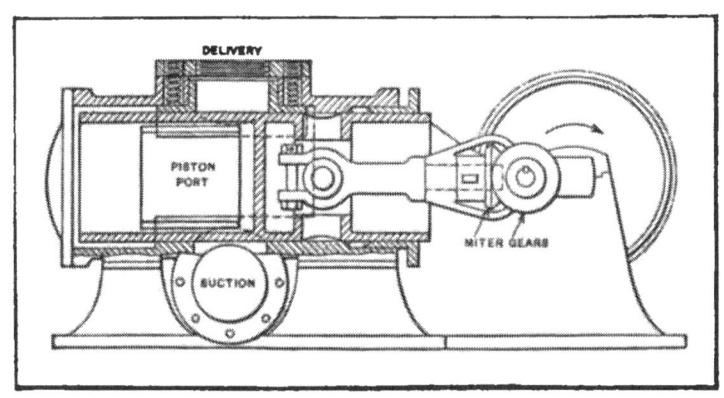

Fig. 19. Piston having Combined Rectilinear and Rotary Movements

pump cylinder. Instead of using suction or discharge valves which would become clogged and cause trouble, the opening and closing of the ports is controlled by the rotary movement of the piston, and any foreign materials of the kinds mentioned are sheared off by the edges of the ports. The rectilinear motion of the piston is obtained from a crank. A miter gear keyed to the end of the crankpin meshes with a mating gear keyed to the end of the connecting-rod, so that, as the piston is moved in and out, it is also given a rotary motion. The piston is of the trunk type with an opening at both ends and a partition in the center. The head end at the left of the partition contains a port which alternately registers with the suction and delivery ports. When the piston is in the position shown, both ports are closed, but, as soon as the pump rotates in the direction indicated by the arrow, the suction port begins to open. When the crank has moved 90 degrees, the piston port will be exactly over the suction port and, when the opposite dead center is reached, both ports will again be closed. When the crank is on the bottom quarter or at the center of the return stroke, the piston port will be opposite the delivery port.

CHAPTER IV

REVERSING MECHANISMS

A REVERSAL of motion is essential to the operation of many different forms of mechanism. Machine parts having a rectilinear or straight-line motion must, of necessity, reverse their movement, and many rotating parts also revolve first in one direction and then the other. The reversal in some cases is applied to a single shaft or slide and, in other instances, an entire train of mechanism is given a reversal of motion. The types of reversing mechanisms vary considerably, both as to principle of operation and as to form or design. Some are so arranged that the reversal of motion occurs at a fixed point in the cycle of movements, whereas, with other designs, the point of reversal may be changed by means of adjustable dogs or tappets which are attached to the movable part and control the action of the reversing mechanism. The adjustable type is required on machine tools for varying the length of the stroke made by a cutting tool or machine table so that the stroke will conform to the length of the work. Reversing mechanisms also differ in that some are hand-controlled and others are operated automatically. A crank-driven slide might be regarded as a form of reversing mechanism, since the member having a rectilinear movement reverses its motion at the end of each stroke. In this chapter, however, the forms of reversing mechanism illustrated and described will be those intended primarily for reversing motion.

Intermediate Spur Gears for Reversing Motion. — A simple method of obtaining a reversal of motion by means of spur gears is shown at A and B in Fig. 1, where the reversing gears used on some designs of lathe headstocks are illustrated diagrammatically. The two intermediate gears b and c are mounted on a swiveling arm which can be adjusted for engaging either one of the intermediate gears with the spindle gear. When the gears are in the position shown at *A*, the drive is from *a* through *c* to *d*. When the arm carrying the intermediate gears is shifted as indicated at *B*, the motion is transmitted through both intermediate gears or from *a* through *b* and *c* to *d*, thus reversing the direction of rotation. This mechanism, as applied to a lathe, is used for reversing the rotation of the lead-screw when cutting left-hand threads, in order to make the tool carriage travel from left to right.

Another method of obtaining a reversal of rotation by means of an intermediate gear is illustrated by diagram *C*, Fig. 1. In this case, there are two sets of gearing between the driving and

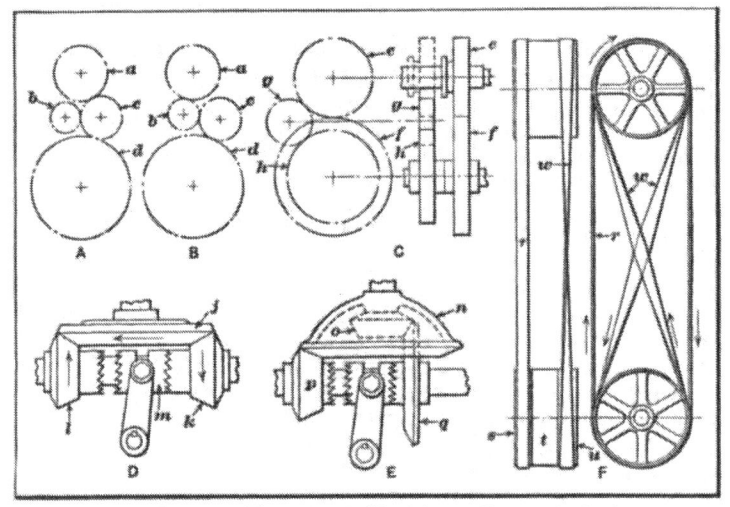

Fig. 1. Common Methods of Obtaining a Reversal of Motion

driven shafts. For the forward motion, the drive is from gear *e* to *f*. When the rotation of the driven shaft is to be reversed, gear *e* is shifted to the left and into mesh with the intermediate gear *g*, as shown by the dotted lines, so that motion is transmitted through *e*, *g*, and *h*. This general arrangement for obtaining a reversal of rotation is applied extensively to the transmission gearing of automobiles.

Bevel-gear Type of Reversing Mechanism. — A combination of three bevel gears, as illustrated by diagram *D*, Fig. 1, is applied to many different classes of mechanisms for obtaining a reversal of motion, especially when the reversing action is automatically controlled. With the usual arrangement, gear j is the driver and it is constantly in mesh with the bevel pinions l and k. These bevel pinions are loose upon the driven shaft and have a clutch m interposed between them. This clutch is free to move endwise along the shaft, but it slides along a key or feather which compels it to revolve with the shaft. Each bevel pinion has teeth corresponding to the clutch teeth, so that the engagement of the clutch with either pinion locks it to the shaft. Since these bevel pinions revolve in opposite directions, as indicated by the arrows, the rotation of the driven shaft is reversed as clutch m is shifted from one gear to the other. When the clutch is in the central or "neutral" position, it does not engage either gear, and no motion is transmitted to the driven shaft. Many of the reversing mechanisms which are equipped with this bevel gear combination differ in regard to the method of operating the clutch. For instance, clutch m might be shifted by the direct action of a slide or table having a rectilinear motion, or an auxiliary mechanism might be utilized to give the clutch a more rapid movement at the point of reversal. Some of these auxiliary features will be referred to later.

Two-speed Reversing Mechanism of Bevel-gear Type. — On some classes of machinery, it is desirable to have a relatively slow motion in one direction followed by a rapid return movement, in order to reduce the idle or non-productive period. One design of reversing mechanism of the bevel-gear type, by means of which a slow forward speed and a rapid return speed may be obtained, is illustrated at E in Fig. 1. In this case, there are two driving as well as two driven gears. The larger driver n is made cup-shaped so that a smaller driver o can be placed inside. When the clutch engages the smaller driven gear p, the fast speed is obtained, and, when the clutch engages gear q, the speed of the driven shaft is reduced an amount depending upon the ratio of the slow-speed gearing. Reversing mechanisms of this general type are not adapted for reversing the motion of heavy slides or work tables nor for fast-running machinery, because of the excessive shocks and stresses incident to a sudden reversal of movement in case of high velocities or heavy loads.

Reversal of Motion with Friction Disks. — When motion is transmitted between shafts located at right angles to each other by the type of frictional transmission shown at B in Fig. 14, Chapter I, a reversal of rotation is easily obtained. As disk c is shifted inward along the face of disk d, the velocity ratio is gradually reduced, and when disk c passes the axis of disk d, the direction of rotation is reversed. This form of transmission has been applied to the feeding mechanisms of certain types of machine tools, and to other classes of machinery, especially where simplicity of design and ease of operation and control are essential factors. One method of arranging this form of drive, as applied to an automobile transmission, is to mount the driving member on a sliding shaft which enables the driving and driven disk to be readily disengaged, thus combining in one simple mechanism the clutching, speed-changing, and reversing functions.

Reversal from Open and Crossed Belts. — Shafts are often connected with open and crossed belts for permitting a reversal of rotation. The arrangement is illustrated by the diagram F in Fig. 1. There are three pulleys on the driven shaft. The central pulley t is keyed or attached to the shaft, whereas the outer pulleys s and u are loose and free to revolve upon the shaft. When the "open" belt r is shifted onto the tight pulley t, the driven shaft revolves in one direction and its rotation is reversed when the crossed belt w replaces the open belt on the tight pulley.

This form of drive is sometimes modified by having two pulleys on the driven shaft and a clutch interposed between the pulleys, so that either of them may be made the driven member. Thus, when the clutch is engaged with the pulley connecting with the open belt, the rotation is the reverse of that which is obtained when the clutch engages the pulley driven by the crossed belt. The countershafts for engine lathes and other machine tools which may require a reversal of movement are commonly arranged in this manner. Open and crossed belts are also applied to belt-driven planers for reversing the motion of the platen or work table. Many planer drives have pulleys which are so proportioned as to give a rapid return movement. A common arrangement is to place a central or tight pulley on the driven shaft which has two steps or diameters, the smaller one of which is for obtaining a fast return motion.

Incidentally, belt drives of the type referred to are often used in place of gearing, for reversing heavy or fast running parts, because the belts slip somewhat if the load becomes excessive, due to the stopping and starting at the points of reversal, and this slipping action automatically protects the mechanism from injurious shocks or stresses.

Operation of Reversing Clutches. — When a reversal of motion depends upon the action of a clutch which is shifted from one gear to another revolving in an opposite direction, it is essential to operate the clutch rapidly and to secure a full engagement of the clutch teeth. Provision should also be made against disengagement of the clutch as the result of vibrations incident to the operation of the machine. There are two common methods of controlling the clutches used in connection with the bevel-gear type of reversing mechanism illustrated at D in Fig. 1. One form of control may be defined as the swinging-latch type and the other as the beveled-plunger type. The general principle of operation is the same in each case, and is as follows: When the work table, or whatever part is to be reversed, approaches the end of its stroke, a spring is compressed, and then a latch or trip allows this compressed spring to suddenly and rapidly throw the reversing clutch from one gear to the other. Reversing mechanisms of this general design are often called the "load-and-fire" type, because the spring is first loaded or compressed and then tripped to secure a rapid movement of the clutch and a reversal of motion at a predetermined point within close limits. The action of the compressed spring also insures a full engagement of the clutch teeth and prevents the clutch from stopping in the central or neutral position, which might occur if a spring were not used and the momentum of the part to be reversed were insufficient to carry the clutch across the space intervening between the two reversing gears.

102   MECHANICAL MOVEMENTS

Latch Type of Reversing Clutch Control. — The reversing mechanism illustrated in Fig. 2 is a bevel-gear type equipped with the swinging latch form of clutch control. This mechanism is applied to a cylindrical grinding machine for reversing the motion of the work table, and is located at the rear of the machine. The rockshaft H extends through to the front of the machine

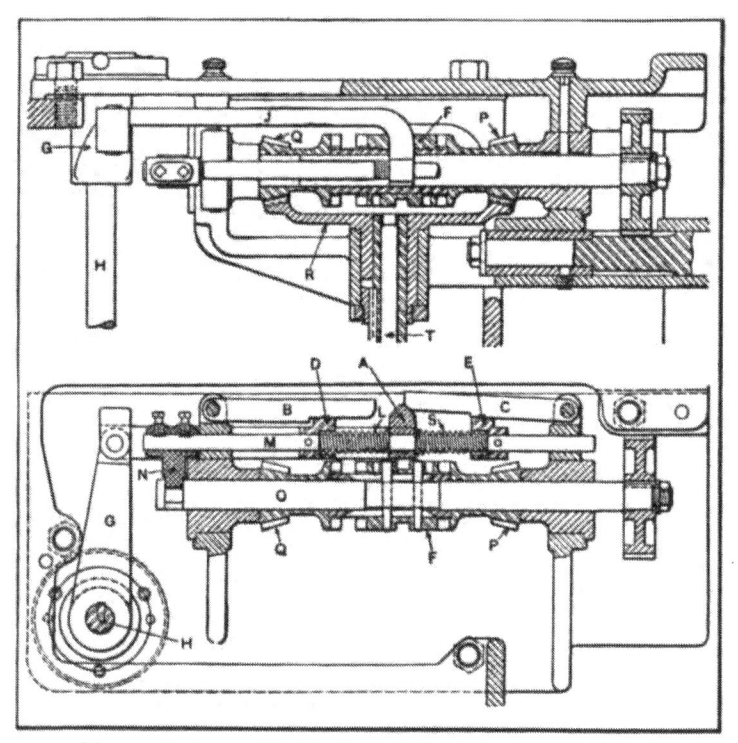

Fig. 2. Spring and Latch Type of Reversing Clutch Control

and has attached to it a lever which is engaged by dogs on the work table, the distance between these dogs being varied according to the length of stroke required. At the rear end of rockshaft H there is a lever G which, by means of link J, transmits motion to the reversing mechanism. As the work table approaches the end of its stroke, lever G swings either to the right or left as the case may be. If the motion is to the left, tappet A, connected to link J, compresses spring L on rod M

and forces block D against a square shoulder on the lower side of latch B. Continued movement of tappet A to the left causes the beveled side of A to lift latch B, thus releasing block D, which, with rod M, is thrown rapidly to the left under the impulse of the compressed spring L.

After the movement of shaft M to the left, the shoulder on latch C drops in behind block E. The fork N on rod M also throws shaft O to the left and with it the reversing clutch F which is keyed to this shaft. The motion which prior to reversal was transmitted through bevel pinion P to the main gear R is now from pinion Q to R so that the movement of the work table is reversed. When the work table approaches the end of its stroke in the other direction, tappet A is moved to the right, thus compressing spring S. Then latch C is lifted by the beveled edge on A and the parts M, N, and O are quickly shifted to the right by spring S, thus again reversing the motion.

If the operator desires to stop the traversing movement at the end of the stroke, this may be done by the movement of a knob located in the center of the table-traversing handwheel at the front of the machine. This knob is connected with a plunger T which, by pressing the knob, may be held under pressure against the reversing clutch F. When this clutch is shifted at the end of the stroke either by springs L or S, plunger T drops into a groove in clutch F, thus holding it in the central or neutral position. The knob previously referred to may be set at any part of the stroke to stop the traversing movement at the end of that stroke. The withdrawal of the knob again starts the traversing movement without requiring any further action on the part of the operator. The shaft connecting with bevel gear R extends to the front of the machine and, through suitable gearing, transmits a rectilinear motion to the work table of the grinding machine.

Beveled Plunger Control for Reversing Clutch.—An example of the beveled plunger type of clutch control for a reversing mechanism is shown in Fig. 3. This design is also intended for a cylindrical grinding machine. The point of reversal is controlled by the tappets A which are adjusted along the work table to vary the length of the stroke. These tappets alternately engage lever *B* at the ends of the stroke and, by swinging this lever about its pivot, shift bar *C* which transmits motion to the reversing clutch. If the work table is moving toward the right, the tappet at the left engages lever *B* as the table approaches the end of its stroke. The movements of the lower end of reversing lever *B* towards the left forces the beveled plunger *D* downward, thus compressing a spring that is located beneath it. When the point of the V-shaped end of lever *B* has passed the point of plunger *D*, the latter is suddenly forced upward by the com-

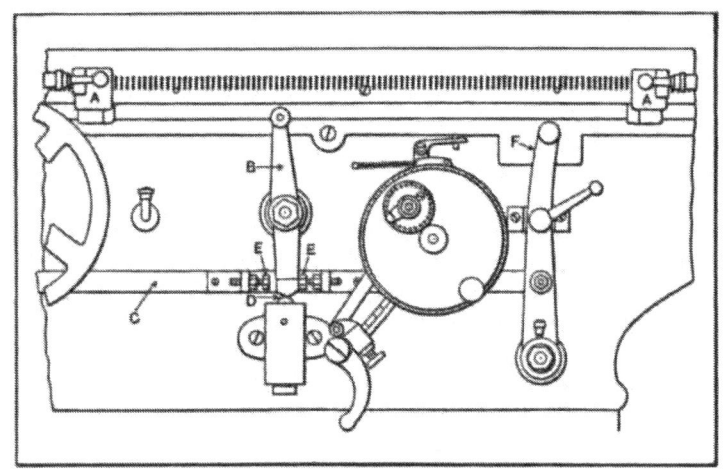

Fig. 3. Spring and Beveled Plunger Control for Reversing Clutch

pressed spring and lever *B*, rod *C*, and the reversing clutch are shifted rapidly.

There is a certain amount of lost motion between the studs *E* on bar *C* and the reversing lever *B*. As the result of this lost motion, the clutch is not entirely disengaged until the V-shaped point of the reversing lever has passed the point of plunger *D*; the reversing clutch is withdrawn slowly from the bevel pinion which it engages until the sudden action of plunger *D* causes it to shift rapidly into engagement with the opposite bevel pinion. The clutch is held in engagement until the next reversal of motion by the upward pressure of the plunger against the beveled end of the reversing lever *B*. With the particular design illustrated, the point of reversal can also be controlled by hand lever F which is connected to rod C; by placing this lever in a central position, the clutch is shifted to neutral and the movement of the work table discontinued.

Controlling Point of Reversal by Special Mechanisms. — The points of reversal for a reciprocating slide are usually controlled by trip dogs mounted directly on the slide and adjusted to give the required length of travel or stroke. It is not always convenient, however, to control the reversal in this way. For instance, if the operating slide is at the rear of a machine where the trip dogs cannot be adjusted readily, some form of mechanism which operates in unison with the slide may be used to permit locating the trip dogs at the front of the machine. A simple method of controlling the points of reversal from the front of the machine is applied to Landis grinders. The wheel slide travels along ways at the rear of the machine and the length of stroke is regulated in accordance with the length of the work by two trip dogs mounted on a wheel or circular rack at the front of the machine. The shaft carrying this wheel extends through the machine and is connected by gearing, so that it has an oscillating or turning movement in first one direction and then the other, which movements correspond to, and are in unison with those of the wheel carriage at the rear. Worm teeth are formed on the periphery of the trip-dog wheel and the dogs are held in position by worms which may be lifted out of engagement when the dogs are to be adjusted considerably. The dogs alternately strike a tappet or lever which controls the movements of the reversing clutch.

Another method of controlling the reversing points of a rear slide is by means of a shaft connected through gearing with the reciprocating slide and having at the front end a pinion meshing with a sliding rack carrying the trip dogs. As the rear slide operates, it turns the pinion shaft in first one direction and then the other, which imparts a reciprocating motion to the rack. The trip dogs attached to the rack, by engaging a lever, cause a reversal of motion by means of a clutch-and-gear type of reversing mechanism.

An indirect or independent method of controlling the points of reversal on a Brown & Sharpe automatic bevel gear cutting machine is illustrated in Fig. 4. The cutter-slide A must be set at an angle corresponding to the inclination of the gear teeth to be cut, so that it would be difficult to have the trip dogs attached directly to this slide. To avoid such an arrangement, a sliding rack B is employed. This rack meshes with a pinion C which rotates in unison with the feeding of the cutter-slide, since this

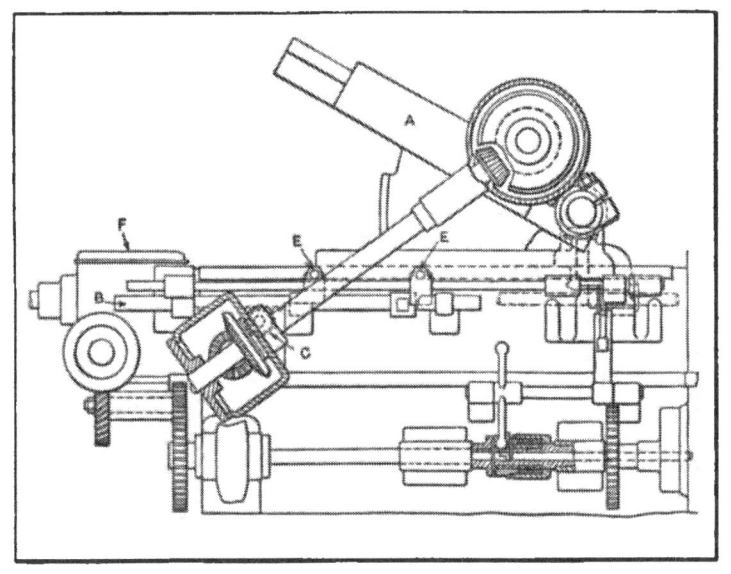

Fig. 4. Independent Method of Controlling Reversal of an Adjustable Slide on a Bevel Gear Cutting Machine

pinion and the slide derive their motion from the same shaft. As pinion C rotates in first one direction and then the other, it traverses the rack B, which, by means of the adjustable dogs E, controls the action of the reversing mechanism enclosed at F. With this arrangement, the traversing movement of the rack can be made less than the travel of the cutter-slide, if this is desirable because of limited space. On the other hand, if the traversing movement of the slide is to be very short and it is essential to reverse it at a given point within close limits, the movements of the reverse controlling rack can be increased considerably as compared with the motion of the cutter-slide.

Mechanism for Shifting Open and Crossed Belts. — The open and crossed belts illustrated by diagram F, Fig. 1, are shifted automatically for obtaining a reversal of motion, when used to drive such machines as planers, broaching machines, or other classes of mechanisms which are designed for continuous operation and equipped with this form of drive. A side elevation

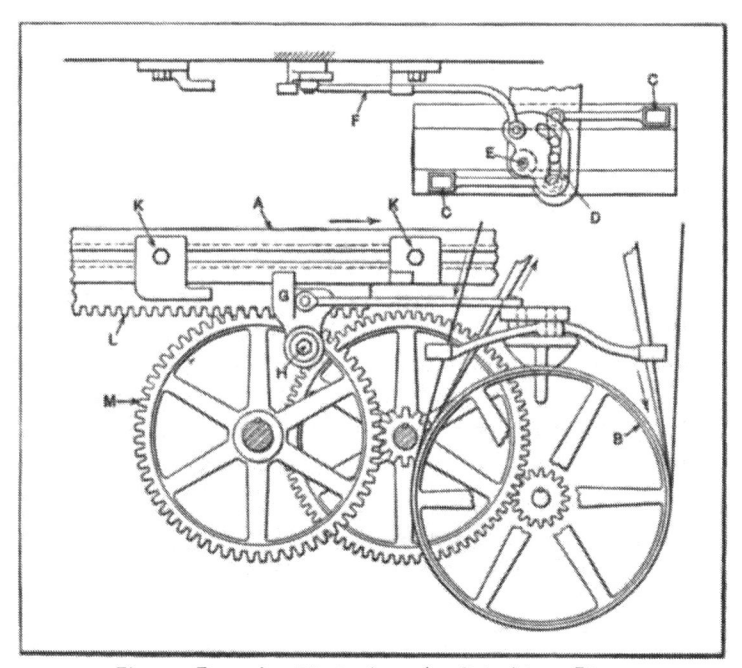

Fig. 5. Reversing Mechanism of a Belt-driven Planer

and plan of the automatic belt-shifting device used on a planer is illustrated in Fig. 5. The shaft on which the belt pulleys B are mounted transmits motion to the planer table A through a train of gearing which gives a suitable speed reduction. In order to reverse the motion of the work table, this entire train of gearing is reversed by alternately shifting the open and crossed belts onto the central pulley, which is attached to the shaft. The length of the stroke is governed by the distance between the two dogs K which may be adjusted along a groove at the side of the table. The position of each belt is controlled by a guide C having an opening at the end through which the belt passes. These two guides or shifters, which are in the form of bellcranks, are pivoted and the inner ends carry small rollers that engage a groove in the cam-plate D. This cam-plate is pivoted at E and is connected by a link F with the arm or lever G which is pivoted at H.

When the planer is in operation, the table moves in a direction depending upon which belt is on the tight pulley. When this movement has continued far enough to bring one of the dogs K

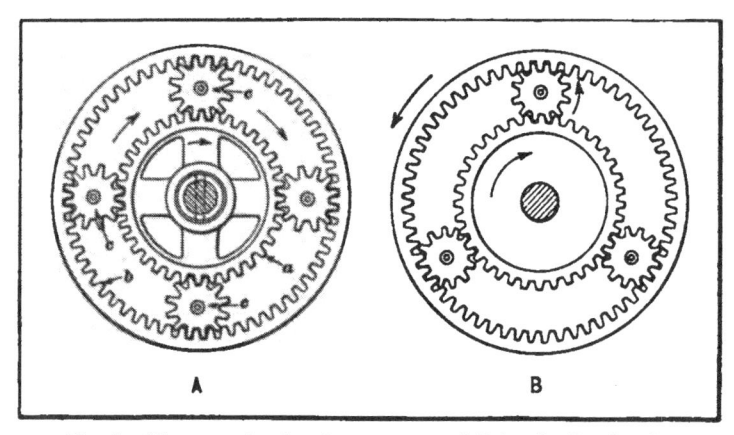

Fig. 6. Diagram showing Arrangement of Epicyclic Gearing for Obtaining Forward and Reverse Motions

into contact with arm G, the latter is pushed over about its pivot, thus imparting a swinging movement to the cam-plate D. The groove in this cam-plate is so formed that the belt on the tight pulley is shifted to the loose pulley and the other belt is moved over to the driving position on the tight pulley. At the end of the return stroke, the other dog engages arm G, thus swinging the cam-plate in the opposite direction and again reversing the motion.

Reversal of Motion through Epicyclic Gearing. — A train of epicyclic or differential gearing may be designed to give a reversal of motion. This form of transmission has been applied

REVERSING MECHANISMS

to some automobiles of the smaller sizes. The principle governing the operation of one of the earlier designs is shown by the diagram, Fig. 6. Two sets of differential gears, indicated at A and B, are mounted inside of drums. These drums may be revolved independently for obtaining the slow forward speed and a reverse motion, or they may be locked together so as to revolve as a unit with the crankshaft for obtaining the direct high-speed drive. The central gear a is the driver in each case, and is keyed to the crankshaft. The slow forward speed is obtained with the combination illustrated at A. To obtain a reduction of

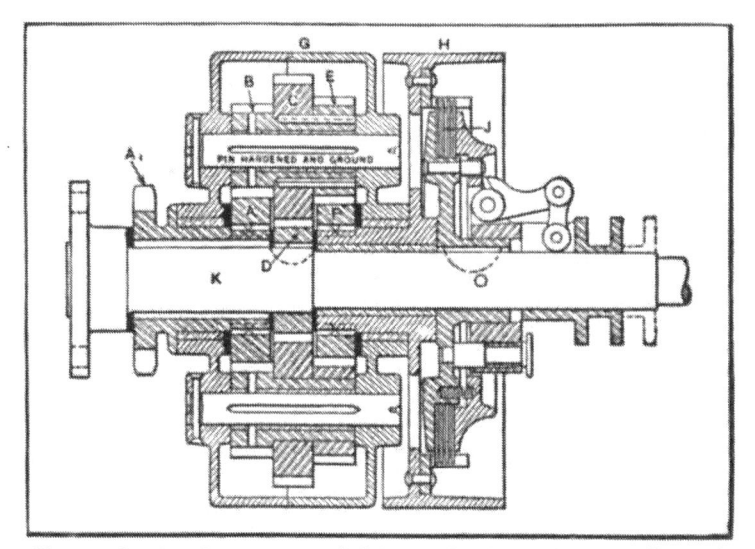

Fig. 7. Another Arrangement of Epicyclic Gearing which gives Forward and Reverse Motions

speed, the internal gear b is held stationary by the application of a brake-band to its periphery; the pinions c carried by the driven member are then forced by the driving gear a to roll around inside of the internal gear, thus transmitting a slow rotary motion to the driven member attached to the pinions. In order to obtain a reversal of motion through the combination of gearing illustrated at B, the disk carrying the pinions is prevented from rotating by the gripping action of another brake-band, so that the pinions merely revolve on their studs and rotate the internal gear in a reverse direction. In this case, the internal gear is the driven member and transmits motion to the driving sprocket.

A reversal of motion may also be obtained with the train of epicyclic gearing shown in Fig. 7. In this case, there is no internal gear. Gear A is mounted on the sleeve of sprocket A_1, gear D is keyed to shaft K, and gear F is attached to the extended hub of drum H. The three gears, B, C, and E are locked together and revolve upon a pin carried by drum G. A duplicate set is also located on the opposite side of the drum, as the illustration shows. When this drum is held stationary by a brake-band, gear A and sprocket A_1 are driven at a slow forward speed through gears D, C, and B, gears D and A revolving in the same direction. The direct high-speed drive is obtained when clutch J is engaged, the whole mechanism then revolving as a unit with shaft K. When drum H is held stationary by a brake-band, gear D causes gear E to revolve about the stationary gear F in a direction opposite to the rotation of D; consequently, gear A is forced to follow in the same direction in which drum G and the planetary gears B, C, and E are moving, thus reversing the motion of gear A and the sprocket.

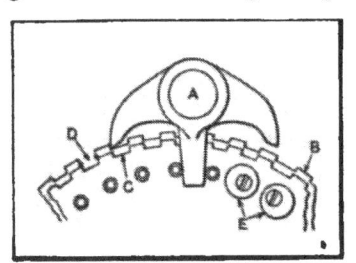

Fig. 8. Ratchet Mechanism which will Automatically Reverse after making a Predetermined Number of Revolutions

Automatic Ratchet Reversing Mechanism. — The simple design of ratchet reversing mechanism illustrated in Fig. 8 enables a ratchet wheel to be automatically reversed after making a predetermined number of revolutions, and the arrangement is such that the time of reversal or the number of revolutions made by the driven ratchet prior to reversal may be varied at will throughout a wide range. The double pawl A is carried by an oscillating arm (not shown), and this pawl engages the driven ratchet B. Mounted concentrically with B there is a smaller controlling ratchet C which is normally restrained from rotating by suitable frictional resistance. The larger diameter of ratchet

B prevents pawl A from engaging the smaller ratchet C, except when the deep notch D is reached by the pawl which then drops down into engagement with C.

The reversal of motion is effected by the engagement of the extension on pawl A with one of the trip dogs E. The number of revolutions made by ratchet B prior to reversal depends upon the number of deep notches D and the position of the trip dogs E. When this mechanism is in operation, ratchet B receives an intermittent motion from the oscillating pawl A and the controlling ratchet C remains stationary until one of the deep notches D is engaged by pawl A; then ratchets B and C rotate together an amount depending upon the motion of the pawl. Controlling ratchet C then remains stationary until another deep notch is engaged. The repeated movements of ratchet C each time the pawl drops into a deep notch, finally bring one of the trip dogs E into contact with the projection on the pawl; the latter is then swung around so that its opposite end engages ratchet B and, consequently, the direction of rotation is reversed. The time of reversal may be controlled by varying the distance between the trip dogs and by having one or more deep notches in the driven ratchet.

Combined Reversing and Feeding Movements. — Some reversing mechanisms are so designed that the longitudinal movement of a reversing rod is accompanied by a rotary motion for imparting a feeding movement at the time reversal occurs. A reversing device of this kind, as applied to a Richards' side-planing machine, is illustrated in Fig. 9. The saddle A is traversed along the bed B by means of a screw, the rotation of which is reversed by open and crossed belts that are alternately shifted from loose pulleys to a tight pulley attached to the screw. The two projecting arms C which are bolted to A strike dogs D mounted on rod E, which, by its longitudinal movement, actuates the belt-shifting mechanism. When rod E is shifted in a lengthwise direction, it is also given a rotary motion in the following manner: Within the bearing F there is a bushing having cam grooves cut into it, as shown by the enlarged detailed view. These grooves receive rollers carried by a pin that passes through the rod E. With this arrangement, any endwise movement of rod E is accompanied by a rotary motion resulting from the engagement of the rollers with the helical grooves in the fixed bushings of bearings F. This rotary movement is transmitted through bevel gears to a rod G which imparts a downward feeding movement to the feed-screw of the tool-slide, through the medium of ratchet gearing.

Automatic Control of Spindle Reversal. — Fig. 10 represents a sectional view through the bed of an automatic screw machine, beneath the headstock, and illustrates the mechanism

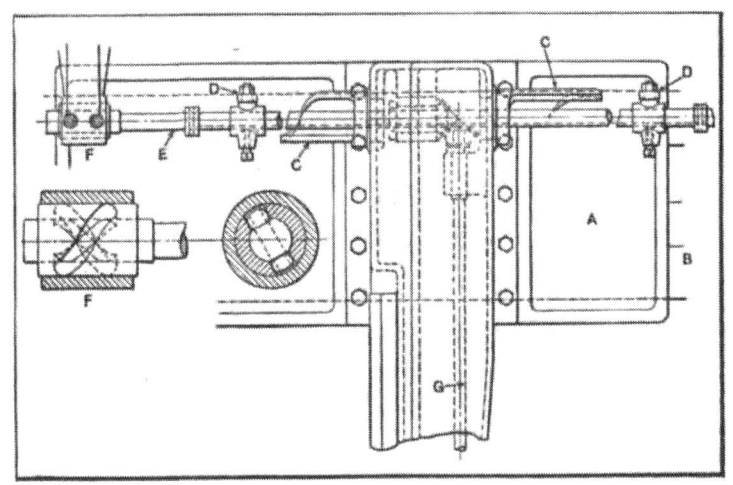

Fig. 9. Reverse Controlling Mechanism so arranged that Motion of Reversing Rod is accompanied by a Rotary Movement for Feeding Tool

for automatically controlling the reversal of the spindle rotation. This machine is driven by a single belt pulley rotating at constant speed. The various movements of the machine, other than revolving the spindle, are derived from a shaft at the rear which rotates at a constant speed. On this shaft H is mounted a series of automatically-controlled clutches which are similar in action to those used on punch-presses. These clutches control the feeding of the stock, the opening and closing of the chuck, the revolving of the turret, the reversing of the main spindle and the changing of the speed from fast to slow, or *vice versa*. This back-shaft H is connected by change-gearing through a worm drive, with a slow moving camshaft A at the front on which are mounted the cams for the turret and cross-slide movements and a series of dog carriers B carrying tappets or dogs which control the action of the different clutches on the back-shaft. The ratio of the change-gears previously referred to determines the duration of the cycle of operations and, consequently, the length of time it takes to make a given piece of work.

The main spindle is reversed by a clutch located between two clutch members revolving in opposite directions. The carrier

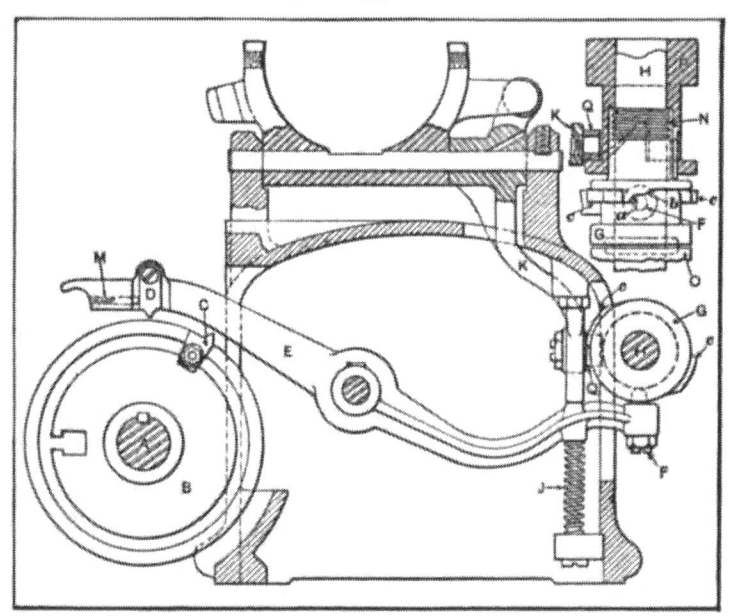

Fig. 10. Arrangement for Automatically Controlling Spindle Reversal

B has an annular T-slot in which adjustable dogs like the one shown at C are mounted. These dogs engage a tappet D on lever E, the rear end of which carries a screw F, the cylindrical point of which enters a cam groove in clutch G. This clutch is mounted loosely on shaft H which revolves continuously. A plan view of the cam is shown in detail above the end view. The cam groove is exactly the same on the other side as on the side shown, the clutch being arranged to engage each half revolution and then automatically disengage. The normal position of the pin F is in the recess at a. When it is lowered entirely out of the groove by the action of dog C on tappet D against the pressure of spring J, this releases clutch G, which is forced forward by a spring N coiled about the shaft, until it engages a mating member O, fastened to shaft H, and begins to revolve. Meanwhile dog C has passed tappet D, allowing pin F to drop into the cam groove again. The clutch G, as it revolves, brings inclined face b of the groove (or a similar incline on the opposite side) into contact with F, and the continued revolution of G, through the action of this inclination on the pin, forces the clutch teeth out of engagement, stopping G again with the pin in position a as at the start. A cam P, also loose on the shaft H, is keyed to G. This cam engages a roll Q on the end of lever K, which operates a clutch fork, controlling the position of the main spindle clutch. When it is time to again reverse the spindle, another dog C is set in the proper position, and the clutch is tripped, revolving for a second time a half revolution and stopping, thus operating lever K and the spindle clutch to change the direction of the spindle rotation. This represents the normal procedure in cases where the time taken to make one piece is short enough so that the rotation of dog carrier B is reasonably rapid. For many pieces, however, this movement is so slow that dog C does not come out from under tappet D in time to allow pin F to drop into the cam groove before the clutch has made the required half revolution. In such cases, incline b would pass without disengaging the clutch and pin F could not enter until the next recess came around and the next incline b; hence the clutch would be stopped at the end of one revolution instead of a half revolution. This difficulty has been very simply overcome by the following means:

Tappet D is pivoted to lever E as shown, and is forced back against a shoulder to the position indicated, by a spring M located in a drilled hole and pressing against a plunger bearing on D. This spring is of such strength as compared with spring J that the first effect of dog C, when it strikes D, is to move the latter backward without raising lever E. When D has been pressed so far back that it strikes the shoulder at the left, further movement being impossible, E is raised, pin F is withdrawn from the cam slot in the clutch G, and the latter is allowed to engage fixed member O on the shaft H, and starts to revolve. A cam surface c is provided on G which, immediately after the clutch begins to rotate, strikes pin F and depresses it still further, thus raising tappet D clear above the point of dog C, and allowing it to swing back to its normal position against the shoulder at the right under the influence of spring M. Lever E is then ready to drop instantly, as D and C are entirely clear of each other. As soon as the end of cam projection c passes, F drops into the groove and the rotation of the cam is arrested after a half revolution, as required. When it is known that shaft H revolves at 120 revolutions per minute, so that the half revolution of G occupies but one-fourth second, it will be seen that the device has a difficult duty to perform, but operates in a very satisfactory manner.

Automatic Variation in Point of Reversal. — One of the many interesting mechanisms found on textile machinery is the one employed on fly frames for controlling the winding of the roving on the bobbin. The way the bobbins are driven at a decreasing rate of speed as the diameter increases is explained in connection with Fig. 13, Chapter VIII, which shows diagrammatically the relation of the different parts. As mentioned in connection with that illustration, the bobbins not only revolve but are given a vertical reciprocating motion, in order to wind the roving onto them in successive helical layers. This winding of the roving onto the bobbin involves, in addition to decreasing the speed as the diameter increases, a decrease in the traversing speed of the bobbin and a gradual shortening of the bobbin travel as one layer of roving is wound upon another. The bobbin should move a distance equal to the diameter of the roving while it rotates relative to the " flyer " a distance equal to one revolution; therefore, as the bobbin speed gradually diminishes, it is also necessary to decrease the rate of traverse, so that each layer of the roving will be coiled closely. The change in the point of reversal in order to shorten the stroke as the bobbin increases in diameter is required in order to form conical ends on the wound bobbin and a firm winding that will not unravel and cause trouble, such as would be the result of attempting to wind each layer the full length of the bobbin. These changes occur simultaneously, although they will be referred to separately in describing the " builder motion " illustrated diagrammatically in Fig. 11.

The plates B and C engage a screw A, which has a right-hand thread extending along one-half its length and a left-hand thread, along the remaining half. These plates and the screw are traversed vertically with the bobbin carriage. The vertical shaft D carries a dog E having two arms located 180 degrees apart. At each end of the stroke, shaft D makes a half turn which motion is utilized for reversing the motion, for shifting the cone belt slightly in order to decrease the speed, and also for shortening the stroke of the bobbin. As the plates B and C move vertically, one end of the tumbling dog E bears against them until it slides off at one end. Prior to the disengagement of the dog with one of the plates, gear F on the cone-pulley shaft revolves idly in a space on the rim of gear G where the teeth are omitted. There are two of these spaces located 180 degrees apart, as the illustration indicates. One of the projecting pins on the disk H at the lower end of shaft D is in engagement with a lever J which has attached to it a spring that holds the lever against a pin and tends to turn shaft D. When dog E slides off one end

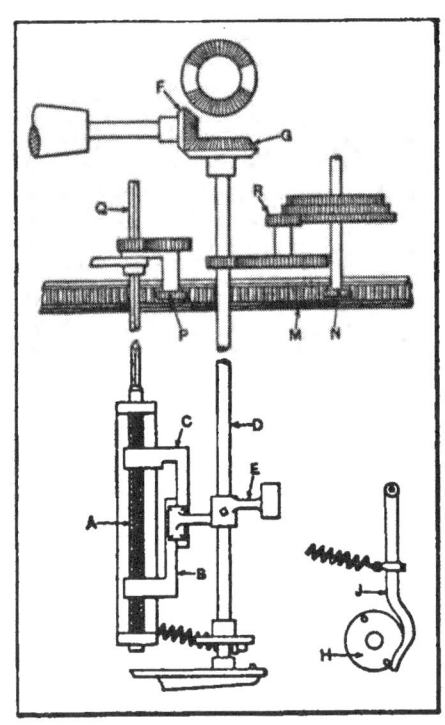

Fig. 11. **Mechanism for Varying Point of Reversal and Speed of Rotation**

of a plate, shaft D is turned far enough by the action of the spring and lever J to bring gear G into mesh with pinion F; consequently, gear G is revolved one-half turn or until pinion F engages the space on the opposite side where there are no teeth. The partial rotation of shaft D shifts the reversing gears through a connection at the lower end and starts the bobbin carriage and plates B and C in the opposite direction. As the opposite end of the tumbling dog E swings around, it engages one of the plates and again causes a reversal of motion as it slides off of the opposite end.

The shifting of the belt on the cone-pulley at each reversal, for gradually decreasing the speed as the bobbin winding increases its diameter, is obtained by connecting rack M with shaft D through the pinion N and the train of gearing shown. This rack M has a fork attached to it that connects with the cone-belt, and it is traversed slightly each time dog E slides off a plate and allows shaft D to turn one-half revolution. The reduction in the length of the carriage traverse is obtained by revolving screw A at each reversal and thus shortening the distance between the plates B and C. This rotation of the screw is effected by pinion P which engages rack M and transmits motion through the other gears shown to the extension Q on the screw, which is made square and is free to slide through the gear hub as the carriage moves vertically. As the plates B and C are moved toward each other, the tumbling gear E has a shorter surface to traverse before it is disengaged. These two plates both move the same distance, so that the point of reversal decreases at each end and the bobbin is wound conical at both ends. The roving delivered by the front roll is either tightened or slackened by engaging pinion R with one of the three gears shown.

Reversal of Motion after Predetermined Number of Revolutions. — With the mechanism illustrated in Fig. 12, a driven shaft may be reversed after making any predetermined number of revolutions from 1 to 100,000 and the motion may be discontinued entirely after the shaft has made any given number of reversals up to 10,000. This mechanism was applied to a textile

118   MECHANICAL MOVEMENTS

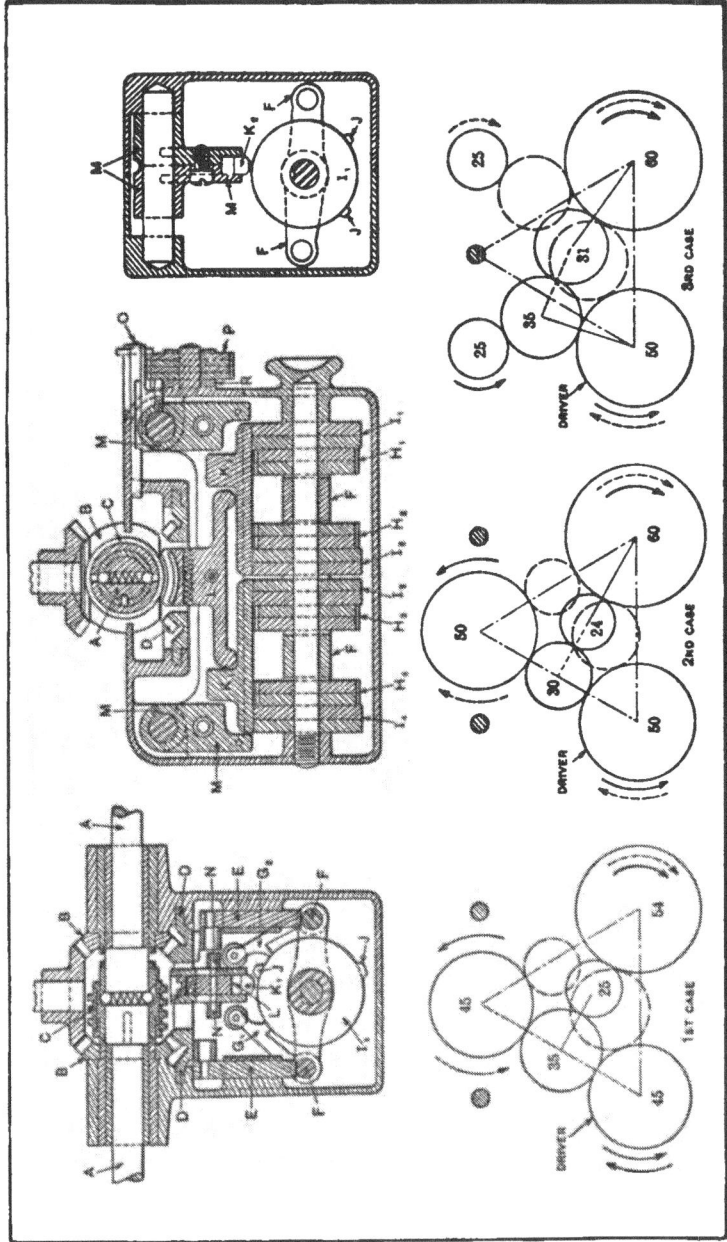

Fig. 12. Mechanism for Reversing Motion after any Predetermined Number of Revolutions between 1 and 100,000, and for Stopping Driven Shaft after any Number of Reversals up to 10,000

machine. The reversing shaft A is driven from the vertical shaft shown through either one of the miter gears B which revolve in opposite directions and are alternately engaged with the shaft by the sliding clutch C. The reversal of rotation after a predetermined number of revolutions is controlled by a system of ratchets and pawls. Another ratchet-and-pawl mechanism is also utilized for stopping the rotation of A after a given number of reversals, by placing the shifting clutch C in the central or neutral position.

The lower miter gear D has a cam which engages the rollers on the upper ends of bars E. The lower ends of these bars oscillate the rockers F which carry two sets of pawls, G_1 and G_2. The set of four pawls G_1 at the left is in the operating or working position, as shown in the illustration. There are four pairs of ratchets H_1, H_2, H_3, and H_4. The teeth of each pair of ratchets are cut oppositely and the four pawls on one side of the ratchet shaft are for engaging the ratchets which control the number of revolutions made by shaft A in one direction, whereas the four pawls on the other side of the shaft are for operating the reverse motion ratchets. These ratchets operate progressively and transmit motion to disks I_1, I_2, I_3, and I_4. These disks have projections or cam surfaces J, which serve to shift the reversing clutch C after shaft A has made a predetermined number of revolutions, which number is regulated by adjusting the ratchets before the mechanism is put into operation. This system of cam disks and ratchets will be referred to as the "combination."

Each ratchet has 20 teeth with one deep cut or tooth. Each tooth of ratchet H_4 is equivalent to 8000 revolutions of shaft A; each tooth of ratchet H_3 is equivalent to 400 revolutions; each tooth of ratchet H_2, 20 revolutions; and each tooth of ratchet H_1 is equivalent to one revolution of shaft A. The mechanism is set for a given number of revolutions by turning each ratchet so that the deep tooth is away from the operating pawl a certain number of teeth, the number depending, in each case, upon the number of revolutions of A represented by each tooth. For instance, to set the combination for a reversal of motion after shaft A makes 49,763 revolutions, ratchet H_4 is so located that there are six teeth between the operating pawl and the deep tooth; these six teeth are equivalent to 48,000 revolutions of A. Ratchet H_3 is then set at four teeth, representing 1600 revolutions of A; ratchet H_2 is set at eight teeth, equivalent to 160 revolutions of A, and, finally, ratchet H_1 is set at three teeth, representing three revolutions of A. The mechanism is now set for a total of $48,000 + 1600 + 160 + 3 = 49,763$ revolutions.

After the mechanism has been set in the manner described, its action is as follows: The pawl G_1 which is actuated once for every revolution of gear D, drops into the deep tooth or notch of ratchet H_1 after engaging three teeth on H_1, since, in this particular case, this ratchet was adjusted so that there were three teeth between the pawl and the deep tooth. As soon as this deep tooth is engaged by the pawl, the ratchet H_2 is turned a distance equivalent to one tooth; ratchet H_2 then remains stationary until H_1 has made a complete turn and its pawl again drops into the deep tooth, when H_2 is again moved one tooth. The pawls are so located that the first one must engage the deep notch before the next successive pawl can engage its ratchet at all, and the relation between the other pawls is the same. Ratchet H_2 continues to be moved a single tooth for each complete revolution of H_1 until it has moved eight teeth, in this particular instance. The pawl of H_2 then drops into a deep tooth and ratchet H_3 is moved one tooth. Ratchet H_3 now remains stationary until H_2, by the continued action of H_1, makes a complete revolution, when H_3 is moved another tooth. After H_3 has moved a distance equivalent to four teeth, its pawl, in turn, drops into the deep notch, and ratchet H_4 is turned one tooth. A complete revolution of H_3 turns H_4 another tooth and, when H_4 has moved six teeth, in this case, the shaft A will have made a total of 49,763 revolutions.

This result will be verified in order to more clearly show the action of the mechanism. As previously mentioned, each ratchet has 20 teeth. Each tooth of H_1 represents one revolution of shaft A and the movement of three teeth prior to engagement with the deep notch equals three revolutions. Since H_2 is set for a movement of eight teeth, H_1 will have to make eight complete turns, which will be equivalent to 160 additional turns of A. Now the four complete turns of H_2 necessary for moving H_3 four teeth require $4 \times 20 \times 20$ or 1600 additional turns of A, giving a total of 1763 revolutions. Finally, the movement of H_4 six teeth requires $6 \times 20 \times 20 \times 20 = 48,000$ additional turns of A, so that the total number of revolutions made by A prior to reversal equals 49,763, when the ratchet mechanism is set as previously described.

The progressive action of the ratchets gradually revolves the cam disks preparatory to shifting the reversing clutch. The cam J on disk I_4 first engages and lifts the floating lever K_1 at the left-hand end and the lever L one-half as much. When the other cam disks act upon K_1 and K_2, these levers, together with part L, are lifted the full amount and spring balls in L cause it to be thrown quickly into mesh with the clutch C. This clutch is threaded and two threads are also formed on the upper side of part L. As levers K_1, K_2, and part L are contained in a carriage M, all are constrained to move parallel to the axis of shaft A, because of the action of the screw threads on clutch C. This results in breaking the combination; that is, the floating levers are all removed from the cams, the four pawls G_1 are disengaged from their ratchets, and the idle set of pawls G_2 comes into action, thereby reversing the rotation of the controlling mechanism. As soon as the travel of carriage M is completed, which requires 1½ revolution of the clutch, the latter is constrained to act along the threads on L while making one revolution, until feathers attached to the clutch over-ride the spring balls in shaft A; the clutch is then instantly thrown out of mesh with one bevel gear and into mesh with the other, thereby reversing the rotation of shaft A. Just as the clutch starts this rapid shifting movement, the cam on gear D engages one of the rollers N on part L and throws the levers all down and the threads on L out of mesh with the clutch.

The rotation of shaft A is stopped after a predetermined number of reversals by means of a separate mechanism which arrests the movement of carriage M midway of its travel. The worm threads on clutch C then act upon part L and withdraw the clutch until it is out of engagement on one side and cannot engage on the other. Carriage M is stopped by a pin O which drops into a groove in M after the four ratchets P, having ten teeth, are properly aligned as regards a deep notch in each ratchet. These ratchets are operated consecutively by a stepped four-fingered pawl on R through the medium of a pin connecting with M.

The three diagrams in the lower part of Fig. 12 illustrate the systems of gearing controlled by the mechanism described in the foregoing. The requirements, as illustrated by these three diagrams, are as follows: 1. That a reversing gear shall drive two others continuously in the same direction but in opposite directions relative to each other. 2. That a reversing gear shall drive one of the two gears continuously in the same direction and the other in the same direction as that of the reversing gear. 3. That a reversing gear shall drive one gear continuously in the same direction and shall drive two others alternately in the same direction as itself. The full arrows and the full circles on these diagrams belong together, and likewise the broken or dotted lines and arrows. The full lines connecting the centers indicate that those gears are linked, whereas the broken lines denote spring connections. The movement of the reversing driver and the friction of the links swing the idler gears.

Reversing Motor Drives. — When a machine is driven by an electric motor, the direction of rotation may be reversed in the case of a direct-current motor by reversing the current in either the armature or the field. The motors used for street railway work are usually reversed by changing the direction of the current flowing through the armature, the flow of the field current remaining the same. If a motor is running, a resistance should be inserted in the armature circuit before reversing the current flowing through the armature, and the speed of the motor should preferably be reduced considerably before reversing the current.

Some motor-driven planers are so arranged that the reversal of motion for the work table is obtained by reversing the motor instead of employing shifting belts. When the planer is in operation, the point of reversal is controlled by dogs similar to those on a belt-driven planer. With one type of equipment, at the instant of reversal a pilot switch is thrown by one of the dogs and the controller short-circuits the armature through suitable resistance, thus causing the motor to act as a generator, and, consequently, as a powerful electric brake for arresting the motion of the planer table. As soon as the speed of the motor has been reduced a predetermined amount, the armature current is reversed and with it the rotation of the motor and the movements of the work table. The pilot switch takes the place of the belt-shifting mechanism on belt-driven planers. The reversal of motion at the end of each stroke is entirely automatic.

When motion is derived from an induction motor, a change in the direction of movement involves reversing the rotation of the revolving magnetism set up by the field windings. If the motor is two-phase, the current in either one of the phases may be reversed to change the direction of rotation, which is accomplished by interchanging the connections of one of the phases with its terminals on the motor. For a three-phase motor, a reversal of rotation is obtained by interchanging the connections of any two of the line wires with the motor terminals.

CHAPTER V

QUICK-RETURN MOTIONS

MANY machines, especially of the type used for cutting metals, are equipped with a driving mechanism which gives a rapid return movement after a working or cutting stroke, in order to reduce the idle period. For instance, shapers, slotters, and planers are so arranged that the tool, after making the cutting stroke, is returned at a greater velocity, thus increasing the efficiency and productive capacity of the machine. The method of obtaining this rapid return varies with different types of machine tools. In some cases, motion for the return movement is obtained by using two belts which alternately come into the driving position and rotate the driven member at two rates of speed. This method is employed with belt-driven planers, the belt for the return movement of the table connecting with pulleys having a higher speed ratio. The rapid return movement for some other types of machines is obtained by transmitting motion through a different combination of gearing which is automatically engaged at the end of the working stroke. The term "quick-return motion," however, as applied to machine tools, generally relates to a driving mechanism so designed that the increased rate of speed for the return movement is obtained through the same combination of parts which actuate the driven member during the forward or working stroke.

Crank and Oscillating Link. — A simple form of quick-return mechanism which has been applied extensively to shapers is shown diagrammatically in Fig. 1. The pinion A drives gear C at a uniform speed, and this gear carries a swiveling block B which engages slotted link L. The lower end of this link is pivoted at D and the upper end connects by means of a link with the ram of the shaper. As the crankpin or swiveling block B revolves with gear C, it slides up and down in the slot of link

QUICK-RETURN MOTIONS 125

L and causes the latter to oscillate about the fixed pivot D at its lower end. The ram of the shaper is mounted in guides or ways so that it is given a rectilinear movement.

A quick-return movement is obtained with this form of drive owing to the fact that the crankpin B moves through an arc a during the cutting stroke, whereas, for the return stroke, it moves through a much shorter arc b. As gear C rotates at a uniform speed, obviously the time required for the return stroke, as compared with the cutting stroke, is in the same proportion as the lengths of the arcs a and b. The radial position of block

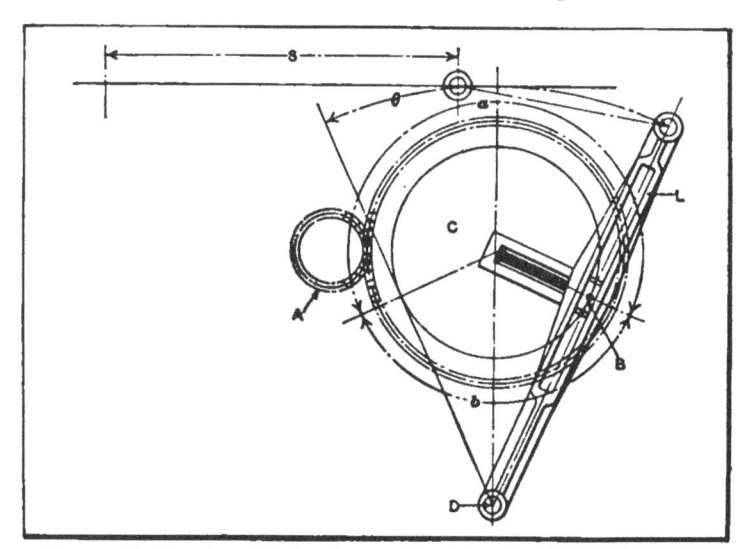

Fig. 1. Quick-return Motion from a Revolving Crank and Oscillating Slotted Lever

B may be varied in order to change the length S of the stroke. This mechanism imparts a variable speed to the ram, the speed increasing toward the center of the stroke and then diminishing. The angle made by the crankpin for the forward stroke equals 180 degrees + the angle θ through which slotted link L moves; for the return stroke, the crankpin moves through an angle equal to 180 degrees − the angular movement θ of the slotted link. The sine of one-half angle θ equals the radius of the crank divided by the distance from pivot D to the center of the gear C.

Whitworth Quick-return Motion. — A type of quick-return motion that has been widely used in slotter construction is illustrated in Fig. 2. This mechanism, which is known as the "Whitworth quick-return," is similar in principle to the crank and oscillating link combination previously referred to, although the construction is entirely different. The pinion A drives gear C at a uniform velocity, and this gear carries a block B which engages a slot or groove in part D, which is connected by a link E with the tool-slide of the machine. The line xx represents the center-line of motion for the tool-slide. The gear C revolves upon a large bearing F which is a part of the machine frame.

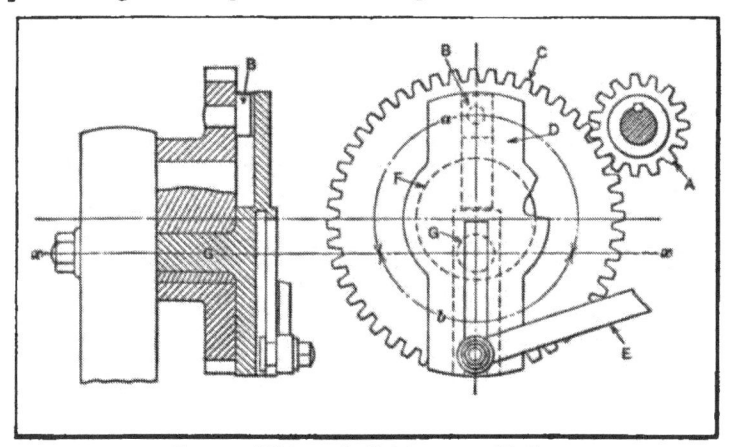

Fig. 2. Whitworth Quick-return Motion

The slotted member D has a bearing G, within F, and the center about which D rotates is offset with relation to the center of driving gear C; consequently, the crankpin or block B moves through an arc a during the cutting stroke and through a shorter arc b for the return stroke, so that the latter requires less time in proportion to the respective lengths of arcs a and b. The stroke is varied by changing the radial position of the pin which connects with link E.

So far as the principle of operation is concerned, the chief difference between the Whitworth motion and the crank and slotted link is that, in the former case, the bearing for the slotted or driven member is inside of the crankpin circle, whereas, with

QUICK-RETURN MOTIONS 127

the crank and slotted link combination, the pivot is outside of the crankpin circle. As the result of this difference in arrangement, part *D* in Fig. 2 has a continuous rotary motion, whereas the slotted link *L*, in Fig. 1, swings through a definite angle. With the Whitworth quick-return, the ratio of the time required for the forward and return strokes is not varied by changing the

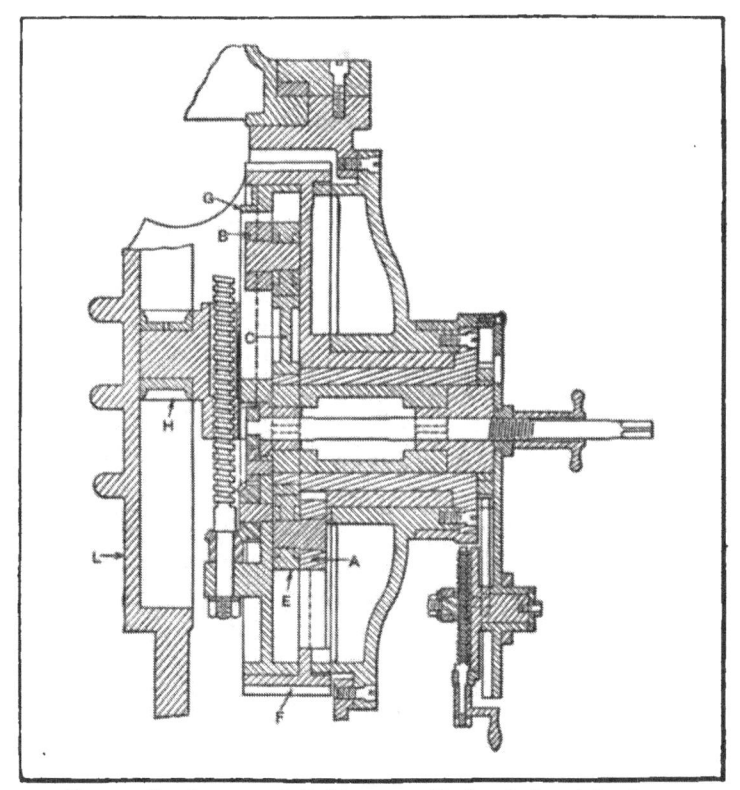

Fig. 3. Crank-operated Quick-return Motion designed to give a Uniform Forward Speed

length of the stroke. With the crank and oscillating link, a change of stroke does affect this ratio, the latter increasing as the length of the stroke is increased.

Modification of Whitworth Motion. — A quick-return mechanism that is a modification of the Whitworth motion combined with the slotted link and rotating crank is illustrated by the sectional view, Fig. 3. This form of drive has been applied to a shaper in order to secure in addition to a quick return a cutting speed that is practically constant throughout the working stroke. The driving gear F transmits its rotary movement through a swiveling block A to a ring E which turns about an eccentric C. On the opposite side of this ring there is a second swiveling block B, which drives the crank-disk G, on which is mounted the main crankpin block H, engaging the vibrating arm or link L that, in turn, is connected with the ram. The eccentric C is offset with relation to the center of the driving gear F, and it remains permanently in a fixed position; therefore, the circular path of the eccentric ring blocks A and B is not concentric with the path described by the main crankpin H. In other words, the circle which these blocks describe as they are driven around by gear F has a constantly varying radius from the center of the gear, which compensates for the irregularity of speed obtained by a plain slotted link, and gives a practically constant movement during the working stroke.

Quick Return from Elliptical Gearing. — Elliptical gearing has been used to obtain a quick-return motion, although such gearing is difficult to cut without special attachments, and comparatively few mechanisms requiring a quick-return motion have this type of drive. The driving and driven gears are of the same proportions and size as shown in Fig. 4, and each gear revolves about one of its foci as a fixed center. The distance between the shaft centers is made equal to the length of the common major axis. The angular velocity ratio varies according to the respective radii of the driving and driven gears at the point of contact. If A is the driving shaft and it rotates at a uniform speed, the angular velocity of shaft B will increase during the first half revolution from the position shown in the illustration, and then decrease during the remaining half revolution. When the gears are in the position shown, the angular velocity of the driven shaft B is minimum, because that side of the driver having the shortest radius is in contact with it; as the driver revolves, the radius at the point of contact gradually increases, and, consequently, the angular velocity increases until tooth C is in mesh, when the angular velocity is maximum. When point C representing the longest radius of the driving gear has passed the point of contact, the angular velocity gradually diminishes until it is again at a minimum.

The actual number of revolutions made by each shaft in a given time is, of course, the same, and the driving and driven gears both require the same time to complete the half revolution between the two positions representing the minimum and maximum angular velocities. The variable motion of the driven gear, however, may be utilized to give a quick-return movement to a driven tool-slide or other part. When two shafts are to be connected by elliptical gearing, either the maximum or the

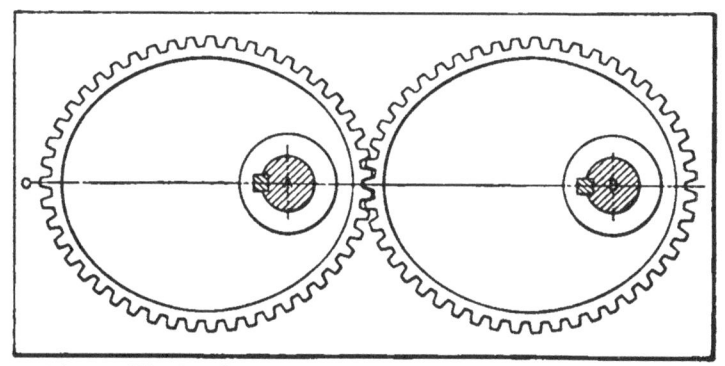

Fig. 4. Elliptical Gearing arranged to Return Driven Part quickly

minimum angular velocities may be selected at will, but, when one has been determined, the other is fixed; the driver is assumed in all cases to have a constant or uniform angular velocity.

This type of quick-return motion has been applied to shapers in order to return the tool quickly after the cutting stroke. The driven gear is connected to the ram by a link. The bolt or crankpin on the gear which connects with the link may be adjusted along a groove for varying the distance from the center of the driven shaft and the length of the stroke. Elliptical gearing has also been used for operating the slide valve of a steam stamp, such as is used for crushing rock. In this case, the variable motion obtained from the gearing is utilized to so control the motion of the valve as to admit steam above the piston throughout almost the entire downward stroke, whereas, on the upward stroke, just enough steam is used to return the stamp shaft, in order to reduce steam consumption.

Eccentric Pinion and Elliptical Gearing for Quick Return. — The combination of eccentric and elliptical gearing, in conjunction with gears mounted concentrically, as illustrated in Fig. 5, has been utilized to secure a quick-return motion. The pinions A and B are keyed to the driving shaft. The smaller

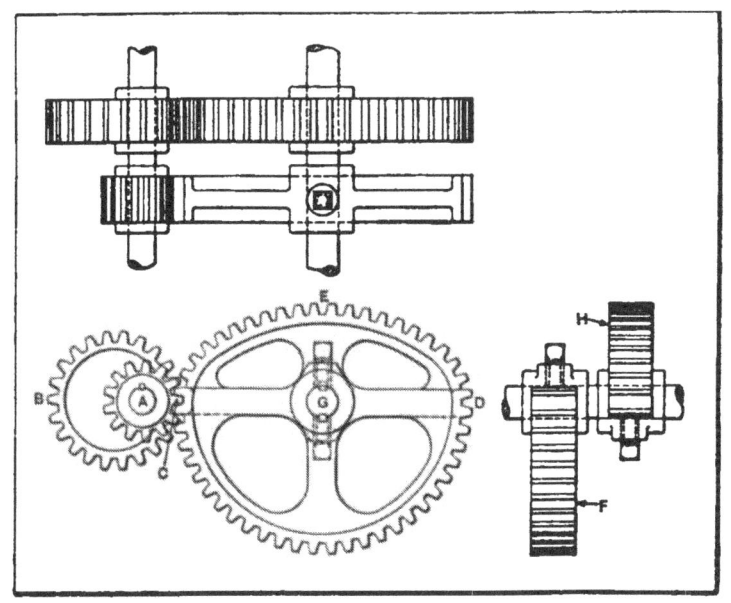

Fig. 5. Eccentric Pinion and Elliptical Gear for Accelerating Return Movement

pinion A is concentric with the shaft and meshes with a half spur gear F. The larger pinion B is eccentrically mounted on the shaft and is in line with a half elliptical gear H, the two gear segments on the driven shaft being offset as shown by the end and plan views.

In the operation of this gearing, the semi-circular gear F is driven by the small pinion A and the elliptical gear by the eccentric pinion B. The elliptical gear makes one-half revolution to each complete revolution of its eccentric driving pinion.

If the driven shaft is revolving in a counter-clockwise direction, the eccentric pinion will be the driver from C to D. At the latter point, the elliptical gear segment leaves the eccentric pinion and the smaller pinion A comes into mesh with the half spur gear and continues to be the driver through the remaining half revolution of the driven shaft, or until the elliptical gear again comes around into mesh with the eccentric pinion. Owing to the difference in the diameters of the half spur gear and its pinion A, the latter must make two revolutions before the eccentric pinion can again engage the teeth of the elliptical gear.

At the point C where the eccentric pinion again becomes the driver, the radius of pinions A and B is equal, and the transfer of the load from A to B does not cause an abrupt change of speed for the driven member. As the eccentric pinion, however, begins to swing the elliptical gear around, the speed of the driven shaft is increased until the maximum radius of the eccentric pinion is opposite the minor axis of the elliptical gear. The speed is then at maximum and, as the movement continues, the speed gradually decreases until the load is transferred to the concentric pinion A which imparts a uniform velocity to the driven member.

With the eccentric-elliptical combination of gearing just described, one revolution of the driven shaft is obtained for every three revolutions of the pinion driving shaft, two revolutions of the concentric pinion A being required for a half revolution, and one revolution of the eccentric pinion B for the remaining half revolution. If this mechanism is applied to a slotter or other machine requiring a similar movement, the cutting stroke will occur while pinion A is the driver, because a relatively slow and uniform speed is imparted to the driven shaft. As the eccentric pinion starts the drive, the speed of the driven shaft is gradually accelerated and, after reaching the maximum, is reduced to the cutting speed, so that the tool-slide is rapidly returned to the starting position ready for the next cutting stroke. The ratio of the quick return to the cutting speed should not be too great, because a jerky motion and excessive vibrations in the machine will result. It has been found, by experiment, that a ratio of 2 to 1 is about the highest that will give satisfactory operation.

When laying out gearing of this kind, there are a few fundamental points which must be observed in all cases: 1. The long radius AB of the eccentric pinion from the shaft center to the pitch line should equal one-half the distance between the centers of the driving and driven shafts. 2. The short radius AC of the eccentric pinion should equal one-half the diameter of the concentric pinion. 3. The major axis CD of the elliptical gear

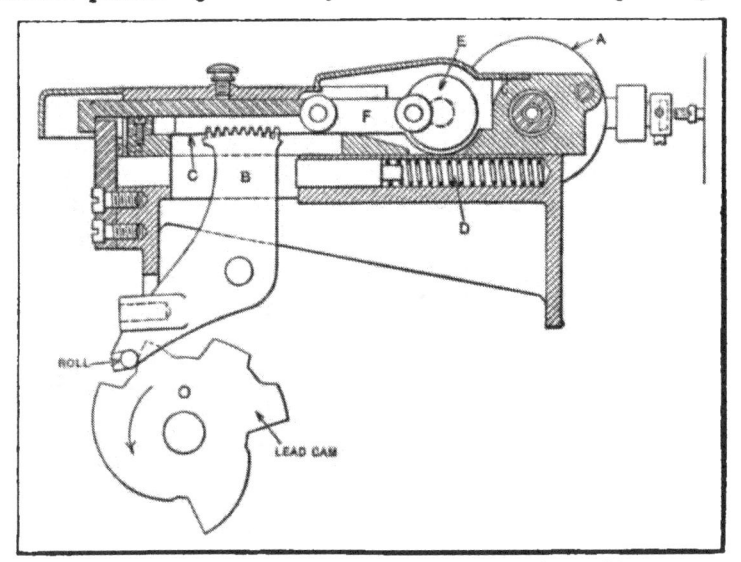

Fig. 6. Independent Quick-return Movement for Screw Machine Turret-slide

should equal twice the distance between the shaft centers, minus twice the short radius AC of the eccentric pinion. 4. The minor axis of the elliptical gear, or twice the distance EG, should equal the distance between the centers of the shafts. 5. The elliptical gear, assuming that it were complete, should have twice the number of teeth that there are in its eccentric driving pinion, and the number of teeth in both the elliptical gear and eccentric pinion should be even. 6. The shaft hole for the elliptical gear should always be located at the intersection of the major and minor axes, or in the center of the gear. This type of gearing is employed when it is especially desirable to secure a uniform motion during the entire cutting stroke.

Independent Quick-return Movement. — On the Brown & Sharpe automatic screw machine, the quick-return and advance movements of the turret-slide are controlled independently of the turret-slide feed cam by means of a crank. The turret A (Fig. 6) is carried by a slide that moves horizontally along the machine bed. The movements of the turret-slide are derived from two different sources. When the turret tools are at work, the slide is operated by a lead cam through lever B, which has teeth at its upper end meshing with rack C. While the turret is being indexed, it is withdrawn rapidly and then quickly advanced to the working position again, by the action of crank E which is revolved once for each indexing movement. The rack C transmits motion to the turret-slide through connecting-rod F, which is pivoted to crank E on the turret-slide. This crank is on the " dead center," as shown in the illustration, while the tools are cutting; when the turret is to be indexed to bring the next successive tool in position, it is first withdrawn far enough for the tool to clear the work, and then the shaft carrying crank E is turned one revolution, through suitable gearing, by the engagement of a clutch the action of which is controlled by a trip dog. When the crank revolves, it allows spring D to draw back the turret-slide without rack C, while making one-half turn, and then advance it during the remaining half turn, the rate of movement being increased by the motion derived from cam A, which is laid out to suit the work. This quick-acting crank operates while the roll on the lower end of lever B is passing from the highest point of the cam lobe to the point for starting the next cut.

CHAPTER VI

INTERMITTENT MOVEMENTS

It is frequently necessary for machine parts to operate intermittently instead of continuously, and there are various forms of mechanisms for obtaining these intermittent motions. A toolslide which is given a feeding movement at regular intervals is an example of a part requiring an intermittent movement. Automatic indexing mechanisms which serve to rotate some member, periodically, a definite part of a revolution, after the machine completes a cycle of operations, represent other applications of intermittent movements. The usual requirements of an intermittent motion, when automatic in its action, are that the motion be properly timed relative to the movement of parts operating continuously and that the member receiving the intermittent motion be traversed a predetermined amount each time it is moved. When the machine part which is traversed intermittently must be located in a certain position with considerable accuracy, some auxiliary locating device may be utilized in conjunction with the mechanism from which the intermittent motion is obtained. The spindle carriers of multiple-spindle automatic screw machines are so arranged that the carrier is first rotated to approximately the required position by an intermittent motion, and then it is accurately aligned with the cutting tools by some form of locating device.

Ratchet Gearing. — One of the simplest and most common methods of obtaining intermittent movements is by means of ratchet gearing. This type of gearing is arranged in various ways, as indicated by the diagrams in Fig. 1. In its simplest form, it consists of a ratchet wheel a (see diagram A), a pawl b, and an arm or lever c to which the pawl is attached. The arm c swings about the center of the ratchet wheel, through a fractional part of a revolution, as indicated by the full and dotted

INTERMITTENT MOVEMENTS 135

lines which represent its extreme positions. When the movement is toward the left, the pawl engages the teeth of the ratchet wheel so that the latter turns with the arm. When the arm swings in the opposite direction, the pawl simply lifts and slides over the points of the teeth without transmitting motion to the ratchet wheel. If a load must be sustained by the

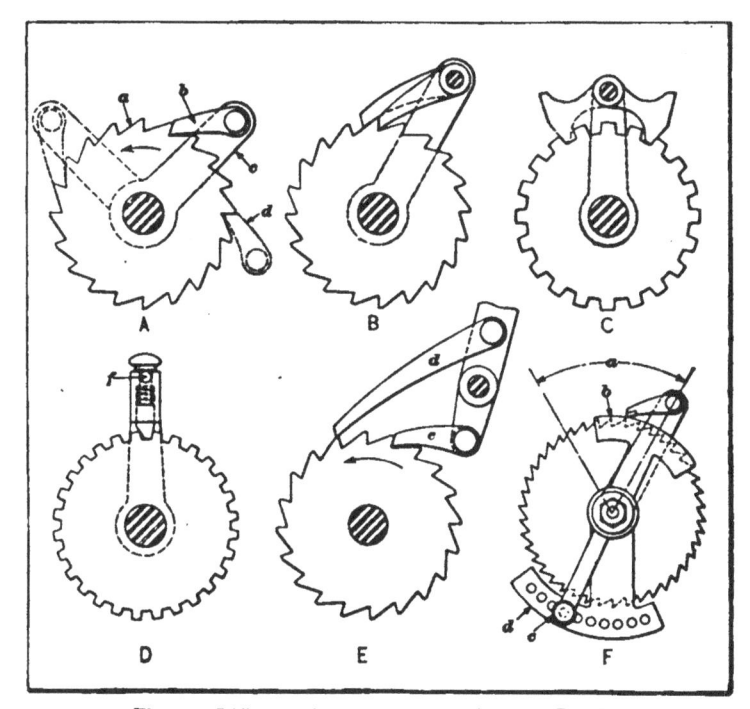

Fig. 1. Different Arrangements of Ratchet Gearing

ratchet gearing, a fixed pawl located at some point, as indicated at d, is used to prevent any backward rotation of the ratchet wheel.

With gearing of this general type, the faces of the ratchet teeth against which the end of the pawl bears should be so formed that the pawl will not tend to fly out of mesh when a load is applied. In order to prevent such disengagement, the teeth should be so inclined that a line at right angles to the face of the tooth in contact with the pawl will pass between the center of the ratchet wheel and the pivot of the pawl. If the face of this tooth should incline at such an angle that a line at right angles to it were above the pawl pivot, pressure against the end of the pawl would tend to force it upward out of engagement with the ratchet wheel.

Multiple Pawls for Ratchets. — When a single pawl is used as shown at A, Fig. 1, the arm which carries it must swing through an arc equal to at least one tooth of the ratchet wheel; hence the pitch of the teeth represents the minimum movement for the wheel. If two or more pawls are used, a relatively small motion of the arm will enable successive teeth to be engaged without decreasing the pitch of the ratchet wheel. The principle is illustrated by diagram B which shows two pawls in position instead of one. As will be seen, one pawl is longer than the other by an amount equal to one-half the pitch of the ratchet teeth. With this arrangement, the movement of the arm may equal only one-half the pitch, if desired, the effect being the same as though a single pawl were applied to a wheel having teeth reduced one-half in pitch. By using three pawls, each varying in length by an amount equal to one-third of the tooth pitch, a still finer feeding movement could be obtained without actually decreasing the pitch of the teeth and thus weakening them.

Reversal of Motion with Ratchet Gearing. — A simple method of obtaining a reversal of motion is illustrated by diagram C, Fig. 1. A double-ended pawl is used and, in order to reverse the motion of the ratchet wheel, this pawl is simply swung from one side of the arm to the other, as indicated by the full and dotted lines. Reversible ratchet wheels must have teeth with bearing faces for the pawl on each side.

Another method of obtaining a reversal of motion is shown at D. The pawl, in this case, is in the form of a small plunger which is backed up by a spiral spring. One side of the pawl is beveled so that the pawl merely slides over the teeth on the backward movement of the arm. When a reversal of movement is required, the pawl is lifted and turned half way around, or until the small pin f drops into the cross-slot provided for it, thus reversing the position of the working face of the pawl.

Frictional Ratchet Mechanisms. — The types of ratchet gearing previously referred to all operate by a positive engagement of the pawl with the teeth of the ratchet wheel. Some ratchet mechanisms are constructed on a different principle in that motion is transmitted from the driving to the driven member by frictional contact. For instance, with one form, the driving member encircles the driven part which has cam surfaces that are engaged by rollers. When the outer driving member is revolved in one direction, the rollers move along the inclined cam surfaces until they are wedged tightly enough to lock the driven part and cause it to turn with the operating lever. When the driver is moved in the opposite direction, the backward motion of the rollers releases them. This general principle has been applied in various ways.

Double-action Ratchet Gearing. — It is sometimes desirable to impart a motion to the ratchet wheel during both the forward and backward motions of the ratchet arm or lever. This result may be obtained by using two pawls arranged as illustrated by diagram E, Fig. 1. These pawls are so located relative to the pivot of the arm that, while one pawl is advancing the ratchet wheel, the other is returning for engagement with the next successive tooth.

Variable Motion from Ratchet Gearing. — Ratchet gearing, especially when applied to machine tools for imparting feeding movements to tool-slides, must be so arranged that the feeding motion can be varied. A common method of obtaining such variations is by changing the swinging movement of the arm that carries the operating pawl. In many cases the link which operates the pawl arm receives its motion either from a crank or a vibrating lever, which is so arranged that the pivot for the rod can be adjusted relative to the center of rotation for changing the movement of the operating pawl and the rate of feed.

One method of adjusting the motion irrespective of the movement of the operating pawl is illustrated at F in Fig. 1. The pawl oscillates constantly through an arc a, and this angle represents the maximum movement for the ratchet wheel. When a reduction of motion is desired, the shield b is moved around so that the pawl is lifted out of engagement with the ratchet wheel and simply slides over it during part of the stroke. Thus, when the shield covers three of the teeth as shown in the illustration the motion of the ratchet wheel is reduced the same as though the swinging action of the pawl lever had been diminished an amount corresponding to three of the teeth. With the particular arrangement illustrated, the shield is held in any position by means of a small spring plunger c that engages holes in a stationary plate d.

Ratchet Mechanisms for Releasing Sprockets. — Some ingenious ratchet mechanisms have been applied to the sprocket wheels of bicycles to permit the pedals to remain stationary while coasting down a grade or hill. A design that has been extensively used is illustrated in principle by the detailed sectional view at A in Fig. 2. The sprocket wheel is not attached directly to the inner member which is shown in section, but motion is transmitted from one part to the other through frictional contact. The inner ring has a series of recesses equally spaced about the circumference. Each of these recesses contains a hardened steel roller or ball, and the bottoms of the recesses are inclined slightly. The rollers are lightly pushed up these inclined surfaces by blocks behind which are small spiral springs. Any relative motion of the inner and outer members of the sprocket causes these steel rollers to either roll up the inclined surfaces and lock the two parts together or to move in the other direction and release the driving and driven members, the action depending upon the direction of the relative movement. For instance, if the outer sprocket is revolved in a clockwise direction, all of the rollers are immediately wedged in their recesses. If the motion of the outer sprocket is suddenly arrested and the inner member continues to revolve, the rollers are immediately released.

An entirely different type of ratchet mechanism designed for use on the sprockets of bicycles is shown by diagrams B to F, inclusive, which illustrate its method of operation. The exterior sprocket is recessed on the inner side for the reception of a crescent-shaped piece a, which acts as the pawl. The depth of the recess

INTERMITTENT MOVEMENTS 139

and the shape of part *a* are such that the teeth on the inner ring *b* can pass freely when moving in the direction indicated by the arrow at *B*; with motion in this direction, part *a* simply is given a rocking movement in its recess to allow the successive teeth to pass. When the relative motion is in the opposite direction, as indicated by diagram *C*, the teeth on the inner member swing part *a* around in its seat, as shown by the successive diagrams, until it is finally wedged firmly between the two parts as shown at *F*. These so-called "free-wheel" mechanisms were subsequently replaced by an arrangement operating on the same

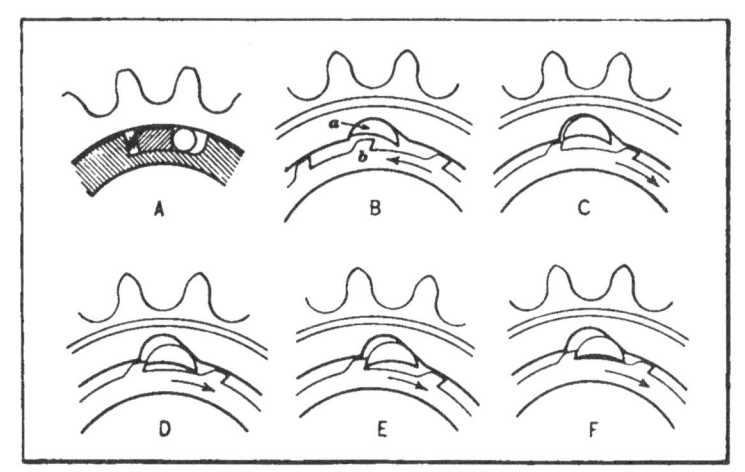

Fig. 2. Ratchet Mechanisms for Releasing Sprockets

general principle so far as the releasing mechanism was concerned, but so designed that a backward movement of the pedal also applied a brake.

Automatic Disengagement of Ratchet Gearing. — The action of ratchet gearing can be stopped automatically after the ratchet wheel has been turned a predetermined amount, by equipping the wheel with an adjustable shield which serves to disengage the pawl after the required motion has been completed. This form of disengaging device, as applied to the cross-feeding mechanism of a cylindrical grinding machine, is shown in Fig. 3. This mechanism is used to automatically feed the grinding wheel in toward the work for taking successive cuts, and it is essential to have the mechanism so arranged that it can be set to stop the feeding movement when the diameter of the work has been reduced a predetermined amount. When the pawl A is in mesh with the ratchet wheel B, the grinding wheel is fed forward an amount depending upon the position of screws (not shown) which control the stroke of pawl A. The automatic feeding movement continues at each reversal of the machine table, until the shield C, which is attached to head D, intercepts the pawl and prevents it from engaging with the ratchet wheel, thus stopping the feeding movement. The arc through which the ratchet

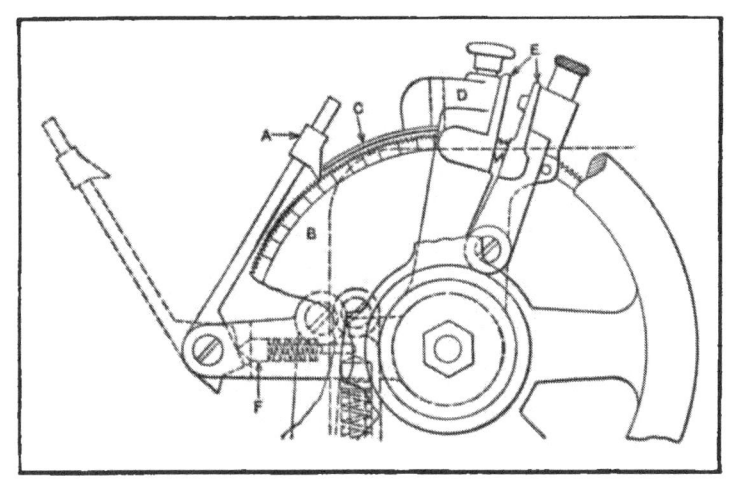

Fig. 3. Ratchet Gearing arranged to Disengage Automatically after a Predetermined Movement

wheel is turned before the pawl is disengaged from it, or the extent of the inward feeding movement of the grinding wheel, depends upon the distance between the tooth of the pawl and the end of the disengaging shield. With the particular mechanism illustrated, a movement of one tooth represents a diameter reduction of 0.00025 inch, so that the amount that the wheel moves inward before the feeding motion is automatically disengaged can be changed by simply varying the distance between the shield and the pawl. To facilitate setting the shield, a thumb-latch E is provided. Each time this thumb-latch is pressed, the shield moves a distance equal to one tooth on the ratchet wheel. For instance, if the shield is at the point of disengagement and the latch is pressed sixteen times, the shield will move a distance equal to sixteen teeth. As each tooth represents 0.00025 inch, a feeding movement of 0.004 inch will be obtained before the pawl is automatically disengaged. This mechanism prevents grinding parts below the required size, and makes it unnecessary for the operator to be continually measuring the diameter of the work. It is located back of a handwheel (which is partly shown in the illustration) that is used for hand adjustment. The pawl is kept in contact with the ratchet wheel and is held in the disengaged position by a small spring-operated plunger F.

Escapements. — An escapement may be considered as a form of ratchet mechanism having an oscillating double-ended pawl for controlling the motion of the ratchet wheel by engaging successive teeth. Escapements are designed to allow intermittent motion to occur at regular intervals of time. The escapement of a clock is illustrated in Fig. 4. As applied to a pendulum clock the escapement serves two purposes, in that it governs the movement of the scape wheel for each swing of the pendulum and also gives the pendulum an impulse each time a tooth of the scape wheel is released. An escapement should be so arranged that the pendulum will receive an impulse for a short period at the lowest part of its swing and then be left free until the next impulse occurs. The time required for a pendulum to swing through small arcs is practically independent of the length of the arc. For instance, if a stationary pendulum receives an impulse, the time necessary for its outward and return movement will be approximately constant regardless of the impulse and arc of swing, within ordinary limits. Thus, if the impulse is of considerable magnitude, the pendulum starts with a relatively high velocity, but the distance that it travels counteracts the increase of speed so that the time remains practically constant for any impulse or arc of swing. A pendulum that is swinging freely will adapt the length of its swing to the impulse it receives, and any interference which might be caused by the locking or unlocking of the escapement will affect the regularity of movement less if it occurs at the center of the swing rather than at the ends. As the arc of swing increases, there is a very slight increase in the time required for the movement, and, therefore, it is desirable that the impulses given to a pendulum should always be equal.

One of the earlier forms of escapements was known as the "anchor" or "recoil" escapement. With this type, the pendulum was never free, but was controlled by the escapement throughout the swing. To avoid this effect, the Graham "dead-beat" escapement, illustrated in Fig. 4, was designed and has been extensively used. When the escapement is in action, the pallets A and B alternately engage the teeth of the scape wheel, which revolves intermittently in the direction indicated by the arrow. With the mechanism in the position illustrated, the point of tooth C is about to slide across the inclined "impulse face" or end of the pallet A, thus giving the pendulum an impulse as it swings to the left. When tooth D strikes the "dead face" of pallet B, the motion of the scape wheel will be arrested until the pendulum reverses its movement and swings far enough to the right to release tooth D; as the point of D slides past the inclined end of B, the pendulum receives another impulse, and this intermittent action continues indefinitely or until the force propelling the scape wheel around, which may be from a spring or weight, is no longer great enough to operate the mechanism. In designing an escapement of this type, the pallets are so located as to embrace about one-third of the circumference of the scape wheel. One of the features of the dead-beat escape-

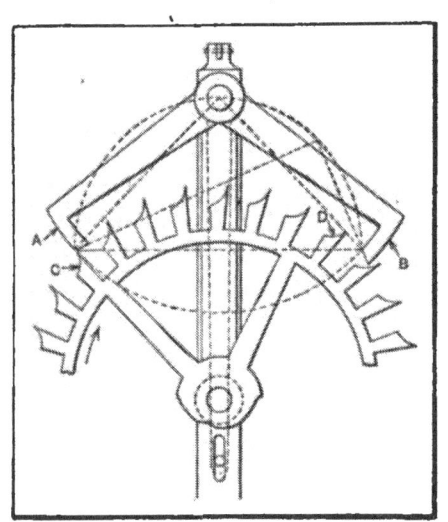

Fig. 4. Escapement for Controlling Action of Clockwork

ment is the effect which friction has on its operation. During each swing of the pendulum, there is a rubbing action between the points of the scape wheel teeth and the surfaces of the pallets, so that the pendulum is retarded constantly by a slight amount of friction. This friction, however, instead of being a defect, is a decided advantage, because, if the driving force of the clock is increased so that the impulse on the pallets becomes greater, the velocity of the pendulum tends to increase, but this effect is counteracted by the frictional retardation caused by a greater pressure of the teeth of the scape wheel on the faces of the pallet. If the driving force be increased, the frictional retardation increases relatively in a greater proportion than the driving effect and, up to a certain point, the time of vibration of the pendulum diminishes. If the force or weight propelling the clock mechanism is continually increased, a neutral point is finally reached, beyond which a greater force causes the time of vibration to increase instead of to diminish. In the design of clock mechanisms, it is desirable to have a driving power of such magnitude that it neither accelerates nor retards the motion of the pendulum. Many modifications of the escapement previously referred to have been devised to meet special requirements. The escapements of watches and of some clocks and portable timekeeping devices have a balance wheel instead of a pendulum to regulate the period of the intermittent action, but all of these escapements operate on the same general principle.

Crank and Ratchet Combination. — An interesting form of ratchet mechanism is illustrated in Fig. 5. This mechanism is used on moving picture cameras and also for feeding films through printing machines. It is commonly referred to as a "claw" mechanism or movement. The claw or hook A is double and engages evenly spaced perforations that are along each edge of the film. When this device is applied to a moving picture camera, the film is drawn, from a roll in the film box, down in front of the lens and then passes to a reel in the receiving box. The film remains stationary during each exposure and is drawn downward between successive exposures which are made at the rate of sixteen a second. The hook A, which engages the film and moves it along intermittently and with such rapidity, receives its motion from a crank and cam combination. The two intermeshing gears B and C revolve in opposite directions. Gear B has a crankpin upon which the hook is pivoted. An extension of this hook has a curved cam slot that engages a pin on gear C. As the two gears revolve, the hook is given a movement corresponding approximately to the D-shaped path indicated by the dotted lines. While this mechanism is shown in a horizontal position in the illustration, it would normally be vertical with the hook uppermost, when in operation. Some of the other claw mechanisms in use differ from the one shown in regard to the arrangement of the operating crank and the cam or curved slot

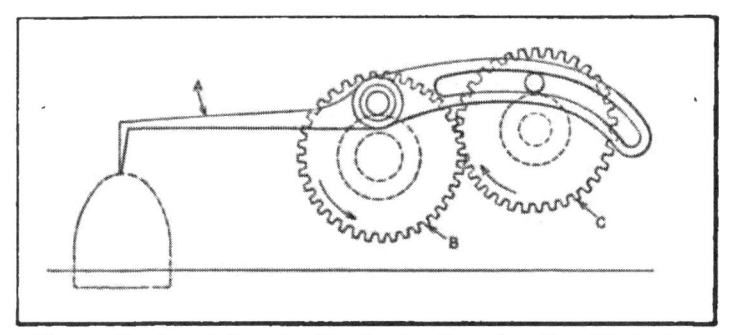

Fig. 5. Crank and Cam Combination for Operating Claw Mechanism of Moving Picture Camera

for modifying the crank motion. For instance, the cam, in some cases, is a separate part that is placed between the crank and the film hook, a pin on the hook lever engaging the cam slot. Another type of claw mechanism derives both the downward motion for moving the film and the in and out movements of the film hook from separate cam surfaces.

Automatic Reduction of Intermittent Movement. — The mechanism to be described is applied to a Bryant chucking grinder for automatically reducing the cross-feeding movement and depth of cut, as the diameter of the part being ground approaches the finished size. The head which carries the grinding wheels (three or four wheels are used on this machine) is given a reciprocating motion on the bed of the machine, and the work-spindle head is mounted on a bracket that can be set at an angle relative to the motion of the wheel-carrying slide for taper grinding. The shaft which transmits motion to the cross-feed mechanism shown in Fig. 6 derives its motion from a cam surface on a swinging member of the wheel-head reversing mechanism, which is of the

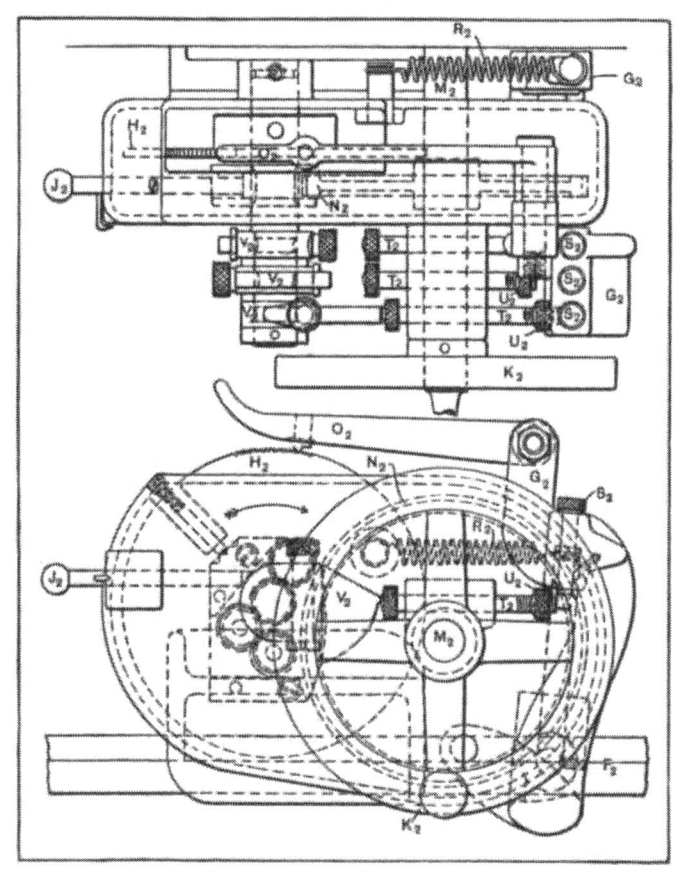

Fig. 6. Ratchet Feeding Mechanism arranged to Automatically Diminish the Feeding Movement

bevel gear and clutch type controlled by a load-and-fire shifting device. The universally jointed telescopic shaft F_2 transmits motion to the cross-feed mechanism at whatever angle the swiveling bracket and work-spindle may be set. The cross-feed screw M_2 has mounted on it a handwheel K_2 and a spur gear N_2.

This spur gear is connected with ratchet wheel H_2 by a tumbler gear arrangement controlled by lever J_2, which thus provides for reversing and disengaging the feeding movement. The ratchet wheel is operated by a pawl O_2, pivoted to lever G_2, which, in turn, receives its movement from rockshaft F_2. This movement is positive in the direction which operates the ratchet wheel H_2, and through it the cross feed. In the other direction, motion is derived from a spring R_2 until the point of plunger S_2 brings up against the adjustable stop T_2. As the position of T_2 governs the extent of the movement of the swinging of lever G_2, a greater or less cross feed is effected at each stroke. The position of stop T_2, and the amount of feed, is governed by two things. In the first place, the knurled nut U_2 furnishes a check to its backward movement, and thus regulates the rate of cross feed. Screwing this nut out increases the feed — screwing it back decreases it. In the second place, the feed is controlled by cam V_2, which is adjustably clamped on the shaft of ratchet wheel H_2, and revolves with it in the direction of the arrow. As the feeding progresses, the lower edge of V_2 comes into contact with the left-hand end of stop T_2, gradually limiting its movement from that permitted by the adjustment of U_2 until finally, in the position shown, the swinging of lever G_2 is stopped altogether, thus stopping the cross feed. The diminishing depth of cut thus provided for, as the desired finished diameter is approached, tends to improve the work in regard to accuracy and finish.

It will be noted in the plan view that there are three stop cams V_2, three stops T_2, and three feed adjusting nuts U_2 and plungers S_2. Any one of these three latter may be pressed down into working position, thus giving a separate cross-feed stop and rate of feed for each of three operations.

Intermittent Gearing. — When a shaft which rotates continuously is to transmit motion to another shaft only at predetermined intervals, intermittent gearing is sometimes used. Gearing of this type is made in many different designs, which may be modified to suit the conditions governing their operation, such as the necessity for locking the driven member while idle, the inertia of the driven part, or the speed of rotation. With some forms of intermittent gearing, the driven gear rotates through a fractional part of a revolution once for each revolution of the driver, whereas, with other designs, the driving gear transmits motion to the driven gear two or more times while making a single revolution. The number of times that the driven gear stops before it is turned completely around is varied

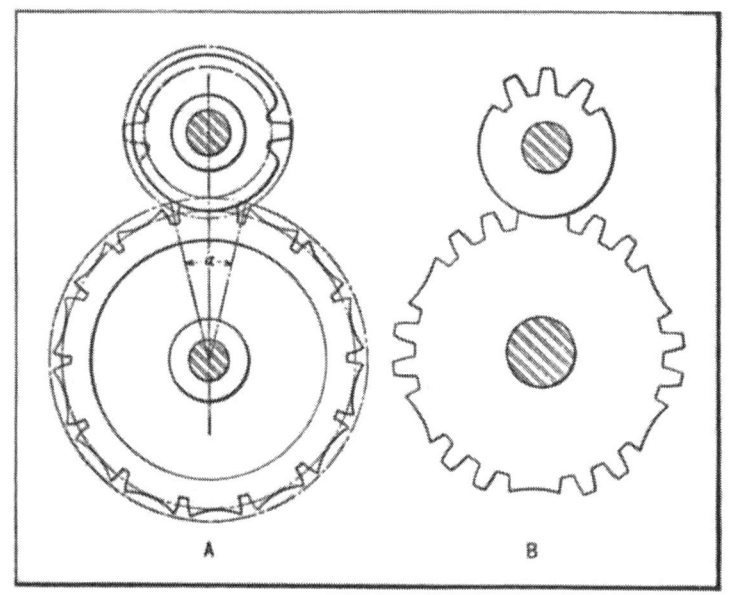

Fig. 7. Gears for Uniformly Intermittent Motion

in each case according to the requirements; the periods of rest may also be uniform or vary considerably.

Gears for Uniformly Intermittent Motion.—The design of intermittent gearing illustrated by diagram A, Fig. 7, is so arranged that the driving gear, which has only one tooth, revolves fourteen times for each revolution of the driven gear. Each time the tooth of the driver engages one of the tooth spaces in the driven gear, the latter is turned through an arc α. The driven gear is locked against rotation when the driving tooth is not in mesh, because the circular part of the driver fits closely into the concave surfaces between the tooth spaces as they are successively turned to this position. The radius of the driver should be small enough to insure adequate locking surfaces between the tooth spaces, but not so small that sharp weak points will be formed at the edges of the tooth spaces. Counting mechanisms are often equipped with gearing of this general type. In order to vary the relative movements of the driving and driven gears, the meshing teeth may be arranged in various ways. For instance, if a second tooth were added to the driver on the opposite side as indicated by the dotted lines, the driven gear would receive motion for each half revolution of the driver. The diagram at *B* illustrates another modification. In this case, the driven gear has a smaller number of rest periods, and it is turned farther for each revolution of the driver, as the latter has three successive teeth.

Variable Intermittent Motion from Gearing. — With some forms of intermittent gearing, the driven gear does not move the same amount each time it is engaged by the driver, the motion being variable instead of uniform or equal. The diagram *A*, Fig. 8, shows an example of the variable motion intermittent type. The driving gear has four driving points around its circumference with numbers of teeth at each place varying from one to four. The tooth spaces on the driven gear are laid out to correspond so that the motion received by the driven gear is either increased or decreased progressively depending upon the direction of rotation of the driver. Gearing of this general type may be arranged in many different ways and is designed to suit the particular mechanism of which it forms a part. After laying out gears of this kind, it is often advisable to make brass templets in order to ascertain by actual experiment if the gears are properly formed and give the required motion.

Intermittent Gearing for High Speeds. — The design of gearing illustrated by diagram *B*, Fig. 8, is considered preferable to the forms previously described, where the driving member revolves at a comparatively high speed. With this gearing, the driven member is stationary during one-half revolution of the driver. The latter has a stud *a* or roller which engages radial slots in the driven gear while passing through the inner half of its circle of travel. The flat spring illustrated at c is used to hold the driven wheel in position so that the driving roller will enter the next successive slot without interference. The projections or teeth on the driven gear may have semi-circular ends as shown, or all of the ends may be concentric as indicated by the dotted line at b. If the semi-circular ends are not provided, there should be some form of positive locking device to insure alignment between the radial slots and the driving pin or roller. The corners should also be rounded to facilitate engagement of the roller.

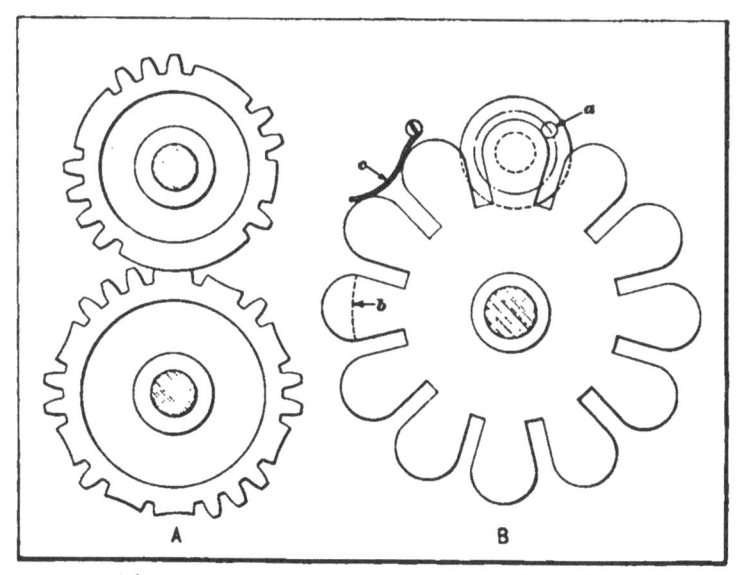

Fig. 8. (A) Gearing for Variable Intermittent Motion; (B) High-speed Intermittent Gearing

Another form of intermittent gearing designed to eliminate shocks when operating at relatively high speeds is illustrated in Fig. 9. The speed ratio between the driving and driven members is 4 to 1, each revolution of the driver turning the driven wheel one-quarter revolution, or 90 degrees. The driver A has a cam groove C which is so shaped that the motion of the driven wheel B is gradually accelerated and retarded at the beginning and end of its movement. This groove is engaged by rollers D on the driven wheel. The rollers enter and leave the cam groove through the open spaces at E, and when the driven wheel is stationary, two of the rollers are in engagement with this groove, thus effectually locking the driven member. The illustration at the left shows the driven wheel at the center of its movement, and the view to the right shows the relative positions of the two parts after the movement is completed. As the roller at D is revolved 45 degrees from the position shown, the following roller enters the cam groove through the left-hand space E.

Intermittent Motion of Moving Picture Projector. — A very rapid intermittent motion is required on moving picture project-

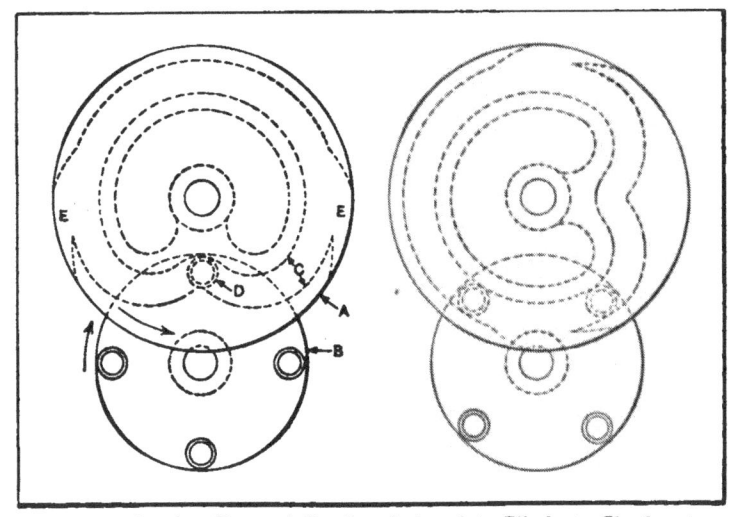

Fig. 9. Another Form of Gearing designed to Eliminate Shocks at High Speeds

ors. The film is not moved continuously, but each view or positive on it is drawn down to the projecting position while the shutter is closed, and the film remains stationary for a fractional part of a second while the picture is exposed on the screen; then, while the shutter is again closed, the next successive view is moved to the projecting position. It is apparent, therefore, that moving pictures are, in reality, a series of stationary pictures thrown upon the screen in such rapid succession that they are, in effect, blended together and any action or movement appears continuous. It is important to give the film a very rapid intermittent motion, because it is necessary to have the shutter closed when this movement occurs; and the length of time that the shutter is closed, should be reduced to a minimum. This shutter is in the form of a wheel or disk, and it has a fan-shaped section which passes the projector lens while the film is being shifted. In order to avoid flicker on the screen, the shutter has two additional fan-shaped sections. With these three equally spaced sections, the light is not only shut off from the screen during each successive film movement, but twice between each movement at uniform intervals. By closing the shutter twice while the picture is on the screen, the flicker that would be visible and annoying if the shutter were only closed while moving the film is multiplied to such an extent that it becomes almost continuous and is practically eliminated as far as the observer is concerned, assuming that the projector is operated at the proper speed. The width and area of that section of the shutter which is passing the lens when the film is being moved is governed by the time required for the film movement. Theoretically, the area of each section or segment of the shutter should be equal, although, in practice, the two extra sections are made of somewhat smaller area than the main one, in order to increase the open space and the percentage of area left for the passage of light.

There is an important relation between this shutter wheel and the intermittent motion or gearing of the projector. This is due to the fact that the shutter must be closed while the film is being shifted. With the mechanism to be described, the film movement is very rapid so that the shutter blades may be proportionately reduced in area, thus leaving more open space for the light. The intermittent motion referred to is shown in Fig. 10 and is used on the Power moving picture projector. This mechanism is composed of a disk or wheel A, having an annular flange or ring B, which has two diagonal slots across it as shown; this wheel, which is the driver, imparts an intermittent motion to the follower H, which carries four equally spaced pins or rollers that engage the ring B on wheel A. Each time this wheel makes one revolution, the follower H is turned one-quarter revolution and in the same direction, as indicated by the arrows. The follower is stationary except when it is engaged by the slots or cam surfaces formed on one side of ring B. During this stationary period, the ring B simply passes between the four pins on the follower, two of these pins being on the outside and two on the inside of the ring.

The quarter-turn movement is obtained in the following manner: When the projection or cam surface G on the revolving wheel A strikes one of the pins, the rotation of the follower begins, and the pins are so spaced that one on the outside moves through a diagonal slot in ring B while a pin on the inside moves

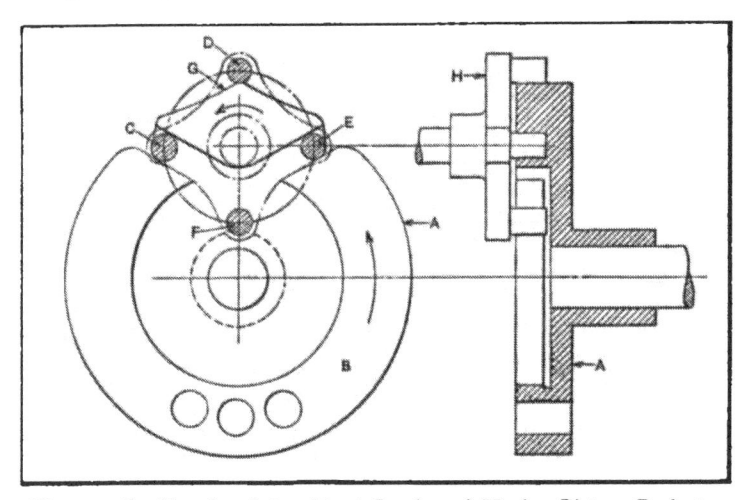

Fig. 10. Rapid-acting Intermittent Gearing of Moving Picture Projector

outward through the other slot. For instance, if the pins C and D are on the outside and E and F on the inside, pin D will first be engaged by cam surface G and, as the follower revolves, pin C will pass in through one diagonal slot while pin E is moving to the outside of the ring through the other slot. At the completion of the quarter-turn movement, pins C and F will be on the inside and D and E on the outside. As wheel A continues to revolve, ring B simply passes between these closely fitting pins which lock the follower against movement until projection G again comes around and strikes the next successive pin on the follower.

The follower operates a toothed wheel or sprocket which connects with the film and moves it downward each time the shutter is closed. Above and below the intermittent gearing there are other sprockets which rotate continuously, and these are so timed that a loop of film is formed above the intermittent gearing that is just large enough to provide for one film movement, which is equivalent to the length of one view or positive. As the film is drawn down rapidly by the intermittent mechanism, a loop is formed below it which is taken up by the lower sprocket as the film is wound upon the lower receiving reel. The normal speed of wheel A is sixteen revolutions per second, and it has been operated at two or three times the normal speed. The time required for turning the follower one-quarter revolution is approximately one-sixth of the time for a complete revolution, or $\frac{1}{96}$ second, when running at normal speed. With the Geneva motion (illustrated in Fig. 12), which has been applied to many projectors, approximately one-quarter of the time is required for the intermittent action; therefore, the shutter blades must be of larger area than when the film movement occurs in one-sixth of the time. Notwithstanding this increase of speed, the mechanism shown in Fig. 10 is claimed to be superior to the Geneva motion in that there is less tendency to subject the film to injurious stresses. The locking of the follower during the stationary period is also more secure, especially at the critical time when near the operating point. The three holes drilled in the ring B are to compensate for the slots on the opposite side and to balance the wheel A.

Intermittent Gear with Swinging Sector. — The gearing illustrated in Fig. 11 operates on a different principle from the gearing previously described. The driven gear has one period of rest for each revolution of the driver; the latter has a sector B which is free to swing in the space provided for it, but is normally held in the position shown by a spiral spring D. The driver revolves at a uniform speed in the direction shown by the arrow and, when the sector B comes into engagement with the driven gear, the latter stops revolving while the sector is swinging across the open space or until side B strikes side F, when the driven gear is again set in motion. As soon as the sector is released by the driven gear, the spring draws it back to the position shown in the illustration, preparatory to again arresting the movement of *E*. The resistance to motion offered by gear *E* should be great enough to overcome the tension of spring *D*, as otherwise the sector would not swing away from the position shown. In order to avoid shocks, this gearing would have to be revolved quite slowly; while the design is not to be recommended, the principle may be of some practical value.

Geneva Wheel for Intermittent Motion. — The general type of intermittent gearing illustrated in Fig. 12 is commonly known

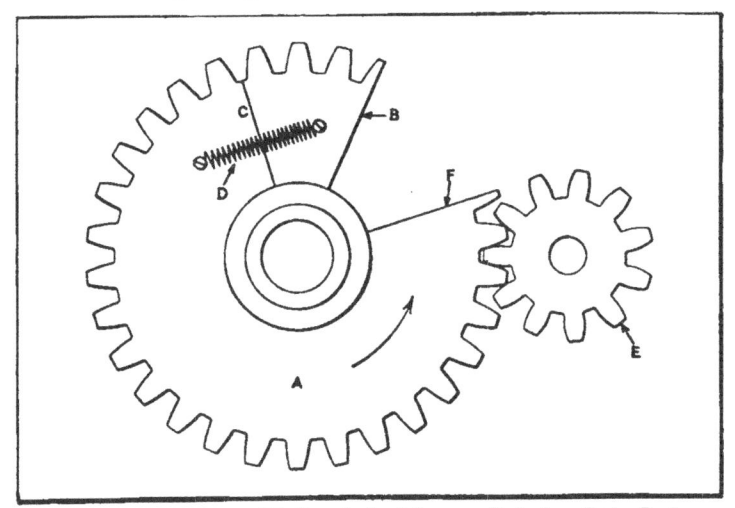

Fig. 11. Intermittent Motion derived from a Swinging Gear Sector

as the "Geneva wheel," because of the similarity to the well-known Geneva stop used to prevent the over-winding of springs in watches, music boxes, etc. Geneva wheels are frequently used on machine tools for indexing or rotating some part of the machine through a fractional part of a revolution. The driven wheel shown at *A* in the illustration has four radial slots located 90 degrees apart, and the driver carries a roller *k* which engages one of these slots each time it makes a revolution, thus turning the driven wheel one-quarter revolution. The concentric surface *b* engages the concave surface *c* between each pair of slots before the driving roller is disengaged from the driven wheel, which prevents the latter from rotating while the roller is moving around to engage the next successive slot. The circular boss b on the driver is cut away at d to provide a clearance space for the projecting arms of the driven wheel.

The Geneva wheel illustrated by diagram B differs from the one just described principally in regard to the method of locking the driven wheel during the idle period. The driven wheel has

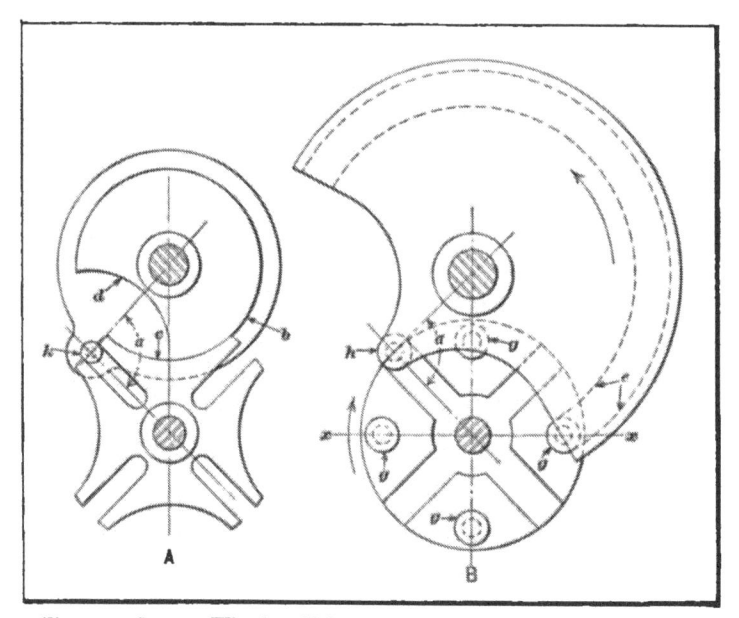

Fig. 12. Geneva Wheels which vary in regard to Method of Locking Driven Member during Idle Period

four rollers g located 90 degrees apart and midway between the radial grooves which are engaged by the roller of the driver. There is a large circular groove e on the driver having a radius equal to the center-to-center distance between two of the rollers g, as measured on the center line xx. This circular groove engages one of the rollers as soon as the driving roller h has passed out of one of the grooves or radial slots. Each time the driver makes one revolution, the two rollers on the center line xx are engaged by the locking groove. The illustration shows the driving roller about to enter a slot and the locking roller at the point of disengagement. When the driven wheel has been moved 90 degrees from the position shown, the roller which is now at the lowest position will have moved around to the left-hand side so that it enters the locking groove as the driving roller leaves the radial slot.

When designing gearing of the general type illustrated in Fig. 12, it is advisable to so proportion the driving and driven members that the angle a will be approximately 90 degrees. The radial slots in the driven part will then be tangent to the circular path of the driving roller at the time the roller enters and leaves the slot. When the gearing is designed in this way, the driven

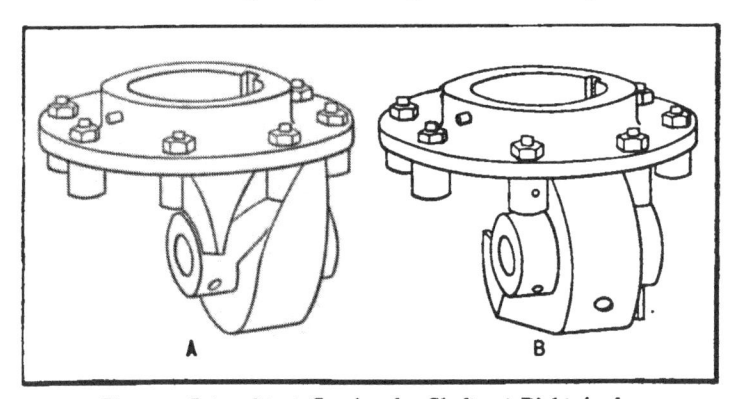

Fig. 13. Intermittent Gearing for Shafts at Right Angles

wheel is started gradually from a state of rest and the motion is also gradually checked.

Intermittent Gearing for Shafts at Right Angles. — When driving and driven shafts are at right angles to each other, intermittent gears which are similar to bevel gears in form, but constructed on the same general principle as the spur gearing illustrated in Fig. 7, may be employed. The smooth or blank space on the driving gear for arresting the motion of the driven member corresponds to the pitch cone and engages concave locking surfaces formed on the driven gear. Owing to the conical shape, such gearing is more difficult to construct than the spur-gear type.

A form of intermittent gearing for shafts at right angles to each other but not lying in the same plane is illustrated in Fig. 13. The driving member is in the form of a cylindrical cam and has a groove which engages, successively, the rollers on the driven wheel. Diagram *A* shows the cam in the driving or operating position, and at *B* the driven wheel is shown locked against rotation during the period of rest. The locking action is obtained by parallel faces on the cam which fit closely between the rollers and are located in planes at right angles to the axis of rotation. This mechanism was designed for a high-speed automatic machine requiring an accurate indexing movement and a positive locking of the driven member during the stationary period.

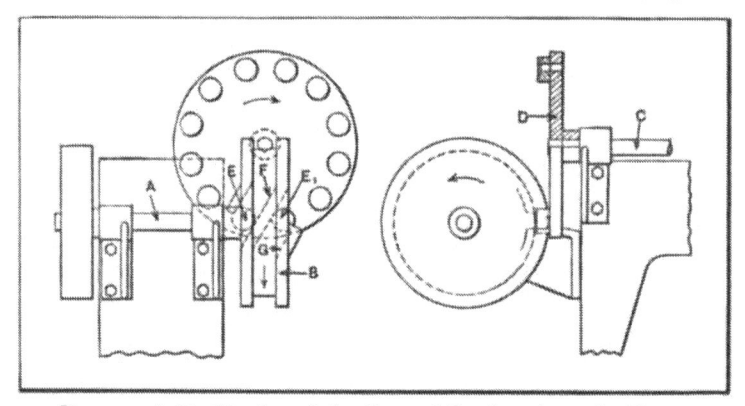

Fig. 14. A Modification of the Type of Gearing shown in Fig. 13

The gearing operated successfully at a speed of 350 revolutions per minute, and it was because of the speed that this design was used in preference to the Geneva-wheel type of gearing previously described. The curvature of the operating groove on the driving cam is such that the driven wheel is started slowly and, after the speed is accelerated, there is a gradual reduction of velocity. The driven wheel has no lost motion for any position and the mechanism operates without appreciable shock or vibration, and is practically noiseless.

Another form of intermittent drive for shafts located at right angles but not lying in the same plane is illustrated in Fig. 14. This mechanism operates on the same general principle as the one just described, but differs in regard to the form of the driving member or cam. This cam B is attached to the end of the driving shaft A and has an annular groove corresponding in width to the diameter of the rollers on the driven wheel D carried by shaft C. This annular groove is not continuous as there are inclined openings on both sides. When the cam revolves in the direction indicated by the arrow, the inclined surface F pushes roller E over to the left, thus causing disk D to

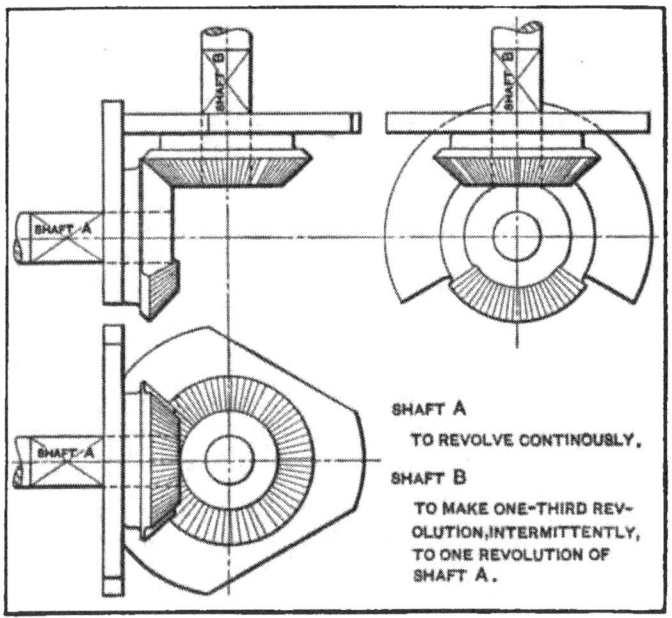

Fig. 15. **Intermittent Bevel Gears provided with Auxiliary Locking Device**

turn; at the same time, roller E_1 enters the opening on the opposite side and is pushed over to the central position by cam surface G. This roller E_1 remains in the groove until the cam has made one revolution, thus locking the driven wheel against rotation. This locking roller then passes out at the opposite side and another roller is engaged by the groove. The ratio of this gearing, which was used to provide a feeding movement on an automatic machine, depends upon the number of rollers on the driven wheel.

Auxiliary Locking Device for Intermittent Bevel Gears. — The intermittent bevel gearing illustrated in Fig. 15 is provided with auxiliary locking plates which regulate the motion of the driven gear and hold it stationary while disengaged from the driver. The driving gear is on shaft A and revolves continuously. It is only provided with enough teeth to rotate the driven gear and shaft B one-third revolution to one complete revolution of the driver. This mechanism is used to actuate feeding rolls requiring an intermittent motion. Formerly the gearing was used without the locking device to be described, but there were slight variations in the movements of the driven shaft so that the gears did not always mesh correctly, which caused them to break, and also interfered with the timing of the feeding movement. These defects were eliminated by applying locking plates to the shafts A and B, one plate being located just back of each gear. The plate on shaft B has three equally spaced flat sides or edges and the plate on shaft A is cut away to provide a clearance space for the protruding sections of the plate on shaft B when this shaft is in motion. As the plan view shows, the flat side of the plate on shaft B, during the idle period, is intercepted by the plate on A so that the driven shaft is not only locked but its motion is limited to one-third revolution for each complete turn of the driving shaft.

Two-speed Intermittent Rotary Motion. — The fast and slow motion of the pattern cylinder of a certain type of loom is derived from the reversible intermittent gearing shown in Fig. 16. The large gear A is mounted on the pattern cylinder shaft, and receives its motion either through the segment gear and crank combination B or through a similar combination C, these two combinations being used to reverse the direction of rotation. Gear D is the driver for this train of mechanism. Whether the motion is transmitted from gear D to the pattern gear A through the crank and segment gear combination B or through combination C depends upon the position of a sliding key F. An intermittent fast and slow motion is obtained with either combination. When key F locks the crank and gear B to the shaft, the pattern wheel is rotated at a relatively slow speed when the segment pinion is acting as the driver, and at a faster speed when the crankpin *E* comes around into engagement with one of the radial slots in the pattern gear. When this direct drive is employed, the gears *G* and *H* revolve idly with the upper crank and gear combination *C*. When a reversal of motion is required, sliding key *F* is pushed in to engage gear *H*, which then drives gear *G* and the combination at *C*.

Intermittent Feed Mechanism. — The solution of an interesting problem in design is indicated in Fig. 17. The requirements were that for every one and one-quarter revolution of

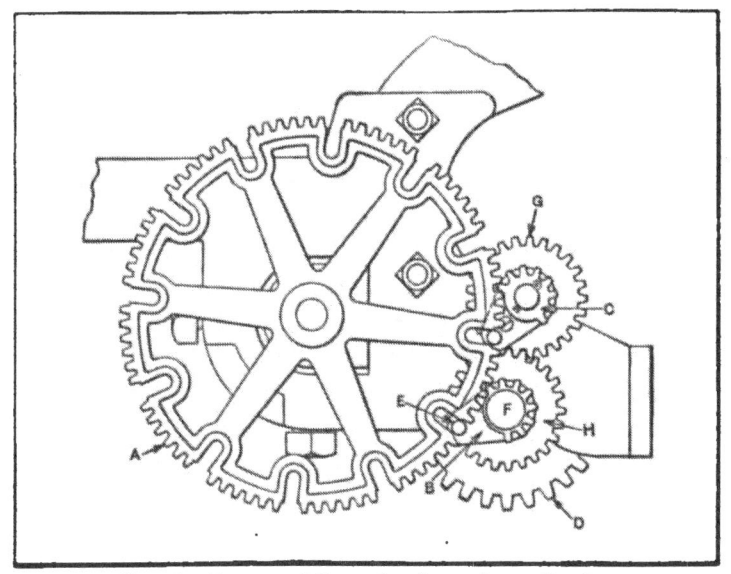

Fig. 16. Two-speed Reversing Intermittent Gearing

a continuously rotating shaft *A* a second shaft *L* in alignment with the driving shaft must rotate intermittently, with equal velocity and in the same direction as shaft *A*, one-twelfth revolution or through an angle of 30 degrees. An eccentric bushing *C* is keyed to the driving shaft *A*. A 96-tooth gear *D* is loosely mounted on eccentric bushing *C*, but is prevented from rotating by lever *E*; the pitch-line of gear *D*, however, is always tangent to the pitch-line of the 120-tooth gear *F* and to that of the planetary pinion *G*. This pinion is carried by a double arm *B* which

INTERMITTENT MOVEMENTS 161

is also keyed to the driving shaft A. As arm B traverses the pinion around gear D, gear F is revolved on shaft A in the ratio of 120 to 96 or 1.25 to 1. The end of arm B opposite the pinion carries a link and roller I which runs on a flange of gear F until a depression in the periphery allows the roller to drop and permits pawl H to engage ratchet wheel J which is keyed to shaft L; each time the pawl engages the ratchet wheel, the latter is turned forward until roll I runs up on top of the flange again. As gear F advances one-fifth revolution for each revolution of the arm and pawl, and since 30 degrees equals one-twelfth revolution, the

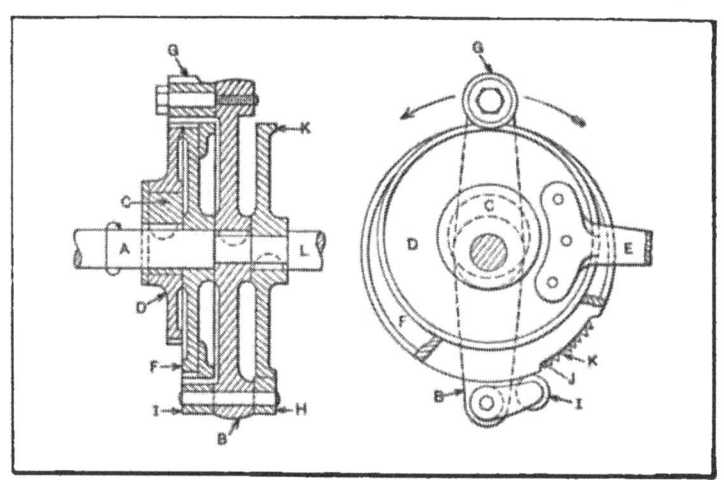

Fig. 17. Mechanism for Rotating Driven Shaft Intermittently and at same Velocity as Driver

opening or depression for the roll must be shortened $\frac{1}{5} \times \frac{1}{12}$ of 30 degrees, or to $29\frac{1}{5}$ degrees.

Constant Intermittent Motion from Variable Motion. — The feeding movement of a planer tool, which occurs at the end of each return stroke, is derived from a shaft which revolves in first one direction and then the other, the number of revolutions depending upon the length of the stroke which is adjusted to suit the work. The simple mechanism to be described makes it possible to obtain the same rotary movement for operating the feed-screw of the tool-slide, regardless of the number of revolutions made by the shaft which drives the feeding mechanism.

The arrangement is such that a feed disk or crank at the end of the driving shaft turns part of a revolution and then remains stationary while the shaft continues to revolve.

One method of securing this fractional part of a turn and then stopping the motion of the feed disk is illustrated at A in Fig. 18. The link f connects the crankpin of the feed disk with a rack which, through suitable gearing, transmits motion to the feedscrew. The main pinion shaft of the gear train for driving the planer table has attached to its end the cup-shaped casting a, which forms one part of a friction clutch. The crank disk b has

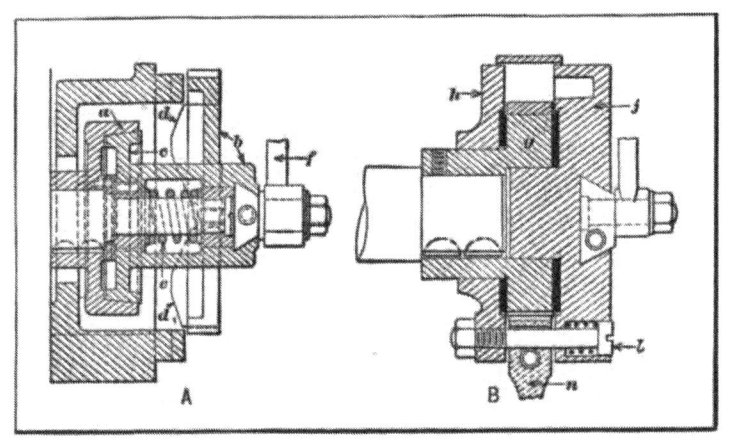

Fig. 18. Mechanisms for Deriving an Unvarying Rotary Movement from a Driving Shaft regardless of the Number of Revolutions made by the Shaft

a hub c, which fits into the tapering seat in part a and forms the other member of the clutch. If this friction clutch is engaged when the planer is started, the crank disk b revolves until one of the tapered projections d strikes a stationary taper lug, thus forcing part c out of engagement with a against the tension of spring e. The crank disk then remains stationary until part a and the driving shaft reverse their direction of rotation at the end of the stroke. This reversal of motion disengages the tapering surface d or d_1, as the case may be, and allows the friction clutch to reëngage; the crank disk is then turned in the opposite direction, until the other tapering projection strikes a second lug which again stops the motion of the feed disk. This intermittent action in first one direction and then the other is continued as long as the planer is in operation, and the feed disk oscillates through the same arc regardless of the length of stroke or the number of revolutions made by the driving shaft.

Another planer feed mechanism which operates on the same general principle as the one just described is illustrated at B, Fig. 18. In this case, the hub g is keyed to the shaft and the flange formed on this hub is between plates h and j. This flange does not come directly into contact with the plates, as there are leather washers on each side as indicated by the heavy black lines. The plates h and j are held in contact with these washers by three bolts l having springs under the heads. The hub g is surrounded by a band which is split on the lower side and has lugs n into which is fitted a pawl of such shape that, when it strikes a fixed stop, the band is opened and released from the hub. This releasing of the band occurs after the crank disk has turned far enough to give the necessary feeding movement. The crank is held in position while the driving shaft continues to revolve, by the friction between plates h and j and the leather washers previously referred to. When reversal occurs at the end of the stroke, the hub g revolves in the opposite direction and the band again grips it until the pawl of lug n strikes the opposite stop.

Adjustable Intermittent Motion. — The intermittent feed mechanism shown in Fig. 19 is so arranged that the intermittent action may be varied according to requirements by means of a simple form of "skipping" device. A pitman connecting with crank B transmits an oscillating movement to lever A. This lever carries a stud on its free or upper end upon which is pivoted a fiber pawl C. This pawl engages the smooth periphery of disk D and turns the latter a fractional part of a revolution when lever A is moving to the left, unless the engagement of the pawl is prevented by the mechanism to be described. The pawl is formed of two pieces attached to opposite sides of a diamond-shaped block F. This block is within the slot and, being slightly thinner than the bar, causes the projecting sides C to frictionally engage the lower side of the bar. Any motion of lever A towards the right causes the pawl to turn to the position shown so that it clears the disk D for the return stroke. The reverse motion of lever A changes the position of block F so that the ends C grip the disk D, which is given the required feeding movement. The skipping of the feed is accomplished by a train of change-gears and a cam G. This cam serves to lift the pin H clear of its seat, so that the bar carrying pawl C is free to slide horizontally as lever A moves to the left; the result is that the pawl is not

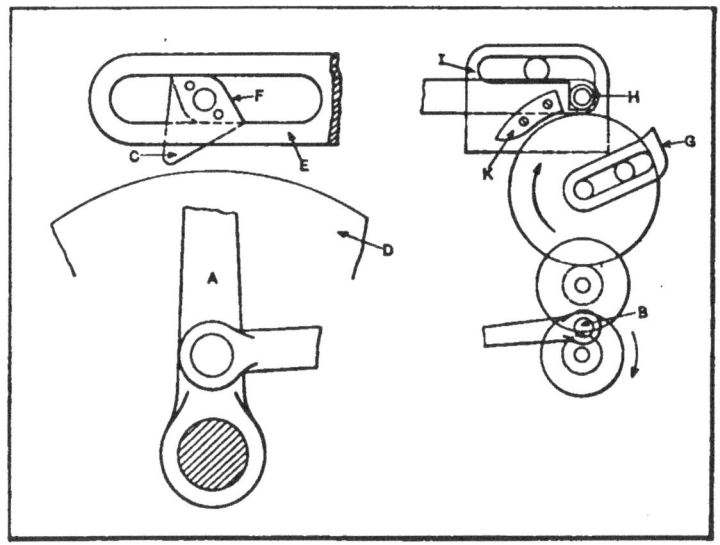

Fig. 19. Feed Mechanism with Skipping Device for Varying the Intermittent Motion

turned by frictional resistance to the gripping position, and it simply makes an idle stroke. The cam G is pushed in when it strikes dog K and is suddenly thrown outward by a spring after passing the dog; this sudden release disengages pin H from its seat, into which it drops again upon the return of bar E. The number of feeding strokes before an idle stroke are governed by the ratio of the change-gears.

Automatic Variation of Intermittent Motion. — The mechanism described in the following is somewhat complicated as it is designed to turn a driven shaft through a small arc for every other revolution of the driving shaft and according to the following requirements: The feeding movement of the driven shaft is to increase by small amounts until a maximum feed is obtained; the feed then decreases to a minimum, again increases to a maximum, and at this point instantly begins at the minimum again. If a line is drawn representing these movements graphically, it will readily be seen that there are two periods of increasing feed and one period of decreasing feed for every cycle of movements. It was necessary to derive the feeding motion from a shaft running at twice the desired speed.

The principle upon which this mechanism operates is shown partly in diagrammatical form, in Fig. 20. The arm C carries a sliding block D which is connected to lever L by a pitman K. Block D is fed to or from the center of B by screw E, working in a divided nut. On the upper end of C are two intermittent motion star-wheels F and G, of six teeth each, with their planes at right angles. Wheel F is pivoted on the side of C, and G is fastened onto E. Wheel F has three projecting pins F_1, F_2, and F_3, placed on alternate teeth and denoted in the illustration by black dots. Suppose star-wheel F is rotated one tooth (denoted by the straight lines). If that tooth is one of the three with the projecting pins on the side, wheel G and screw E will be rotated one-sixth revolution. Conversely, if the tooth on F has no projecting pin, G will not rotate. This method gives the alternating feed through K and L, as the arm C revolves about the center of B.

The center of F revolves about B in a path as shown by the broken line, which passes midway between the two circles at H. These circles represent the controlling star with six teeth or points (denoted by straight lines). A pin (not shown) upon the block D is caused to engage two teeth of H, on two successive revolutions before it is retracted. This is done only when the slide is at the upper end of its travel. Star-wheel H merely operates star F. Three projecting points (denoted by black dots) engage point after point of F as it comes around. Suppose it is projections H_1 or H_3 that engage with F. Then, by reason of their being on the outer side of the center of F, star-wheel F must revolve in an opposite direction to that in which it would revolve if H_2 were the projection engaging F, because H_2 is on the inner side of the center path of F.

It is now apparent that block D moves up (or down) through the action of H upon F and F upon G; and the motion takes place only for every other revolution of B. When block D reaches the outer limit, the pin upon the block is released as mentioned, which, in turn, revolves H two teeth before it is retracted, thereby

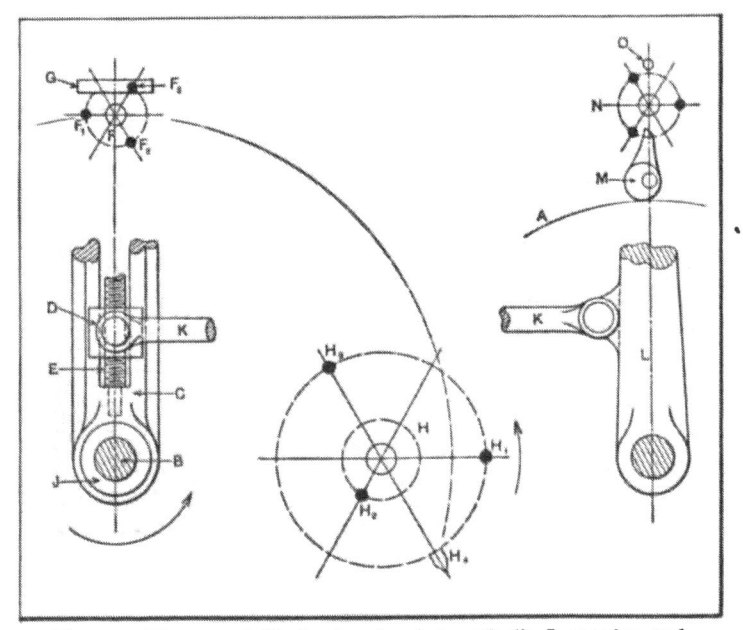

Fig. 20. Diagram of Mechanism for Automatically Increasing and Decreasing Intermittent Motion of Driven Shaft

engaging the opposite side of F, reversing the direction of rotation of F and G, and returning D toward the center. Pin H_3 is now brought into action and D goes outward again to the extreme position. The controlling star is rotated as before, returning H_1 to position and bringing H_4 into action to open the split nut at screw E, which allows a spiral spring in J to return the block D and pitman K instantly to the center, thus completing one cycle. Through link K, lever L, and pawl M, ratchet A is rotated. A star N is carried by L, which is operated by the hinge tappet O and which is provided with three projecting pins to lift the eccentric pawl from the ratchet every alternate stroke of L.

Automatic Indexing Mechanism. — The indexing or dividing of circular work requiring equally spaced grooves milled across the periphery may be controlled automatically by the dividing-head illustrated in Fig. 21. In addition to the transverse and longitudinal sections shown, there are three detail views which illustrate important features. The mechanism for controlling the indexing automatically derives its motion from a spindle L driven through coupling W from a special pulley carried on a bracket attached to the bed of the milling machine. The clutch M (see detail view) on spindle L locks worm K to the spindle when the worm is pressed against the clutch M by a spring H, acting through rod I and finger J. This engagement with clutch M occurs when lock-bolt B is withdrawn from plate C, so that worm-wheel E is free to revolve. The movement of plate C at each indexing is controlled by a counter mechanism consisting of a dividing-plate C having teeth on the periphery which engage the teeth of disk N, thus rotating stop-plate O which controls the engagement of lock-bolt B and the extent of the indexing movement.

The table of the milling machine on which this mechanism is used should be arranged to return automatically. When one groove has been milled across the work, the table returns and, when near the end of the return stroke, lock-bolt B is withdrawn by a suitable mechanism (not shown in the illustration). When this bolt is disengaged from dividing-plate C, the worm-wheel E is free to revolve. The pressure of spring H forces rod I, finger J, and worm K to the left, the worm engaging clutch M on spindle L which is constantly revolving. As worm K and worm-wheel E revolve, rotary motion is transmitted to dividing-plate C, and also to spindle G through epicyclic gearing consisting of bevel pinions T mounted on pins U attached to part V which is keyed to the spindle G. The indexing movement continues until bolt B enters one of the succeeding holes in plate C. The movement of worm-wheel E is then arrested and the worm,

168 MECHANICAL MOVEMENTS

as it continues to revolve, disengages itself from clutch M and stops rotating. The dividing-plate C has a number of teeth c, the number corresponding to the number of its holes. Whenever this plate is set in motion, these teeth engage disk N and turn

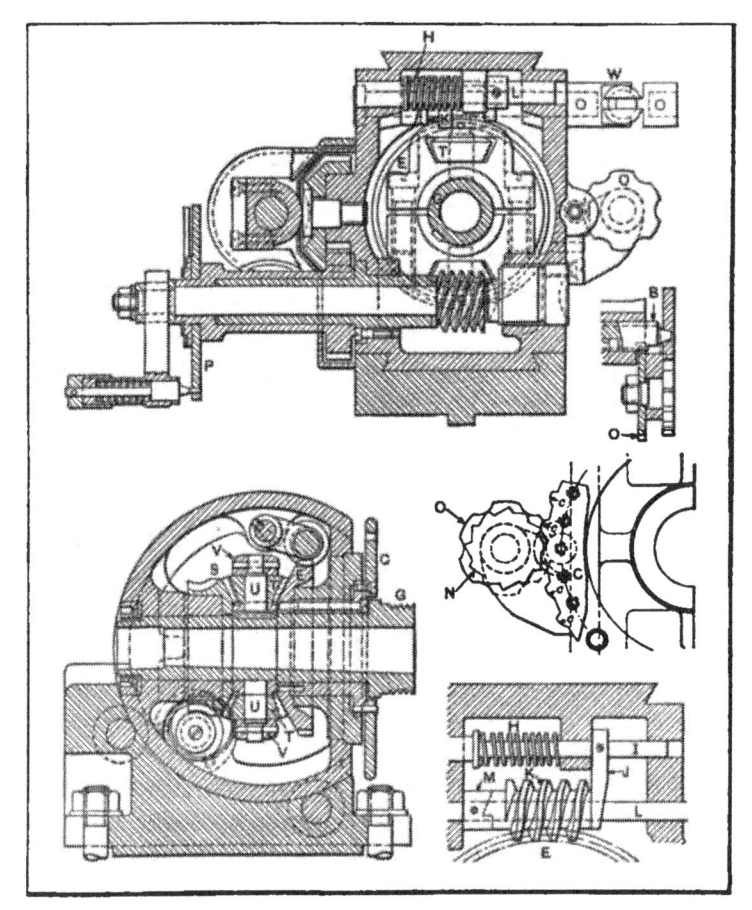

Fig. 21. Automatic Indexing or Dividing Mechanism

the counter O. A solid portion of this counter is thus placed in front of lock-bolt B, which prevents the bolt from reëngaging with plate C until a rotation equal to the required number of holes has been completed. One of the concave notches in counter O then releases bolt B which engages plate C. The number of teeth in plates C and N and the notches in counter O depend upon the number of divisions required. This dividing-head may be used the same as the hand-operated design. The hand-operated indexing movements, as well as the automatic movements, are transmitted to spindle G through the train of epicyclic gearing previously referred to.

Indexing Mechanism of Screw-slotting Machine. — The automatic machine to which the indexing mechanism shown in Fig. 22 is applied mills the screw-driver slots across the heads of screws. The screws to be slotted are placed in a slowly revolving hopper from which they are conveyed by a chute to the work-holder or turret M, which, in turn, locates each successive screw beneath the narrow cutter or saw, which mills the screw-driver slot. The work-holding and cutter-feeding movements are derived from a camshaft at the back of the machine which is connected with the main driving pulley through change gearing so that the rate of operation may be varied to suit the size of the work.

Fig. 22 is a plan view showing the turret operating mechanism. After a screw is released from the chute, it falls into the position shown at A where it is held between a seat in bushing B and spring C, which is attached to escapement lever D. This escapement permits the blank to fall into position in the work-holding turret and also holds the screw blank in place in bushing B. The lever D receives its motion from cam E on a camshaft at the rear of the machine, which is driven through change-gears. At F is a vertical shaft extending down through the bed of the machine, which is driven through bevel gearing from the shaft on which cam E is mounted. This vertical shaft carries a revolving arm G that strikes locking lever H pivoted at J, and raises it from the slot in disk K in which it is seated. All of these parts are shown by dotted lines, as they are located beneath the turret or work-holder of the machine. As arm G continues its movement, it strikes against one of the teeth of star-wheel L and revolves it one-sixth revolution. When this indexing movement has been completed, locking lever H again drops into a slot in K, thus locking the turret in position.

170   MECHANICAL MOVEMENTS

The turret carries six equally spaced bushings B, although only one is shown in the illustration. The slotting saw (not shown) is located on the side opposite bushing B and the screw blanks, after being placed in the work-holder at A, are indexed around to the saw by the intermittent action of the indexing mechanism, which movement occurs after each screw-head is slotted. As the screw blanks leave position A they are held loosely in place in the bushings by guard N which may be adjusted in or out to agree with the body diameter of the screw blank. As each screw arrives at the operating position beneath the slotting saw, it is held firmly against its seat in the bushings by the inner end of lever O. This lever receives its motion from the left-hand face of cam E. This cam does not bear directly against the end of the lever O, but acts through the intermediate lever P which is adjustable by means of the thumb-screw shown. It is thus possible to regulate the pressure with which O bears against the work, the adjustment being varied according to the size of the screw blank.

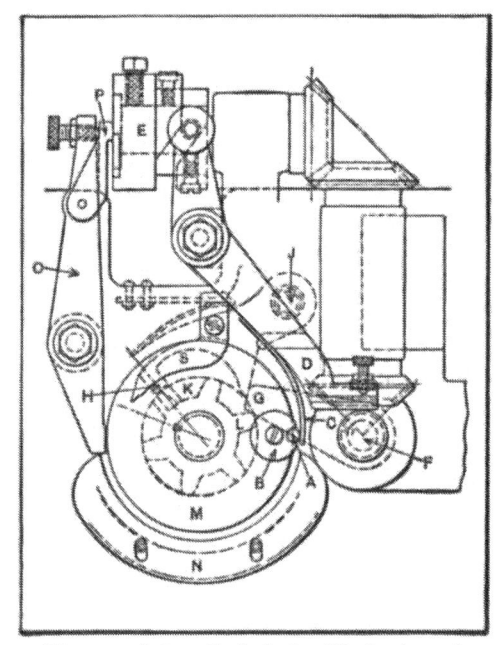

Fig. 22. Automatic Indexing Mechanism of a Screw-slotting Machine

The slide carrying the slotting saw moves vertically and is fed downward by a cam as each successive blank is located beneath it. After the slot is milled, the saw is moved upward rapidly by a spring action, and lever O releases the slotted screw which drops through a chute and into a receptacle. If the screw blank does not release readily, the continued rotation of the turret brings it into contact with the curved edge of the ejector S. Incidentally, the bushings B are provided with a number of seats in their periphery so that, by simply turning these seats outward, the bushings are adapted for holding screws of a number of different sizes. The indexing mechanism is so arranged that any inaccuracy which may occur is in a direction lengthwise of the screw slots and not at right angles to the face of the saw, so that the centering of the slot in the head of the screw is not affected.

Combined Indexing and Locking Mechanism. — The automatic indexing and locking mechanism illustrated in Fig. 23 was designed for a multiple-spindle automatic screw machine. The motions of this machine are all controlled by cams on a camshaft which transmits motion for indexing by means of a chain and sprocket gearing. The sprocket wheel A on the camshaft is directly connected by a chain with a sprocket wheel fast to the spindle head B. Sprocket wheel A is normally loose on its seat on cam C, but it is engaged with the cam for indexing by means of a dog D contained in a slot in the cam. One end of this dog is arranged to engage a recess inside the hub of sprocket wheel A and the outer or projecting end is in position to be acted upon by stationary cam E. Normally the dog D is out of engagement with the sprocket wheel, but for the indexing movement, cam E throws the dog into engagement, thus revolving the sprocket and the spindle head to a new position. As there are five spindles in the head, in this case, the spindle head must be revolved one-fifth revolution at a time. After the indexing movement is completed, cam E disconnects the dog from the sprocket automatically.

As it is necessary on machines of this class to locate the spindle head very accurately each time it is indexed, some form of auxiliary locating and locking mechanism is employed. In this case, the locking bolt is at G, and is forced into its seat by the spiral spring shown. The action of the bolt is controlled by a lever H and cam F. This cam allows the bolt to drop in place as soon as the indexing motion is completed. The conical point of bolt

G engages a seat of corresponding form, in whichever plug K is in position. These plugs are spaced equidistantly about the periphery of the spindle head. The tapered seat for the end of bolt G is formed partly in the plug K and partly in the bushing J through which the plug passes, as indicated by the detailed view. With this arrangement, the location of the spindle head does not depend upon the closeness of the fit of the cylindrical part of the locking bolt in bushing J.

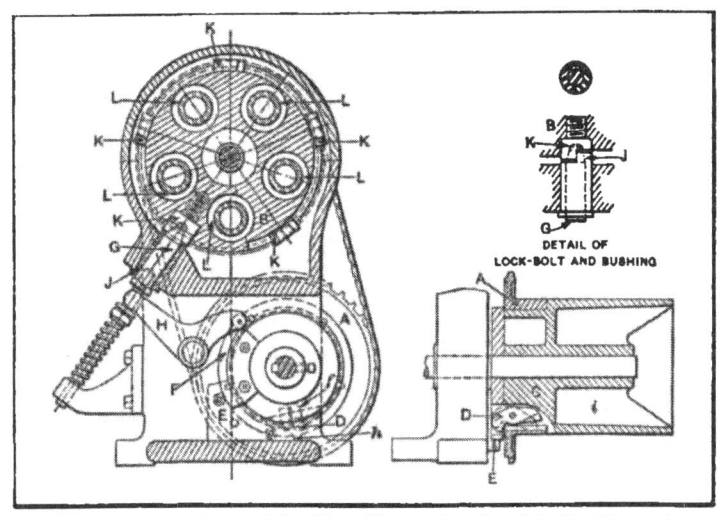

Fig. 23. Indexing and Locking Mechanism for Spindle Head of Multiple-spindle Automatic Screw Machine

Action of an Adding Mechanism. — The adding mechanism to be described is applied to a machine which is a typewriter and adding machine combined. With this machine (the Ellis), debit and credit accounts may be written down indiscriminately; each set of items added, and the total amount printed beneath each vertical column. The writing is done on the typewriter in the regular way, and the figures are set up and printed with the adding mechanism at the same time that the reading matter is written. Two adding mechanisms or " accumulators " are required, one being for the debit and the other for the credit column. This machine may also be used in various other ways. For instance, a list of items may be printed in a series of vertical columns and these columns added to obtain the total amount in both horizontal and vertical directions; finally, these totals, both horizontal and vertical, may be added together to obtain the grand total. Discounts may also be reckoned, amounts may be subtracted from each other, and many other operations performed in connection with commercial work.

The adding keyboard is composed of nine vertical rows of nine keys each. The lower key of each row is numbered one, the next two, and so on up to nine. Of the nine vertical rows, the first on the right is for units, the next, for tens, etc., or, since the reckoning is usually in dollars and cents, the first row is for cents, the next, for dimes, and the succeeding rows, for dollars. Figs. 24 and 25 show diagrammatical sections through the machine along the line of any one of the vertical rows of adding keys, which are shown at G. Other important parts of the mechanism are the rack A, the type sector F, by means of which the numbers are printed on paper carried by roller K, and the accumulator wheels B, by which the addition is performed. These parts, as well as the other moving mechanism shown, are duplicated for each one of the nine rows of keys, there being nine racks, nine type bars, nine sets of accumulator wheels, etc., in all.

The adding mechanism is operated by the movement of rack A. This movement takes place under the influence of spring O whenever stop N is swung back as shown in Fig. 25 by the operation of the handle of the machine. The length of the movement which spring O thus gives to rack A is determined by keys G. If the figure $476.34 is set up on the keyboard, for instance, key "4" will be depressed in the cents column, and, when the movement of the rack takes place, the rack teeth beneath the accumulator wheel will have moved four spaces.

This is more clearly seen in Fig. 24 where each of the keys G is shown to be mounted on a stem which carries a stop H at the lower end. When the keys are depressed, these stops come into line with corresponding steps formed at the left-hand end of the rack A. These steps are so proportioned that when key 1 is depressed, for instance, the rack is allowed to move one tooth before striking its abutment. When key 2 is depressed,

174 MECHANICAL MOVEMENTS

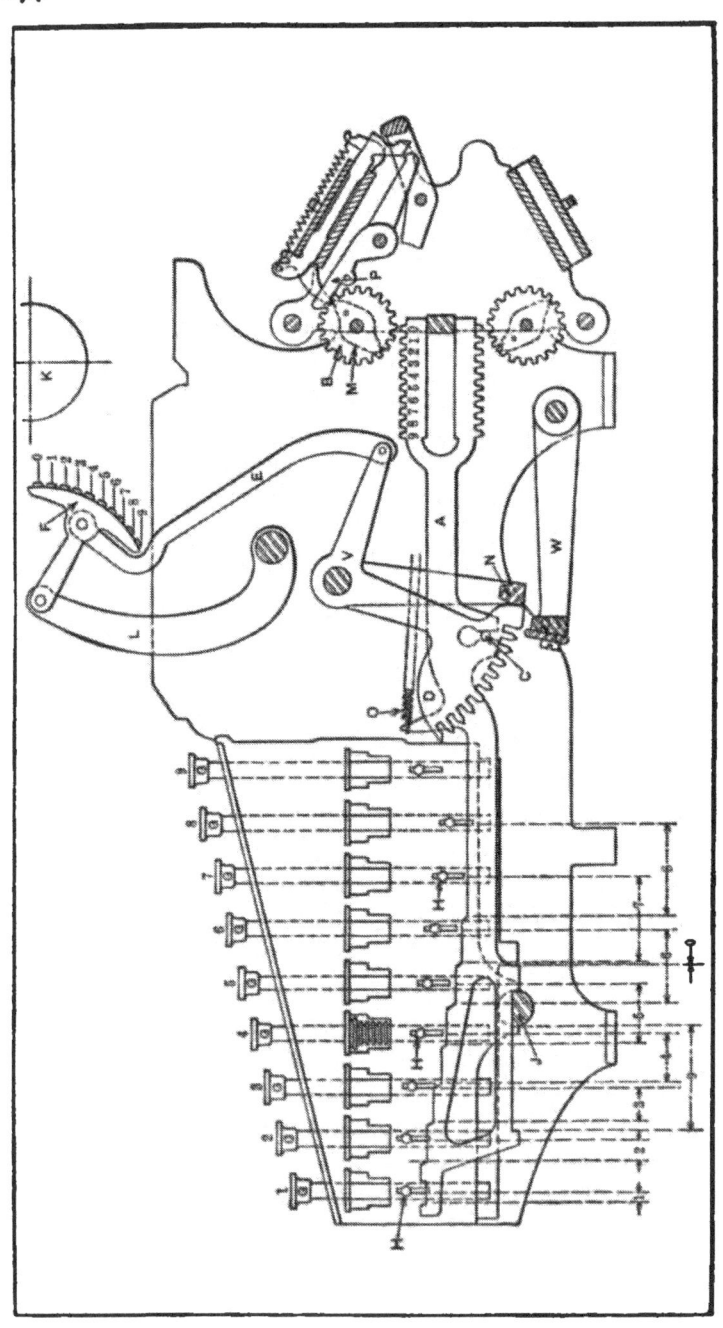

Fig. 24. Diagrammatical Cross-section of Adding Mechanism showing Relation of Keys, Racks, Accumulators, and Printing Device

it moves two teeth and so on, as shown by the numbered arrows at the lower part of the illustration. When no key is depressed, indicating zero, then a stop is interposed which prevents any movement of the rack. When key 9 is depressed, the rack takes the full movement of nine teeth allowed by the striking of the projections on the under side of the rack against supporting bar J.

Each rack A has cut in it a slot engaging pin C in sector D. Each sector is, in turn, connected by link E with the type bar F having numbers from 0 to 9. Whenever a key (key 4, for instance) is depressed as shown in Fig. 25, and the rack is allowed to move four teeth backward under the influence of spring O, the type bar F is thereby set at the corresponding figure. The throwing forward of lever L to which the type bar is pivoted then prints this figure "4" on paper wrapped about roll K. It is important to remember that rack A and type bar F are positively connected under all conditions. It should, perhaps, be mentioned that the teeth in sector D simply provide for more accurate alignment of the type in printing than would otherwise be possible. Just before the printing stroke takes place, arm W swings up, carrying a plate which enters the corresponding tooth space in each one of the nine sectors D, aligning all the figures on type bars F and giving a good, evenly printed number on paper.

The Accumulator Mechanism. — The accumulator mechanism, by means of which the adding is done on the machine previously referred to, will now be described. There are ordinarily nine accumulator wheels for each of the nine racks. This particular machine, however, has two sets of nine wheels each, one set being above rack A (see Fig. 25), and the other below it. The upper one is the debit accumulator for addition in the debit column and the other is the credit accumulator for the credit column. Only the upper or debit accumulator will now be considered. This set of nine accumulator wheels, of which only one is shown at B, may be swung into and out of engagement with the teeth of racks A, at will. These accumulator wheels have 20 teeth each; they could have ten, except for the

176 MECHANICAL MOVEMENTS

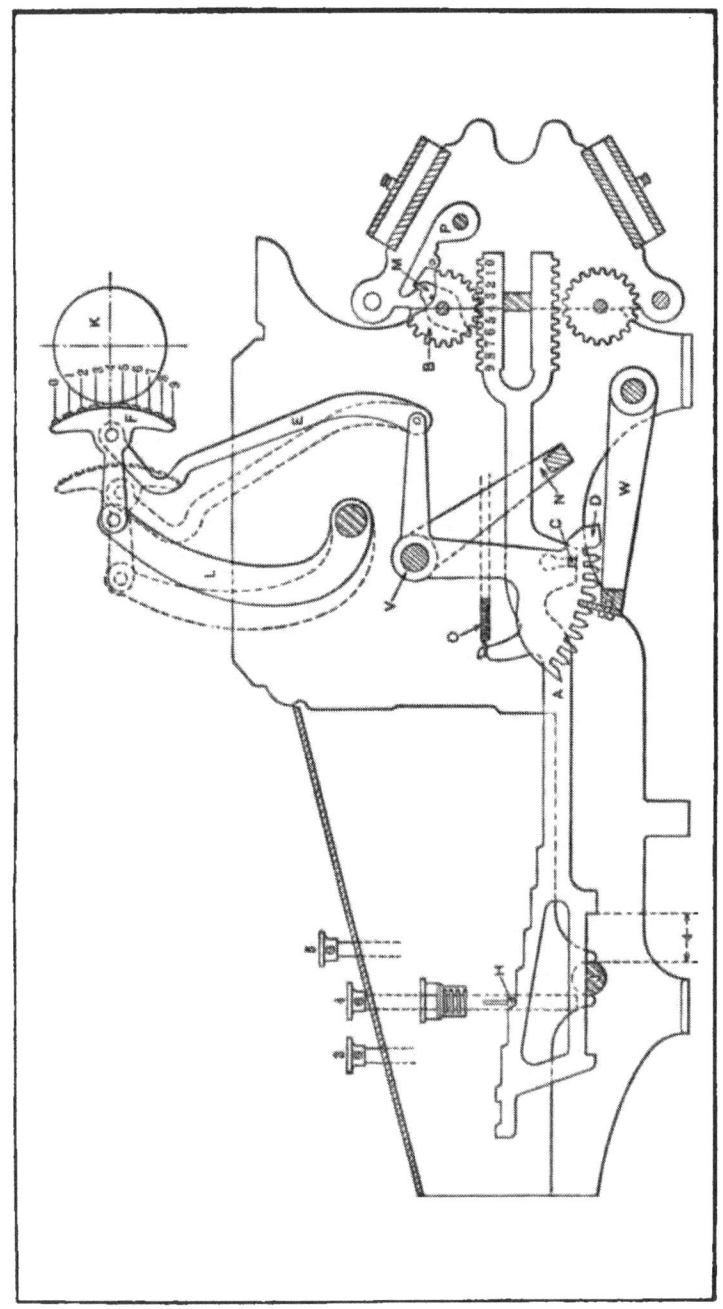

Fig. 25. Adding Mechanism arranged for Printing the Number 4 and adding it into the Accumulator

fact that it would make them inconveniently small. Each wheel is provided with a two-tooth ratchet M positively pinned to it. This ratchet spans ten of the wheel teeth between its points. Pawl P is adapted to engage the teeth of ratchet M, and is connected with the mechanism by means of which the tens are carried from one column to another (that is, from one accumulator wheel to another) as will be described later.

Order of Operations for Adding. — Figs. 26 and 27 show, in diagrammatical form, the method of procedure followed in the simple problem of adding 4 to 9, and obtaining the sum 13. At A, Fig. 26, the machine is shown " clear," that is, with the accumulator wheels at zero, which means that one tooth of the two-tooth ratchet is up against the hook of the pawl. Key 4, corresponding to the number to be added, in this case, into the accumulator wheel, is now depressed and the operating handle of the machine is pulled over. The first thing that takes place is that the rack is allowed to move four teeth to the right, as shown at B (see also Fig. 25). In this position, the number " 4 " is printed. Next (as shown at C in Fig. 26) the mechanism automatically throws the accumulator wheel down into engagement with the rack. Then as the operator allows the handle to return, the rack moves back to the zero position again as shown at D, carrying the accumulator wheel with it a space of four teeth from its zero position. The mechanism then disengages the accumulator wheel, leaving the machine ready for the next operation with the 4 added into the accumulator, as shown at E.

To add 9 to the 4, key 9 is depressed and the operator pulls the handle. This results in a movement of nine teeth of the rack as shown at F in Fig. 27. The figure 9 is then printed. The accumulator wheel is next engaged, as at G. Then the rack is returned to the zero position as at H, and the accumulator wheel is disengaged as at I. This evidently moves the accumulator wheel $9 + 4 = 13$ teeth as shown at H. In doing this, one of the teeth of the two-tooth ratchet lifts the pawl as it passes under it. This raising of the pawl operates a spring-loaded mechanism, which shifts the next accumulator wheel (that for the tens col-

178 MECHANICAL MOVEMENTS

umn) one tooth, when the wheels are returned from engagement in operation *I*. This operation corresponds to that of "carrying" when adding with pencil and paper, except that it is done automatically. This carrying mechanism will not be described in detail as the parts are small and rather complicated, although

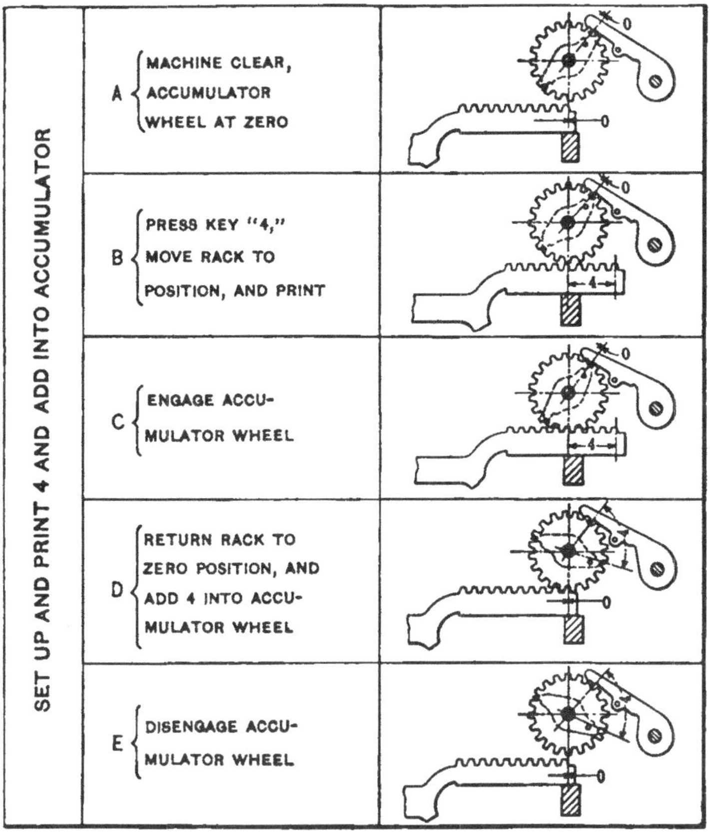

Fig. 26. Diagrams illustrating Principle Governing Action of Adding Mechanism

the action is simple. The mechanism may be understood more clearly by considering the actions of the wheels when every one of them in the accumulator, from cents up to the millions of dollars, is set at 9 — that is, when they are set up for 9,999,999.99. Now suppose that one cent is added, so that the first wheel is moved beyond 9 — that is, to 0. The tooth of the ratchet M will then pass under the first pawl, raising it. When the accumulator wheels return from engagement, this raising of the first pawl releases a spring-loaded mechanism which moves the next wheel from 9 to 0. This, in turn, moves the next wheel from 9 to 0 and so on until each one of the row has been advanced one tooth, setting the whole row at 0,000,000.00. This operation is done so rapidly that one cannot distinguish between the successive operations, but each one is dependent upon the preceding one. The operations required for finding a total are shown at J, K, L, and M, Fig. 27. The first thing the operator does is to depress the " credit total " key at the left of the keyboard, the sum having been added into the upper or credit accumulator. He then pulls the operating handle, and the accumulator wheels are engaged with the racks as shown at J. The next operation is the release of the racks so that the springs move them toward the right. There are, in this case, no keys depressed in the keyboard, so that the racks would move the full distance of nine teeth, were it not for the fact that they have to carry the accumulator wheels with them, and the ratchets on these wheels come in contact with the pawls, thus arresting their movement and stopping the movement of the racks.

The previous operation of adding 9 to the 4 in the wheel set the " units wheel " three teeth beyond the point of the ratchet, and the " tens wheel," one tooth beyond the point of the ratchet. It is evident, then, that in operation K the units rack will be allowed to move three teeth and the tens rack one tooth. This will evidently set up the unit type bar at " 3 " and the tens type bar at " 1." On the return of the handle, the printing mechanism is operated, transferring the total " 13 " to the paper. The accumulator wheel will then be released, and the rack will be allowed to return to the zero position as shown at M. This leaves all the accumulator wheels back in the zero position, with the teeth of the ratchets back against the pawls, leaving the machine " clear " and ready for the next operation.

It might have been desired to print a sub-total instead of a total; that is, a total for the addition as far as it had proceeded,

180 MECHANICAL MOVEMENTS

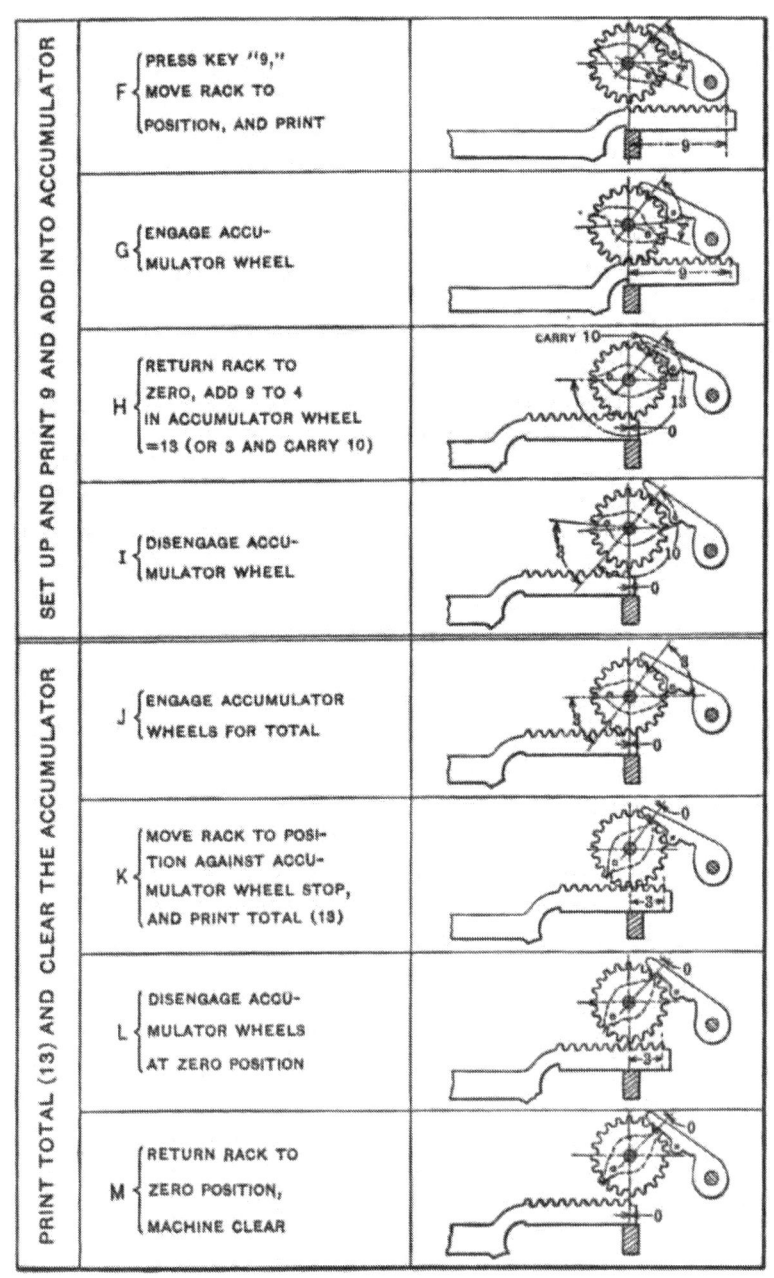

SET UP AND PRINT 9 AND ADD INTO ACCUMULATOR	F { PRESS KEY "9," MOVE RACK TO POSITION, AND PRINT	
	G { ENGAGE ACCU- MULATOR WHEEL	
	H { RETURN RACK TO ZERO, ADD 9 TO 4 IN ACCUMULATOR WHEEL =13 (OR 3 AND CARRY 10)	CARRY 10
	I { DISENGAGE ACCU- MULATOR WHEEL	
PRINT TOTAL (13) AND CLEAR THE ACCUMULATOR	J { ENGAGE ACCUMULATOR WHEELS FOR TOTAL	
	K { MOVE RACK TO POSI- TION AGAINST ACCU- MULATOR WHEEL STOP, AND PRINT TOTAL (13)	
	L { DISENGAGE ACCU- MULATOR WHEELS AT ZERO POSITION	
	M { RETURN RACK TO ZERO POSITION, MACHINE CLEAR	

Fig. 27. Continuation of Diagrams illustrating Operation of Adding Mechanism

but not to clear the machine, thus permitting more figures to be set up and printed and added into the same sum. Sub-totals can be printed at any point in the adding up of a line of figures, as required, by a simple change in the operation shown at J, K, L, and M in Fig. 27. This consists simply in allowing the wheels to remain in engagement at L, so that the racks, when they return in operation M, will bring the wheels to the same position as they had in J, thus leaving the totals still set up in the accumulator. Since there are two independent accumulators, it is evident that a number can be added into either one or both of them; or a total or sub-total can be taken from one of them and added into the other — all depending upon the manipulation of the keys and the time of throwing the accumulator wheels into and out of action.

This adding machine has what are known as "controlling keys." These are named "non-add," "debit add," "debit sub-total," "debit total," "credit add," "credit sub-total," "credit total," "repeat," and "error." The pressing down of the non-adding key permits the printing of a number without adding. In other words, this keeps the accumulators permanently out of engagement with the racks. The debit and credit add keys permit a number to be printed and added into the corresponding accumulator, even though the carriage is not set in the proper position for that accumulator. The use of these keys, therefore, gives a flexibility to the machine which is necessary for special operations such as horizontal adding. The debit and credit sub-total keys take and print a total from either the debit or credit accumulators without clearing the accumulators. The debit and credit total keys, on the other hand, take the total from either the debit or credit accumulators, as the case may be, and clear the accumulator after the total is printed. The pressing down of the repeat key holds in the downward position whichever of the number keys have been depressed, allowing the same number to be repeatedly printed and added as many times as the operating handle is pulled. This is useful in multiplying by repeated additions and for other similar uses. The pressing of the error key will release every other key on the keyboard, both of the number keys and of the operating keys as well.

The keyboard is provided with an interlocking mechanism connected with the controlling keys of the machine and with the operating lever. This mechanism, among other things, prevents the keys from being pressed down or changed after the operating lever movement is started. The keyboard also has a connection with an error key, the pressing of which releases all the keys that may be depressed at the time. Means are also

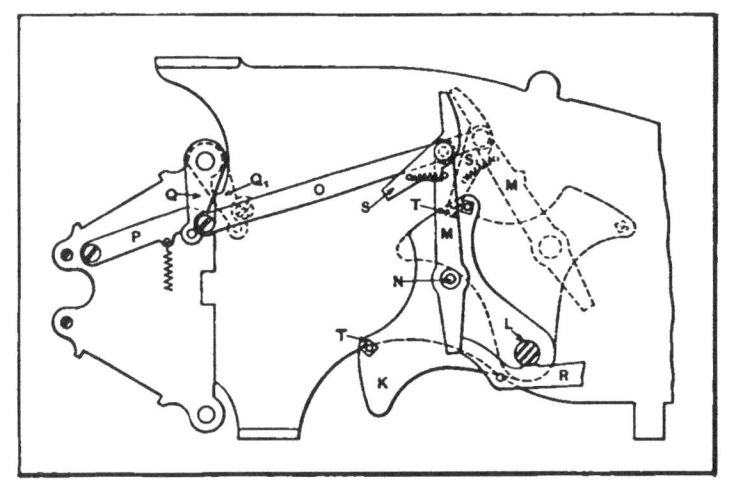

Fig. 28. Flying Lever Connection between Operating Shaft and Accumulators of Adding Mechanism

provided for automatically releasing and returning the keys after each operation.

Accumulator Controlling Mechanism. — The engagement of the accumulators with the racks, and their release, in the operation of the adding mechanism previously described, is effected as follows: The sector K (see Fig. 28) is directly connected with the operating shaft L controlled by the operating handle. It is provided with connections with both accumulators, although this illustration only shows the connections with the debit accumulator. Flying lever M is connected with the debit accumulator by means of links O_1 and bellcrank Q. Member

P is simply a spring detent to locate *Q* for either the engaged or disengaged position of the accumulator wheels.

As sector *K* starts on its stroke toward the dotted position, flying lever *M* is carried with it, owing to the resistance which the end of the latter meets with against abutment *R*. When *K* has gone far enough so that the end of the lever has dropped off *R*, the lever *M* becomes free. The movement has been sufficient, however, to move accumulator lever *Q* to position Q_1 which throws the wheels into engagement. If it had been desired to throw the wheels into engagement at the end of the stroke instead of at the beginning, detent *R* would have been withdrawn from the position shown, leaving flying lever *M* free. Near the end of the stroke of *K*, however, the end of the pawl *S* would have struck stud *T*, making *M* and *K* solid, for all practical purposes, and moving *Q* to the position Q_1 at the end of the stroke. If it had been desired to keep the accumulator wheels out of engagement altogether, *R* would have been lowered out of the position shown, and *S* would have been moved to a position clear of stud *T*. Then flying lever *M* would have been entirely free of *K*, and no movement of *Q* would have taken place. The provisions for throwing the accumulator out of engagement at either the commencement or end of the return stroke are similar to those just described.

CHAPTER VII

IRREGULAR MOTIONS

MANY machine parts require either an intermittent or an irregular motion instead of moving continuously or at a uniform velocity. The most common method of obtaining an irregular motion is by means of cams which have grooves or surfaces of such shape or form that the required motion is imparted to the driven member when the cam is in motion. The exact movement derived from any cam depends upon the shape of its operating groove or edge which may be designed according to the motion required.

Cams may be classified according to the relative movements of the cam and follower and also according to the motion of the follower itself. In one general class may be included those cams which move or revolve either in the same plane as the follower or a parallel plane, and in a second general class, those cams which cause the follower to move in a different plane which ordinarily is perpendicular to the plane of the motion of the cam. The follower of a cam belonging to either class may either move in a straight line or receive a swinging motion about a shaft or bearing. The follower may also have either a uniform motion or a uniformly accelerated motion. The working edge or groove of a uniform motion cam is so shaped that the follower moves at the same velocity from the beginning to the end of the stroke. Such cams are only adapted to comparatively slow speeds, owing to the shock resulting from the sudden movement of the follower at the beginning of the stroke and the abrupt way in which the motion is stopped at the end of the stroke. If the cam is to rotate quite rapidly, the speed of the follower should be slow at first and be accelerated at a uniform rate until the maximum speed is attained, after which the motion of the follower should be uniformly decreased until motion ceases, or a reversal takes place; such cams are known as "uniformly accelerated motion cams."

Plate Cam. — Several different forms of cams are shown in Fig. 1. The form illustrated at A is commonly called a "plate cam," because the body of the cam is in the form of a narrow plate, the edge of which is shaped to give the required motion to the follower. This follower may be mounted in suitable guides and have a reciprocating motion (as indicated in the illustration) or it may be in the form of an arm or lever which oscillates as the cam revolves. When the follower is in a vertical position as shown, it may be held in contact with the cam either by the action of gravity alone or a spring may be used to increase the contact pressure, especially if there are rather abrupt changes in the profile of the cam and the speed is comparatively fast.

Positive Motion Cam. — The cam illustrated by diagram B, Fig. 1, is similar to the type just described, except that the roller of the follower engages a groove instead of merely resting against the periphery. Cams of this general form are known as "face cams" and their distinctive feature is that the follower is given a positive motion in both directions, instead of relying upon a spring or the action of gravity to return the follower. The follower, in this particular case, is in the form of a bellcrank lever and is given an oscillating motion. One of the defects of the face cam is that the outer edge of the cam groove tends to rotate the roller in one direction and the inner edge tends to rotate it in the opposite direction. A certain amount of clearance must be provided in the groove and, as the roll changes its contact from the inner edge to the outer edge, there is an instantaneous reversal of rotation which is resisted, due to the inertia of the rapidly revolving roll; the resulting friction tends to wear both the cam and the roll. This wearing action, however, may not be serious when the cam rotates at a slow speed. If the speed is high, there is also more or less shock each time the follower is reversed, owing to the clearance between the roller and the cam groove.

Plate Cam arranged for Positive Motion. — In order to avoid the defects referred to in connection with the face cam,

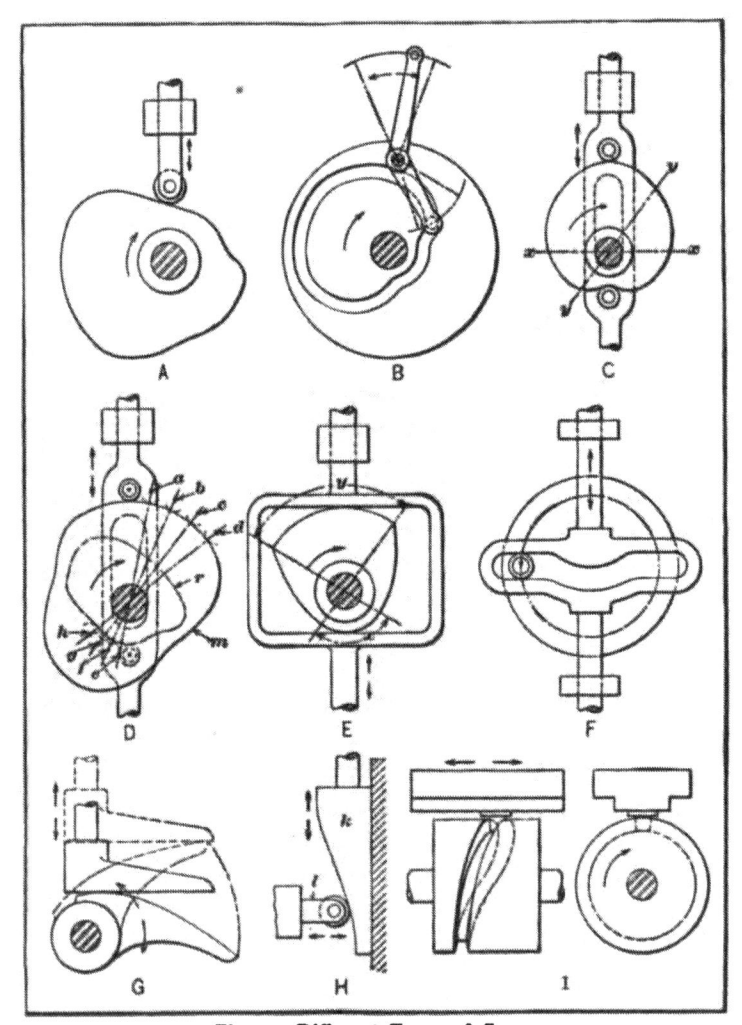

Fig. 1. Different Types of Cams

the follower of a plate cam is sometimes equipped with two rollers which operate on opposite sides of the cam, as shown at C, Fig. 1. With such an arrangement, the curve of the cam for moving the follower in one direction must be complementary to the curve of the remaining half of the cam, since the distance between the rollers remains constant. In other words, this cam may be designed to give any motion throughout 180 degrees of its movement, but the curvature of the remaining half of the cam must correspond to that of the first. When a cam is laid out in this way, the distance between the sides as measured along any center line, as at xx or yy, is constant and represents the distance between the rollers of the follower. For this reason, the term *constant diameter cam* is sometimes applied to this class which is adapted for heavier work than the grooved face cam illustrated at B. The follower or driven member is slotted to receive the camshaft, and this slot acts as a guide and keeps the rollers in alignment with the center of the cam.

Return Cam for Follower. — When the curvature of one-half of a cam does not correspond to the curvature of the other half, a special return cam is necessary, if the follower is equipped with two rollers in order to secure a positive drive. A main and return cam is illustrated at D, Fig. 1. The main cam may be laid out to give any required motion for a complete revolution of 360 degrees, and the return cam has a curvature which corresponds to the motion of the return roller on the follower. After the main cam is laid out to give whatever motion is required, points as at a, b, c, d, etc., are located on the path followed by the center of the roller, and, with these points as centers, the points e, f, g, and h are located diametrically opposite, and at a distance equal to the center-to-center distance between the rollers. These latter points lie in the path followed by the center of the return roller, and by striking arcs from them having a radius equal to the roller radius, the curvature or working surface of the return cam may be laid out. One method of arranging these two cams is to place the follower between them and attach the rollers on opposite sides of the followers. The camshaft, in some cases, carries a square block which is fitted to the elongated slot in the follower to serve as a guide and a bearing surface.

Yoke Type of Follower. — Another form of positive motion cam is shown at E, Fig. 1. In this case, the follower has a surface which is straight or tangential to the curvature of the cam. With a follower of this kind, there is a limitation to the motion which can be imparted to it, because, when the contact surface is flat or plane, it is evident that no part of the cam can be concave since a concave surface could not become tangent to the straight face of the follower, and even though the follower is curved or convex any concave part of the cam must have a radius which is at least as great as the radius of any part of the follower. The type of cam shown at E, like the one illustrated at C, can only be laid out for a motion representing 180 degrees of cam rotation; the curvature of the remaining half of the cam must be complementary to the first half or correspond to it. The follower of the cam shown at E has a dwell or period of rest at each end of its stroke, the parts x and y being concentric with the axis of the camshaft. This general type of cam has been used for operating light mechanisms and also to actuate the valves of engines in stern-wheel river steamers.

Inverse Cams. — On all of the cams previously referred to, the curved surface for controlling the motion has been on the driving member. With a cam of the inverse type, such as is shown at F (Fig. 1) the cam groove is in the follower and the roller which engages this groove is attached to the driving member. The motion of this cam can be laid out for only 180 degrees of movement. The inverse type of cam is used chiefly on light mechanisms, the particular cam illustrated at F being designed to operate a reciprocating bar or slide. The curved part of the slot in the follower has the same radius as the path of the driving roller, and serves to arrest the motion of the slide momentarily. The well-known Scotch yoke or slotted crosshead is similar to an inverse cam having a straight slot that is perpendicular to the center line of the follower. (The motion obtained with the Scotch yoke and its practical application is referred to in Chapter III.)

Wiper and Involute Cams. — The form of cam shown at G, Fig. 1, is simply a lever which has a curved surface and operates with an oscillating movement through an arc great enough to give the required lift to the follower. A cam of this kind is called a "lifting toe" or a "wiper" cam, and has been employed on river and harbor steamboats for operating the engine valves. Many involute cams are somewhat similar in form to the type illustrated at G, and they are so named because the cam curve is of involute form. Such cams are used on the ore crushers in stamp mills. Several cams are placed on one shaft and as they revolve the rods carrying the stamps are raised throughout part of the cam revolution. Disengagement of the cam and follower then causes the latter to drop.

Cams having Rectilinear Motion. — Some cams instead of rotating are simply given a rectilinear or straight-line motion. The principle upon which such cams operate is shown by diagram H, Fig. 1. The cam or block k is given a reciprocating motion in some form of guide, and one edge is shaped so as to impart the required motion to the follower l. An automatic screw machine of the multiple-spindle type is equipped with a cam of this general type for operating side-working tools, the tool-slide receiving its motion from the cam which, in turn, is actuated by the turret-slide. This type of cam is also applied to an automatic lathe for operating the radial arm or tool-holder.

Cams for Motion Perpendicular to Plane of Cam. — The cams previously referred to all impart motion to a follower which moves in a plane which either coincides with or is parallel to the plane of the motion of the cam. The second general class of cams previously referred to, which cause the follower to move in a plane usually perpendicular to the plane of the motion of the cam, is illustrated by the design shown at I, Fig. 1. This form is known as a "cylinder" or "barrel" cam. There are two general methods of making cams of this type. In one case, a continuous groove of the required shape is milled in the cam body, as shown in the illustration, and this groove is engaged by a roller attached to the follower. Another very common method of constructing cylinder cams, especially for use on automatic screw machines, is to attach plates to the body of the cam, which have edges shaped to impart the required motion to the follower. When a groove is formed in the cam body, it should have tapering sides and be engaged by a tapering roller, rather than by one of cylindrical shape, in order to reduce the friction and wear.

Automatic Variation of Cam Motion. — Ordinarily the motion derived from a cam is always the same, the cam being designed and constructed especially for a given movement. It is possible, however, to vary the motion, and this may be done by changing the relative positions of the driving and driven members by some auxiliary device. This variation may be in the extent or magnitude of the movement or a change in the kind of motion derived from the cam. The cam mechanism shown at A in Fig. 2 is so arranged that every other movement of each of the two followers is varied. The bellcrank levers a and b, which are the followers, have cam surfaces on the lower ends, and they are given a

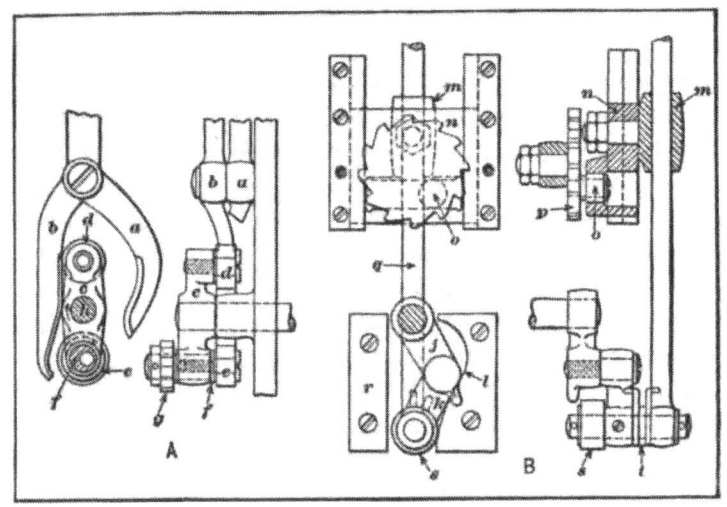

Fig. 2. Mechanisms for Varying Motion Normally derived from Cams

swinging motion by rolls d and e pivoted to arm c which revolves with the shaft h seen in the center of the arm.

The requirements are that each lever have first a uniform motion and then a variable motion; it is also necessary to have a change in the variable stroke until twelve strokes have been completed, when the cycle of variable motions is repeated. For instance, every other vibration of each lever is through a certain angle, and for twelve alternate vibrations the stroke is changed from a maximum to a minimum, and *vice versa*, the angle of the uniform vibration being the mean or average movement for the variable strokes. The uniform vibration is obtained when roll d engages the cam surface on either lever a or b, and the variable movement is derived from roll *e* on the opposite end. This roll is mounted eccentrically on bushing *f* which is rotated in its seat by star-wheel *g*, one-twelfth revolution for each revolution of arm *c*; consequently, the roll is moved either toward or away from the axis of shaft *h*, thus varying the angle of vibration accordingly.

Another mechanism which serves to vary the motion derived from a cam surface is shown at *B* in Fig. 2. This mechanism is used in conjunction with the one previously described. A motion represented by the curvature *l* of a plate cam is reproduced by the upper end of the rod or lever *q*. One movement of the rod end is an exact duplicate of the cam curvature, and this movement represents the mean of a cycle of twelve movements, each of which is a reproduction of the curvature on an increasing or diminishing scale from maximum to minimum, or *vice versa*. The lever returns to the starting position with a rectilinear or straight-line motion. The lever is given a reciprocating movement by crank *j* and connecting link *k*. The roll *s* at the lower end of the lever is kept in contact with cam surface *l* by spring *t*. The lever *q* is fulcrumed and slides in the oscillating bearing *m* which is supported by the slotted cross-head *n*. This cross-head is operated by roll *o* which is carried by a crankpin on a twelve-tooth ratchet wheel *p*. When the mechanism is in action, the crank *j* throws connecting link *k* out of line with lever *q* and the resulting tension on spring *t* causes roll *s* to follow the outline or curvature *l* of the cam until the upper end of the travel is reached; then the connecting link *k* is thrown out of line with lever *q* in the opposite direction, which causes spring *t* to force roll *s* against the straight return guide *r*. For each revolution of the crank, a pawl turns the ratchet wheel *p* one tooth, so that the slotted cross-head *n* and the bearing *m* are gradually raised and then lowered. As the result of this upward and downward movement of bearing *m*, which is the fulcrum for lever *q*, the motion is increased and then diminished the desired amount.

Varying Dwell of Cam Follower. — The mechanism illustrated in Fig. 3 is for varying the dwell of a cam follower or the length of time it remains stationary. The cam *A* lifts lever *B* during three-fourths of a revolution, and during the dwell the follower B is held up by the latch C. This latch is controlled by pawl D, cam E, and spring F. The cam E has ratchet-shaped notches in its edge and is made integral or in one piece with a twenty-four-tooth gear G. The ratchet and gear are revolved upon the hub of a twenty-five-tooth stationary gear H, by the planetary pinion K, once for every twenty-four revolutions of cam A. With this particular mechanism, the lever B is given a dwell of 90 degrees for the first revolution; thereafter the dwell increases 360 degrees after each rise of the follower, until the fourth period

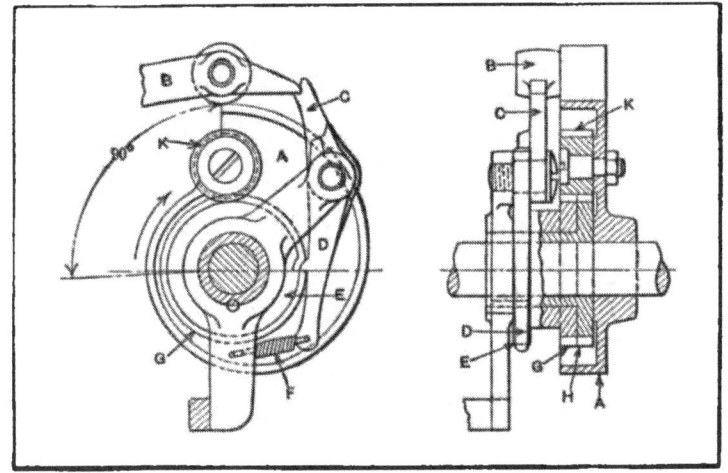

Fig. 3. Arrangement for Varying Dwell of Cam Follower

(which gives 1530 degrees dwell) when the dwell decreases until it is again 90 degrees; that is, during the fourth period the rise occurs while the cam makes three-fourths revolution, and then there is a dwell equivalent to 4¼ revolutions. Twenty-four revolutions are required to complete a cycle of movements. When milling the teeth in cam E, the index-head was arranged for twenty-four divisions, but teeth were cut only at the following divisions: 1–2–4–7–11–16–20–23. When the mechanism is in use, latch C is disengaged whenever pawl D enters a notch in cam E, thus allowing lever B to drop suddenly.

Automatic Variation of Cam Rise and Drop. — The special design of cam illustrated in Fig. 4 normally has a 120-degree

IRREGULAR MOTIONS 193

rise, a 60-degree dwell, a 90-degree drop, and a 90-degree dwell. In the operation of the machine to which this cam was applied, however, it was necessary to vary the motion derived from the cam in accordance with the pressure exerted upon a certain part of the machine; for instance, if the pressure exceeds a given limit during a dwell, the rise must take place in 90 degrees instead of 120 degrees; whereas, if the pressure decreases below the desired amount, the drop must be lengthened to 120 degrees.

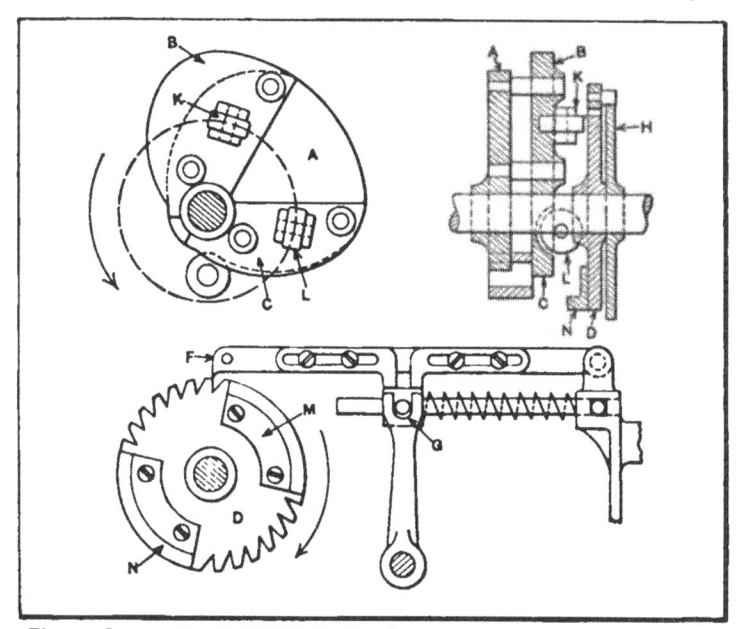

Fig. 4. Cam equipped with Mechanism for Varying Rise and Drop according to Predetermined Pressure on another Part of the Machine

The mechanism for automatically varying the cam motion is comparatively simple, as the illustration indicates.

The main cam A carries two auxiliary cams B and C. These cams are driven by pins, which pass through them as shown by the sectional view, and they are free to slide upon these pins and the shaft, parallel to the axis of the shaft. Cam B carries a roller K and cam C, a roller L. Adjacent to these movable cams, there is a disk D having two sets of ratchet teeth and two side cams M and N. (The end view of this disk is shown at the lower part of the illustration.) A pawl F rests upon the block G until the increase or decrease of pressure interferes with the balance of the spring shown and causes pawl F to drop into engagement with a ratchet tooth. As soon as this engagement occurs, disk D stops rotating and cams M and N come into engagement with rollers K and L and force cams B and C over toward cam A, so that they engage the wide cam-roller on the follower, and give it the required variation of movement. The cam H returns pawl F to the neutral position.

Sectional Interchangeable Cams for Varying Motion. — A flexible cam system was required that made it possible to vary the motion relative to the complete cycle of movements by substituting one interchangeable cam section for another, instead of using a large single cam for each variation. Two distinct methods of obtaining practically indentical results were successfully evolved. One mechanism was a rotary type and the other involved the use of rectilinear motion for the cam sections. Both mechanisms might properly be called " magazine " cams, because the cam sections are continually placed in action and then replaced by others in successive order.

The rotary design is illustrated in Fig. 5. The cam sections shown at A are semi-circular. The continuity of the cam surface is obtained by making each semi-circular section in the form of a half turn of a spiral with close-fitting joints, the complete cam appearing like a worm. The sections are fed longitudinally along the shaft and successively under the lever roller at a rate of advance equaling the lead of the spiral. Four feathers C are provided to guide and retain the cams. The two screws D producing the longitudinal movement are driven by pinions E meshing with an internal gear F, which is fastened to the bearing. As the feathers extend only to within the width of one cam from the left bearing, two sections drop from the shaft at every revolution, the dropping sections being guided by the guides G. The double cam upon the driving gear I, the lever J, and the carrier-slide K provide the means for hanging the semi-circular cams upon the magazine bar H. The slide K catches each piece by the pins L and, by pushing one, causes the further one to slide onto the lifting slide M which engages its grooved hub. The gears N and O, in the ratio of 1 to 2, and disk P operate a slide for returning the cams to their shaft. The rollers on P successively engage the steps M_1 and M_2, thus raising the slide which drops back automatically.

To facilitate engagement between the cam threads and the screws, the square threads of the latter are V-shaped at the entering ends, and, to insure locking the cams to the shaft quickly, the ends of the feathers recede into pockets and fly out by the action of springs. Any part of the system may be

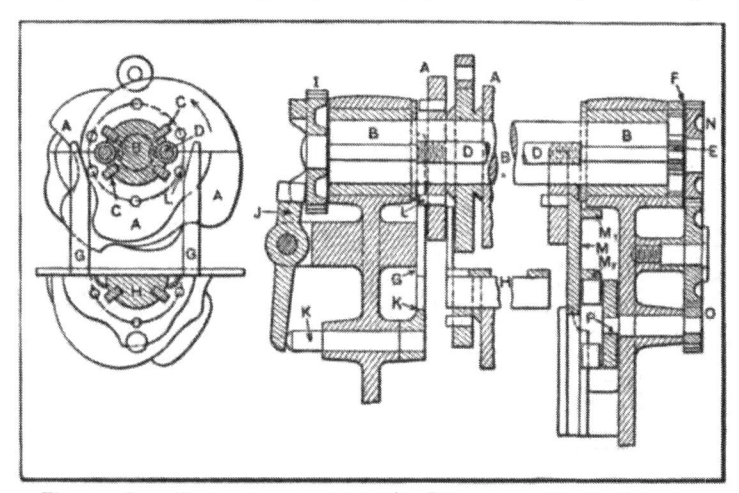

Fig. 5. Cam Mechanism provided with Interchangeable Sections for Varying Motion of Follower

changed by placing the desired section in a holder and introducing it between the slide K and the magazine bar. The cam to be removed — the dropping cam — comes out upon an inclined runway of the holder.

The alternate design is the rectilinear cam system shown in Fig. 6. The mechanism consists of the cam sections A, provided with rack teeth at B. (See also detail sectional view.) Each section has four lugs C which act as guides in the ways D. A pinion E feeds the sections along beneath the lever roller, and the frictionally driven pinion F assembles them. When any section has passed beneath the roller, it is automatically hung upon the magazine chute. The forward lugs C are made slightly longer than the rear ones, to span the gap G; but the rear lugs enter the gap just as the forward lugs clear the ways. The sections are taken from the lower part of the ways in the magazine by spring-controlled forks H upon the chain I which engage the lugs and lift the cams until the smaller lugs strike at the corner J. The linked gear K meanwhile engages the rack, and as it swings about the center L, it lifts the cam up against the ways; here the resistance offered to further motion of the links causes K to rotate about its own center and slide the cam into

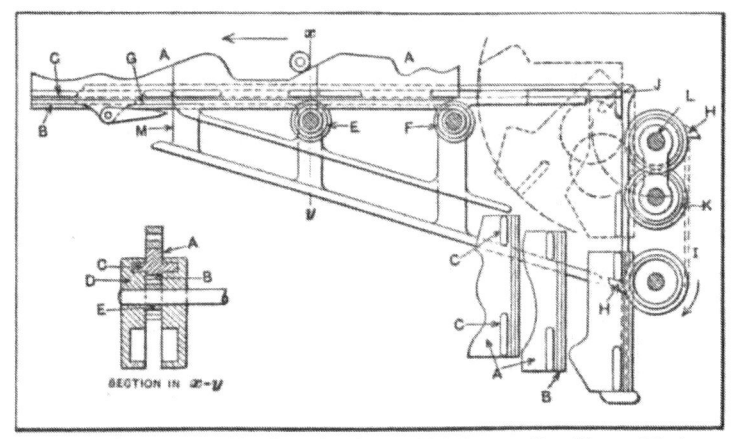

Fig. 6. Interchangeable Cam Sections which have a Rectilinear Motion

place. Substitute sections are introduced at M, and the replaced sections are lifted from the ways.

Variable Rotary Motion derived from Cam. — An unusual application of a cam is illustrated in Fig. 7. In this case, a cam is used to impart a variable speed to a shaft which makes the same number of revolutions as its driving shaft. The driving shaft carries a casting A to which is fulcrumed the lever B which, in turn, has a roll on each end. One roll engages a cam C which is supported upon the shaft but does not revolve with it. The other roll bears upon a lug on the side of gear D which is also free upon the shaft, but is constrained to revolve with it either faster or slower, according to the relative positions of lever B and cam C.

IRREGULAR MOTIONS

Group of Cams engaged Successively. — The mechanism to be described was designed to engage with the driving shaft first one and then another of the cams in a group of five mounted upon the same shaft. It was necessary to have these cams operate their respective levers successively back and forth from one end of the group to the other, and while any one cam was in action the others must remain stationary with their lever rolls on a 90-degree dwell. Eight revolutions of the shaft were required to complete one cycle of movements. The device for

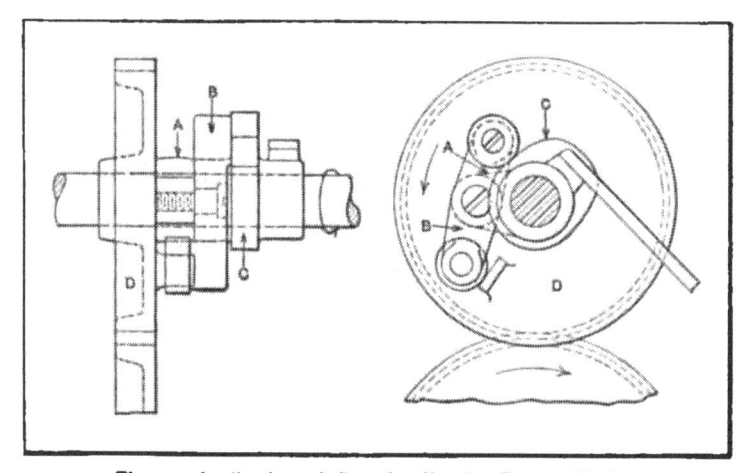

Fig. 7. Application of Cam for Varying Rotary Motion

controlling the action of these cams is shown in Fig. 8. The cams A, B, C, etc., are mounted upon a hollow shaft D carried in bearings E. The engagement of successive cams with the hollow shaft is effected by a roll-key G which is caused to move inside of the shaft from end to end. This motion of the roll-key is obtained from ratchets K and K_1. (See longitudinal section at lower part of illustration, which is taken at an angle of 90 degrees to upper section in order to show more clearly the construction.) As the roll-key is moved along, it follows the inclined surfaces H which bring it into engagement with the respective cam keyways, as at M. Within the roll-key there is a double-ended pawl L (see also detail view) which is held into engagement with either ratchet K or K_1 by balls and springs. The ratchets are cut oppositely and are given a reciprocating movement by cam O, roll N, and roll screw P which causes both ratchets to reciprocate together. A similar equipment on the opposite end of the ratchet makes the motion positive. When the roll-key has engaged the last cam in one direction, the return of the ratchet causes the pawl L to rise onto a higher surface,

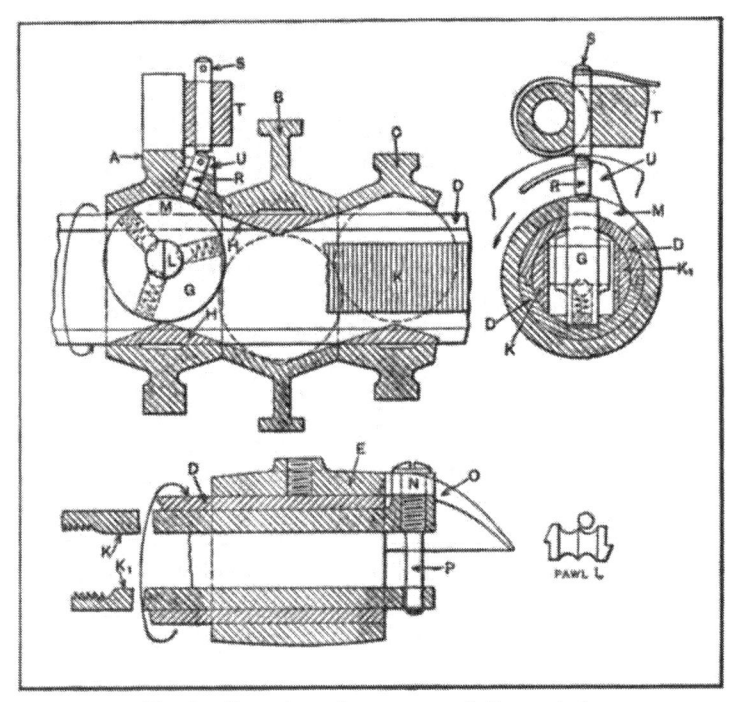

Fig. 8. Cams in a Group engaged Successively

thereby throwing it into mesh with the other ratchet and effecting the reversal.

Obtaining Resultant Motion of Several Cams. — A driven member or follower is given a motion corresponding to the resultant motion of four other cam-operated followers by the mechanism to be described. These followers are in the form of levers, which are equally spaced and fulcrumed upon one bar. Four of the levers are operated independently by four positive-motion cams. The fifth lever, which is in the center of the group, receives the resultant motion of all the others; that is, the forces acting upon the other four levers are automatically resolved and their resultant in magnitude and direction is transmitted positively to the fifth lever. It is not necessary to show the cams or levers to illustrate the principle involved, but the ingenious apparatus by means of which the resultant motion is obtained is shown in horizontal section in Fig. 9. Each of the four levers is connected by a knuckle joint to one of the racks A, B, C, and D. These racks are free to slide up and down independently and are arranged in two pairs. One pair meshes with pinion E and the other pair with pinion F. As the arrangement of the mechanism is symmetrical it will only be necessary to describe the action of one side. Any movements of the levers connecting

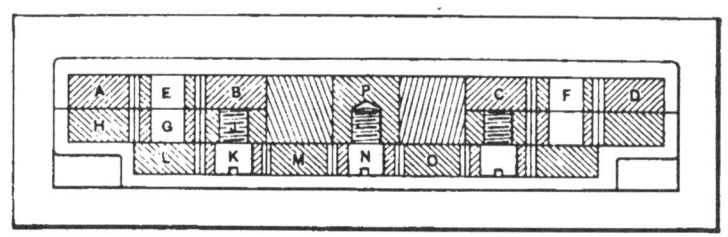

Fig. 9. Mechanism for Obtaining Resultant Motion of Several Cams

with racks A and B will be transmitted to pinions E and G, which are mounted on one stud and rotate together. A stationary rack H and a sliding rack J engage pinion G. The sliding rack J carries a pinion K which, in turn, engages a stationary rack L and a sliding rack M. Pinion N is located on sliding bar P to which is attached the fifth lever previously referred to.

In order to illustrate the action of this mechanism, assume that rack A lifts one inch, rack B drops one-half inch, rack C is stationary, and rack D lifts one-quarter inch. The resultant is a three-quarter inch rise. In analyzing the motion, it should be remembered that a pinion moving along a stationary rack will cause a movable rack on the opposite side to travel with twice the pitch-line velocity of the pinion, which fact and its converse are here applied. The racks A and B acting upon pinion E will cause it to rise $\frac{1}{2} \times (1 - \frac{1}{2}) = \frac{1}{4}$ inch. This movement is doubled in the sliding rack J which, therefore, travels one-half inch, and it is again doubled in sliding rack M which has a movement of one inch. Rack M, in turn, moves pin N and the fifth lever slide P one-half inch. If the action of racks C and D is analyzed in a similar manner, it will be found that rack O has a movement of one-half inch, and rack N, one-quarter inch, which gives a total rise of the lever attached to slide P of three-fourths inch. To further illustrate the action, if all of the cam levers should drop one inch simultaneously, the result would be a drop of four inches for the middle lever attached to slide P.

Double Two-revolution Cam of Shifting Type. — The cam mechanism illustrated at A in Fig. 10 is so arranged that two

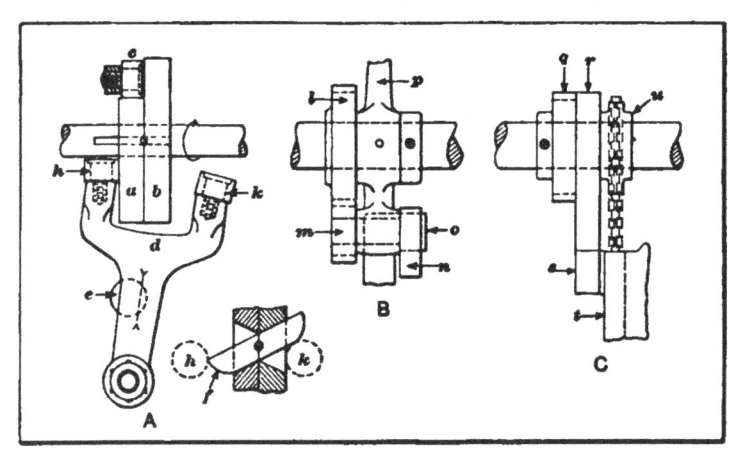

Fig. 10. (A) Double-shifting Cam; (B) Lever vibrated from Shaft on which it is fulcrumed; (C) Shaft oscillated by Cam located on it

revolutions of a double cam are necessary in order to give the required motion to a follower. One revolution is required for the rise or upward movement of the follower and a second revolution for the "dwell," during which the follower remains stationary. The cam sections a and b are fastened together and are free to slide upon their shafts a distance equal to the face width of one section. The two cam sections are driven by means of a spline. Roll c is attached to the follower or driven member and, in the illustration, is shown in contact with the spiral cam a, from which the upward movement is derived. The cam b is simply a circular disk mounted concentric with the shaft. The lever *d* for shifting the double cam is operated by a "load-and-fire" mechanism having a spring plunger at *e*. (The load-and-fire principle is explained in Chapter IV on "Reversing Mechanisms.")

When the mechanism is in operation, cam *a* lifts roll *c* to its highest position, when lever *d* shifts the double cam along the shaft, leaving roll *c* upon cam *b*, where it remains during a dwell of one revolution; the cam is then immediately shifted in the opposite direction, thus allowing roller *c* and the driven member to drop instantaneously upon cam section *a*. The movement of shifting lever *d* is derived from the double-ended lever *f* (see detailed view) which extends through a slot in the cams. This lever is pivoted at the center and is free to swing in one direction or the other, until it rests against the sides of the opening. With the double cam in the position shown in the illustration, end *f* engages roll *h* and forces it to the left until spring plunger *e* comes into action and suddenly throws the lever over the full distance. The opposite end of lever *f* swings far enough to clear roll *k* before this roll is thrown over.

Lever Vibrated from Shaft on which it is Fulcrumed. — A cam which is used for vibrating a lever twice for each revolution of a shaft on which it is fulcrumed is illustrated at *B* in Fig. 10. A gear *l* attached to the shaft drives a pinion *m* which is one-half the size of the gear. This pinion revolves cam *n*, and the shaft for the pinion and cam has a bearing in the end of lever *p*. The cam revolves in contact with a stationary roll *o* which causes the lever to vibrate about the shaft as a center twice for every revolution.

Shaft Oscillated by Cam located on it. — Fig. 10 shows, at *C*, how a shaft can be given an oscillating or rocking movement by a cam which is mounted on the shaft. The cam *r* is attached to gear *q* which is driven from an outside source. As the cam revolves in contact with roll *s*, a reciprocating motion is imparted to slide *t*. A chain attached to this slide passes over a sprocket *u* which is fast to the shaft. The other end of the chain is fastened to a tension spring beneath the slide, which serves to hold the roll *s* into engagement with the cam.

CHAPTER VIII

DIFFERENTIAL MOTIONS

WHEN a motion is the resultant of or difference between two original motions, it is often referred to as a differential motion. The differential screw is a simple example of a motion of this kind. This is a compound screw from which a movement is derived that is equal to the difference between the movements obtained from each screw. The diagram A, Fig. 1, illustrates the principle. A shaft has two screw threads on it at e and f, respectively, which wind in the same direction but differ in pitch. Screw f passes through a fixed nut and screw e through a nut that is free to move. The motion of the movable nut for each revolution of the screw equals the difference between the pitches of the threads at e and f.

This combination makes it possible to obtain a very slight motion without using a screw having an exceptionally fine pitch and a weak thread. Another form of differential screw is shown at B, which illustrates a stop that enables fine adjustments to be obtained readily. The screw bushing g is threaded externally through some stationary part and is also threaded internally to receive screw h which is free to move axially but cannot turn. Both screws in this case are right-hand, but they vary as to pitch. If bushing g has a pitch of $\frac{1}{32}$ inch or 0.03125 inch and screw h a pitch of $\frac{1}{36}$ inch or 0.02777 inch, one complete turn of g will advance screws h only 0.00348 inch (0.03125 − 0.02777 = 0.00348), because, as bushing g advances $\frac{1}{32}$ inch, it moves screw h back a distance equal to the difference between the pitches of the two threads. By turning the bushing only a fractional part of a turn very small adjustments may be obtained.

Differential Motion of Chinese Windlass. — The Chinese windlass shown by the diagram C, Fig. 1, is another simple example of a differential motion. The hoisting rope is arranged to unwind from one part of a drum or pulley onto another part differing somewhat in diameter. The distance that the load or hook moves for one revolution of the compound hoisting drum is equal to half the difference between the circumferences of the two drum sections.

The well-known differential chain hoist illustrated at D operates on the same general principle as the Chinese windlass. The double sheave a has two chain grooves differing slightly in di-

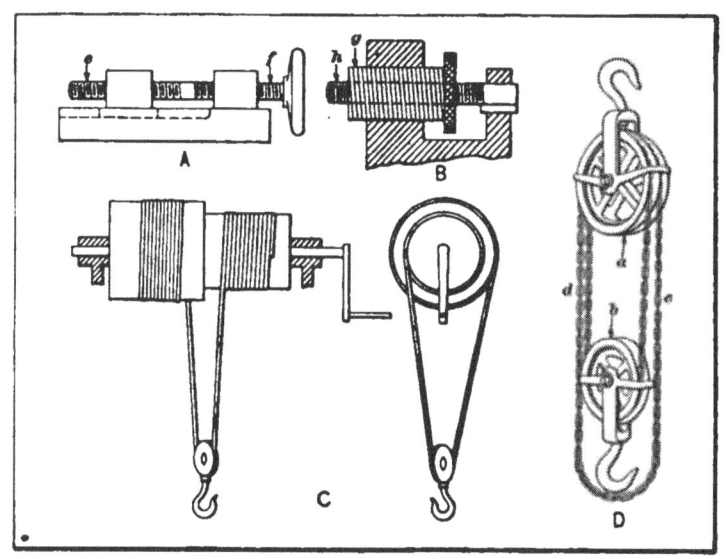

Fig. 1. (A and B) Differential Screws; (C) Chinese Windlass; (D) Differential Hoist

ameter, and an endless chain passes over these grooves and around a single pulley b. This pulley b and the hook attached to it is raised or lowered, because, for a given movement, a greater length of chain passes over the larger part of sheave a than over the smaller part. If the upper sheave is revolved by pulling down on the side d of the chain that leads to the groove of smaller diameter, the loop of chain passing around pulley b will be lengthened, thus lowering the pulley; the opposite result will be obtained by pulling down on chain c which leads up to the larger diameter of the sheave.

Differential Motions from Gearing.— Most differential motions are derived from combinations of bevel or spur gearing. The epicyclic bevel gear train illustrated by diagram A, Fig. 2, is applied to many mechanisms of the differential type, and its action under different conditions should be thoroughly understood. The shaft a has mounted on it two bevel gears b and c and an arm d. The arm is attached to the shaft and carries a pinion e which meshes with each gear and is free to revolve upon the arm. There are several conditions that can exist with a gear train of this kind.

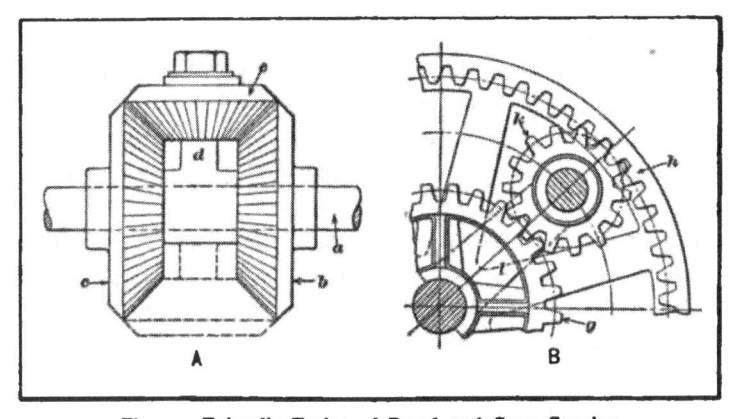

Fig. 2. Epicyclic Trains of Bevel and Spur Gearing

First, assume that gear b is stationary and c loose on the shaft. If the shaft and arm d is revolved, motion will be transmitted from the stationary gear b to gear c, through pinion e, and gear c will make two turns for every one of arm d and in the same direction as the arm. If gear b should rotate instead of being stationary, this motion, combined with that of the arm, would modify the motion of gear c and it would also make a difference whether gear b turned in the same direction as the arm or in an opposite direction.

Second, suppose the preceding conditions are reversed and one of the bevel gears b or c is revolved while the other gear remains stationary, and that arm d carrying the bevel pinion constitutes the driven element. With only one gear revolving, the arm will turn in a direction corresponding to that of the gear and at half its speed. If both gears rotate in the same direction at different speeds, the arm will follow in that direction and with a speed intermediate between the two. If the gears are driven in opposite directions at different speeds, the arm will follow the more rapidly moving gear, and if the speeds are equal, pinion e will revolve upon the arm, but the latter will remain stationary.

Third, assume that arm d remains stationary and gears b and c are loose on the shaft. If gear b is the driver, the pinion e will simply transmit motion to gear c in the opposite direction, the three gears in this case forming a simple train with pinion e acting as the idler. The force tending to rotate arm d will be one-half the force transmitted from gear b to gear c. A practical application of this last principle is found in the Webber differential dynamometer. The arm of this dynamometer which supports the scale pan and weights corresponds to arm d and is pivoted on a shaft carrying two bevel gears. On the arm and meshing with these two bevel gears are bevel pinions and the amount of power transmitted through this train of gearing is measured by the weights in the scale pan. The combination of gearing illustrated by diagram A usually has two or more pinions meshing with the bevel gears. In many cases, there are two pinions located diametrically opposite, as indicated by the full and dotted lines. The addition of other pinions, however, does not affect the action of the gearing.

The diagram B, Fig. 2, shows an arrangement of spur gearing which gives a differential motion. This combination consists of ordinary spur gear g, an internal gear h, and a pinion k. This pinion is free to turn on a stud that is attached to arm l. In the application of this gearing, there are three possible conditions. In the first place, the internal gear h may be stationary, and the gears g and k may revolve. Second, the arm l may be stationary, in which case either the internal gear h or gear g may be the driver. Third, gear g may be stationary and the motion be transmitted in either direction between gear h and arm l. Fig. 3 shows a practical application of this gear combination. In this design, there are two intermediate pinions (corresponding to

206   MECHANICAL MOVEMENTS

k in diagram *B*, Fig. 2) which are mounted on an arm and located diametrically opposite. This arm is keyed to the end of a shaft. The large internal gear is stationary and forms part of a casing enclosing the gears. The central gear is keyed to another shaft which is in line with the shaft carrying the pinion arm. This arrangement is simply used to obtain a reduction of speed. The design is compact, although differential or epicyclic gearing, in general, is inefficient as a transmitter of power. Such gear combinations, however, have certain mechanical advantages, and they are often utilized by designers for a variety of

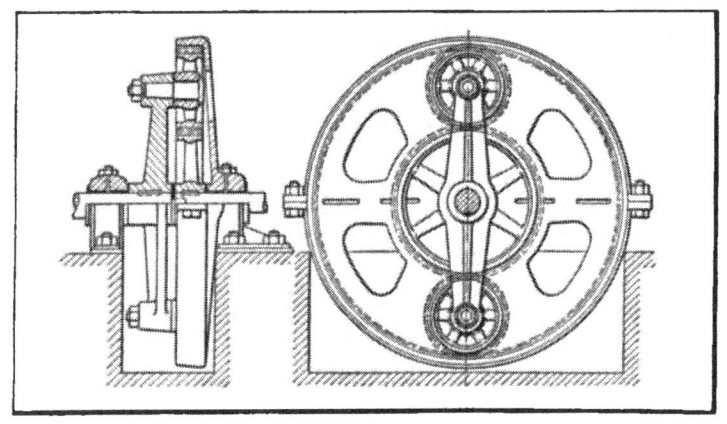

Fig. 3. Epicyclic Gearing for Obtaining Speed Reduction by Differential Motion

purposes as indicated by the different mechanisms to be described.

Compound Differential Gears for Varying Speeds. — The differential speed-changing mechanism shown in Fig. 4 has spur gears and pinions but no internal gear. This is a compound or reverted train and is intended for an automatic screw machine of the heavier class (the Cleveland) in order to provide a slow and powerful movement to the spindle for heavy thread-cutting operations, or for any other heavy work which requires a powerful drive. The gearing is contained within the spindle driving pulleys on the back shaft of the spindle head. There are three pulleys and the slow speed is obtained by shifting the belt to the

DIFFERENTIAL MOTIONS 207

center pulley A, and engaging the sliding clutch B with gear C; as this clutch slides upon a square shaft and cannot revolve, the gear C is held stationary. There are two sets of planetary pinions D and E located diametrically opposite. The pinions on each stud are locked together but they are free to revolve about the stud. Pinions D rotate around the fixed gear C, while pinions E revolve the driven gear F at a slow speed, but with considerable power. The gear F is keyed to the extension of pinion G which meshes directly with the front spindle gear of the machine. When this slow speed is not required, the clutch

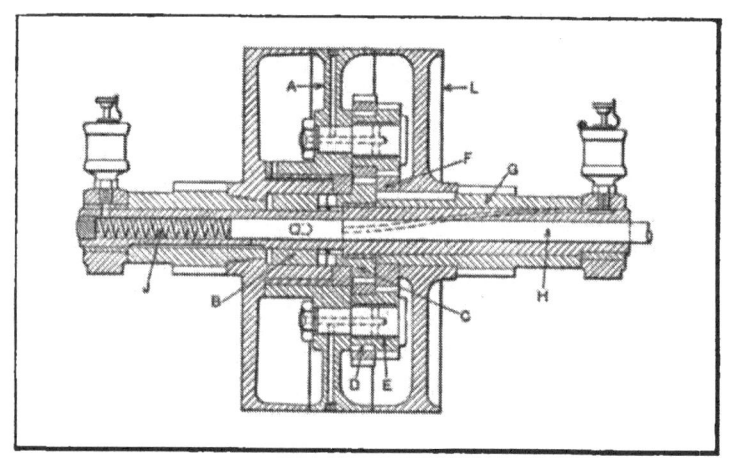

Fig. 4. Compound or Reverted Train of Epicyclic Gearing for Reducing Speed

B is disengaged, so that the entire train of differential gears is free upon the loose center pulley A. Two spring plungers (not shown) attached to pulley A engage the rim of pulley L and cause both pulleys to revolve together when the slow-speed attachment is not engaged, so that the planetary pinions will not revolve upon their studs at this time. The clutch B is shifted by a cam-operated rod H acting in conjunction with a spring J.

With this arrangement of gearing, the differential action and reduction of speed is the result of the difference in the diameters of pinions D and E and their mating gears. When the slow-speed attachment is operating, the larger pinions D roll around the stationary gear C and force gear F to follow slowly in the same direction. This action will be more apparent if that part of the larger pinion D which is in engagement with stationary gear C, at any time, is considered as a lever pivoted at the point where the teeth mesh with the stationary gear. As the pinion D revolves and the imaginary lever swings around its fulcrum, the teeth of the smaller pinion E in contact with gear F force the latter to move in the same direction in which the rolling pinions D and E and pulley A are moving. (See "Reversal of Motion through Epicyclic Gearing," Chapter IV.)

Differential Motion between Screw and Nut. — Variations of movement are sometimes obtained by the differential motion between a revolving screw and a nut which is rotating about the screw at a different speed. One application of this principle is illustrated by the variable-speed mechanism of a milling machine shown in Fig. 5. This mechanism is designed to increase the efficiency of a machine by accelerating the speed of the table when the cutters are not at work. The machine table moves rapidly up to the cutting point, then the speed is reduced while milling and, after the operation is completed, the table is quickly returned to the loading position.

This mechanism is located beneath the machine table C, which is traversed by a screw D, that passes through the plain bearings E, F, and G, mounted upon the base of the machine. The pinion H is confined longitudinally between bearings E and F, and it is splined to screw D, so that the latter must turn with the pinion but is free to slide in a lengthwise direction. The hole through gear I is threaded to fit screw D so that it is practically a nut and gear combined. The auxiliary shaft J supported in bearings K carries two pinions, L and M, which are loosely mounted upon the shaft. This shaft J is rotated continuously in one direction through spiral gears W from the driving shaft V. Within the housings N and O are clutch sleeves which encircle the shaft J. The sleeves are splined to the shaft, but are free to slide upon it, and they may be locked with teeth formed on pinions L and M. These clutches are controlled by levers T and U at the front of the machine which are connected by the

DIFFERENTIAL MOTIONS 209

shafts shown, with the clutch shifting devices at R and Q. The action of the clutches is controlled automatically by adjustable stops located on the front of the machine table.

The clutch connecting with gear L is first engaged by hand lever T. The table then moves forward rapidly (in the direction indicated by arrow A) as gear H revolves screw D and causes it to turn through the gear nut I which is held stationary at this time. Just before the milling cutter begins to act upon the work, lever U strikes a stop, thus engaging the clutch with gear M. The gear nut I is then revolved in the same direction as

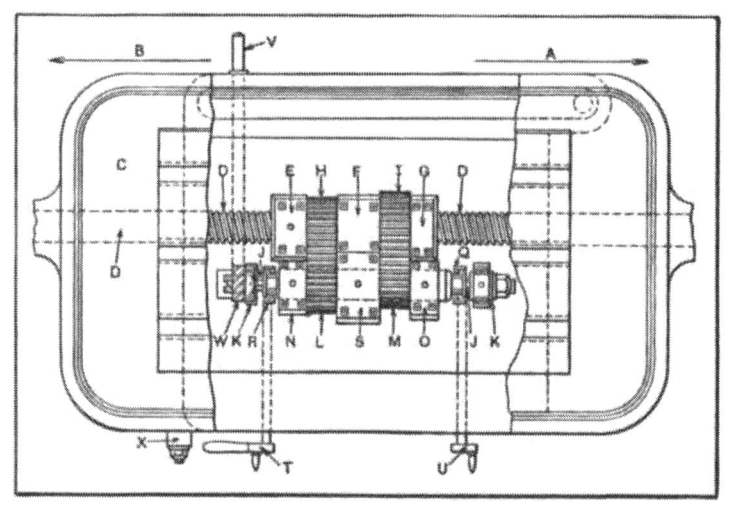

Fig. 5. Variable Feeding Mechanism which is partly controlled by the Differential Movement between a Revolving Screw and Nut

gear H but at a slower speed, so that the forward movement of screw D is reduced, because of the differential action between the screw and nut. Both sets of gears continue to operate while the cut is being taken; when the milling operation is completed, another stop engages lever T, thus stopping the rotation of gears L and H. As the gear nut I continues to revolve about the screw, the movement of the machine table is reversed, since screw D is not rotating. The motion continues in the direction indicated by arrow B until a third stop to the right of lever U trips the latter, thereby stopping gear I and the table movement.

The table is now in position for removing the finished parts and replacing them with others that require milling.

Differential Feeding Mechanism for Revolving Spindle. — The spindle of a horizontal boring, drilling, tapping, and milling machine is given a lengthwise feeding movement by the differential action between the revolving spindle and a revolving nut which engages a helical groove in the spindle. The spindle is driven by a large gear A (see Fig. 6) which connects with the back gearing of the machine. The hub of this gear has two keys

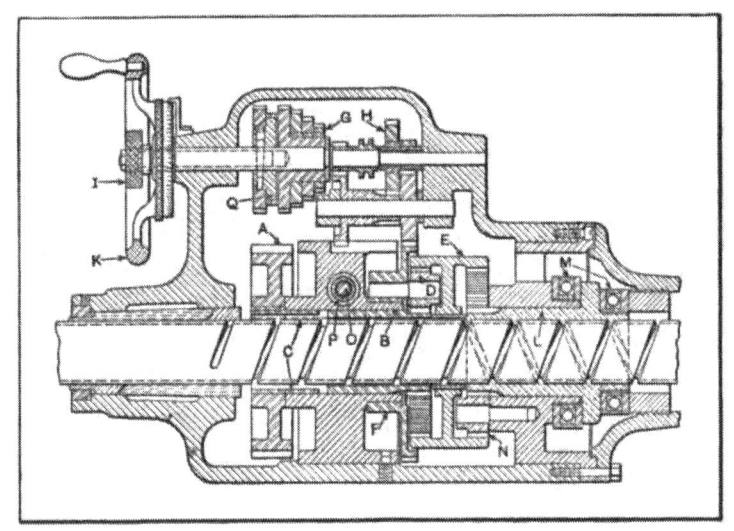

Fig. 6. Mechanism of Differential Type for Feeding Spindle in Lengthwise Direction

which engage the splined spindle. The sleeve B on which gear A is mounted has gear teeth cut in one end which mesh with three planetary pinions D that engage one side of the double internal gear E. The other side of this internal gear meshes with pinions N. These pinions, in turn, mesh with gear teeth formed on the rotary nut L which engages directly with a spiral or helical groove cut in the spindle. A flange on this nut rotates between large ball thrust bearings, as shown, in order to take the end thrust in either direction.

When nut L rotates at the same speed as the spindle, the latter does not move in a lengthwise direction, but, by revolving nut L either faster or slower than the spindle, a feeding movement in one direction or the other is obtained. The rotation of nut L is regulated by the gearing at G. When the feeding movement is stopped, gear F, which carries the planetary pinions D, does not revolve and nut L rotates with the spindle, which, therefore, remains in the same longitudinal position. When gear F which is connected indirectly with the feed change-gears G is revolved by these gears, the nut L is revolved independently of the spindle and at a different rate of speed.

Application of Floating Lever Principle. — What are known as "floating" or "differential" levers are utilized in some forms of mechanisms to control, by the application of a small amount of power or force, a much greater force such as would be required for moving or shifting heavy parts. Floating levers are commonly applied to mechanisms controlling the action of parts that require adjustment or changes of position at intervals varying according to the function of the apparatus subject to control. The initial movement or force may be derived from a hand-operated lever or wheel, and the purpose of the floating lever is to so control the source of power that whatever part is to be shifted or adjusted will follow the hand-controlled movements practically the same as though there were a direct mechanical connection. A floating lever is so called because it is not attached to fixed pivots and does not have a stationary fulcrum, but is free to move bodily, or to "float" within certain limits and in accordance with the relative forces acting upon the different connections.

Fig. 7 illustrates one application of the floating lever. The diagram at the left represents an auxiliary braking apparatus for a large hoist. The brake shoe A is applied to the brake drum B whenever the dead weight C rests upon the lever D. This lever is connected by rod E with a cross-head attached to the upper end of a piston rod extending through the oil cylinder F and into the steam cylinder G. When steam is admitted beneath the piston in cylinder G by opening a valve at H, the weight is raised and the brake released, and, if for any reason the steam pressure should be suddenly reduced, weight C would fall and the brake be applied automatically. The movements of the piston in cylinder G and, consequently, of weight C are controlled by hand lever L through floating lever J, in such a manner that the weight rises and falls, as the lever is shifted, practically the same as though the force for moving the weight were derived directly from the lever by means of a rigid mechanical connection.

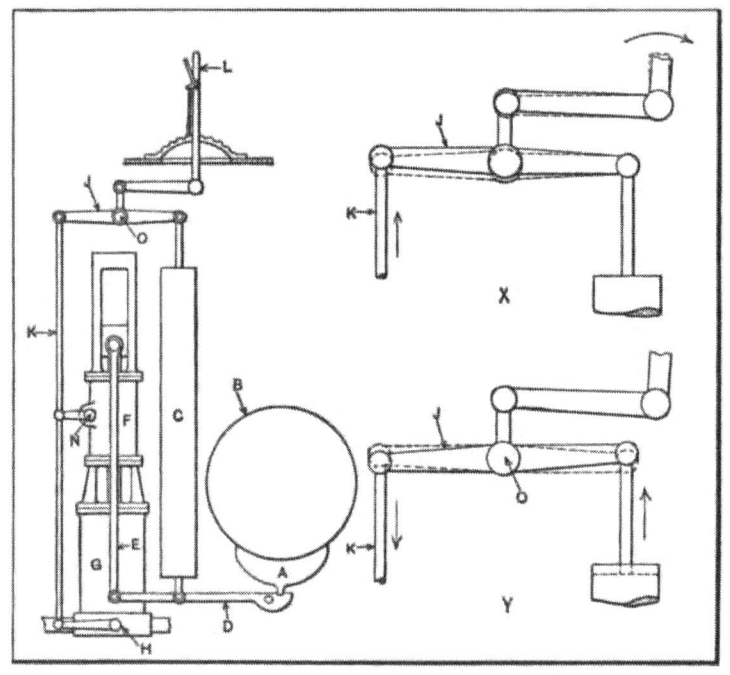

Fig. 7. Diagrams illustrating Application and Action of Floating Lever

The action of the mechanism is as follows: If the weight is down and the brake applied, and lever L is moved from its central position to the right, the left-hand end of lever J will be raised (as shown on an exaggerated scale by diagram X), thus lifting rod K and opening valve H; this valve has no lap, so that any movement of the lever admits steam to the cylinder. As soon as the piston begins to rise, the right-hand end of lever J also rises (see diagram Y) and turning about pivot O immediately begins to close the steam valve. If the lever L is moved through a small arc, the valve is closed quickly and the weight only rises a short distance; on the contrary, if the lever is thrown over to the extreme position, the piston and weight must move upward a proportionately greater distance before the valve is closed. If the lever, after being thrown to the right, is moved towards the left, valve H opens the exhaust port and the weight descends; as soon as it begins to move downward, the left-hand end of the floating lever is raised, which tends to close the exhaust port and prevent further downward motion.

An apparatus of this kind responds so quickly to adjustment that the weight follows the motion of the hand lever almost instantaneously and the end of the floating lever connected to rod K has very little actual movement. The oil cylinder F is used to stabilize the action of the weight and prevent overtravel which would occur if there were only the cushioning effect of steam. The by-pass valve N controls the flow of oil from one end of the cylinder to the other as the piston moves up or down, so that the motion of the weight ceases as soon as the steam and oil valves are closed.

Controlling Mechanism of Steering Gear. — The practical effect of the floating lever previously described for controlling the movements of power-driven apparatus may be obtained by other mechanical devices, examples of which are found on steamships for controlling the action of the steering engines. Engines used for this purpose are commonly equipped with a control valve which distributes steam to the engine valves. The latter are generally of the hollow piston type and are arranged to receive steam either at the ends or in the center, the exhaust varying accordingly. The admission of steam either to the ends or in the center is governed by the position of the control valve. For instance, if the control valve is moved in one direction, steam may be admitted to the ends of the engine valves and be exhausted in the center. If the control valve were moved in the opposite direction, this order would be reversed and also the direction in which the engine rotates; therefore, each engine valve requires but one eccentric, the control valve acting as a reversing gear. The mechanism which operates this control valve is so designed that, when the engine is set in motion to move the rudder either to port or starboard, this same motion is utilized to shift the control valve in such a way that the movement of the rudder coincides with the motion of the steering wheel. While the floating lever has been used in connection with this controlling mechanism, the common form of control depends upon the action (which is often differential) either of gearing or of a screw and nut.

With the arrangement illustrated at A, Fig. 8, the control valve of a steering engine is governed by the action of a screw that is operated by the steering wheel, and a nut that is revolved by

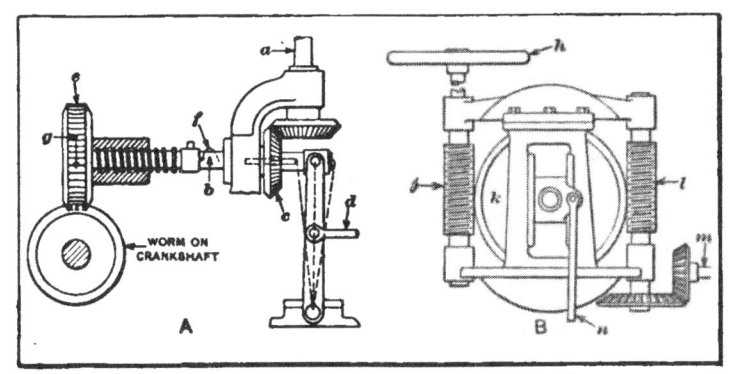

Fig. 8. (A) Controlling Device for Steering Gear; (B) Mechanism used as Substitute for a Floating Lever

the engine. The shaft a is connected with the steering wheel and transmits rotary motion to screw b which is splined to, and free to slide through, gear c. The rod d serves to operate the control valve of the steering engine. Any rotary motion of shaft a moves screw b in a lengthwise direction in or out of the nut on worm-wheel e, unless this nut is revolving at the same speed as the screw. The action of the mechanism is as follows: If worm-wheel e, which meshes with a worm on the steering engine crankshaft, is stationary, the rotation of shaft a will turn screw b in or out of the nut and shift the control valve, thus starting the engine in one direction or the other, depending upon which way the control valve was moved. As soon as the engine starts, worm-wheel e and the nut begin to revolve, which tends

DIFFERENTIAL MOTIONS 215

to move the screw and control lever in the opposite direction. Suppose screw *b* were revolved in the direction shown by the arrow *f*, thus moving the screw and control lever to the right; then, as the engine starts, worm-wheel *e* and the nut revolve as shown by the arrow *g*. Now as soon as the rotation of shaft *a* and screw *b* is stopped or is reduced until the speed of rotation is less than that of worm-wheel *e*, the screw is drawn back into the nut and the control valve is closed. If the steering wheel and screw *b* were turned slightly and then stopped entirely, the rudder would only be moved a corresponding amount, because the

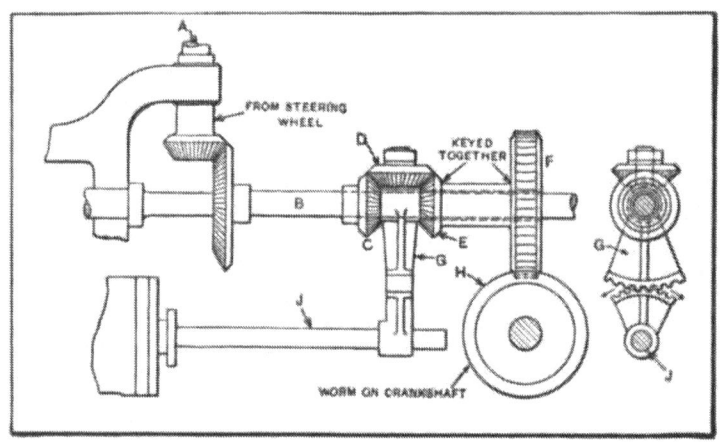

Fig. 9. Steering Gear Control Mechanism having Differential Bevel Gearing

control valve would soon be shifted, by the action of worm-wheel *e*, to the closed position. Steering engines, in general, are equipped with some form of stopping device which automatically limits the movement of the rudder and prevents overtravel and damaging the mechanism.

Control Mechanism having Differential Bevel Gearing. — The steering gear controlling mechanism illustrated in Fig. 9 operates on the same general principle as the design previously described, although the construction is quite different. The control valve, in this case, operates with a rotary motion, instead of moving in a lengthwise direction. Shaft *A* is revolved by the steering wheel and transmits rotary motion to shaft *B* through the gearing shown. The differential action for regulating the position of the control valve is obtained by means of three gears C, D, and E. Gear C is keyed to shaft B, and gear E on the extended hub of worm-wheel F is free to revolve about shaft B. Gear D interposed between gears C and E is mounted upon a segment gear G which engages another segment gear on the control valve spindle J. If shaft B is revolved while gear E and the worm-wheel are stationary, gear D rolls around between the gears and, through the segment gear, turns the control valve, thus starting the steering engine and with it the worm H on the crankshaft which drives worm-wheel F and gear E. As soon as the rotation of shaft B is stopped, gear E which has been revolving in the opposite direction to that of C rolls gear D back to the top position, thus closing the control valve and stopping the engine. If gears C and E are revolved at the same speed, gear D simply rotates between them and the control valve remains open. If the speed of gear E exceeds that of C, the valve begins to close, and if C revolves faster than E, the valve is opened wider and the engine continues to operate.

Rolling Worm-wheel Type of Controlling Mechanism. — The ingenious substitute for the floating lever illustrated at B in Fig. 8 depends for its action upon a worm-wheel which is interposed between two worms. The handwheel h controls the rotation of worm j, which meshes with the worm-wheel k. The worm l on the opposite side of the worm-wheel is rotated by whatever apparatus is to be controlled. The shaft of the worm-wheel is journaled in boxes which are free to slide up and down the vertical slides in the framework shown. Any vertical displacement of the worm-wheel is transmitted to rod n which operates the valve, clutch, or other mechanical device used for starting, stopping, and reversing the driving machinery. Assume that the mechanism is at rest with the worm-wheel midway between its upper and lower positions in the vertical slides of the housing. When the handwheel h is revolved in a direction corresponding to the motion desired, worm j revolves, and worm l is stationary, since the mechanism is not yet in motion; therefore, the rotation of the handwheel has the effect of rolling the worm-wheel k between the two worms either up or down, depending upon the direction in which the handwheel is rotated. Any vertical displacement of the worm-wheel will, through the medium of controlling rod n, start the power-driven machinery. This motion is immediately transmitted to shaft m and worm l which acts to move worm-wheel k in the opposite direction vertically, provided worm j is stationary or is revolving slower than l. The result is that the power-driven member is moved or adjusted proportionately to the rotation of the handwheel h. The handwheel, for instance, might be turned to a position corresponding to a certain required adjustment, which would then be made automatically. This controlling device operates on the same general principle as the steering gear controlling mechanisms previously described.

Differential Governors for Water Turbines. — Many of the automatic governing devices used for controlling the speed of water turbines have a differential action. A simple form of governor is illustrated in principle by the diagram A, Fig. 10. An auxiliary water motor drives the bevel gear a by belt d, and bevel gear c is driven by belt e from a shaft operated by the turbine to be governed. Both gears a and c are loose on their shaft, but the arm n which carries the bevel pinions b is fast to the shaft. On one end of the shaft there is a pinion f which meshes with a rack g that operates the turbine gate, and thus controls the flow of water to the turbine. As the auxiliary motor has no work to do except to drive part of the governing mechanism, it runs at practically a constant speed; the variations due to the rise or fall of the water level are so small a percentage of the total head of water that the speed of this motor is little affected. It will be assumed then that the speed of gear a is practically uniform. The speed of gear c, however, changes with an increase or decrease of the load upon the turbine, and, as gear c runs faster or slower than gear a, the arm n follows it around one way or the other and thus opens or closes the turbine gate.

The governor shown at B also has a differential action, but it is controlled by centrifugal force acting on a fly-ball governing device. The governor is operated by a belt a connected with the turbine. This belt passes around idler pulleys and over the wide-faced pulleys b and c. These pulleys, through bevel gearing, drive the differential gearing composed of gears d, e, and f. Gears d and e are loose from their shafts and pinion f is pivoted on an arm that is keyed to the shaft. Gear e is connected by the gearing shown with a centrifugal governing device at g. The belt pulley b is conical and the diameter at the center is the same as that at pulley c. When the turbine is operating at normal speed, the belt is at the center of the conical pulley b and, con-

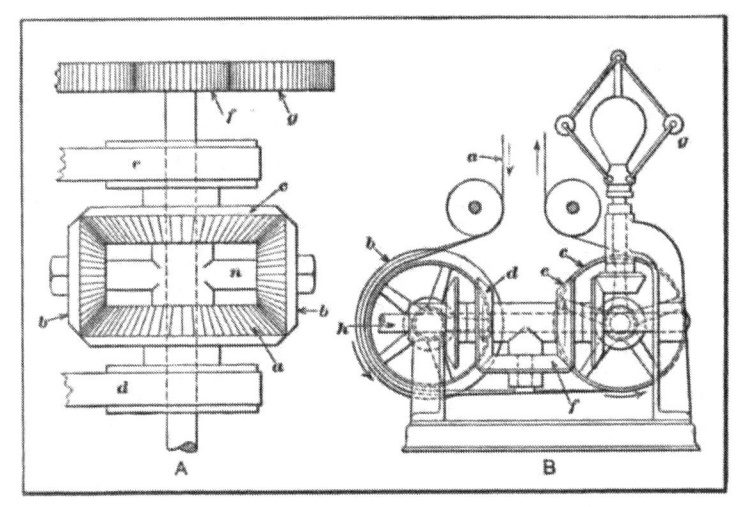

Fig. 10. Differential Governing Devices for Water Turbines

sequently, gears d and e revolve at the same rate of speed in opposite directions. The result is that the arm carrying pinion f remains stationary. If the turbine begins to run too fast, the balls at g move outward under the action of centrifugal force, and belt a is shifted by a mechanism not shown to a smaller part of the conical pulley b. The resulting increase in the speed of gear d causes the arm carrying pinion f and the shaft h to which it is attached to revolve in the same direction as gear d. As a result of this movement, the turbine gate is lowered by means of gearing not shown, and the speed of the turbine wheel is reduced. If the turbine should begin to run more slowly than the normal

DIFFERENTIAL MOTIONS 219

speed, the shifting of belt *a* by governor *g* would cause gear *d* also to revolve slower, thus turning shaft *h* in the opposite direction and raising the gate.

Another modification of the differential governor is shown by the diagram, Fig. 11. This particular type of governor was installed in one of the large power plants at Niagara Falls. It is equipped with two sets of epicyclic gearing. The gears *A* and *B* are free to turn on the shaft, but may be retarded by brake bands at *E* and *F*. The inner gears *C* and *D* are driven by belts connected in some way with the turbine. One of these belts is open and the other crossed, so that the gears revolve in opposite

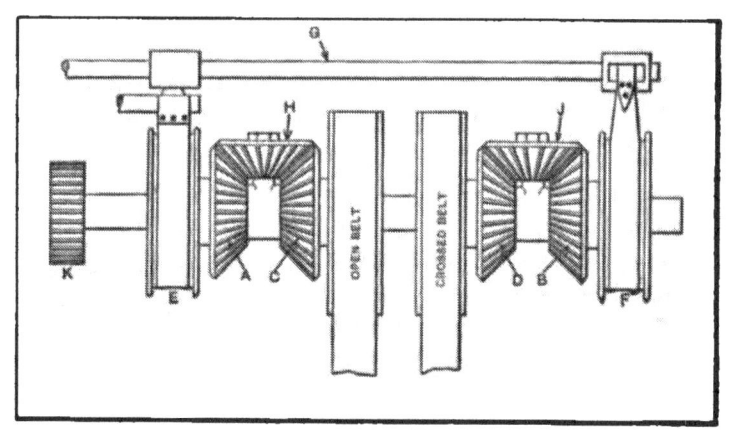

Fig. 11. Differential Governing Mechanism controlled by Ratchet-operated Brakes

directions. The brake bands are so arranged that, when one tightens, the other loosens its grip on the brake drum. Both of these bands are operated by a shaft *G* and the tightening of the bands is effected by a double ratchet mechanism (not shown) having two pawls. One pawl rotates shaft *G* in one direction and the other in the opposite direction. When the speed increases or decreases, one pawl or the other is operated by a fly-ball governor driven from the turbine. As the result of this motion of the pawl, one band is tightened and the other released, so that one of the gears *A* or *B* is held with a greater or less degree of friction or is prevented from turning altogether, while the other one runs free. If gear *A* is held by the brake, the arm carrying pinion *H* will begin to turn in the same direction in which gear *C* turns, whereas, if gear *B* remains stationary, the arm carrying pinion *J* will follow gear *D*; consequently, the pinion *K* on the end of the shaft will by means of a rack raise or lower the turbine gate. This governor depends for its sensitiveness upon the fly-ball governing device, and for its power upon the open and cross-belts which may be proportioned to transmit any required amount of power.

Differential Gearing of Automobiles. — One of the important applications of differential gearing, at the present time, is found on automobiles. The object of transmitting motion from the engine to the rear axle through differential gearing is to give an equal tractive force to each of the two wheels and, at the same time, permit either of them to run ahead or lag behind the other as may be required in rounding curves or riding over obstructions. The axle is not formed of one solid piece, but motion is transmitted to the right- and left-hand wheels by means of separate sections, the inner ends of which are attached to different members of the differential mechanism. The principle of this mechanical movement will be understood by referring to Fig. 12. Two general types of differential gearing are shown in this illustration. The design at the left is equipped with bevel gearing and is the type generally employed. The propeller shaft extends from the transmission case where speed changes are obtained, and revolves the bevel pinion *N* which drives the large bevel gear *M*. This gear *M* and the casing *O* to which it is bolted revolve freely on the hub of gears *F* and *E*. Attached to the casing *O* are radial pivots on which revolve loosely bevel pinions *D*. These pinions engage the bevel gears *E* and *F* which are connected with the right- and left-hand axles or shafts *T*.

Under ordinary conditions, the rotation of gear *M* causes gears *F* and *E* to both revolve at the same rate of speed, since the connecting pinions *D* are moved around with the casing *O*, but do not revolve. To illustrate the action, assume that the wheels are jacked up and are simply revolving in one position;

then, if one wheel is held from turning so that, say, gear E is stationary, the rotation of bevel gear M will roll pinions D around on gear E, with the result that gear F will revolve twice as fast as when gear E is revolving with it and at the same speed. On the other hand, if the opposite wheel and gear F were held stationary, the gear E would run at twice its normal speed; moreover, if the speed of either of the gears is reduced, the other side is speeded up a corresponding amount.

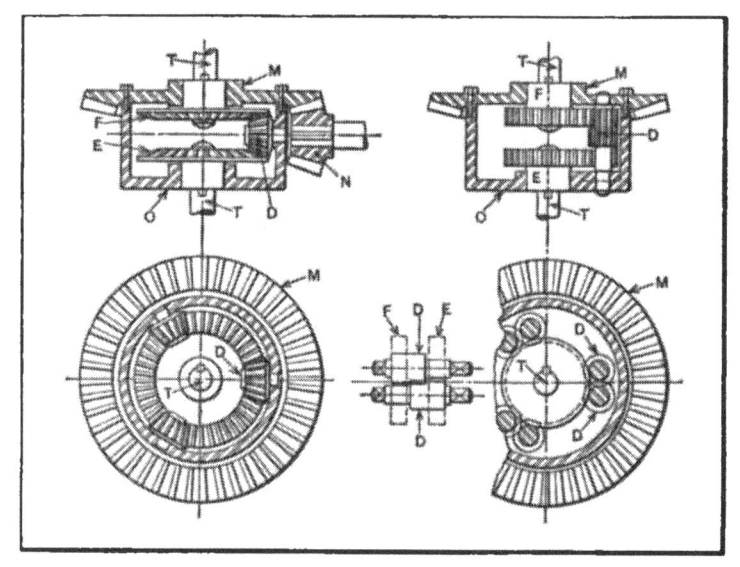

Fig. 12. Automobile Differential Gearing of Bevel and Spur Gear Types

While the bevel form of differential gearing is largely used, some designs have been equipped with spur gearing. The diagram at the right in Fig. 12 illustrates the difference in arrangement. Each of the bevel pinions is replaced by a pair of spur pinions D connecting with each other and with spur gears E and F. These pinions do not extend over as far as the opposite gear so that connection between the gears F and E is from one pinion to the other, as shown by the detailed view. The action of this form of differential is identical with the bevel pinion type previously described. The differential gearing is ordinarily incorporated in the rear axle, except when power is transmitted to the wheel by means of side chains, in which case the differential is in the countershaft.

Speed Regulation through Differential Gearing. — When the speed of a driven part is governed by drives from two different sources, differential gearing may be used to combine these drives and allow any variations in speed that may be required. An application of this kind is found on the fly frames used in cotton spinning for drawing out or attenuating the untwisted fiber or

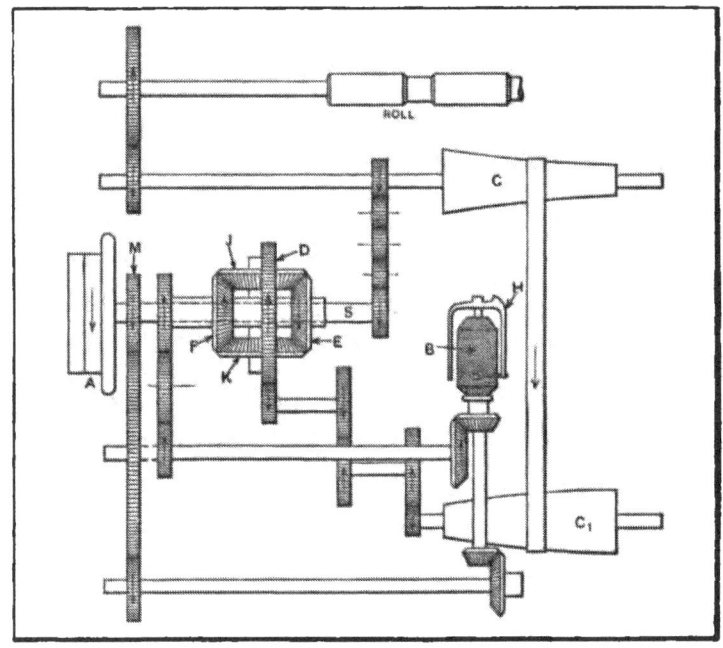

Fig. 13. Diagram of Mechanism having Differential Gearing through which Speed Changes are Transmitted

roving, by passing it between different pairs of rolls which move, successively, at increased speeds. After the fiber is attenuated, it is wound on bobbins and at the same time given a slight twist. The diagram, Fig. 13, represents a mechanism for controlling the speed of the bobbins, one of which is indicated at B. This bobbin receives its motion through a train of gearing connecting with the main shaft of the machine and also through another combination of gearing which is driven by a pair of cone-pulleys for decreasing the speed of the bobbin as the roving is wound upon it and the diameter increases.

The main shaft is driven by pulley A and motion is transmitted through shaft S and the gearing shown to the cone C and the rolls, one of which is indicated at the upper part of the diagram. The cone C and the rolls move at a constant speed, and the roving is delivered by the rolls at a uniform rate of speed. On the shaft S there is a bevel gear E, which is one of the gears of an epicyclic train that is commonly known as the "differential motion." The large gear D corresponds to the arm of the gear train, since it carries the two intermediate bevel pinions J and K. This gear D is driven from the lower cone C_1 which is connected by belt with the upper cone. Bevel gear F which meshes with the pinions carried by gear D is loose on shaft S and is connected through gearing with the bobbin B. With this arrangement, the speed of the bobbin depends first upon the speed of bevel gear E, which is constant, and also upon the speed of gear D, which may be varied by shifting the position of the belt on the cones. Any variations in the relative speeds of gears D and E will produce twice the variations in the speed of the bobbin.

The roving is wound on the bobbin in successive helical layers by means of the flyer H driven at a constant speed by gear M on shaft S. The roving passes from the rolls to the flyer, and entering the top of its hollow spindle, is threaded down through one arm of the flyer and then wound on the bobbin. The flyer and bobbin revolve in the same direction, but the bobbin has a higher velocity and, for that reason, draws the roving from the flyer and winds it in successive layers as the bobbin travels up and down, so as to cover its entire surface. As each successive layer is added, the bobbin increases in diameter, and its speed relative to that of the flyer must be decreased in order to prevent breaking the roving. This change of speed is transmitted to the bobbin through the differential gearing referred to by shifting the belt on the cone-pulleys.

Differential Gear and Cam Combination. — The differential gear and cam combination described in the following is used on fly-frames in conjunction with the same general class of mechanism illustrated by the diagram, Fig. 13. This mechanism differs from the differential ordinarily used in that it has no epicyclic train of gearing. As previously explained, a differential motion is employed in connection with a shifting belt and cone-pulleys for changing the speed of the bobbins. The differential action is obtained, in this case, by means of a crown gear A (Fig. 14) which is attached to the main driving shaft B; the crown gear C secured to sleeve E, which carries the bobbin driving gear F, and the double crown gear D, which is mounted on a spherical seat and engages gears A and C at points diametrically opposite. This double crown gear operates in an oblique position, so that a small part of the gear meshes with gear A

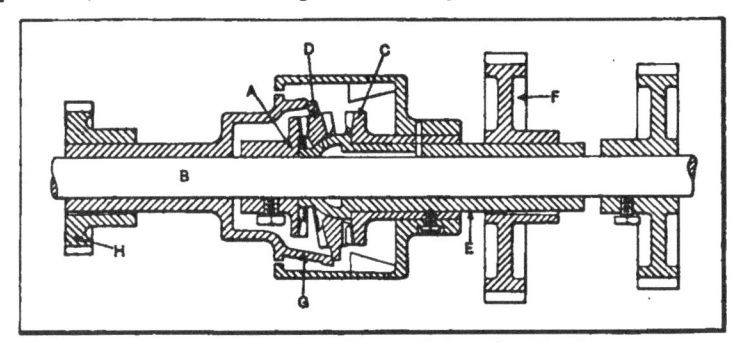

Fig. 14. Differential Gear and Cam Combination

on one side and a small part on the other side meshes with gear C. The spherical bearing allows the intermediate crown gear D to swivel in any direction, and it is held in position by a cam surface on the edge of sleeve G. The gear C has the same number of teeth as the intermediate gear D, but gear A has a somewhat smaller number of teeth.

The differential action is obtained by the relative motions between gear A and cam G. This cam is driven from the lower belt-cone of the machine which is connected with gear H. If cam G were revolving at the same speed as gear A, the same teeth on gears A and D would remain in contact and the entire gear combination would act practically the same as a clutch. As soon as the speed of the cam differs from that of gear A, the position of intermediate gear D is changed so that different teeth are successively engaged. As the result of this differential action, the speed transmitted to gear C is either increased or decreased. The extent of the differential motion depends upon the difference between the speeds of gear A and cam G. As this difference diminishes, the speed of gears D and C increases; inversely, as the speed of cam G is reduced, the speed of gear C is also reduced, since the motion from gear A is lost as the result of differential action. The advantages claimed for this mechanism are quiet operation and reduction of friction.

Differential Mechanism of Gear-cutting Machine. — On a certain kind of gear-cutting machine, a differential mechanism is employed so that when cutting spiral gears the rotary motion

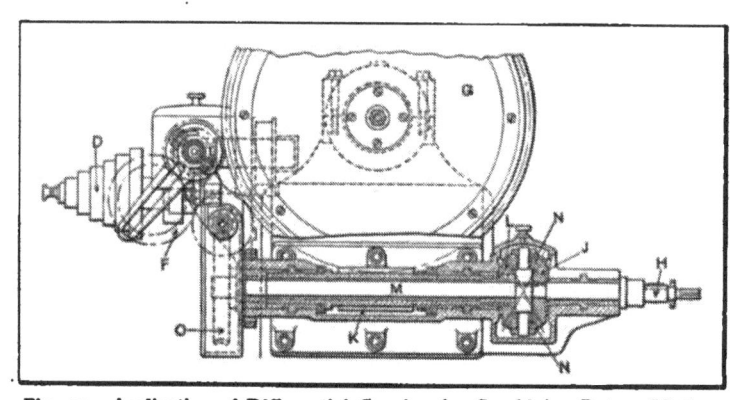

Fig. 15. Application of Differential Gearing for Combining Rotary Motions

for generating helical teeth will be combined with the rotary motion for indexing the work, for cutting successive teeth. This machine operates on the same general principle as a universal milling machine when the latter is used for cutting spiral gears. The mechanism, however, for generating the helical teeth and indexing the work form integral parts of the machine. The screw which feeds the cutter-slide along the horizontal bed of the machine is driven from cone-pulley D (see Fig. 15) through connecting shafts and gears. This cone-pulley is also connected with change gearing F which transmits motion to the indexing worm K for revolving wheel G and the work at a rate suitable for generating the required helix angle. These change-gears

226   MECHANICAL MOVEMENTS

F serve the same purpose as those used on a universal milling machine for connecting the spiral head with the table feed-screw. The worm-wheel *G* is not only used for rotating the work in order to generate the helix, but for indexing as well. The way these two motions are imparted to wheel *G* without interfering with each other will now be explained.

The change-gears for controlling the indexing movement connect at *H* with a shaft leading to the differential or epicyclic gearing, consisting of bevel gears *J* and *L* with intermediate pinions *N*. Bevel gear *J* is attached to the shaft connecting with the change-gears at *H*, whereas the opposite bevel gear *L*

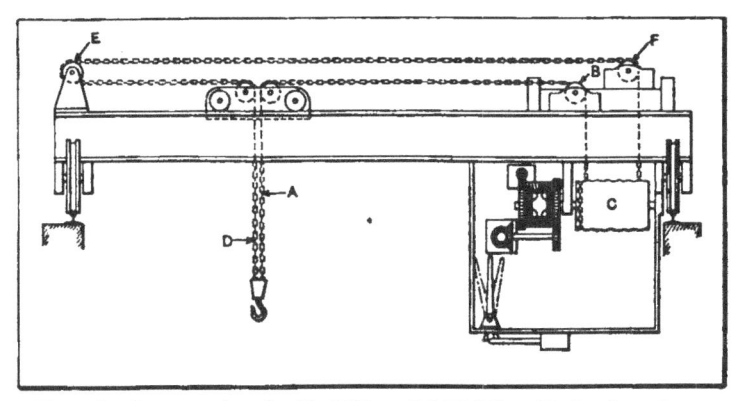

Fig. 16. Crane equipped with Differential Hoisting Mechanism shown Diagrammatically in Fig. 17

is attached to a hollow sleeve upon which worm *K* is mounted. The bevel pinions *N* are carried by an arm attached to shaft *M*. This shaft *M* is driven by worm-wheel *O* connecting with the cutter-slide through change-gears *F*. The action of this differential mechanism or "jack-in-the-box" is such that, if shaft *M* is stationary, the change-gears at *H* may be operated for indexing, motion being transmitted from gear *J* to *L* through pinions *N* as idlers, thus revolving worm *K*. On the other hand, if the indexing mechanism is stationary and the cutter-slide feeding, the movement thus imparted to shaft *M* may be transmitted to worm *K* as pinions *N* roll around the stationary bevel gear *J* and impart motion to gear *L*. As will be seen, it would be possible with this mechanism to index the work and rotate it for generating helical teeth independently. The two motions can also be operated together or combined without interference. The change-gears at H are connected through a one-revolution friction trip with the main driving shaft. As the cutter feeds across the gear blank, a helical groove is generated by the rotary motion derived from change-gears F, shaft M, the differential gearing, and worm K. After a tooth groove is finished, the cutter is dropped down to clear the work and returned for milling another tooth groove. The indexing mechanism is then tripped by hand and the work is rotated sufficiently

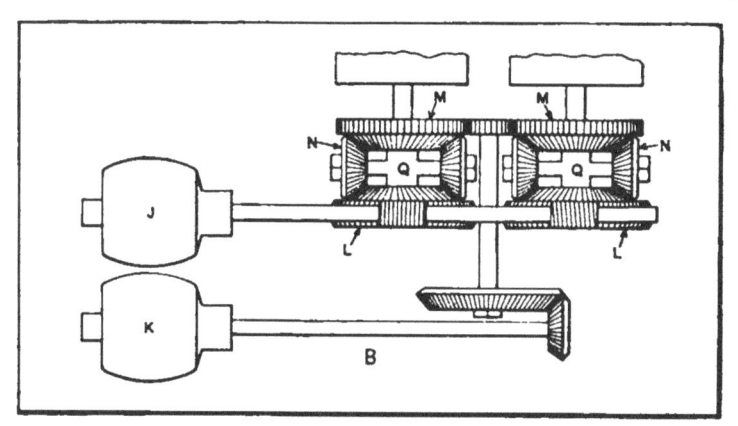

Fig. 17. Differential Hoisting Mechanism

for the next successive tooth by the change-gears at H acting through the differential gearing and worm K.

Differential Hoisting Mechanism. — An ingenious method of utilizing differential action to vary the speed of a hoisting mechanism is illustrated by the diagram, Fig. 16, which represents the crane to which this mechanism is applied. There are two chains attached to the crane hook. One of these chains A passes over a pulley on the trolley and over pulley B to the winding drum C. The other chain D passes upward over its trolley pulley to the left, and over pulley E to pulley F, and then down to a drum located back of drum C. These chains may be wound upon their respective drums either in opposite directions or in the same direction, and at varying rates of speed. If both drums are rotated in opposite directions at the same speed, the effect will be to raise or lower the hoisting hook, whereas, if the drums rotate in the same direction and at equal speed, the chain will be taken in by one and given off by the other, thus causing the hook and its load to be carried horizontally without raising or lowering it. Any difference in the speed of the two drums when moving either in the same or opposite directions will evidently cause the hook to move both vertically and horizontally at the same time.

The mechanism for operating the two hoisting drums is illustrated diagrammatically in Fig. 17. There are two electric motors J and K. Motor J drives the worm-wheels L in opposite directions and also the attached bevel gears. The other motor K drives the spur gears M and the upper bevel gears. The intermediate pinions N between the bevel gears revolve on arms Q which are keyed to the shafts of their respective drums. The bevel gears with which the pinions mesh are loose on their shafts. With this arrangement, if motor K is stationary, motor J will drive the drums in opposite directions and raise or lower the hook as previously explained. On the other hand, with motor J

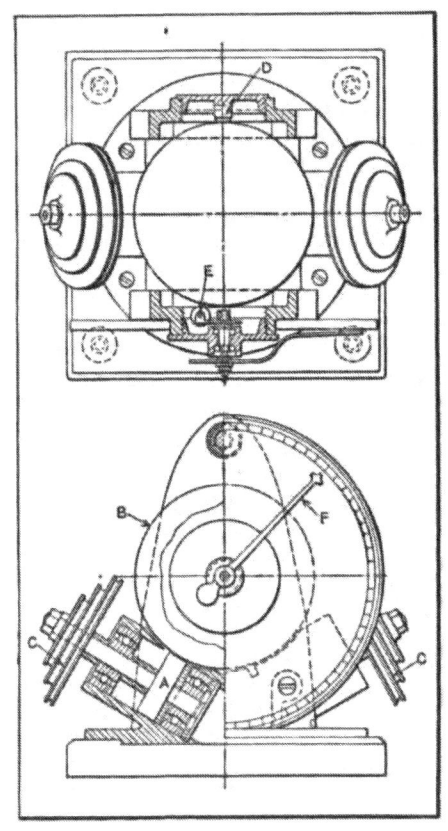

Fig. 18. Differential Speed Indicator

stationary, motor K will operate the drums in the same direction and move the crane hook horizontally. As these motors may be reversed or operated together at varying speeds, any desired combination of movements and speeds for the hook and its load may be obtained.

Differential Speed Indicator. — A sensitive speed-indicating device which shows variations of speed between two rotating parts is shown, partly in section, in Fig. 18. This indicator operates on the differential principle. It is equipped with two cylindrical rollers; one roller is shown at A and the other is located in a similar position on the opposite side of the vertical center line. The axes of the roller shafts are in the same vertical plane, and on the ends of these shafts are mounted belt pulleys C. These pulleys are connected with the shafts the relative speeds of which are to be compared. Each roller A is in contact with a spherical steel ball B three inches in diameter. The ball is held in position by a small stop D at the rear and by a small roller E at the front. This roller is mounted on an arm fixed to a spindle which is free to rotate and to the outer end of which is attached the pointer F. When both the supporting rollers A are driven at the same speed and in the same direction, the spherical ball will rotate about a transverse horizontal axis and will carry the wheel E vertically up or down, as the case may be. The direction of movement will be indicated by the pointer F.

If either of the supporting rollers runs faster than the other, the ball will rotate about some inclined axis and wheel E will naturally turn so that its axis is parallel to that about which the sphere rotates. This instrument is said to be very sensitive as an indicator of speed variations. For instance, it is claimed that a difference in the speed of the rollers due to a variation of 0.001 inch in the diameter of driving pulleys having a nominal diameter of $2\frac{1}{2}$ inches can be detected. While this degree of sensitiveness may be obtained, it would seem preferable to transmit the motion from the driving shaft by some positive drive instead of by belts, inasmuch as any slipping of a belt would affect the action of the indicator.

CHAPTER IX

CLUTCHES AND TRIPPING MECHANISMS

THE different devices used for controlling motion which is transmitted by various kinds of mechanism may either be manually or automatically operated, and be adjustable for varying the time of disengagement, or non-adjustable so that the tripping action occurs at the same point in the cycle of operations. Tripping and disengaging devices also vary in that some operate periodically or at regular intervals, whereas others act once and then must be re-set by hand preparatory to another disengagement. The application of disengaging mechanisms varies greatly. With some classes of machinery, an automatic trip of some form is used to stop the machine completely after it has performed a certain operation or cycle of movements. On many machine tools, trips are used to disconnect a feeding movement at a predetermined point, not only to prevent the tool from feeding too far, but to make it unnecessary for the operator to watch the machine constantly, in order to avoid spoiling work. (When a feeding motion must be disconnected at a certain point within close limits, it is common practice to use some form of positive stop for locating a slide or carriage after the feeding movement has been discontinued by a trip acting through suitable mechanism.) The function of some tripping devices is to safeguard the mechanism by stopping either the entire machine or a part of it, in case there is an unusual resistance to motion, which might subject the machine to injurious strains.

The three mechanical methods of arresting motion which are most commonly employed are by means of clutches, by shifting belts, and by the disengagement of gearing. When the tripping action is automatic, some design of clutch is generally used to disconnect the driven member from the driver or source of power.

The action of the clutch is controlled in various ways. Shifting belts are not ordinarily applied to machines as a part of the regular mechanism, but are very generally used to control the starting or stopping of an entire machine; clutches are also used extensively for this purpose. Gearing which is engaged or disengaged to start or stop a driven member is used in some cases. Feeding mechanisms of some types have a worm-wheel driven by a worm which is dropped out of mesh when the feeding action is discontinued. The method of controlling motion may depend upon the speed of the driving and driven members, and the necessity of eliminating shocks in starting, or upon some other factor, such as the inertia of the driven part or the frequency with which starting and stopping is required.

In considering some of the more common forms of mechanical devices of the class used for starting and stopping, the types of mechanisms employed to disconnect driving and driven members, and also the means of governing the time at which disengagement takes place when such engagement is automatically controlled, will be dealt with. As various tripping devices are used in conjunction with reversing mechanisms to change the direction of motion, instead of stopping it entirely, the chapter on "Reversing Mechanisms" shows additional applications of automatic tripping appliances.

Controlling Motion by Means of Clutches. — A clutch is a form of coupling which is designed to connect or disconnect a driving or driven member for starting or stopping the driven part. A clutch consists principally of two main sections which are engaged or disengaged either at will by a hand-operated controlling device, or automatically by the action of some power-driven mechanical apparatus, such as a cam connected by suitable means with the shifting clutch member. There are several distinct types of clutches which are made in a great variety of designs. The common types of clutches may be divided into two general classes; namely, (1) those having teeth which interlock, or positive clutches, and (2), those which transmit motion from the driving to the driven part of the clutch by frictional contact. No attempt will be made to describe all classes, but rather to illustrate some of the more common types and include a few special forms as examples indicating variations in clutch design.

Two examples of the positive or tooth clutches are shown at A and B in Fig. 1. The form illustrated at A has teeth with sides that incline to make them engage or disengage more readily. One part a of the clutch is fast to one shaft, whereas the other part b is keyed to the opposite shaft section, so that it revolves with it, but is free to move in a lengthwise direction. The shifting of the movable part to engage or disengage it is ordinarily done by means of a forked lever c which may be operated either by hand or mechanically. This lever has prongs which either engage a groove in the shifting member or are pivoted to a ring d which fits into the groove, the arrangement in either case allowing the clutch to revolve between the U-shaped prongs. Many clutches of this general type have straight instead of tapering teeth.

What is commonly known as a "saw-tooth" clutch is illustrated at B. This type is very easily engaged but the driving member can only be rotated in one direction. There are other forms of positive clutches which differ in regard to the shapes of the teeth or the angle of the engaging surfaces. The positive or tooth type is used when it is not objectionable to start the driven member suddenly and when the resistance to motion is not so great as to cause an injurious shock each time the clutch teeth come into engagement.

Friction Clutches. — When motion is transmitted from the driving to the driven parts of a clutch simply by frictional contact, the load may be started gradually and without shock, such as often occurs when a positive clutch is engaged. The different types of friction clutches vary in regard to the form of the friction surfaces and with respect to the kinds of material used to obtain sufficient frictional resistance. The frictional surfaces may be either conical or cylindrical, or in the form of one or more flat rings or disks. A simple design of conical clutch is illustrated at C, Fig. 1. Motion is transmitted from part g to h by the frictional resistance of the conical surfaces. The effectiveness of any friction clutch as a transmitter of power varies with the coefficient or degree of friction between the engaged surfaces. The frictional surfaces may both be of metal, but, in many cases, one member has a metal surface and the other is partially or entirely covered with some material such as leather or an asbestos fabric. The cast iron and leather combination is common, and pieces of cork inserted in holes drilled in one member is another common method of increasing fric-

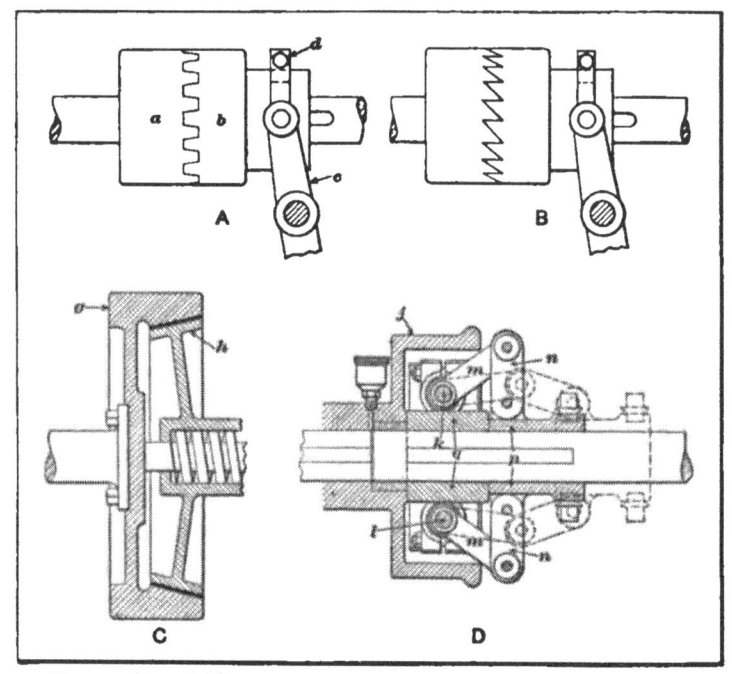

Fig. 1. (A and B) Positive Clutches; (C and D) Friction Clutches

tional resistance. It is common practice to maintain the driving and driven members of friction clutches in engagement by means of springs which are compressed in order to release the clutch. The angle of the conical surfaces is usually about 12 or 13 degrees.

The conical type of friction clutch is simple in construction but rather bulky or large when compared with other types of equal capacity as transmitters of power. One of the disadvantages of a large clutch, aside from the increase in weight and the space which it occupies, is the natural tendency for a heavy rotating body to continue in motion. For instance, when a heavy clutch, which is of necessity made quite large in diameter to obtain the required amount of frictional surface, is revolving rapidly and is disengaged in order to either stop or reduce the speed of the driven member, it may continue to revolve for some time after disengagement, which might be objectionable on some classes of machinery. To avoid trouble from this source, some automobile clutches are equipped with a brake which is interconnected with the foot pedal and only comes into action when the clutch is disengaged.

Expanding Type of Friction Clutch. — The radially expanding type of clutch illustrated at D in Fig. 1 is a form that has been used very generally, the details of the design being varied more or less. This clutch consists of an outer casing j in which there are two expanders or segment-shaped pieces connected by right- and left-hand screws at k and l, respectively. These screws are attached to levers m, which, in turn, are connected to the sliding sleeve p, by links n, thus forming toggles between the sleeve and the screws. The two expanders and the toggle mechanism are caused to revolve with the shaft by a central driving hub q. The clutch is operated by shifting the sliding sleeve and toggles as indicated by the full and dotted lines; this movement turns the screws having right- and left-hand threads far enough to either expand the inner members tightly against the outer casing or to withdraw them from frictional contact. The expanders referred to are lined with maple grips, in this particular case, to increase the frictional resistance.

Ring or Plate Clutches. — The type of friction clutch shown in Fig. 2 has two friction rings A and B which are gripped between flange C and the rings D and E when the clutch is in engagement. The rings A and B are not rigidly attached to the outer casing, but are driven around with the casing by keys or feathers. The driving plates or rings D and E are keyed to the hub of flange C and this hub, in turn, is keyed to the shaft. The two driving rings D and E are free to move along the hub, and the outer ring E is connected to the toggle mechanism shown. When the sliding collar engages the ends of the toggle levers, outside driving plate E moves back against the driven plate B which forces the central driving plate D and the driven plate A back against flange C with considerable pressure, thus engaging four frictional surfaces. The two driven rings A and B contain wooden inserts or blocks to increase the frictional resistance. Some clutches of this general type have one ring which is gripped between a stationary and movable ring, thus giving two frictional surfaces. There are also other modifications of this type.

Multiple-disk Clutches. — By using quite a number of disks or rings instead of one or two, the diameter of the clutch may

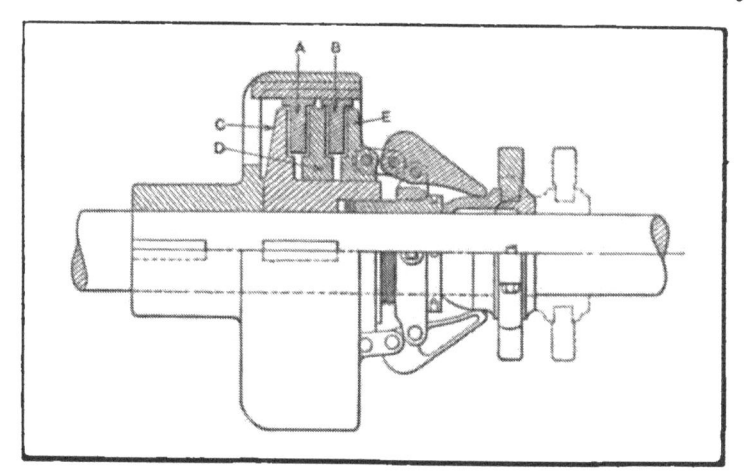

Fig. 2. Plate or Ring Clutch

be reduced without sacrificing the contact area or the amount of frictional surface. The advantage of the smaller and more compact clutch, especially on automobiles, has been referred to. Clutches of the disk type are now applied to many automobiles. The driving member of the clutch has a number of disks which alternate with other disks connected to the driven member. One set of disks may be of soft steel and the other set of phosphor-bronze, or some other combination may be employed. For instance, some disks are provided with cork inserts.

The general arrangement of a multiple-disk clutch as applied to an automobile is illustrated in Fig. 3. The engine flywheel A transmits motion through keys to the driving disks B. These disks alternate with the driven disks which engage keys on drum C; this drum, in turn, transmits its motion through a connecting shaft to the gear set enclosed in casing D where the speed changes are obtained. While the clutch disks must revolve with their respective driving and driven members, they are free to move laterally, so that all the disks may be firmly pressed together in order to engage the clutch. The pressure required to force all the disks into contact is derived from a spring E. The clutch is controlled by a pedal attached to lever F which releases the

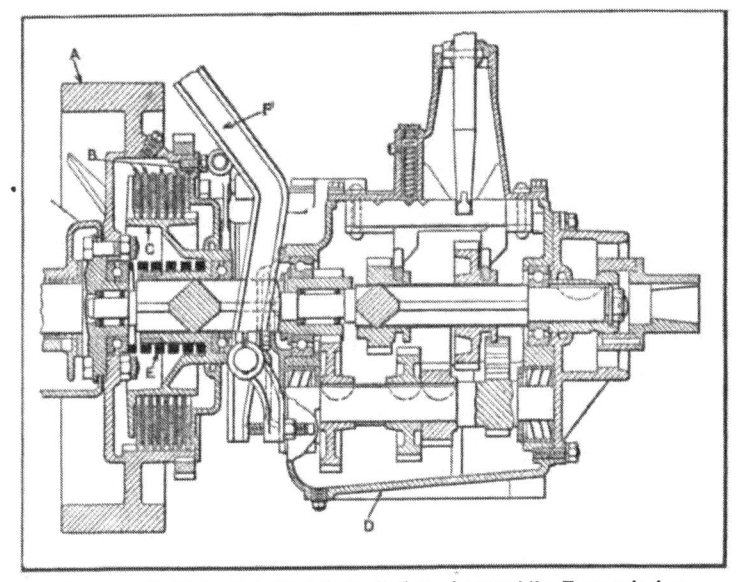

Fig. 3. Multiple-disk Clutch applied to Automobile Transmission

spring for engaging the clutch and compresses the spring for releasing the pressure on the disks. Clutches of this kind are generally enclosed in an oil-tight case, so that the disks can be kept well lubricated. Some disk clutches, however, do not operate in an oil bath. These "dry-plate" clutches have one series or set of disks which is faced with some special friction material, such as asbestos-wire fabric.

Pneumatically-operated Multiple-disk Clutch. — While most clutches are engaged and disengaged by mechanical means, compressed air or water under pressure may be employed. A multiple-disk clutch designed for pneumatic operation is shown in Fig. 4. The driving shaft A has keyed to it casing B, which engages six friction disks C. These disks alternate with an equal number connecting with a hub attached to the driven shaft D. The disks are enclosed in the casing by cover E which is bolted to casing B and is free to turn on the driven shaft D. Surrounding the driving shaft is a sleeve F, which is connected at G with a pipe for supplying the compressed air. The annular groove in the center of this sleeve connects with a hole that extends to the end of the driving shaft, and through which air

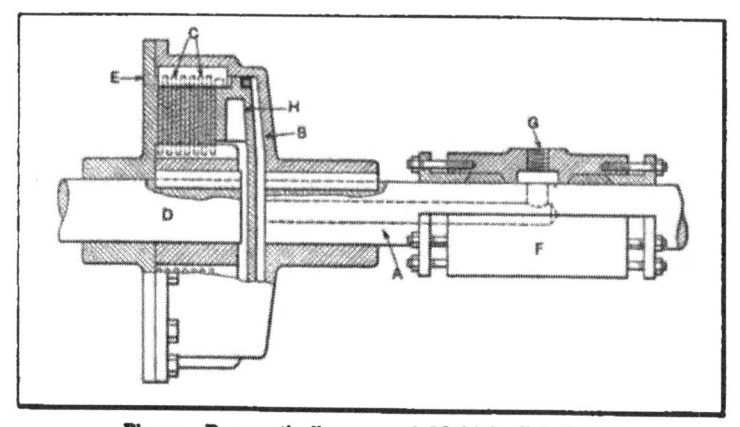

Fig. 4. Pneumatically-operated Multiple-disk Clutch

is admitted back of the circular piston H, which holds the disks firmly together when the clutch is engaged. The sleeve F is provided with a stuffing-box and gland at each end to prevent the escape of air. This sleeve remains stationary and the shaft revolves in it. The clutch may also be operated by water under pressure.

Multiple-disk Clutch equipped with Brake. — It is sometimes necessary to start and stop machines or certain parts of machines smoothly, with great rapidity, and in synchronism with other moving parts. With light or slow moving apparatus, the problem is relatively simple, but the difficulties multiply as weight and speed are increased. The clutch mechanism shown in Fig. 5 has proved very efficient for the class of service mentioned.

This design of clutch is used on a machine transmitting a load of 20 horsepower and operating about 3600 times per day, under unusually trying conditions. This machine picks up its load from dead rest, makes three revolutions and comes to rest again in three-fifths second, or at an average rate of 300 revolutions per minute, without the slightest shock or effort. When it is considered that the clutch drum is driven at only 340 revolutions per minute, and the engagement is only a fraction of a second, it will be seen that the slip is very slight indeed. The absence of shock may be attributed to the perfect cushioning of the pressure applied to the clutch and to the liberal friction area provided, there being nearly a square inch for each pound of pull at the average radius of the disks.

The device consists essentially of two multiple-disk friction clutches of the dry type mounted tandem on a single sleeve which is fitted to slide, but not to turn, on a shaft that is directly coupled to the intermittent load. The driving clutch is shown at A and the brake clutch, at B. The two clutches are built up in the usual form for disk clutches, that is, with two alternate series of disks, one keyed to the driving member and the other to the driven member; one set is preferably faced with friction fabric. One series of disks in a set is provided with internal projections to engage longitudinal slots on the sleeve, while the other disks have external projections loosely fitting the internal slots of the driving and braking clutch drums. The projecting lugs on the disks are reinforced to provide greater bearing surface on the sides of the slots in which they travel. As both clutches are mounted on the same sleeve, and the outer part of the driving clutch is continuously driven, the sleeve becomes the driven member of the driving clutch and the driving member of the brake clutch. The driven member of the brake clutch is solidly bolted to the frame of the machine of which the clutch constitutes a part, so that, in reality, it is not driven, but acts as a brake to bring the sleeve to rest when this clutch is engaged.

Both the clutch drums are built in skeleton form to facilitate the egress of material wearing off the friction facings, and to permit of the easy application of castor oil to the facings. If this treatment is not neglected, a set of facings may last two years or more in constant service, but, if the facings are allowed to become entirely dry, they will be less durable. The sleeve is provided with a flange on each end so that, when it is moved endwise, the disks of one of the clutches will be clamped between one of the sleeve flanges and the head of one of the clutch drums, while the pressure on the disks of the other clutch will be released. Movement of the sleeve in the opposite direction will

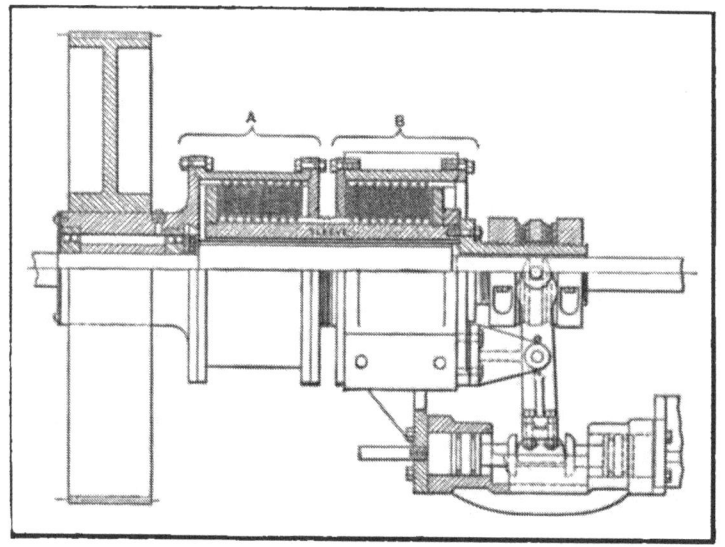

Fig. 5. Quick-acting Multiple-disk Clutch and Brake Combination

release the disks of the first clutch and clamp those of the second. In the illustration, the parts are shown in the position of rest, or with the driving clutch disengaged and the brake clutch set.

The controlling mechanism is operated pneumatically and may be made automatic by connecting with other moving parts to actuate the valves. The actual movement of the sleeve which engages and disengages the clutches is derived from two opposed pneumatic cylinders and the connections shown. It will be apparent that the cylinders must work alternately, that is, when one is under pressure the other must be open or free to exhaust. The distribution of air is controlled by two valves, together with a series of interconnecting pipes. With the valves in the "up" position, compressed air is free to pass through the pipe to one of the cylinders and to the top of the other valve for forcing it down, cutting off the air supply of the cylinder it serves, and opening it to exhaust.

A small hole near the live-air inlet leads to the annular space below the valve proper, around the stem, and is open continuously, admitting air to hold the valve in the "up" position when so placed. As the only connections between the controlling valves and the cylinders are pipes, the control may be somewhat remote and placed in any convenient position. Experiments have been made to determine the practicability of operating the valves magnetically, and also of moving the clutch sleeve by means of magnets, but both have been found far less efficient and much slower than air, the slowness of the electrical operation being due to the time required for the magnets to "build up." The drift of the shaft after the operation of the stopping valve has been found to be very small and practically constant, the shaft stopping within a few degrees of the same position every time. Any wear on the friction disks or their facings is automatically compensated for by additional travel of the pneumatic pistons, so that mechanical adjustments are rarely required.

Magnetic Clutch with Automatic Band Brake. — The magnetic clutch illustrated in Fig. 6 is equipped with an electrically operated brake which acts automatically when the clutch is released, in order to stop the driven part as quickly as possible. The driving shaft carries the field A which is provided with a magnetizing coil B. The hub C on the driven shaft has attached to it a flexible spring-steel disk or plate D. This plate carries the armature E which is prevented from coming directly into contact with the magnetizing coil by a ring of frictional material at F. This friction ring, which is made of woven asbestos and brass wire, provides a frictional surface for driving. The ends of the winding of the magnetizing coil are attached to the rings G which are in contact with a pair of brushes H connected with the electrical circuit. The automatic brake, which is of the band type, engages drum J, and the ends of the band are pivoted to lever K at two points as shown. The plunger of a solenoid enclosed in cylinder L is attached to lever K, and at the outer end of this lever there is a weight which serves to apply the brake when the clutch is disengaged.

In the operation of this clutch, the current is gradually admitted to the magnetizing coil by means of a rheostat. The magnetic attraction between this coil and the armature causes the friction ring F to be held firmly against the driving member, so that motion is transmitted between the driving and driven shafts. The solenoid is also energized so that lever K is pulled upward and the band brake about drum J released. This brake

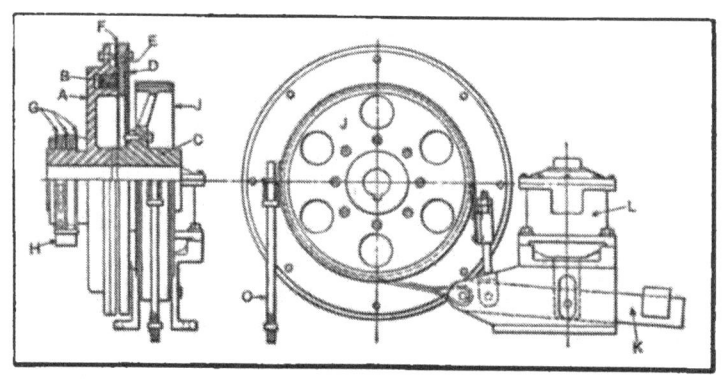

Fig. 6. **Magnetic Clutch equipped with Automatic Band Brake which operates when Clutch releases**

is held in circular form and out of contact with the drum by a spring and rod O. As soon as the circuit is broken, the clutch is released, and the solenoid allows the weighted lever K to fall, thus supplying the brake automatically to the driven part. This feature is of particular advantage when the driven side of the clutch is connected to some part which tends to revolve quite a long time after disengagement.

Induction Clutch. — The induction clutch shown in Fig. 7 is similar in its operation to an induction motor. This particular form of clutch is applied to an electrically-driven planer. The copper ring C is the driven member and it is held by a spider A, the hub of which contains the bushing b. This spider runs loose on the shaft and its hub carries a pinion through which power is transmitted. All the other parts shown belong to the driving member which is keyed to the continuously running motor shaft. This driving member, which acts also as a flywheel, consists of the two-part steel castings E and F, the coil G, and the collector rings D. The copper ring C has running clearance between castings E and F, and, since it is nonmagnetic, it has no tendency to be drawn over towards the poles on either side. This ring has, however, a high conductivity and, because of this fact and its position with relation to the revolving magnetic driving member, it is pulled along by this driving member on the same principle as that of the induction motor. Two of these clutches

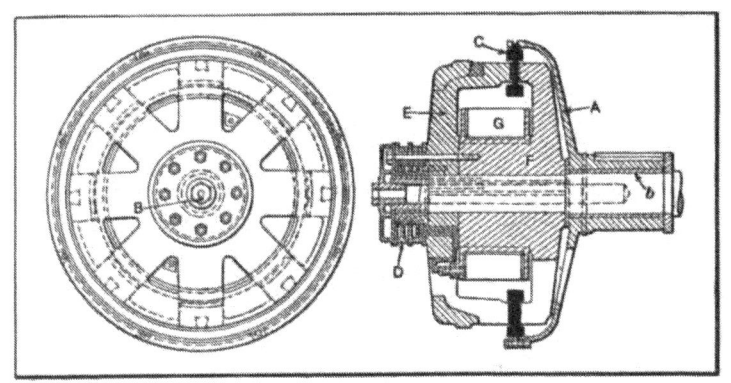

Fig. 7. Induction Clutch which operates on the Principle of the Induction Motor

are employed, one for the cutting and the other for the return stroke, and a switch worked by dogs admits a small current to one clutch on the cutting stroke and to the other clutch on the return stroke. The induction clutch transmits power without contact between its driving and driven members.

Clutches that Automatically Disengage. — The clutches used on power presses are designed to automatically disengage after making one or more revolutions. The clutch connects the flywheel or driving gear of the press with the driven shaft, whenever it is tripped, by pressing down a foot-treadle. As long as this treadle is held down, the clutch remains in engagement and the press continues to run; if the treadle is released, the clutch is disengaged when the ram or slide of the press is approximately at the top of its stroke. The downward movement of the treadle releases a pin, key, or some other form of locking device which quickly engages the driving member; when the treadle is released, the locking device encounters some form of trip or cam surface which withdraws it and stops the press. There are many designs of clutches of this general type and the examples to be described will illustrate the general principles governing their operation.

Automatic Clutches of the Key Type. — Fig. 8 shows a clutch of the type having a key which is engaged or disengaged with the hub A of the flywheel. This flywheel revolves freely on the shaft until the dog D is pulled down by the action of the foot-treadle; then the key C is forced downward into engagement with the flywheel by a strong steel spring E. When the foot-treadle is released, the dog D is forced up, and when key C comes into contact with the dog, it is pushed back into the shaft, thus allowing the flywheel to again run freely. If the treadle is depressed and then released, the press will make one revolution before stopping, but if the treadle is held downward, the press will continue to run. This clutch is equipped with a safety device to prevent the ram or slide of the press from descending unexpectedly while setting dies or making adjustments. This safety device consists of a steel ring F having a keyway or slot in it for receiving the key C. When the press slide is at the top of its stroke and dog D is up, the key is entirely within the shaft and may be held in this position by turning ring F, thus preventing accidental engagement of the clutch. Ring F has an extension arm that enables it to be turned readily.

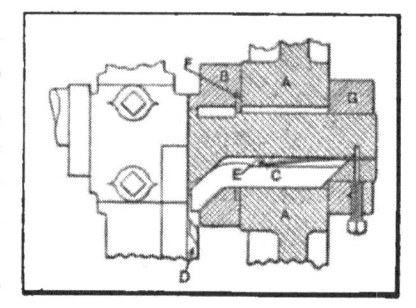

Fig. 8. Automatic Clutch of Shifting-key Type

A clutch is shown in Fig. 9 that has a rocking key instead of one that moves radially. This key A extends across the shaft and, when the press is not in motion, the key rests in a semi-

244   MECHANICAL MOVEMENTS

circular seat and occupies the position shown in the end view. When in this position, the lever B at one end of the key is in engagement with the latch C, which is connected with the foot-treadle. As soon as latch C is swung out of the way by depressing the treadle, lever B and the key tend to turn as they are acted upon by the compressed spring E. When the flywheel has turned far enough to bring one of the recesses F opposite the key, the latter, by making a quarter turn in its seat, engages the recess and locks the flywheel and shaft together. If the

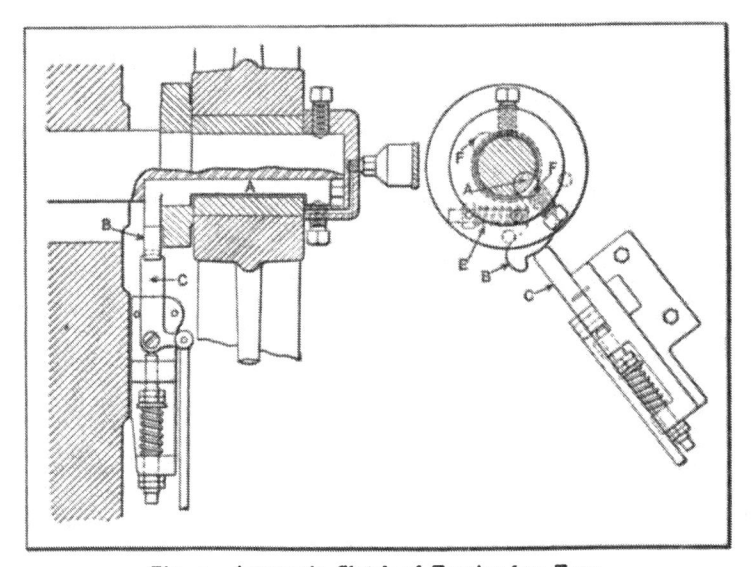

Fig. 9. Automatic Clutch of Turning-key Type

treadle is immediately released, thus allowing latch C to swing back to the vertical position, it will engage lever B when it comes around and force this lever and the key back out of engagement with the flywheel.

Clutches Engaged by a Wedging Action. — Some designs of automatic clutches are engaged by a wedging action of some locking member between cam or eccentric surfaces, instead of employing pins or keys. An example of the cam type of clutch is shown at A, Fig. 10. A cam a, having a series of eccentric or cam surfaces, is keyed to the crankshaft, and surrounding this

TRIPPING MECHANISMS 245

cam there is a slotted ring c containing rollers b, which, in turn, are surrounded by a hardened tool steel ring d. These parts are inserted in a recess formed in the hub of the flywheel. On the slotted ring c, there is a lug f which is in engagement with the pivoted stop lever e when the press is not in operation. As soon as the stop lever is drawn downward by means of the foot pedal, the rollers are carried around by the action of the flywheel until they are wedged tightly between the cam surfaces and the outer ring d; the crankshaft is then driven with the flywheel and continues to revolve until lever e is released and, by striking stop f,

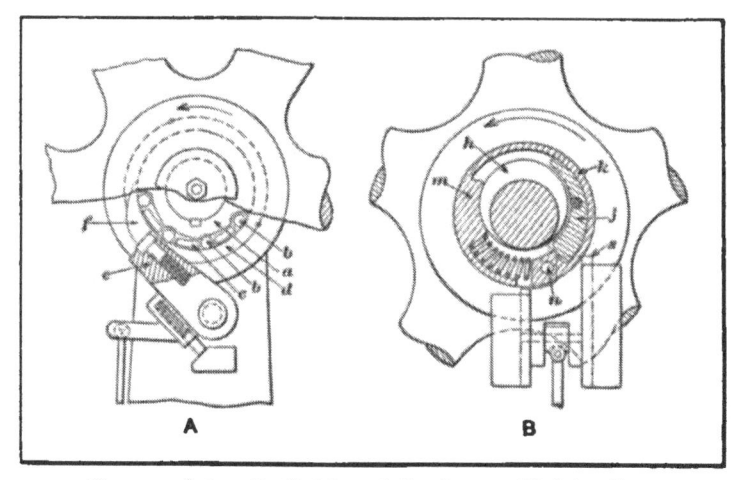

Fig. 10. Automatic Clutches of the Cam or Wedging Type

throws the rollers out of engagement. The slotted ring c has a spring attached to it (not shown) which turns the ring and rollers toward the high points of the cam when the ring is released by the lowering of lever e.

The design of clutch illustrated at B is equipped with an eccentric h which is solid with the crankshaft and a wedge-shaped member j which serves to lock the flywheel and crankshaft together. This wedge j is located between the eccentric and a ring k inserted in a recess in the hub of the flywheel. The ring is split and compressed somewhat so as to exert a pressure against the wall of the recess. When the stop s is in engagement with pin n, the flywheel simply revolves about the expansion ring k. When stop s is withdrawn, the ring k expands, and, as it begins to revolve with the flywheel, the wedge j is forced between the eccentric h and the inside of the ring; consequently, the flywheel, expansion ring, and the shaft are firmly locked together. When the foot pedal is released and stop s engages pin n, the ring contracts and remains stationary while the flywheel continues to revolve. The surface at m serves as a brake, so that the crankshaft is stopped when the slide is approximately at the top of its stroke.

Variable Clutch Control by "Pattern Chain." — When clutches are engaged or disengaged automatically, their action is usually controlled either by cams or some form of revolving carrier having one or more lugs or dogs that engage the clutch-operating lever. The ingenious method of controlling clutches illustrated at A in Fig. 11 is applied to a textile machine known as a "twister" and used for producing fancy yarns. The variations in the yarn are obtained by controlling the action of two sets of delivery rolls. The lower rolls r and s of each set support the upper rolls c and d. Splined to the end of roll r is a shifting clutch member e which revolves the roll when engaged with the clutch teeth on the hub of gear f. A similar clutch and gear combination is located at g for driving the lower set of delivery rolls. The upper clutch is connected with lever q pivoted at h, and the lower clutch, with lever j pivoted at k. The action of these clutch levers is governed by a pattern chain l suspended on a drum m. As this drum revolves, the rollers of the pattern chain come into engagement with the lower ends of the clutch levers, thus shifting the clutches in and out of engagement. By changing the position of the rolls or risers of the pattern chain, the pattern of the yarn may be varied and different fancy effects be obtained. The chain drum is revolved by means of change gearing for varying the speed according to requirements. The clutch gears are rotated continuously, and the delivery rolls are only stopped when a knob or knot is being formed, both sets of rolls being rotated while the yarns are being twisted together between the knots.

TRIPPING MECHANISMS

Another application of an endless chain for controlling the engagement and disengagement of a clutch at predetermined intervals is illustrated at B, Fig. 11. This mechanism is applied to a loom. The vertical shaft a is driven through bevel gearing (not shown) at the lower end, from the driving shaft of the loom. The upper end of shaft a carries a clutch member b, which is engaged by the shifting clutch member c splined to shaft d. Shaft d, through the bevel and spur gearing shown, is connected with

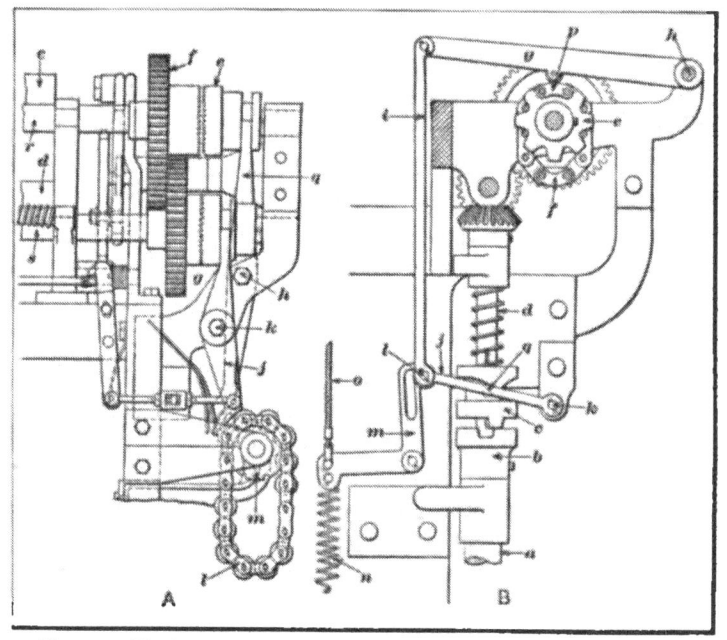

Fig. 11. Mechanisms equipped with Endless Chains for Controlling Engagement and Disengagement of Clutches

the chain drum or cylinder e carrying the clutch controlling chain f. Above this chain, there is a lever g pivoted at h and connected by link i with another lever j pivoted at k. The pin l connecting the link and lever engages a slot in bellcrank m, the movements of which are controlled by a spring n and a connector o which extends to another part of the machine. The vertical slot in lever m has a short horizontal section at the upper end.

The action of the mechanism is as follows: When the clutch

members are engaged, the chain drum and chain revolve, and when one of the links *p* engages lever *g*, the lower lever *j* is raised, thus locating pin *q* in the upper part of the annular groove of the shifting clutch member. As soon as pin *l* at the end of lever *j* reaches the upper end of the vertical slot, the bellcrank lever *m* swings over under the action of spring *n*, thus engaging pin *l* with the horizontal part of the slot and locking the lever *j* in the upper position. As soon as the lever *j* is raised, a projection engages pin *q* and disconnects the clutch, thus stopping the rotation of shaft *d*. The link *p* on the pattern chain is no longer under the roller of lever *g*, but this lever is still held in the upper position, by the engagement of pin *l* with the horizontal slot in bellcrank lever *m*. The clutch remains disengaged until the connector *o* swings the vertical part of lever *m* to the right, thus allowing the upper clutch member *c* to reëngage the lower part. The movements of the connector are controlled by another chain which operates on the same general principle as the one referred to.

Tripping Mechanisms. — What are known as "tripping" mechanisms are applied to various kinds of machinery to stop the movement either of the entire machine or of some part of it. Automatic tripping devices generally operate in conjunction with a clutch, or they are used to disengage intermeshing gears. The trip may be adjustable and be set beforehand to act after a certain part has moved a given distance, or it may only act when a machine begins to operate under abnormal conditions. The adjustable form of trip, if for a part having a rectilinear motion, may consist simply of a stop which is placed in such a position that it will disengage a clutch after the part under the control of the trip has moved the required distance. If a rotary motion is involved, the same principle may be applied with whatever modification of the mechanism is necessary. When the trip is designed to act automatically only when the machine is operating under adverse conditions, the action may be governed by variations of pressure or resistance to motion, or the product on which the machine is working may cause the trip to act in case the operation is not as it should be. The following examples will illustrate a few of the applications and the possibilities of tripping mechanisms of different types.

Trip which Disengages a Clutch. — One of the simplest forms of automatic tripping mechanisms is illustrated diagrammatically at A, Fig. 12. - This general type is applied to some classes of machine tools for disengaging the feeding movements of a tool-slide at a predetermined point. The tool-slide, which may be the carriage of an engine lathe, is moved along the bed by a feed-screw a or a splined rod which is rotated through a clutch b. The shifting member of this clutch is operated by a lever c the lower end of which connects with rod d. This rod extends along the bed a distance equivalent to the carriage movement and

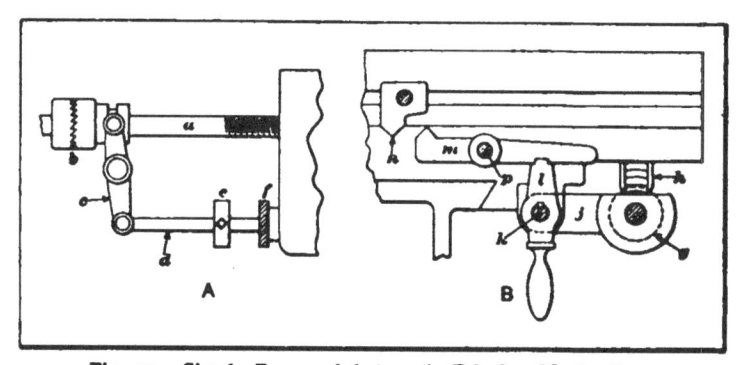

Fig. 12. Simple Forms of Automatic Tripping Mechanisms

carries an adjustable stop collar e, which is engaged by some projecting part f on the carriage; when this engagement occurs, the rod is shifted in a lengthwise direction, thus throwing the clutch out of mesh and stopping the feeding movement. Obviously, the point at which disengagement occurs depends upon the position of stop collar e which is set in accordance with the length of the part to be turned. There are other trip mechanisms of the clutch-shifting type which differ from the kind described in regard to the details of the mechanism for shifting the clutch.

Trip which Disengages Gearing. — Diagram B, Fig. 12, illustrates a form of automatic trip which serves to disengage worm gearing instead of a clutch. The worm g revolves worm-wheel *h* and the table feed-screw. This worm is carried by an arm *j* pivoted at *k* and held in position by the engagement of lever *l* with a notch in lever *m*. When the adjustable trip dog *n*, attached to the work table, strikes lever *m* and swings it about pivot *p*, the worm *g* drops out of engagement with worm-wheel *h* and the feeding motion stops. The point of this engagement may be varied at will by simply changing the position of the trip dog *n*. Some of the trip mechanisms on vertical drilling machines operate on this same general principle.

Many different designs of automatic tripping mechanisms, especially of the type used on machine tools for controlling feeding movements, are of the same principle as those described, in that trip dogs are attached either directly to the driven member or to some auxiliary mechanism such as a revolving disk geared to the driven part, and these dogs stop the feeding movement either by disengaging a clutch or gearing. If the feeding movement is intermittent and is obtained through ratchet gearing, the pawl may be prevented from engaging the gear teeth of the ratchet wheel after the latter has turned a predetermined amount. An example of this type of tripping device is described in Chapter VI (see Fig. 3).

Automatic Stops for Drilling Machine. — Fig. 13 shows a side elevation and plan of an automatic stop or trip for a vertical-spindle drilling machine, which operates by disengaging a friction clutch. The feeding movement is transmitted to the spindle from the friction gear *c* to the disk *d* and through worm gearing at *k* to a pinion meshing with rack *l* attached to the spindle sleeve. The position of friction gear *c* is controlled by hand lever *g* which, through link *e*, lever *f*, shaft *a*, and collar *b* moves the friction gear in or out of engagement with disk *d*. Lever *g* is held in the engaged position by the latch or trigger *n*. An adjustable stop collar *h* is set by means of graduations to automatically disengage the feed after a hole has been drilled to whatever depth is required. This collar acts by simply striking the end of latch *n*, thus releasing lever *g* and the friction gear *c*. Any wear in the friction clutch is compensated for by adjusting set-screw *j* in the end of connecting link *e*.

TRIPPING MECHANISMS

Duplex Automatic Tripping Mechanism. — Another form of tripping device for a vertical-spindle drilling machine is illustrated at B, Fig. 13. This stop may be set to disengage the worm e from the worm-wheel on the pinion shaft, or it may be utilized to disengage miter gear g which drives the worm-shaft. The tripping dog is attached to a bracket or arm a clamped to the feed rack on the sleeve. The dog b may be swung so as to engage either levers c or d; as shown in the plan view, it is in the latter

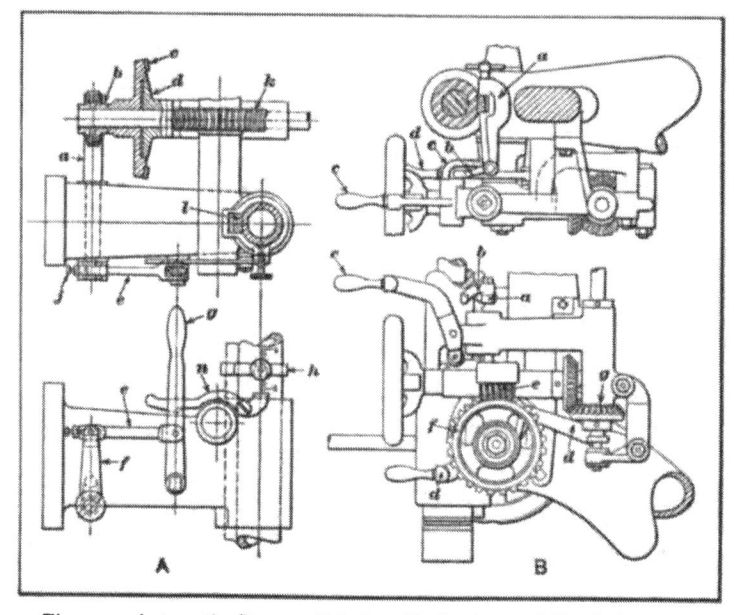

Fig. 13. Automatic Stop or Tripping Mechanisms of Vertical-spindle Drilling Machines

position. Lever c controls the engagement of worm e with wheel f, whereas d serves to disengage the bevel gear g. When the worm is cut of mesh, the spindle may be moved vertically by the hand-feed lever, for facing or similar operations, after a hole has been drilled. Ordinarily, gear g is disengaged, but this does not leave the spindle free for rapid adjustment.

Adjustable Dial Type of Tripping Mechanism. — The automatic tripping mechanism shown in Fig. 14 is applied to Colburn drilling machines and may be adjusted to disengage the downward feeding motion of the drill at any depth up to 14 inches. The feeding movement is transmitted through the drill spindle from shaft A, through worm gearing, to shaft B which has a pinion engaging the rack on the spindle quill. The automatic disengagement of the feed is controlled by the engagement of pawl H with lever N. The distance that the spindle feeds downward before the feed is tripped is regulated by the graduated adjustable dial I. The graduations on this dial indicate $\frac{1}{32}$ inch of the spindle travel, and one complete revolution represents 7 inches of spindle travel. The pawl H is so designed that it

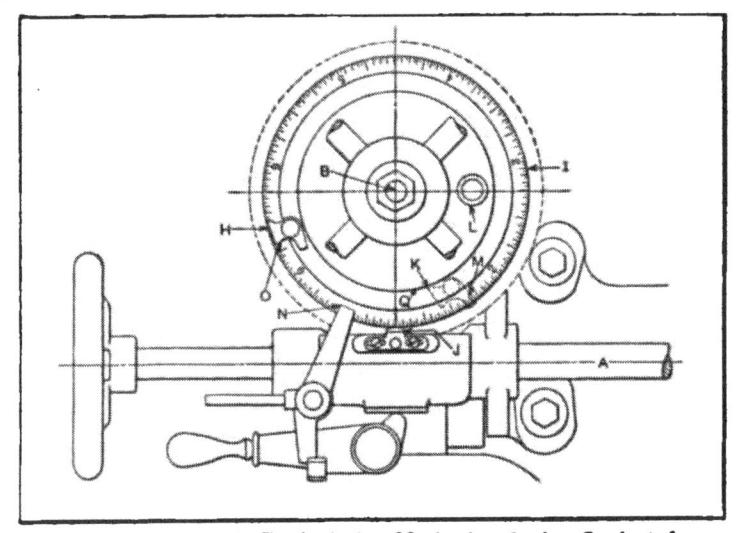

Fig. 14. Automatic Feed-tripping Mechanism having Graduated Adjusting Dial for Controlling Time of Disengagement

can be set to allow two revolutions of the dial before engaging lever N.

The operation of the mechanism is as follows: If the feed is to be tripped automatically in 7 inches or less, pawl H is set as indicated by the dotted lines at K; if it is desired to trip the feed at a distance greater than 7 inches, pawl H is turned to the position shown by the full lines. For example, if it should be required to automatically trip the feed at a depth of 3 inches, the knurled nut L would first be loosened and the graduated dial I turned until the figure 3 on it was opposite the mark on pointer *J*, after which nut *L* would be tightened. The pawl *H* would then be set in the position shown by the dotted lines, with the result that, when the drill had traveled 3 inches, the surface *M* would come into contact with the side *N* of the trip arm and disengage the feed. On the other hand, if it were required to drill to a depth of 9 inches before the feed was automatically tripped, the dial *I* would be set with figure 2 opposite the mark on pointer *J*, and pawl *H* would be turned to the position shown by the full lines. With the pawl in this position, the contact of surface *O* with lever *N* would not throw out the feed, as the pawl, being loose on its stud, would simply turn and pass the

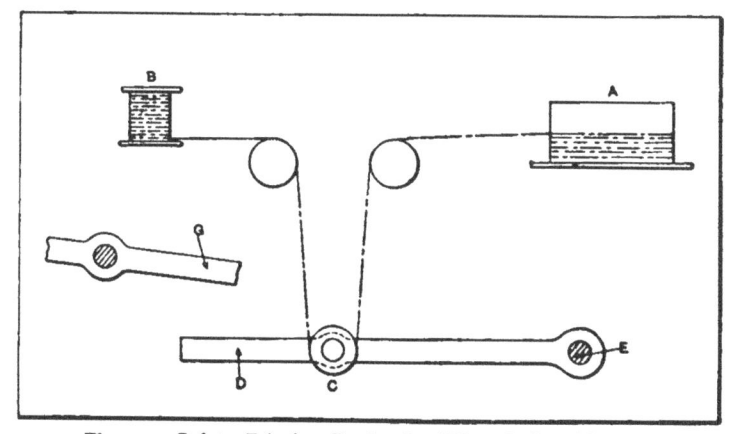

Fig. 15. Safety Tripping Device for Wire-winding Machine

tripping arm without moving it. After the pawl had passed the arm, it would then be in the position shown by the dotted lines, that is, with the end in contact with a projecting sleeve, as at *K*, thus preventing further rotary movement, so that, when it again came around to the tripping lever, the feed would be disengaged. If the knurled nut *L* is loose, the feed cannot be automatically tripped at any point.

Trip for Wire-winding Machine. — The diagram, Fig. 15, shows an automatic tripping device that is applied to a machine used for winding small wire onto spools. In this illustration, *A* represents the reel which contains the stock of wire, and *B* is the spool upon which the wire is wound. This spool is driven at a constant speed. If, for some reason, the wire should not uncoil easily from reel A, it might be broken or the mechanism damaged, assuming that the wire passed directly from the reel to the spool. In order to avoid trouble from any resistance to uncoiling which may occur, the wire, after leaving the reel, is guided by idler pulleys, so as to form a loop; at the end of this loop, there is an idler pulley C mounted on a lever D which is free to swing about fulcrum E. When the uncoiling and winding is proceeding under normal conditions, the weight of lever D is sufficient to prevent the wire from lifting it; any abnormal resistance, however, such as might be caused by a kink on reel A, will result in swinging lever D upward into contact with trip G, which, by disengaging a clutch, stops the machine.

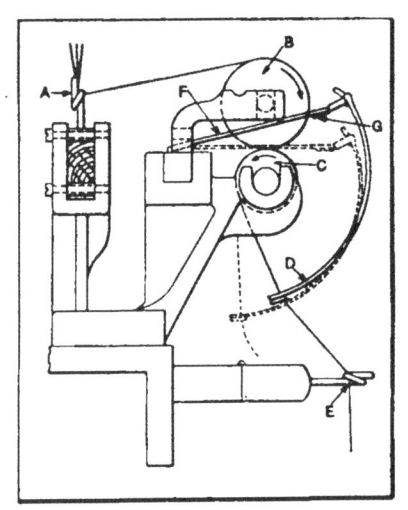

Fig. 16. Tripping Device for a Textile Machine

Tripping Devices for Textile Machines. — Some very ingenious tripping mechanisms or "stop motions" are applied to different classes of textile machines. The examples described illustrate the possibilities of the use of comparatively simple devices for automatically controlling the action of machines under conditions which might, at first, seem to be very complex and difficult.

The stop motion shown in Fig. 16 is applied to a machine used for twisting yarn. The yarn passes from the guide wire at A around the rolls B and C, through an eye in wire D and out through the guide at E. The wire D is attached to another wire F, which is normally held by the yarn in the position shown by the full lines. If the yarn or thread should break, the wires fall to the position shown by the dotted lines, thus bringing wire F into engagement with the lower roll C. Contact with this

TRIPPING MECHANISMS 255

roll immediately moves the wires to the left until a tongue G enters between the rolls and raises B out of contact with C, which prevents it from revolving and stops the delivery of yarn.

Another stop motion which acts when a thread is broken is shown in Fig. 17. This mechanism is applied to a machine used for winding thread on spools. It is designed to raise the spool out of contact with a flange which drives it by friction, if a thread breaks, thus arresting the motion of the spool without stopping the spindle on which the spool is mounted. The device is also arranged so that the wire which drops when a thread breaks is raised automatically to its normal position for re-threading.

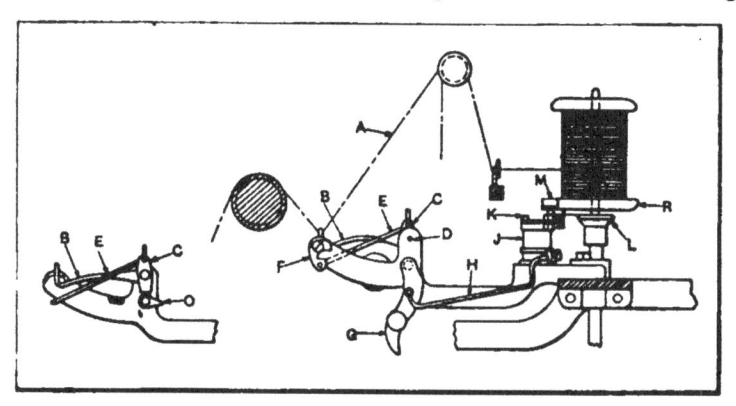

Fig. 17. Another Tripping Device or "Stop Motion" for a Textile Machine

The thread A passes through the eye of a drop wire B and serves to hold this wire in its normal position. Attached to this wire there is a lever C pivoted at D and connected by link E with the catch F. The lever G is normally held in a horizontal position by catch F. If a thread breaks, however, the dropping of wire B releases catch F and lever G falls to the position shown in the illustration. This lever is connected by a rod H with a sleeve J pivoted at K. The downward movement of lever G swings the sleeve about its pivot and brings a pin under the flange R of the spool, thus raising it from the supporting disk L, as shown in the illustration; at the same time, the flange of the spool engages a rubber disk m which stops the rotation. Attached to the shaft of lever G, there is a small finger O which is given a partial turn when the catch lever falls. As the result of this movement, the finger engages lever *C* and swings it with the drop wire *B* back to the normal position ready for re-threading. As soon as the catch lever has been reëngaged with the catch *F*, the spool drops into contact with its driving flange and again begins to wind the yarn.

Electrical Control for Textile Machines. — Certain classes of textile machines are equipped with some form of electrical control for automatically stopping the machine when it is operating under abnormal conditions. A simple method of controlling a machine electrically is found on some drawing frames. The

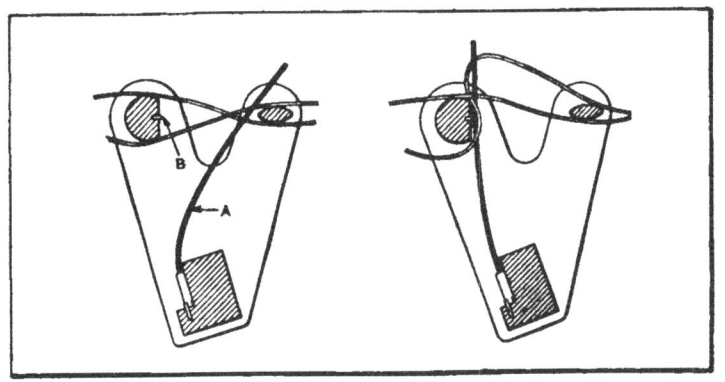

Fig. 18. Simple Form of Electrical Control for Stopping a Loom when a Thread Breaks

upper and lower sections of the machine frame are insulated from each other, and one pole of a small dynamo is connected to one frame section and the other pole to the other section. The cotton, which is a non-conductor and is constantly passing between the different pairs of rolls, prevents the completion of the electrical circuit except when the cotton breaks and both rolls of a pair come directly into contact with each other. When this occurs, the electrical circuit thus formed, acting in conjunction with an electromagnet, swings a lever into the path of a revolving trip or catch which, as its rotation is stopped, either shifts a belt from the tight to the loose pulley or disengages a clutch by means of suitable mechanism.

A very simple form of electrical controlling device is shown in Fig. 18. This device is applied to looms and operates whenever a thread breaks. The steel spring wire A is normally held between two threads in the bent position shown to the left. If one of the warp threads should break, the spring wire is immediately released and flies over to the left into engagement with rod B, as shown to the right, thus closing an electrical circuit. This circuit is a comparatively weak one and stops the machine by means of an electromechanical type of mechanism. The actual force required for stopping the machine is sometimes considerable, and it is derived by a moving part of the loom, the electrical mechanism simply being used to cause a locking effect that enables the other part of the mechanism to operate.

Tripping Mechanism of Drop-hammer. — When a board type of drop-hammer has fallen and is rebounding, the friction rolls grip the board and elevate the hammer preparatory to the delivery of another blow. The eccentrically mounted gripping roll is moved inward against the board for elevating the hammer, when a " friction bar " is released by a tripping mechanism and allowed to fall. Most of these tripping devices operate on the same general principle as the design illustrated at A in Fig. 19. The friction bar a is attached at its upper end to a lever that controls the position of the eccentrically mounted friction roll; when the bar falls, the lifting board is gripped between this front roll and one at the rear that revolves in one position. Before the friction bar is released, the lower end rests upon a seat which prevents it from falling. When the hammer c descends, an incline surface d on it engages bracket b and pushes bar a off of its seat. The weight of this bar is sufficient to give the roll referred to the required gripping pressure on the board f, so that the hammer is lifted to the top of its stroke. As the hammer rises, it engages a lever and raises the friction bar which, in this particular case, is returned to its seat by a spring-operated guide g. In order to operate the hammer properly, it is necessary to release the friction bar at exactly the right time, which must be varied according to the thickness of the hammer dies.

The tripping mechanism must be so set that, as the hammer rebounds, its upward movement is continued by the action of the friction rolls. If the release of the friction bar occurs too soon, the rolls will grip the board either before the hammer strikes its blow or before it has had time to rebound. On the other hand, if the release occurs too late, the hammer will fall back after rebounding and the roll will have to pick up a "dead" or stationary load. The point of release depends upon the vertical position of bracket b.

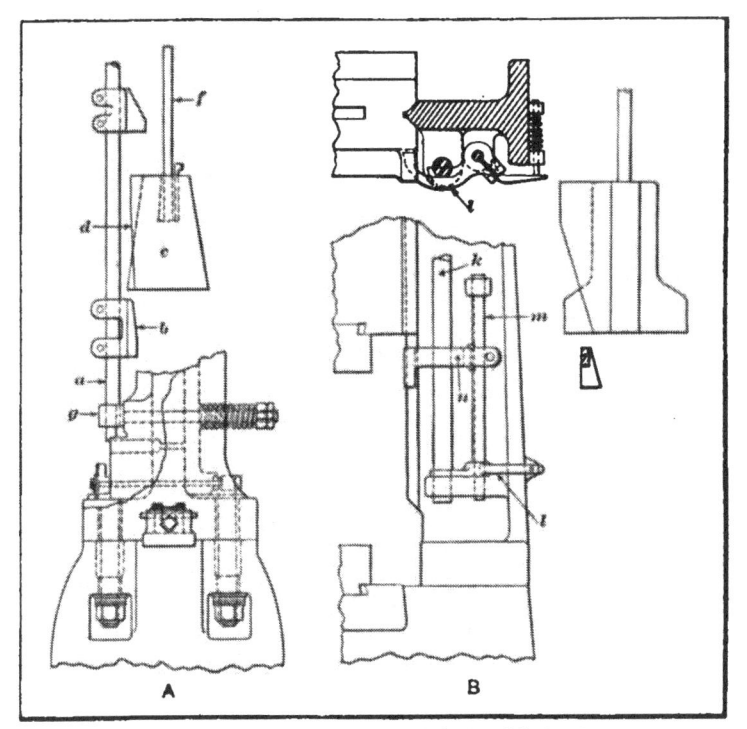

Fig. 19. Board Drop-hammer Tripping Mechanisms

A trip mechanism of the swinging latch type is shown at B, Fig. 19. In this case, the friction bar k is held in the upper position by a catch l which engages a slot in the bar and is attached to the short vertical shaft m. This shaft also carries a lever n that extends out far enough to engage an inclined surface on the hammer. As the hammer descends, lever n, bar m, and catch l are turned, thus releasing the friction bar k and allowing the rolls to grip the board for elevating the hammer. The point at which release occurs may be varied by changing the vertical position of lever n.

Breakable Pins to Prevent Overload. — Some types of machines are so arranged that any unusual resistance to motion will automatically stop either the entire machine or whatever part is affected, in order to prevent damaging the mechanism or straining it excessively. A simple form of safety device consists of a pin which shears off or breaks in case the overload becomes excessive. The sprocket A shown in Fig. 20 is provided with a pin of this kind. This pin C connects the driving hub B with the hub of the sprocket. The sprocket, instead of being keyed to the shaft, is loosely mounted on it, and the hub B is keyed to the shaft instead. The pin C is grooved or reduced in diameter an amount depending upon the maximum amount of power to be transmitted. If this pin is subjected to an unusual strain, it will break, thus leaving the wheel free and protecting the driven parts.

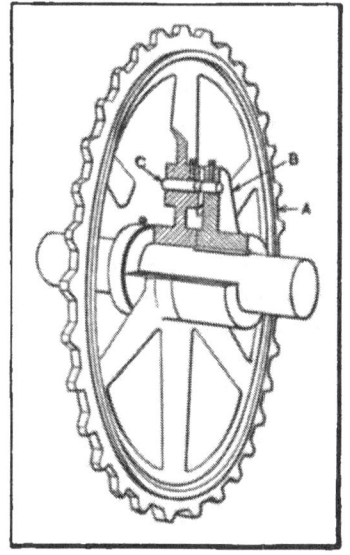

Fig. 20. Sprocket driven through Pin which breaks in Case of Excessive Overload

This same method of protection against overload has been applied in various ways, and, while it is simple, there are certain disadvantages. In order to avoid replacing a broken pin, the machine operator sometimes inserts a pin that is stronger than it should be to afford adequate protection against injurious strains. The ideal safety device is one which does not break in case of overload, but simply disengages and is so arranged that it can readily be reëngaged. In electrical work, this principle has been applied by substituting circuit-breakers for fuses which melt when the current becomes excessive.

Automatic Clutch Control to Prevent Overload.

— The principle governing the operation of an automatic device for disengaging a clutch when the overload becomes excessive is illustrated by the diagram, Fig. 21. This mechanism was applied to a metal-cutting machine, the object being to automatically disengage the feed in case the resistance to the rotation of the tool becomes abnormally high. The mechanism is also arranged to reverse the feeding movement if, for any reason, the excessive resistance should continue after the feed has been disengaged.

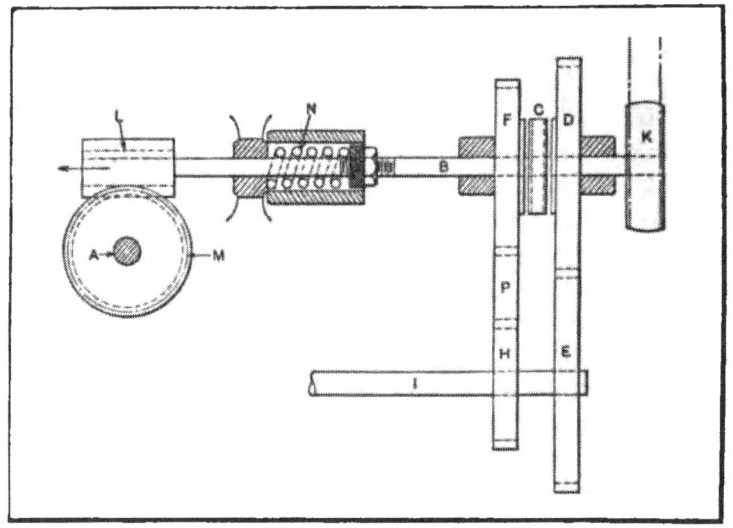

Fig. 21. Device for Automatically Stopping Feeding Motion when Resistance to Rotation becomes Excessive

The spindle to which the cutting tool is attached is represented at A. This spindle is driven through worm-wheel M and worm L from the driving shaft B, which receives its motion from a countershaft through a belt operating on pulley K. The driving shaft B is free to move in a lengthwise direction within certain limits. The clutch C is keyed to this shaft so that it will rotate and move axially with the shaft. The gears D and F on each side of clutch C are free to revolve upon the shaft, but are prevented from moving in a lengthwise direction. The inner side of each gear is provided with clutch teeth corresponding to those on clutch C, which is used to lock either gear to shaft B. The shaft I, which transmits feeding movement to the cutting tool, is driven either through gears D and E or through gears F, P, and H. When clutch C engages gear D, the cutting tool is fed forward by shaft I, and a reversal of the feeding movement is obtained when clutch C is shifted into engagement with gear F.

When clutch C engages with gear D, excessive resistance to the motion of the cutting tool will cause the clutch to be shifted to the neutral position, thus stopping the feeding movement. This automatic action is obtained as follows: The shaft B is normally held by spring N in such a position that clutch C engages gear D, so that the feeding movement is forward. The tension on this spring is regulated by the nut shown. In case the resistance to the rotation of the cutting tool and spindle A should become excessive, the pressure between the teeth of the worm L and the worm-wheel M causes the worm to move in the direction indicated by the arrow, the worm-wheel acting somewhat like a nut. This lengthwise movement of worm-wheel L and shaft B, against the tension of spring N, disengages clutch C from gear D and stops the feeding movement. If the resistance to rotation again becomes normal, clutch C is automatically returned into engagement with gear D. On the other hand, if the resistance to rotation increases, clutch C may be drawn over into engagement with gear F, thus reversing the feeding movement.

Other mechanical devices for automatically disengaging the driven member whenever the resistance to motion increases excessively are shown at A and B in Fig. 22. These devices operate on the same general principle as the one previously described, but differ somewhat in regard to the arrangement. The mechanism illustrated by diagram A is designed to allow a worm-wheel to make one revolution and then stop; the movement, however, may be discontinued before the revolution is completed, if the resistance to rotation becomes excessive. The sleeve a is revolved constantly by a pulley on its outer end. The inner end of this sleeve has clutch teeth intended to engage

262   MECHANICAL MOVEMENTS

corresponding teeth on the end of sleeve b. The latter is attached to the shaft and both are free to move slightly in an endwise direction. The body of sleeve b is threaded to form a worm which engages worm-wheel c. The spring e tends to shift sleeve b to the left and into engagement with clutch teeth on sleeve a. The stop at d is utilized in this particular case to disengage the driving clutch after the worm-wheel has made a revolution. If stop d is withdrawn, the spring e revolves the worm-wheel slightly and moves the worm and clutch b to the

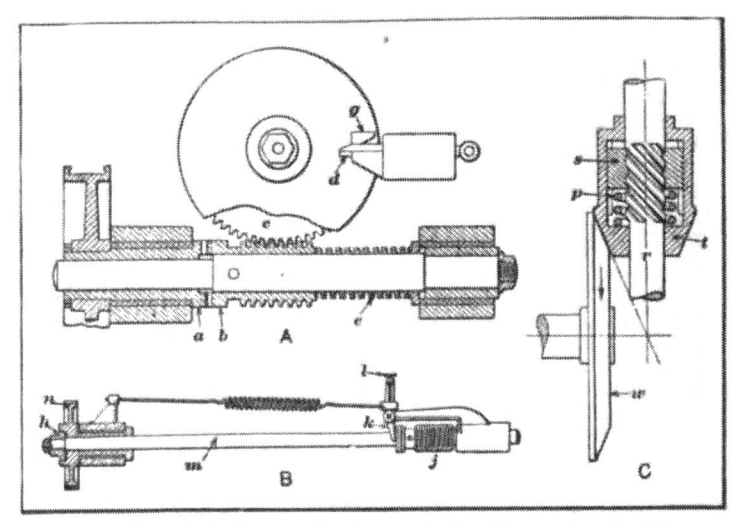

Fig. 22. (A and B) Devices for Automatically Disengaging the Driven Member whenever Resistance to Motion Increases Excessively; (C) Friction Gearing designed to Vary Contact Pressure According to Load

left and into engagement with the constantly revolving clutch a. The worm-wheel then begins to revolve and continues until the lug g strikes the stop d or until some unusual resistance too great to be overcome by the spring is encountered; then, as the worm-wheel remains stationary, it forms a nut for the worm which screws itself out of engagement with clutch a. The strength of spring e is proportioned with reference to the safe or maximum load to be transmitted. One of the advantages of this type of mechanism is that the motion is positively transmitted until an excessive load causes the driving clutch to be disengaged. Provision may readily be made for the adjustment of spring e so that the tension can be varied according to conditions.

Diagram B, Fig. 22, illustrates a modification of the same general type of mechanism. The shaft m is free to move slightly in an endwise direction and is keyed to the tapering disk h, which fits into a seat of corresponding taper in the hub of gear n, thus forming a friction clutch. Motion is applied to gear n and is transmitted by worm j to a worm-wheel (not shown), for any desired purpose. Shaft m turns freely in the hub of gear n, but is attached to worm j. The lever k, which has a spring fastened to it above the fulcrum or pivot, supplies the necessary amount of thrust to keep h in engagement with n under ordinary conditions. This thrust may be regulated by the thumb-screw l which changes the position of the block to which the spring is fastened. If the resistance to the motion of the worm-wheel becomes excessive, the worm moves bodily along the teeth of the wheel, as though it were a nut, and, by moving shaft m and disk h to the left, disengages the friction clutch. The endwise thrust from lever k might be obtained by means of a weight instead of a spring.

Pressure of Friction Gearing Varied According to Load. — A novel design of friction gearing, in which the pressure between the two friction wheels is automatically regulated by the amount of power transmitted, is shown at C in Fig. 22. The wheel w which is the driver revolves in the direction shown by the arrow. The driven pinion t is free to either rotate or slide in a lengthwise direction upon shaft r within certain limits. This shaft has a screw of coarse pitch which passes through nut s. This nut slides in grooves in the friction pinion t so that the pinion and nut revolve together. A spiral spring p inserted between nut s and the pinion forces the latter against the driver w with a pressure depending upon the position of the nut. If wheel w is revolving in the direction shown by the arrow and the driven shaft meets with an unusual degree of resistance to rotation, as soon as shaft r lags behind or stops revolving, nut s moves downward, owing to the action of the screw, and increases the compression on spring p and also the pressure between pinion *t* and wheel *w*. When the resistance to rotation again becomes normal, the spring moves the nut slightly upward and reduces the endwise thrust. While this device may not be entirely practicable, it embodies an interesting principle.

Automatic Relief Mechanisms for Forging Machines. — Forging machines are equipped with a tripping or relief mechanism which prevents excessive straining or breakage of the parts controlling the motion of the movable die, in case the stock to be forged is not placed in the grooves of the dies, but is caught between the flat faces. These relieving mechanisms differ somewhat in design, but the object in each case is to temporarily and automatically release the movable die from the action of the driving mechanism, in case the operating parts are subjected to a strain or pressure that is abnormally high. The release may be obtained by inserting bolts or "breaker castings" in the mechanism, which will shear off or break if there is an excessive strain; another type of relief mechanism depends for its action upon a spring which is proportioned to resist compression for all ordinary strains but to compress sufficiently to release the pressure on the dies when that pressure increases beyond a safe maximum. Two forms of spring-controlled relief mechanisms will be described.

Spring and Toggle Relief Mechanism. — The plan view of a forging machine, shown in Fig. 23, illustrates one method of arranging a spring and toggle relief mechanism. When this machine is in operation, the stock is gripped between the stationary die A and the movable die B. The heading slide C, which carries a ram or plunger for performing the forging operation, is actuated by a crank on the crankshaft D. The gripping slide E to which die B is attached is moved inward for gripping the stock and outward for releasing it, by means of two cams F and G. These cams transmit motion to slide H, which is connected with slide E through a toggle and link mechanism. Cam F, acting upon roll T, moves the slide E for gripping the stock, whereas cam G, in engagement with roll V, withdraws the die after the forging operation is completed. The upper detail view to the right shows the relief mechanism in its normal position, and the lower view shows it after being tripped to relieve any abnormal pressure on the dies.

TRIPPING MECHANISMS 265

When the machine is operating normally, link *J*, which connects with link *K* of the main gripping toggle, oscillates link *K* about pivot *L* and, through link *M*, imparts a reciprocating motion to the gripping slide *E*. If a piece of stock or some other part is caught between the flat die faces, the gripping action con-

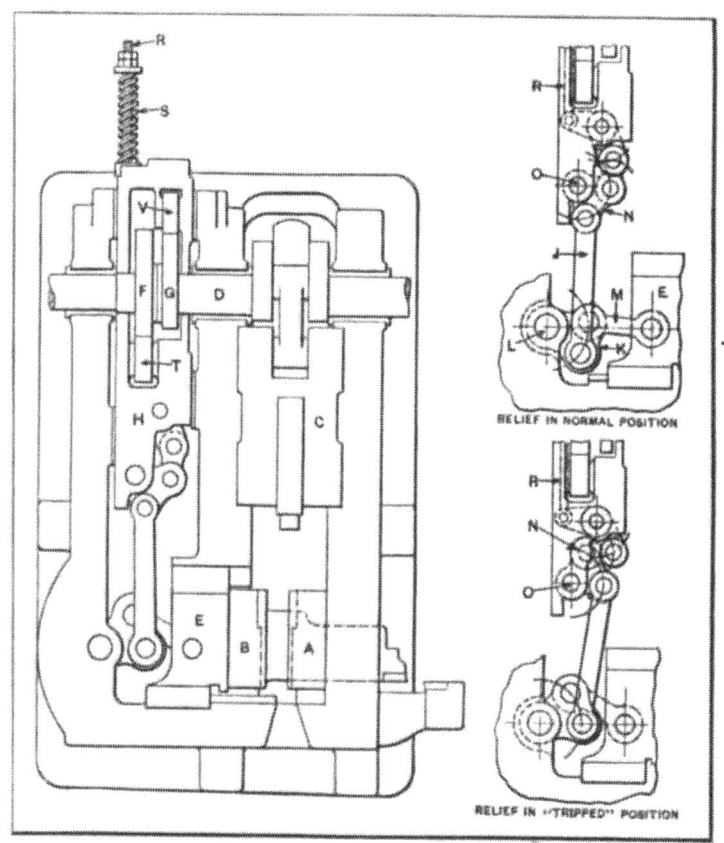

Fig. 23. Plan and Detail Views of Forging Machine showing Automatic Relief or Tripping Mechanism

tinues until the strain exceeds a certain amount; then the backward thrust upon link *N* causes it to swing about pivot *O* (see lower detailed view) carrying with it the other links of the " by-pass toggle " and compressing the spring *S* which is shown in the plan view at the left. As the result of this change in the position of the by-pass toggle, pressure on the gripping die is released. Meanwhile the heading tool attached to slide C completes its full stroke and, upon the return stroke, the by-pass toggle is re-set automatically by spring S which expands and, through rod R, swings the toggle links back to their normal position shown in the upper detailed view. This automatic re-setting of the toggle makes it unnecessary to stop the machine, as is necessary with safety devices of the breaking-bolt type.

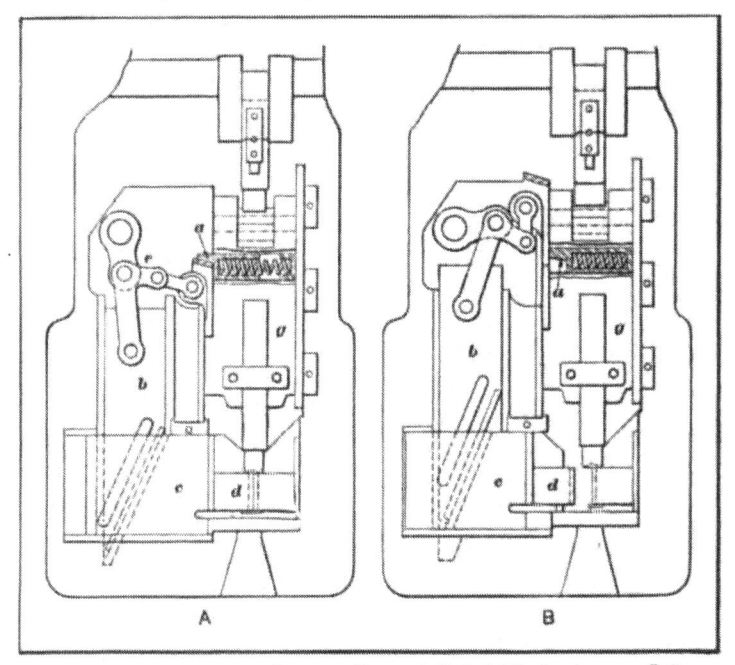

Fig. 24. Bevel Spring Plunger Type of Relief Mechanism on Bolt and Rivet Header

There is no movement of the by-pass toggle, except when a "sticker" — to use the shop expression — is caught between the gripping dies. While this relief mechanism safeguards the working parts from excessive strains, it is capable of transmitting enormous pressures to the gripping dies.

Beveled Spring-plunger Relief Mechanism. — A type of relief mechanism which differs from the design described in the foregoing is illustrated in Fig. 24. This relieving device is ap-

plied to a wedge-grip bolt and rivet header. The movable die
d is attached to a slide c which is beveled to correspond with the
tapering end of slide b. Slide b is given a reciprocating movement
by the toggle mechanism at e, and, when slide c is pushed inward for closing the dies, the beveled end of slide b forms a
solid metal backing, which securely locks the movable die during
the heading operation. When forming the heads on bolts or
rivets, it is necessary to place the stock directly in the impression
in the gripping dies, and not between their opposing faces,
as these dies are intended to come together, so that the stock is
firmly held in the impression between them while the rivet or
bolt head is formed by the tool attached to slide g. The relief
mechanism, which comes into action in case the stock is caught
between the dies, consists of a spring plunger a, which has a
beveled end and is held outward by the spring shown. The
beveled end of this plunger bears against an angular projection
on a slide for transmitting motion, through the toggle mechanism,
to slide b and the movable die. If this die, however, is prevented
from moving inward by a piece of stock that is not in the die
impression, but caught between the faces, the increased pressure
on plunger a forces it back against the tension of the spring and
off of the beveled seat, as indicated by illustration B.

Automatic Speed-limiting Device. — A speed-limiting device
which is governed by the inertia of a weight and the tension of a
spring is shown in Fig. 25. This automatic stop was designed
for application to steam engines but devices operating on the same
general principle could doubtless be applied to other classes of
machinery. This mechanism is primarily a safety device and is
intended to stop the engine and prevent damage such as might
be caused by a bursting flywheel, in case the governor failed to
operate. The lever A is pivoted at B to the engine cross-head
and is normally prevented from swinging about pivot B by the
spring C attached near the upper end. The inertia of weight D,
which may be adjusted along the lever A, tends to swing the lever
to the right when the motion is suddenly reversed and the crosshead moves to the left. When the cross-head is at one end of
its stroke, the upper end of lever A is quite close to the catch

268   MECHANICAL MOVEMENTS

E, which engages latch F. Rod G attached to this latch connects through whatever additional rods or levers may be needed, with the tripping mechanism used in conjunction with a quick-closing valve which controls the flow of steam to the engine cylinder. This valve and its operating mechanism is shown in detail at the left of the illustration. Rod G is connected in any convenient way with bellcrank lever H, from which rod J carrying weights at its lower end is suspended. This rod passes through trip-lever K, which normally engages lever L connected with the

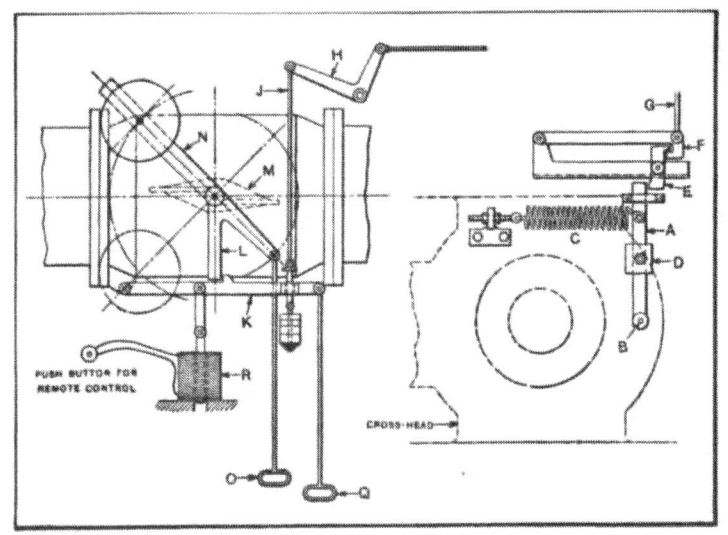

Fig. 25. Automatic Speed-limiting Mechanism for Steam Engines

quick-closing valve M. If, for any reason, the speed of the engine becomes excessive, the lever A and its attached weight resists the sudden reversal of motion at the end of its stroke sufficiently to overcome the tension of spring C, and lever A strikes catch E, thus releasing latch F; as rod J drops, the flange on it strikes trip K and allows the steam valve to be closed by the weighted lever N. This speed-limiting device may be adjusted by varying the tension of spring C and also by changing the position of weight D. The greater the spring tension and the nearer the weight is to the pivot B, the faster the speed will have to be to overcome the tension of the spring at the point of reversal. The handle O is for re-setting the steam valve and handle Q, for tripping the valve by hand. If remote control is required, this may be obtained by the use of rods or cables directly connected to latch K, or by the use of a solenoid R, as indicated by the illustration. This automatic safety stop is recommended as being simple, positive in action, adjustable, inexpensive, and easily applied to almost any engine.

Centrifugal Type of Safety Stop. — The automatic speed-limiting device described in the following was designed for application to gas or gasoline engines. In case the speed becomes

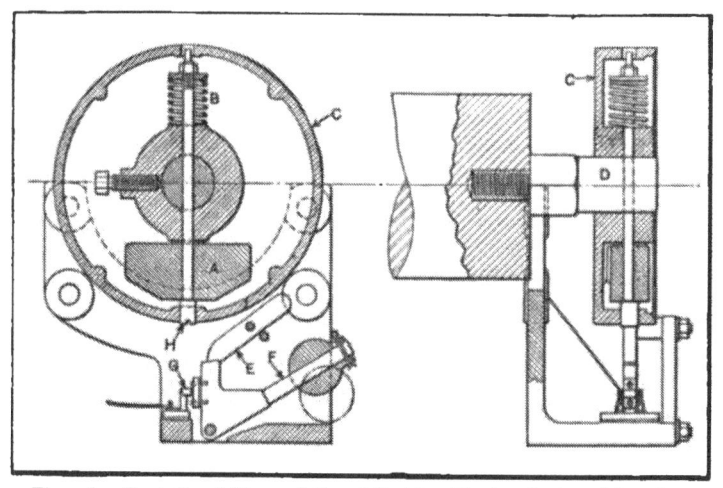

Fig. 26. Centrifugal Type of Speed-limiting Device designed for Gas or Gasoline Engines

excessive, owing to the failure of the governor, this tripping mechanism, which is of the centrifugal type, operates by breaking the ignition circuit. It may be attached either to the secondary shaft or to the main shaft. The controlling element is a weight A (Fig. 26) which is attached to a rod connecting with a spring B on the opposite side of the hub. This weight is located within a casing C carried by a stud D screwed into the end of the shaft. Pivoted near the casing is a latch E which normally holds the weighted trip-lever F in the position shown. The ignition switch is located at G and, when the lever F is held up by latch E, the ignition circuit is closed. If the speed of the engine is increased to such an extent that the action of centrifugal force causes weight A to fly outward against the tension of spring B, the end of rod H, by striking catch E, releases lever F and allows it to fall, thus breaking the ignition circuit.

Electromagnetic Tripping Devices. — In designing automatic machinery or automatic devices for standard machines, the designer is often confronted by the problem of providing a suitable mechanism for making a machine "fool-proof" and reliable. This is particularly true in the case of automatic machines where one operator looks after several units. While it is not claimed that purely mechanical means cannot accomplish the same results which are secured through the use of electromagnetic tripping devices, the mechanisms would, in some cases, be so complicated, as compared to electrical devices for the same purpose, that they would be a source of trouble, if not impractical. Another advantage of the electrical devices lies in the fact that they may be used as a check on the accuracy of preceding operations and thus avoid finishing pieces of work that are defective. The application of electricity to automatic machines may be regarded as a complication in itself, but this is far from being the case if these tripping devices are properly applied.

The following examples are typical applications of electromagnetic tripping devices to automatic machines, and by studying these designs, one may readily understand how similar tripping mechanisms could be applied to other classes of machinery. In most of these examples, the tripping devices constitute part of attachments for standard machines that were converted into " automatics," thus dispensing with the necessity of an operator for each machine.

Methods of Closing Electromagnetic Circuit. — A metallic cartridge shell is shown in Fig. 27 (view to right) in place on a machine which pierces the primer hole, and a shell is illustrated at H on which the piercing operation has been performed. After the hole has been pierced, the primer is inserted in the primer cavity J. These operations are performed on a standard Waterbury-Farrel cartridge primer. The shells were formerly placed on dial pins by hand and indexed under the cross-head for piercing and inserting the primer; they were then removed from the dial pins automatically. An improvement was made in the method of operation by applying an automatic feed mechanism to place the shells on the dial pins, but this did not dispense with the necessity of an operator for each machine, as there are three possible conditions that may result in the production of imperfect work: 1. The feed mechanism might fail to deliver the shell to the dial pin, or the supply of shells might become exhausted, while primers would continue to feed and thus be wasted. 2. The piercing punch might break and the machine would

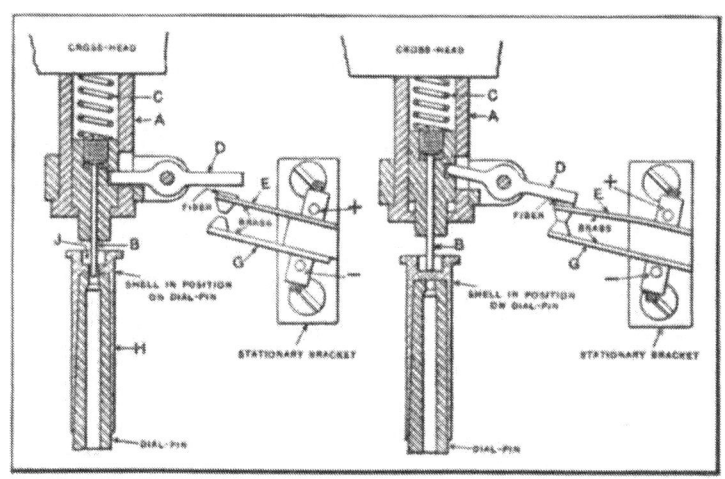

Fig. 27. Mechanism for Closing Circuit and Stopping Machine in Case Punch fails to Pierce the Shell

then continue to place primers in the cavities of shells which had not been pierced, and such shells would obviously be useless. 3. The primer feed might fail to work properly, or the supply of primers might become exhausted.

The application of a suitable electromagnetic tripping mechanism to this machine takes care of all of these contingencies. First, consider the possibility of the feed mechanism failing to deliver a shell to the dial pin. Referring to diagram A, Fig. 28, it will be seen that the shells are carried on pins on the dial and are indexed under the punch a. If a shell is in its place on the dial pin, it contracts the spring b when the ram descends, but should the mechanism fail to deliver a shell to the pin, the sleeve g passes down over the dial pin and pushes the upper contact d of the tripping mechanism down upon the lower contact e. This closes the electrical circuit and stops the cross-head on the up-stroke. The contacts are fastened to the frame of the machine and the method by which the tripping mechanism operates will be described in detail later.

The way in which the piercing operation is safeguarded by the electromagnetic tripping mechanism is illustrated in Fig. 27. The punch-holder A is located at the index point immediately after the completion of the piercing operation. If a shell is

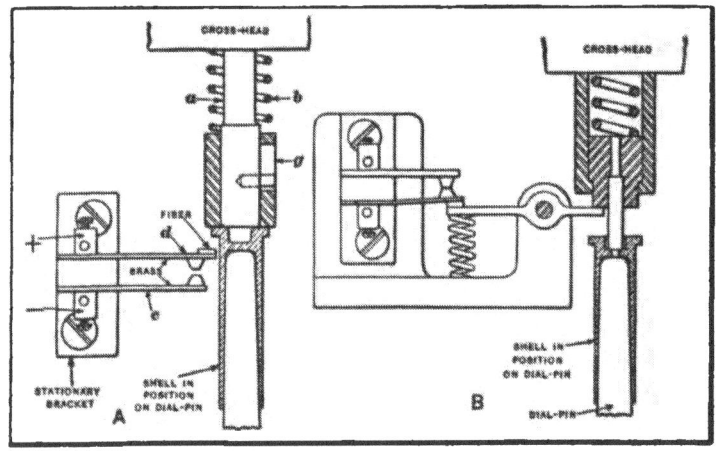

Fig. 28. (A) Circuit-closing Device which acts when Shell has not been placed on Dial Pin; (B) Trip which prevents passing a Shell without a Primer

pierced, the pin B descends through the hole in the shell, as shown at the left of the illustration; but if the piercing operation does not take place, the punch is held in the position indicated in the right-hand illustration, thus contracting the light spring C and throwing the lever D against the contact E. This closes the electrical circuit and causes the machine to be stopped so that shells cannot have primers inserted in them when the primer hole has not been properly pierced.

The failure of the machine to feed a primer into the primer cavity of the shell is guarded against by the mechanism illustrated at B in Fig. 28. The design of this tripping mechanism is practically the same as that used to control the piercing operation, and will be readily understood without further description.

Fig. 29 illustrates the mechanism used on a press for assembling the brass cups A and B, the cup A being inserted in the cup B. These cups are held in hoppers on each side of the machine from which they are taken by notched dials. The cups A are dropped

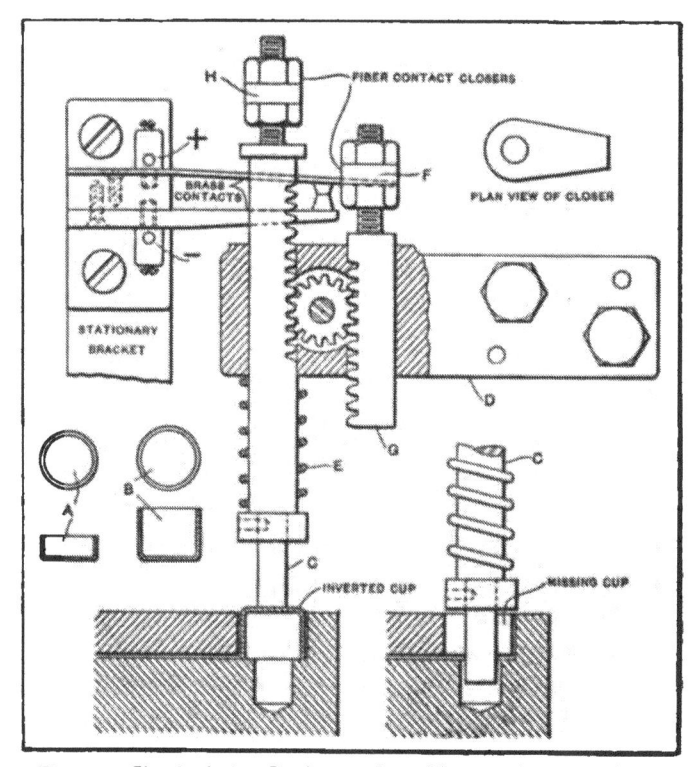

Fig. 29. Circuit-closing Device used on Machine for Assembling Shells A and B

into holes in the machine dial which passes over the dial carrying the cups B. The operation of the machine will not be described; it should be mentioned, however, that a plunger descends in such a manner that the cup A is forced into place in cup B. Several conditions may occur that will result in loss or damage. The feed mechanism could fail to deliver either one or both cups to their respective dials, or it could deliver them to the dials in an inverted position. Either the absence or inversion of either or both cups is detected by an electromagnetic tripping device which automatically stops the machine until the error has been corrected. The punch C is located at an index point preceding the assembling punch, and is carried by a bracket which is fastened to the cross-head. In the case of an inverted cup, the punch C is held on the bottom of the cup and pulls the rod G down through the action of the pinion, which engages with rack

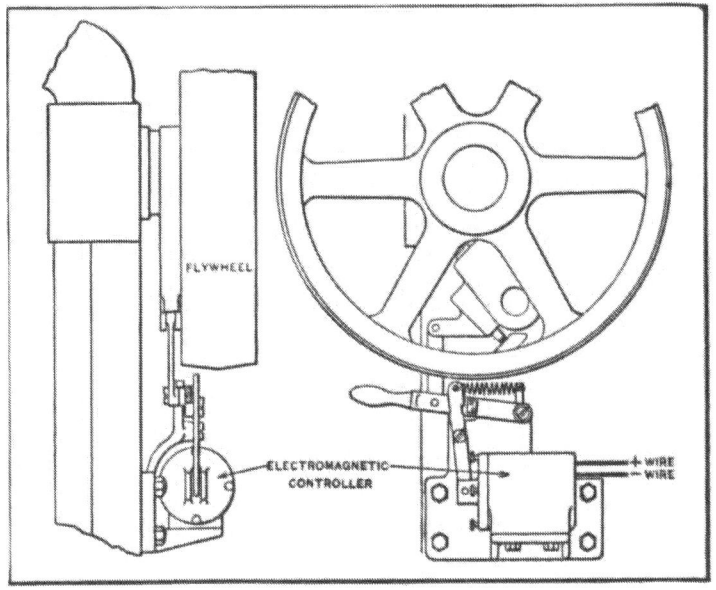

Fig. 30. Electromagnetic Controller applied to Power Press for Operating Clutch

teeth cut in the rods C and G. The descent of the rod G causes the contact closer F to pull down the upper electrical contact until it closes the circuit and causes the machine to be stopped.

The detail view at the right shows the punch and die when the feed mechanism has failed to deliver a cup to the dial plate. In this case, the upper electrical contact is pulled down by the contact closer H and causes the machine to be stopped as previously described.

Electromagnetic Controller. — Fig. 30 shows the electromagnetic tripping device used on the machines referred to in the foregoing, for stopping the machine. In this illustration, the tripping device is shown in place on a power press equipped with a Horton clutch. The arrangement of the tripping mechanism will be more readily understood by referring to Fig. 31, which shows an end and cross-sectional view. This tripping mechanism is self-contained and can be applied to any style of press or type of machine. The bracket A carries the magnet B, pole-piece C, and levers D and E. The brass pole G is wound with No. 14 double-covered wire and the connecting wires extend through the back of the spool. The brass pins H help to support the pole-piece C and provide adjustment for different widths of air gap, which should be as small as possible.

In order to start the press, the lever E is pulled down. This engages the flywheel clutch (see Fig. 30) and allows the spring J to pull the lever D over the hardened knife-edge, thus setting the pole-piece C at the proper working distance from the magnet. The inside dimensions of the device are given in Fig. 31. When the magnet is energized by two dry cells, it gives an initial pull of from twelve to fifteen pounds. As the dry cells are used on open-circuit — except for the fractional part of a second during which the contacts meet — they have a long life.

The initial pull provided by an electromagnet of this kind varies with the material used for the magnet and the pole-piece. Where cast iron is used, the pull of the magnet can be calculated by the formula:

$$NI = 3000 Z \sqrt{P \div D},$$

in which

N = number of coils of wire on the spool (ampere-turns);
I = current in amperes;
P = pull in pounds;
Z = air gap in inches;
D = diameter of plunger in inches.

The electromagnet shown in Fig. 31 was designed to give a pull of 15 pounds, and it will be seen that $Z = \frac{5}{16}$ inch and $D = 1.125$ inch. Then:

$$NI = 3000 \times \tfrac{5}{16} \sqrt{15 \div 1.125} = 3423.19 \text{ ampere-turns.}$$

Assuming that there are 375 turns of wire on a spool, the amount of current required will be found to be $\frac{3423.19}{375} = 9.14$ or, say, 10 amperes. Two good dry cells connected in series will average 15 amperes during their useful life and give a considerably higher current when new. As 10 amperes is sufficient to enable the electromagnet to do the work required of it, it will be seen that an ample factor of safety is provided. When designing devices of this kind, moving wires and moving contacts should be avoided and the mechanism should be made as simple as possible. The dry cells should be used on open circuit, the

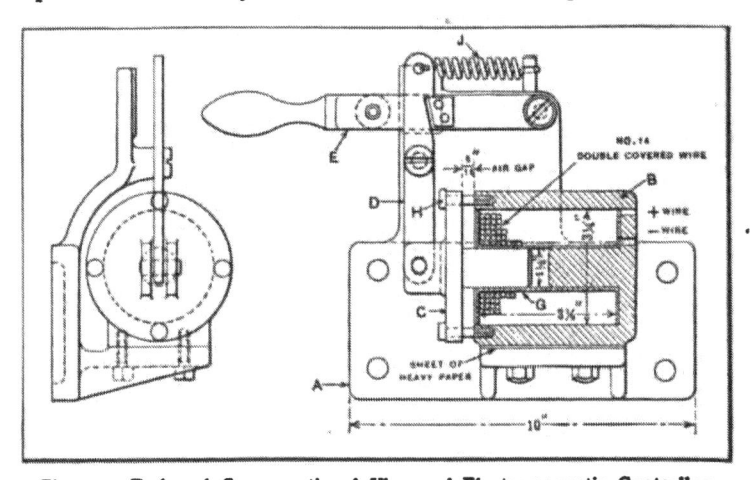

Fig. 31. End and Cross-sectional Views of Electromagnetic Controller

contacts carefully insulated from the machine, and covers provided for contacts and terminals.

Controlling Device for a Delicate Mechanism. — The delicate and intricate mechanism of an adding machine is safeguarded from injury resulting from careless or rough operation, by the ingenious mechanism shown in Fig. 32. This controlling device is so arranged that the force or power exerted upon a hand lever by the operator is not transmitted directly to the mechanism, but the operation of the machine is subject to spring action at a certain known rate and with a known driving force. The operator is only allowed to supply the power for stretching certain

TRIPPING MECHANISMS 277

springs and releasing their action, the arrangement being such that he cannot apply his strength directly to the mechanism.

The inner end of the operating lever is shown at Y. The upper view marked "position No. 1" shows the lever after it has

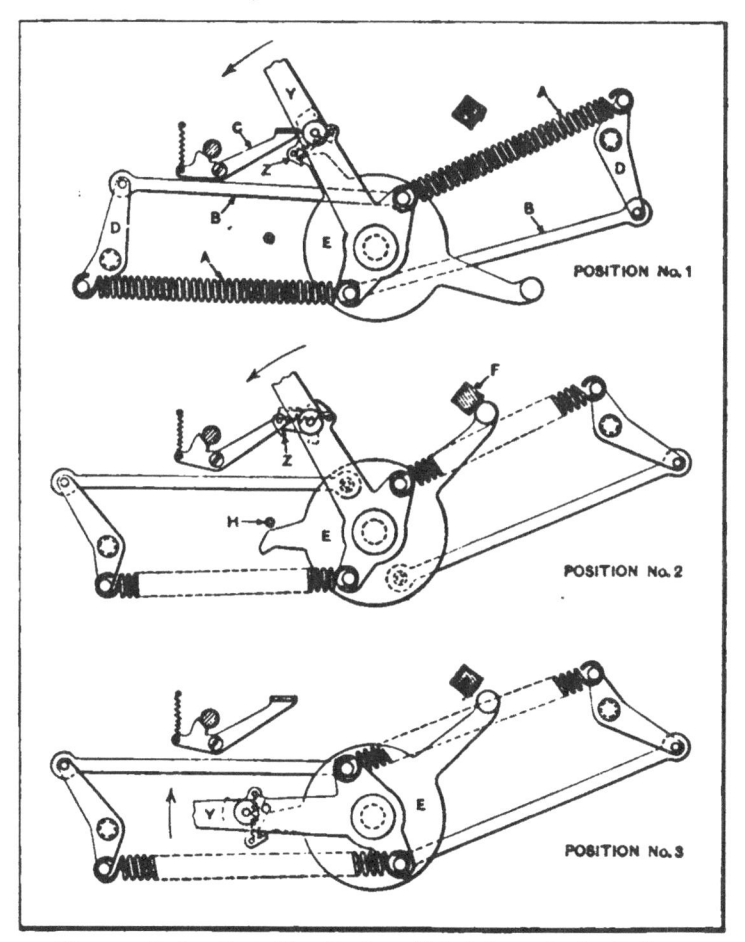

Fig. 32. Spring Controlling Device which Safeguards the Delicate Mechanism of an Adding Machine

been pulled forward for operating the machine. This lever revolves freely on its shaft and the operating parts are driven by the member E. As lever Y is pulled forward, catch C releases pawl Z, thus allowing member E to fly forward as springs A contract and transmit motion to E through levers D and links B. This free movement of part E operates the forward stroke of the machine, and the rate of action is controlled by an oil by-pass governor (not shown). The movement of E is stopped by abutment F in position No. 2. The forward movement of operating lever Y, which is now free of the mechanism, is continued by the operator until the lever arrives at position No. 3. At this point, the end of pawl Z strikes pin H, throwing the pawl back into engagement with the projecting lug on part E. As the lever moves from position No. 2 to position No. 3, the springs A are extended, and acting through levers D and links B they return lever Y to the starting position, the lever

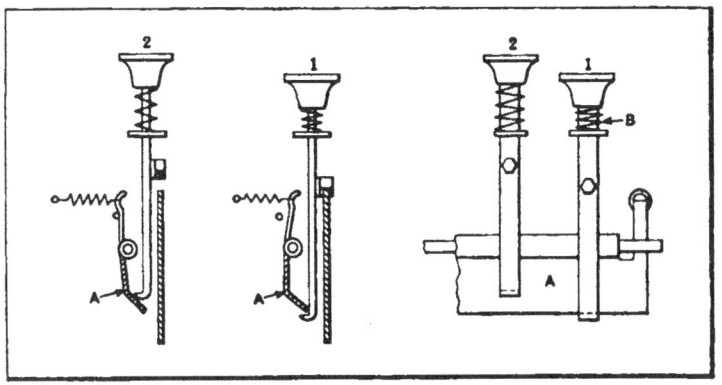

Fig. 33. Simple Arrangement for Holding in the Downward Position only One Key at a Time in a Row of Adding Machine Keys

carrying with it part E and the mechanism of the machine. This reverse movement is also under the control of the oil governor. Near the end of the return movement, latch C rises to permit pawl Z to pass, and the various parts return to position No. 1 ready for another stroke.

The provision of two springs A is simply for balancing the strain on the mechanism. The double action of these springs, which makes it possible for them to operate the mechanism on both the forward and backward strokes, is due to the fact that they are connected to movable members at each end. In one case, the connection is to levers D and in the other to operating lever Y. The contraction of these springs between positions

TRIPPING MECHANISMS

No. 1 and No. 2 operates the forward motion, and their contraction from position No. 3 to No. 1 operates the backward motion.

Control for Flexible Keyboard. — The keyboard of an adding machine is said to be "flexible" when so arranged that, if a key has been depressed, it will stay down, but the pressing down of another key in the same vertical column will release the first key. With this arrangement, if an attempt were made to depress two keys successively, the releasing of one by the downward action of the other would eliminate a possible error. As a further advantage, if the wrong key were pressed, the depression

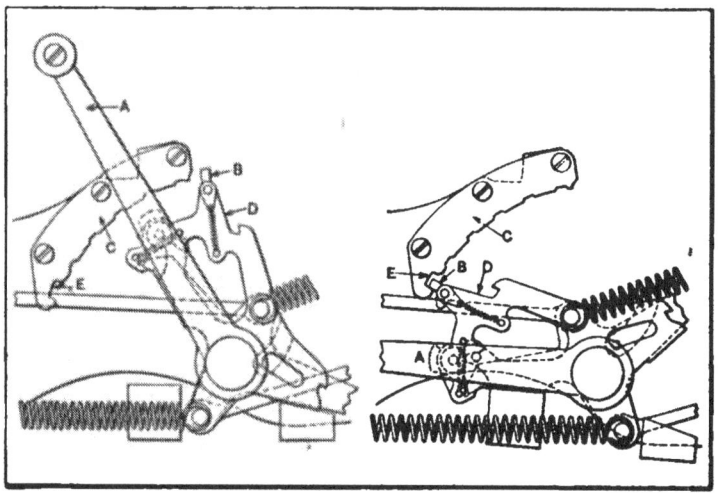

Fig. 34. Full-stroke Mechanism to Prevent starting the Operating Lever and not completing Its Movement

of the right one restores the wrong one to its normal position. The simple, but ingenious, device for controlling the action of the keys on one of the commercial adding machines is illustrated in Fig. 33. If key No. 1 is depressed, the lower hooked end of the stem on which it is mounted springs past the end of a long pivoted strip *A* that extends throughout the entire length of the vertical row of keys. The result is that the key is held in the downward position by this hooked end until some other key is depressed. For instance, if the operator presses down on key No. 2, this will swing the strip *A* about its pivot to allow the hooked end of the stem to pass, and this movement of strip A releases the hooked end of key No. 1 which immediately is forced upward to its normal position by a spring B. In the same manner, any key which may be pressed down will throw back the strip and release any other key which may at the time be depressed.

Full-stroke Mechanisms. — Mechanisms are sometimes so arranged that hand-operated movements are, to some extent, controlled mechanically, to prevent motion in the wrong direction or incomplete action. The full-stroke ratchet mechanism shown in Fig. 34 is used on the Ellis adding typewriter to prevent the operator from starting handle A and not completing the required movement. For instance, if handle A is in the upper position, as shown at the left, any downward movement must be continued until the handle has made a complete stroke before it can be reversed for returning it to the original or upper position. Similarly, if the lever is at the lower end of its stroke, as shown by the view to the right, any upward movement must be completed before the direction of motion can be reversed. This positive control of the action of handle A is obtained in a very simple manner. As the handle is moved downward or upward, pawl B is carried with it. This pawl is pivoted to part D and normally held in a vertical position by a spring. When handle A is at the upper end of its stroke, as shown at the left, and a downward movement is started, pawl B engages sector C and its upper end swings to the right; as the downward movement of handle A continues, pawl B engages successive notches in sector C, and locks into one of these notches if an attempt is made to return handle A before the downward stroke is completed. When handle A has been pushed all the way down (as shown to the right), pawl B drops into the enlarged notch E of sector C where there is enough room to permit the pawl to swing around to the vertical position; consequently, as soon as handle A is moved upward, the top of pawl B swings to the left and again engages successive notches in sector C, thus preventing any return of handle A to the lower position until the pawl has cleared the upper end of the sector and again swings to a vertical position.

CHAPTER X

AUTOMATIC FEEDING MECHANISMS

MACHINES which operate on large numbers of duplicate parts which are separate or in the form of individual pieces are often equipped with a mechanism for automatically transferring the parts from a magazine or other retaining device, to the tools that perform the necessary operations. The magazine used in conjunction with mechanisms of this kind is arranged for holding enough parts to supply the machine for a certain period, and it is equipped with a mechanical device for removing the parts separately from the magazine and placing them in the correct position wherever the operations are to be performed. The magazine may be in the form of a hopper, or the supply of parts to be operated upon by the machine may be held in some other way. The transfer of the parts from the hopper or main source of supply to the operating tools may be through a chute or passageway leading directly to the tools, or it may be necessary to convey the parts to the tools by an auxiliary transferring mechanism which acts in unison with the magazine feeding attachment. These automatic feeding mechanisms are usually designed especially for handling a certain product, although some types are capable of application to a limited range of work. The feeding mechanisms described in the following include designs which differ considerably, and illustrate, in a general way, the possibilities of automatic devices of this kind.

Attachments having Inclined Chutes. — One of the important applications of magazine feeding attachments is in connection with the automatic screw machine. Most of the parts made on these machines are produced directly from bars of stock, but secondary operations on separate pieces are sometimes necessary, and then an automatic or semi-automatic attachment may be employed to transfer the parts successively to the machine chuck where the tools can operate upon them. Many of these attachments have magazines which are in the form of an inclined chute that holds the parts in the correct position and from which they are removed, one at a time, by a transferring device. An example of this type of magazine attachment is shown in Fig. 1. This attachment was designed for feeding the handles of safety razors on a Brown & Sharpe automatic screw machine. The preliminary screw machine operations involve turning, forming, knurling, drilling, tapping, and cutting off the handle, thus producing a piece of the form shown at A in the illustration. These partly finished handles are then placed in the chute or slide of the feeding attachment, from which they are transferred to the chuck, so that a hole can be drilled clear through the handle as indicated at B, and one end of the hole be slightly enlarged. The upper and lower plates C of the chute have grooves milled in them to correspond to the enlarged parts of the handle. As each successive handle reaches the lower end of the chute and drops into the small pocket shown, a spring plunger L attached to the turret advances and pushes the work out into the chuck of the machine.

As the ends of the handles have shoulders, the pocket at the bottom is automatically enlarged to permit the passage of this shoulder. The work-carrier consists principally of two blocks D and E and a finger F. Block D is held in the cross-slide and block E is attached to the top of block D. The forward end of block E is cut out to fit the work, which is held in place by finger F. This finger is fastened to lever G, pivoted on block D, and normally held in position by a pawl H engaged by plunger I and pin J. When a piece of work drops into the pocket in block E and the front cross-slide has advanced far enough to bring the work in line with the hole in the chuck, the enlarged part of the plunger L trips the finger F after the work has been partly inserted in the chuck. This action is caused by the contact of plunger L with a beveled edge on pawl H which disengages the V-shaped end of the pawl from a groove in lever G and, at the same time, pushes back spring plunger I, thus allowing finger F to drop away from block E. The pawl H serves as a locater for the work and, when disconnected from lever G, it swings down and the work is pushed into the chuck by plunger L which is held in the advancing turret. After a piece has been inserted in the chuck, the cross-slide, as it moves outward, brings

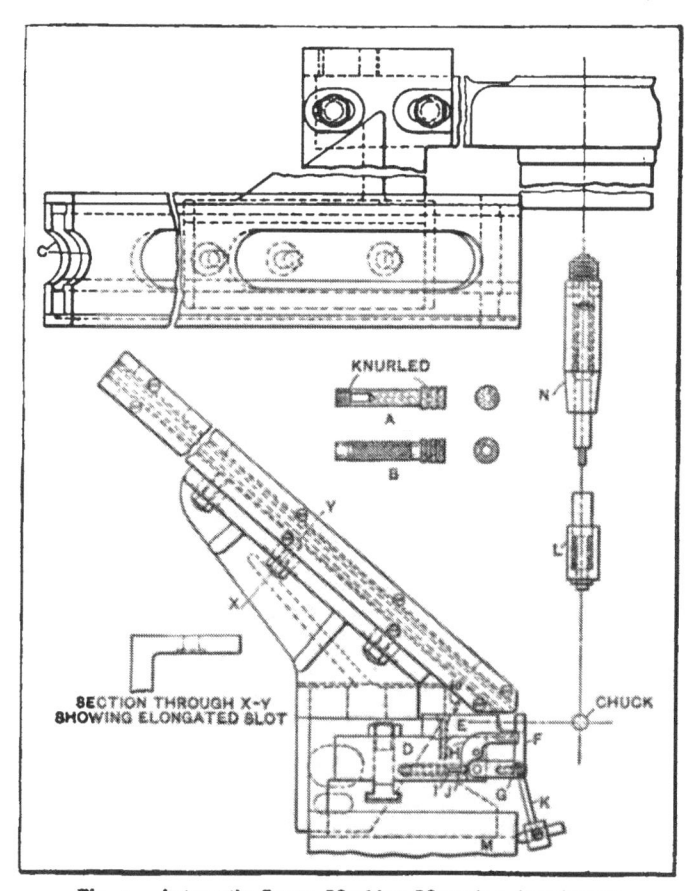

Fig. 1. Automatic Screw Machine Magazine Attachment

trip K against casting M which, through the combined action of lever G, pawl H, and spring plunger I, closes the work-carrier. The piece in the chuck is forced in against a spring plunger held by feed finger N. This spring plunger ejects the work when the machining operation has been finished and the chuck is opened.

Feeding Attachment for Pinion Staffs. — Another magazine feeding attachment having an inclined chute is shown in Fig. 2. This attachment was designed for handling pinion staffs of the

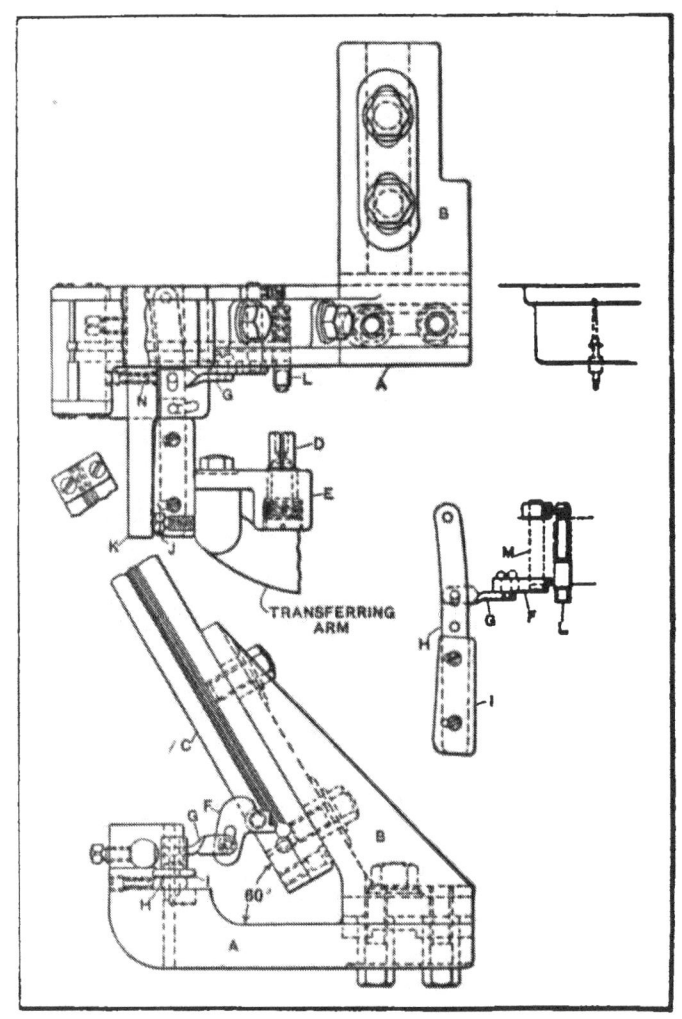

Fig. 2. Magazine Attachment for Pinion Staffs

form illustrated by the dotted lines in the upper right-hand corner of the illustration. The chute C is supported by a bracket B which is attached to a boss provided on Brown & Sharpe automatic screw machines for holding special attachments. The bracket *A* is attached to *B* and carries the mechanism for feeding the pinion staffs successively to the place where they can be removed by the transferring arm. The two main parts of the chute are grooved to fit the pinion staffs, so that the latter are held in the correct position. The operation of this attachment is as follows: The chute is filled with pinion staffs and the lower one is held back temporarily by trip *F*. This trip is connected to link *G*, which carries a pin that engages a slot cut in lever *H* (see detailed view). Lever *H* has fastened to its upper side a trip-lever plate *I* the inclination of which may be varied. When the transferring arm swings upward, it is stopped in the correct position by set-screw *J*, which engages stop *K*, the arm itself bearing against plate *I* and forcing it back, together with lever *H*. This action, through connecting link *G*, operates trip *F* and allows one piece to drop into the pocket formed at the end of this trip. The transferring arm carrying a split bushing *D* then advances and pushing back the nest *L* passes over the end of a pinion staff and grips it. The transferring arm then recedes and swings down to the chuck in which the pinion staff is placed. When the transferring arm descends, the spring *N* returns trip-lever plate *I* and lever *H* to their former position. Trip-lever *F* also swings back in order to catch another piece, the pinion staff in the trip being deposited in the nest *L* ready for transferring to the split bushing *D* the next time the transferring arm ascends.

Magazine Attachment for Narrow Bushings. — The narrow bushings shown at *A*, Fig. 3, are blanked out and drawn in a die to the shape shown; they are then turned, faced, and threaded (as indicated at *B*) in a Brown & Sharpe automatic screw machine. Two separate operations are required, but the magazine attachment shown in this illustration is used for both. The bushings are placed in the inclined slide or chute, and the lower one is retained temporarily by a finger *i*, which is held upward by spring *k*, the exact position of the finger depending upon the adjustments of set-screw *j* which engages a projecting end. The transferring arm, which removes the work from the lower end of the chute and conveys it to the chuck, has a swinging or circular movement, as indicated by the dotted line. The work is gripped as the holder (shown in detail at C) advances, and then, as the transfer arm starts to swing downward toward the chuck, the finger i is depressed, thus allowing the bushing to slide out of the chute. The work-holder has a taper shank b which fits into the main body c. On this body is held a ring d through which a pin is driven. The pin h in this ring d fits into an elongated hole in body c and enters spring plunger e. A slot in body c receives a flat spring g, which is provided to grip the work securely. This spring also compensates for slight variations of diameter.

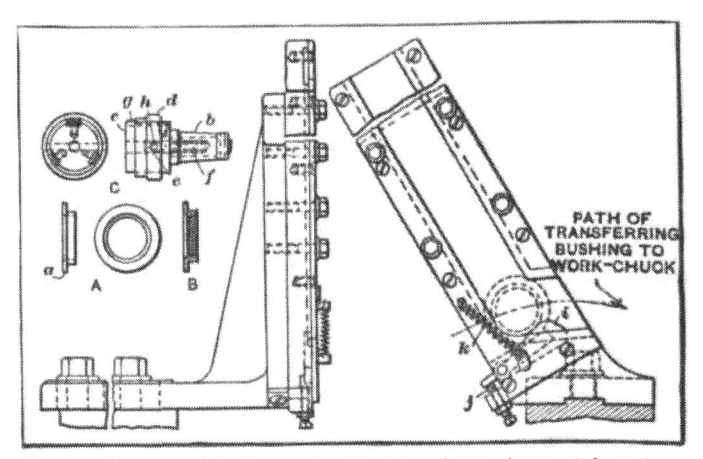

Fig. 3. Magazine Attachment for Handling Parts shown at A and B

The degree of inclination for chutes of magazine attachments varies from 20 to 60 degrees and depends upon the size and shape of the work. The chute should incline at a greater angle for small work than for large work. The chutes of attachments used for handling flat pieces, such, for example, as might be cut out in a blanking die, are usually held in a vertical chute instead of one that is inclined.

Revolving Magazine Attachment. — The automatic feeding attachment shown in Fig. 4 differs from the types previously described in that the blanks to be operated on are held in a revolving carrier or magazine B. This attachment is used for feeding the

AUTOMATIC FEEDING MECHANISMS 287

blanks from which the barrels for watch springs are made. The shape of these barrels, which are about $\frac{3}{4}$ inch in diameter, is indicated at M. The magazine wheel B is recessed, as shown by the side view, to form a pocket for the blanks, and it is provided with slots around the edge in which the blanks' fit, as indicated at N. The blanks are inserted in the attachment or magazine wheel through slot C which connects with pocket D. The wheel B is rotated by a belt which transmits motion from a pulley on the front camshaft to a pulley located on shaft S. As these two pulleys are of the same diameter, the magazine wheel rotates at

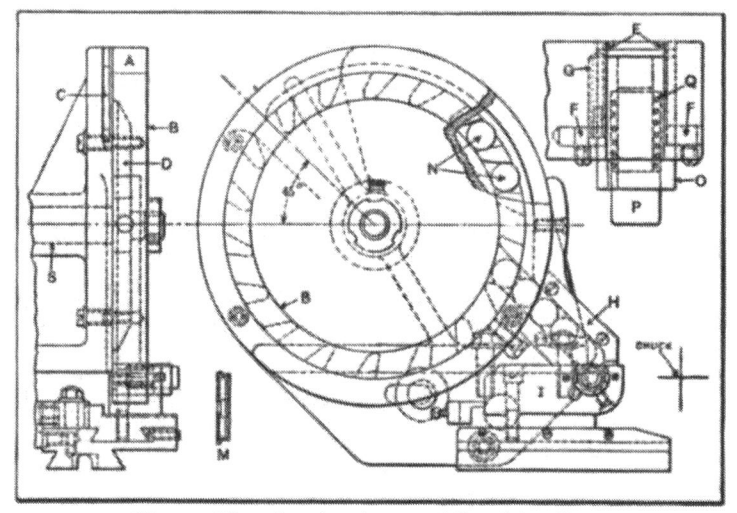

Fig. 4. Magazine Attachment of Revolving Type

the same speed as the front camshaft. The blanks, as they are carried around by the wheel, drop into slide H and from there into a pocket in a bushing held by a carrier. The block I of this carrier (see enlarged detail view) is counterbored to receive a bushing O which contains plunger P, and the bushing is cut out to receive the spring fingers E. These fingers are attached to plugs F which are held in drilled holes in block I. The bushing O is free to slide in block I and is held back by spring G, which bears against a pin driven into the bushing. As a blank rolls down the slide H, it is deposited in bushing O. The cross-slide upon which the attachment is mounted then advances to locate the blank in line with the hole in the chuck. When in this position, the turret advances and a stop on it pushes plunger P forward, thus forcing the blank from the fingers E and depositing it in the chuck. The spring Q which returns plunger P is made much heavier than the spring G used for holding back the bushing O. The object of this arrangement is to insure that the bushing will be pushed out close to the face of the chuck before the plunger forces the blank out of the spring fingers.

Hopper Feeding Mechanism for Screw Blanks. — The automatic feeding mechanism to be described is used on a thread rolling machine of the type having straight dies between which the blanks are rolled to form the threads. The faces of the dies are in a vertical position and one die is given a reciprocating motion in a direction at right angles to the axis of the screw blank. The automatic feeding mechanism shown in Fig. 5 is arranged to transfer the screw blanks from the hopper A to the dies at B in such a way that each successive blank is in a vertical position when caught between the dies. The hopper A, which is at the top of the machine, is equipped with a plate or center-board C which passes through a slot in the bottom of the hopper and is given a reciprocating motion by a gear-driven cam. This center-board has a vertical slot extending along the upper edge (see detail sectional view) which is a little wider than the diameter of the screw blank bodies. As the center-board moves up through the mass of screw blanks, one or more of these blanks are liable to drop into the slot and hang suspended by their heads. If a blank does not happen to be caught for any one stroke of the center-board, the mass of blanks is disturbed and it is likely that one or more blanks will fall into the slot on the next successive stroke of the center-board.

As some blanks are picked up while in a crosswise or other incorrect position, an auxiliary device is employed to dislodge such blanks. This device consists of three revolving wheels at D which have teeth like ratchet wheels. The arrangement of these wheels is shown by the detailed view. The center wheel, which is the smallest, revolves above the heads of the blanks which are moving down the slot of the center-board in the proper position, as indicated at *E*. The two outer wheels, which are larger than the central one, revolve close to the outer edges of the center-board. If a blank is not in the correct position, it will be caught by these wheels and be thrown back into the hopper, but all blanks that hang in the slot pass between the outer wheels and beneath the central one without being disturbed. After the blanks leave the center-board, they pass down the inclined chute *G*, which is provided with a guide *F* that holds them

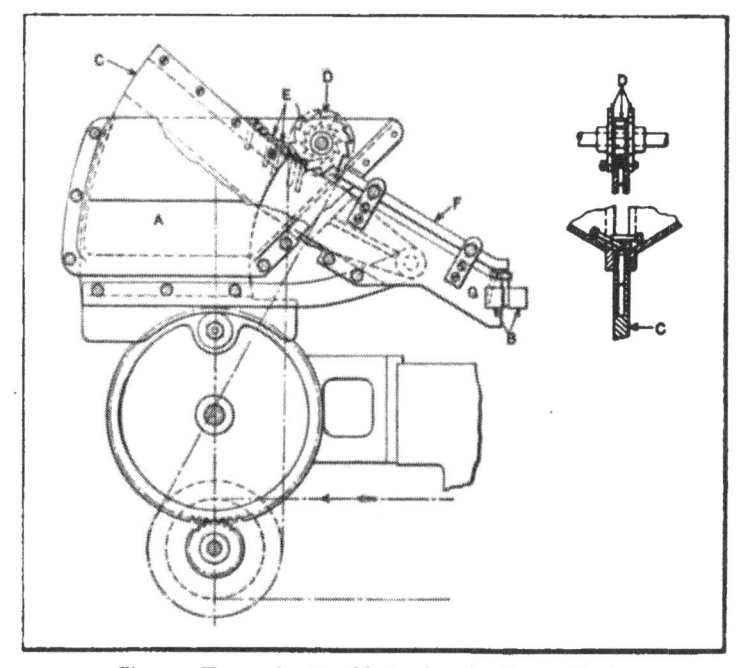

Fig. 5. Hopper-feeding Mechanism for Screw Blanks

in position. As each successive blank reaches the lower end of the chute, it swings around to a vertical position and is caught between the dies which roll screw threads on the ends.

Feeding Shells with Closed Ends Foremost. — The possibilities of mechanical motion and control are almost boundless, if there is no limit to the number of parts that may be incorporated in a mechanism, but as complication means higher manufacturing cost, and usually greater liability of derangement, the skillful designer tries to accomplish the desired results by the simplest means possible; it is this simplifying process that often requires a high degree of mechanical ingenuity. The feed-chute shown in Fig. 6 illustrates how a very simple device may sometimes be employed to accomplish what might appear at first to be difficult. This is an attachment used in conjunction with an automatic feeding mechanism for drawing shells in a punch-press. These shells are fed from a hopper, and it is essential to have them enter the die with the closed ends down. If a shell descends from the hopper with the open end foremost, it is auto-

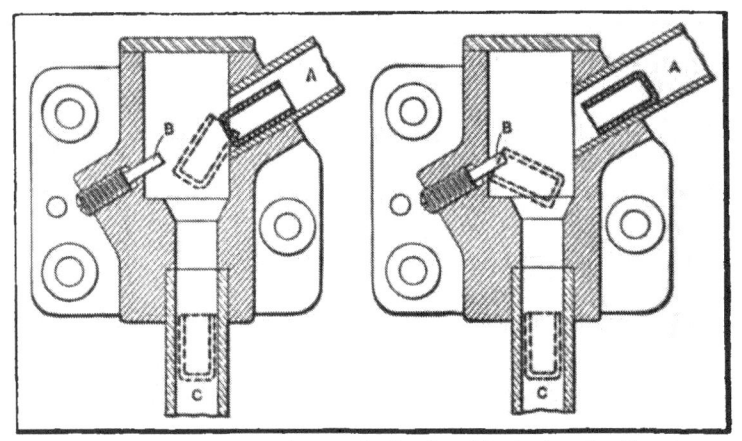

Fig. 6. Attachment of an Automatic Feeding Mechanism for Turning Shells which enter Open End Foremost

matically turned around by the simple device shown. The view to the left illustrates the movements of a shell which comes down in the proper position or with the closed end foremost. In this case, the bottom of the shell simply strikes pin B and, after rebounding, drops down through tube C. If the open end of a shell is foremost, as illustrated at the right, it catches on pin B and is turned around as the illustration indicates. If a shell enters the die with the closed end upward, the drawing punch will probably be broken.

Feeding Bullets with Pointed Ends Foremost. — An attachment for feeding lead bullets or slugs to press tools with the pointed ends foremost, regardless of the position in which the bullets are received from the magazine or hopper, is illustrated in Fig. 7. This attachment is applied to a press having a 4½-inch stroke. The bullets enter the tube A which connects with a hopper located above the press. An "agitator tube" moves up and down through the mass of bullets in the hopper and the bullets which enter the agitator tube drop into tube A. As each bullet reaches the lower end of this tube, it is transferred by slide C (operated by cam D attached to the cross-head) to a position under the rod E. The rod-holder L is also carried by the cross-head. Whenever a bullet enters tube A with the rounded or pointed end downward, it is simply pushed through a hole in dial F and into feed-pipe G leading to the dial feed-plate of the press. This feed-plate, in turn, conveys the bullets to the press tools where such operations as swaging or sizing are performed.

The arrangement of dial F is shown by the detailed sectional views at the lower part of the illustration. Whenever a bullet enters the dial with the pointed end foremost, the plungers H are pushed back against the tension of springs J and the bullet drops into the tube beneath. If the blunt or flat end is foremost, the plungers are not forced back, and as rod E is prevented from descending further, it simply moves upward against the tension of spring K as the cross-head continues its downward motion. A mechanism is provided for turning dial F one-half revolution, so that every bullet that is not pushed through the dial will be turned around with the pointed end foremost before it drops into the feed-tube G. This rotary motion of the dial is derived from a rack M attached to bracket L, and a pinion N with which the rack meshes. The location of the dial is governed by an index plate O and a plunger T which enters one of the notches in the index plate; the latter is attached to dial F. A clutch P (see also detailed sectional view) is fastened to sleeve R. Fiber friction washers S are used to prevent breakage in case anything unusual should happen.

When the cross-head descends, the rack M revolves the clutch in the direction shown by the arrow. When within one-quarter inch of the lower end of the stroke (this position is shown in the illustration), the rack *M* strikes lever *U* and disengages the index plunger *T*. The rack descends far enough to give it time on the return stroke to move dial *F* sufficiently to prevent the returning index plunger from reëntering the hole it just occupied.

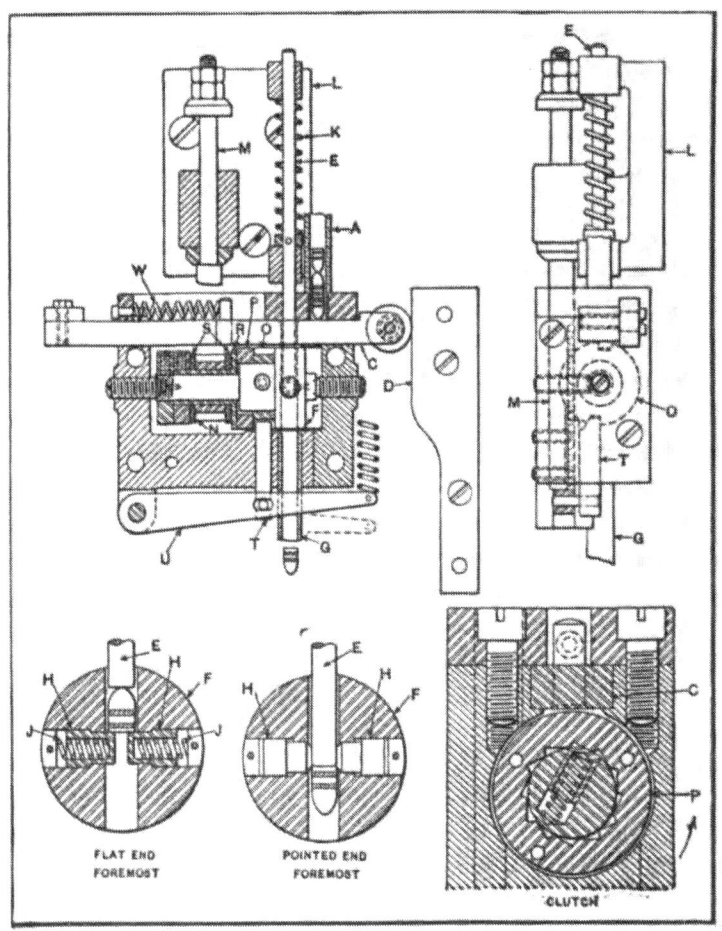

Fig. 7. Attachment for Hopper Feeding Mechanism which delivers all Bullets to a Dial Feed Plate with Pointed Ends Foremost

On the return stroke, the lost motion of the rack in its bracket provides time for the withdrawal of rod *E* before dial *F* is revolved. This lost motion can be adjusted so that the highest point of the upward stroke is reached just as dial *F* has turned

180 degrees, thus bringing the other index slot in line with plunger T. If the rack should move too high, the friction washers S will allow for this excess movement by slipping. This half revolution of dial F turns a bullet that is not pushed through it end for end, so that it drops down in the pipe G with the pointed end foremost. The slide C is returned for receiving another bullet from tube A by the action of spring W which holds the slide roller firmly against the cam-plate D.

Feeding Shells Successively and in Any Position. — A feeding mechanism designed to feed shells or cartridge cases one at a time and in any position is shown in Fig. 8. Owing to the weight of the heads of cartridge cases, they may readily be arranged upon a table heads downward, and the particular mechanism to be described is arranged for changing the shells from a vertical to a horizontal position before dropping them into a trough by means of which they are conveyed to the operating tools. The table A upon which the shells are placed is slightly inclined so that the shells readily slide towards a horizontal disk B which is rotated constantly by a belt and pulley. As the disk revolves, the shells are carried towards the funnel-shaped mouth of a guide-way C where there is a wheel D having teeth of irregular form. This wheel is revolved in the same direction as disk B so that it continually pushes back some of the shells and prevents jamming. The shells which move too near the center of disk B to enter the mouth of the guide-way are carried around until they meet the edge of an inclined fence E, which is just above the disk near the center, but is arched near the periphery so that shells can pass under it. This fence causes the shells to move out towards the circumference of disk B, so that they may enter the guide-way as they again come around.

Just beyond the wheel D there is a feed-wheel F which has teeth of regular form that fit between the cartridge cases. This wheel is rotated in the direction shown by the arrow, so as to feed the shells forward at a definite rate along the guide-way C. This guide-way, excepting at the mouth, is only slightly wider than the shell diameter, so that all the shells in it form a continuous and orderly row. The guide-way may be curved gradu-

294 MECHANICAL MOVEMENTS

ally in any direction, so that the shells which enter it with their axes vertical may be turned to any desired position as they pass along. As previously mentioned, the guide-way, in this case, changes from a vertical to a horizontal position. At the end of the guide-way there is a pair of stops that act alternately to allow one shell to issue at a time from the guide-way. The first stop consists of a pair of fingers G which rise up through the floor

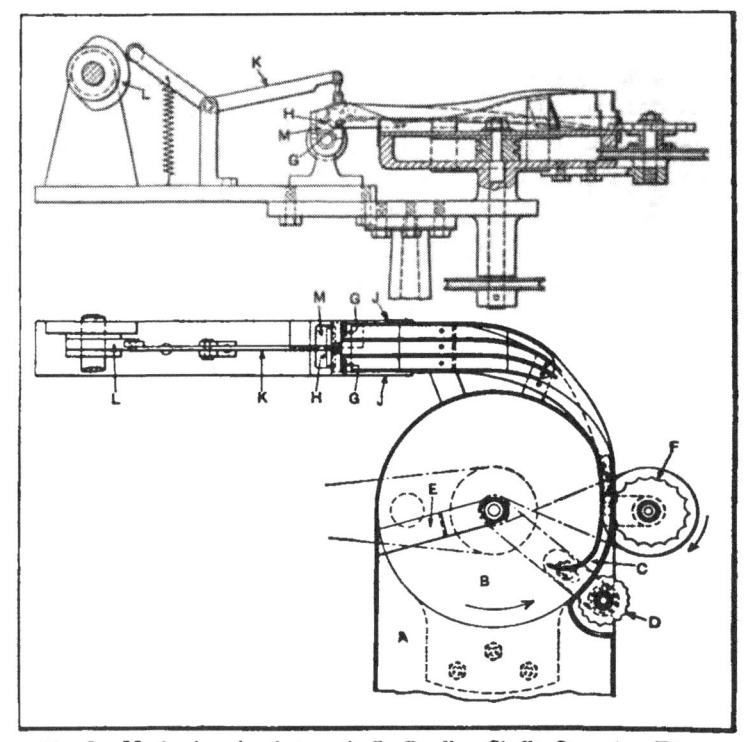

Fig. 8. Mechanism for Automatically Feeding Shells One at a Time

of the guide, and the second stop is in the form of a gate H which moves down in front of the foremost shell of the row. These two stops are carried on a pivoted frame J so arranged that, as the gate rises to allow the foremost shell to pass from the mouth of the tube, the fingers G rise in front of the second shell to hold back the whole row. The frame J is connected with a lever K which is intermittently rocked by the cam L. The successive shells drop into the trough M as they are discharged from the guide-way.

Feeding Shells Successively and Gaging the Diameters. — The mechanism described in the following is part of a cartridge-making machine, and its function is to feed cartridge cases or shells from a tube, one at a time, and provide means of detecting shells having heads that are over the standard diameter. The shells are placed heads downward onto a fixed table from which they are pushed by hand onto a revolving disk A, Fig. 9. This feed disk operates on the same general principle as the one illustrated in Fig. 8. As each successive shell passes from the guide-way of the revolving disk, it is placed directly over a push-rod B. This push-rod is pivoted to the end of a lever which is oscillated by a cam, thus causing the push-rod to move vertically through a guide C and through one of the slots D formed in the periphery of the feed disk A. Each time the push-rod B moves upward, it pushes a shell into the end of tube E. This tube has two gravity fingers F and, as the shell rises, its rim lifts these fingers and separates them far enough to allow the rim to pass; the fingers then drop back behind the rim and prevent the shell from falling when the push-rod recedes. When this push-rod makes the next successive stroke, the shell lifted by it pushes the first shell up into tube E which is bent over to form an arch and terminates at E_1.

When the vertical section of tube E is filled and the shells passed over the top of the arch, they fall open end first down into the vertical section E_1. Just below the end of tube E_1, there is a device for releasing the shells one at a time. This consists of a three-armed lever G, which is pivoted at H and is given an oscillating or rocking movement by vertical rod J having a roller in contact with cam K, against which the rod is held by a spring. As lever G oscillates, it withdraws, alternately, two fingers L and M which project into the passageway for the shells. These fingers are withdrawn against the tension of suitable springs and the upper one catches the cartridge shells by the rim, whereas the other one extends beneath the open end. When the upper finger is withdrawn, a shell drops against the lower

296   MECHANICAL MOVEMENTS

finger and, when the latter is withdrawn, this shell is released and, at the same time, the upper finger moves in and prevents the next successive shell from dropping out until it is released by the backward motion of finger L. As each successive shell drops, it passes through a gage N and then falls over one of the vertical pins O, which are equally spaced around the periphery of the machine table. This table is revolved intermittently in order

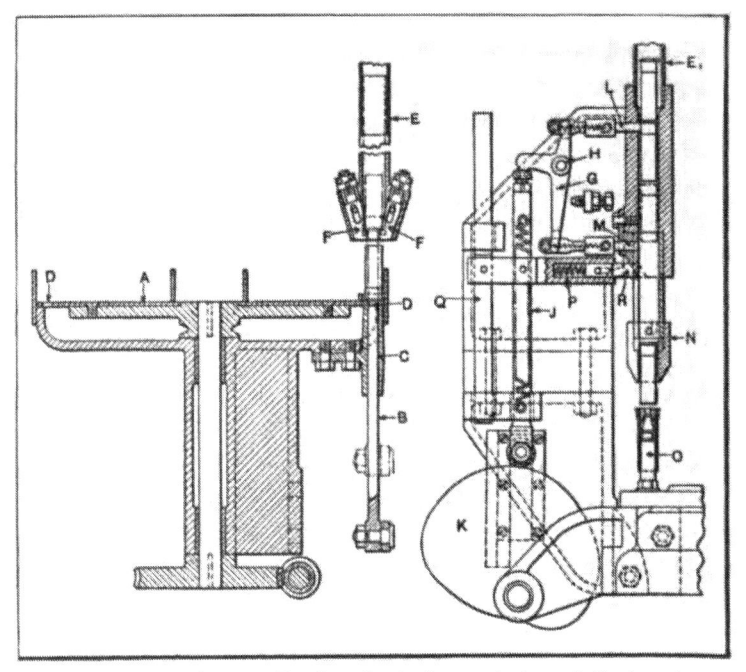

Fig. 9. Mechanism for Feeding Shells Successively and Gaging the Diameters

to locate the shells beneath a series of tools carried by a toolholder having a vertical reciprocating motion.

Attached to the rod J, there is a bar P the movements of which are steadied by a bar Q mounted in suitable guides The bar P carries a spring plunger R having a beveled end which engages a beveled surface as shown; consequently, as rod J and bar P are lifted by cam K, plunger R is pushed back far enough to clear the rim of the descending cartridge. When rod J

descends, however, plunger R moves inward and bears downward on the head of the cartridge beneath it, thus pushing it through the gage N and onto one of the series of pins O. If the rim of a cartridge should be so large that it would not readily pass through the gage, the resistance overcomes the tension of the spring that holds J into contact with the cam, and the cartridge remains in the gage until the next stroke of the machine. As the table moves around, the attendant will notice that there is a pin without a shell upon it and, therefore, he will remove the next successive shell, because, ordinarily, the shells are not so large as to resist being forced through the gage by a second stroke of the push-down bar P. If an exceptionally large head will not pass through the gage, the machine must be stopped and the shell removed by hand.

INDEX

	PAGE
Acceleration, meaning of	4
Accumulator mechanism of adding machine	175
Adding machine, device for protecting delicate mechanism	276
full-stroke mechanism	280
key controlling device	279
Adding mechanism, general principle of operation	172
Aeroplane motor, of revolving cylinder type	65
with revolving cylinders and eccentric track	66
Air springs or cushions of printing press bed	79
American or continuous system of rope transmission	29
Anchor or recoil escapement for clockwork	142
Angular velocity	5
Automatic clutches for power presses	242
Automatic control of reversing mechanism	112
Automatic relief mechanisms of forging machines	264
Automatic screw machine feeding attachments	281
Automatic speed-limiting devices for engines	267
Automatic variation in points of reversal	115
Automobile differential gearing	220
Backgearing, methods of arranging	44
Bands, flexible, use of, for transmitting motion	30
Barrel or cylinder cam	189
Bellcrank lever	8
Belts, reversing, mechanism for shifting open and crossed	107
use of, for transmitting power	28
use of open and crossed, for reversing motion	100
Bevel gearing	26
Bevel type of friction gearing	24
Bolt and rivet header relief mechanism	266
Brake and magnetic clutch combination	240
Brake, multiple disk combined with clutch	237
Breakable pins to prevent over-load	259
Brown & Sharpe multiple-disk speed-changing mechanism	53
Brown & Sharpe quick-return motion for screw machine	133
Brush wheel of friction gearing	23
Builder motion of a textile machine	115
Camera, claw mechanism of moving picture	143
Cam motion, automatic variation of	189
automatic variation of cam rise and drop	192

Cam motion, mechanism for varying dwell of follower	191
sectional cams for varying	194
Cams, arranged to vary rotary motion	196
definition of, and general application	22
double two-revolution shifting type	200
face or positive motion	185
for motion perpendicular to plane of cam	189
general classification of	184
having rectilinear motion	189
having yoke type of follower	187
in group engaged successively	197
obtaining resultant motion of several	198
plate	185
plate, arranged for positive motion	185
sectional, for varying motion	194
special, for returning follower	187
wiper and involute	188
Center-line of motion	8
Centrifugal and inertia governors	57
Centrifugal type of safety stop for gas engines	269
Chain and sprocket form of transmission	29
Chinese windlass, differential motion of	202
Claw mechanism of moving picture camera	143
Clutch control, variable by pattern chain	246
Clutches, automatic disengaging of, to prevent over-load	260
automatic power press, engaged by wedging action	244
automatic power press, of the key type	243
controlling motion by	231
friction	232
friction, multiple-disk type	235
friction, ring or plate type	234
induction type	241
magnetic, with automatic band clutch	240
multiple-disk equipped with automatic brake	237
of reversing mechanisms, methods of operating	101
pneumatically-operated multiple disk	236
that automatically disengage	242
trip for automatically disengaging	249
types of positive or toothed	231
type which expands radially	234
Clutch method of controlling speeds	46
Compound gearing	32
Compound train of epicyclic gearing	37
Concave friction disks and inclined intermediate wheel	55
Cone-pulley and epicyclic gear combination	44
Cone-pulley and spur gear combination	43
Cone-pulley drives, arrangement of	41
Connecting-rod and crank combination	60

CONSTRAINED — DRILLING

	PAGE
Constrained motion	2
Continuous motion	1
Continuous or American system of rope transmission	29
Controller, electromagnetic, for tripping mechanism	274
Crank and connecting-rod	60
Crank and epicyclic gear combination	86
Crank and oscillating link	124
Crank and slotted cross-head	63
Crank, application of, for reversing press bed motion	75
Crank mechanism for doubling stroke	68
Crank motion, for automatically varying the stroke	83
Crankpin and cross-head, relative motions of	61
Crankshaft of stationary type and revolving cylinders	65
Crosby straight-line motion for indicator	16
Cross-feeding movement, automatic reduction of	144
Cross-feed mechanism of grinding machine	139
Cross-head, motion relative to crankpin	61
Crown gear and shifting pinion for changing speeds	49
Curvilinear translation	3
Cycle of motions	6
Cylinder or barrel cam	189
Dead-beat or Graham escapement for clockwork	142
Dead-center positions of crank	60
Differential back-gear for varying speeds	45
Differential controlling mechanism of steering gear	213, 215
Differential feeding mechanism for revolving spindle	210
Differential gear and cam combination	223
Differential gearing, compound train for varying speeds	38, 206
of automobiles	220
speed regulation through	222
Differential governors for water turbines	217
Differential hoisting mechanism	227
Differential mechanism of gear-cutting machine	225
Differential motions	202
between screw and nut	208
from gearing	204
Differential or floating levers	211
substitute for	216
Differential speed indicator	229
Differential speed-reducing mechanism	38, 205
Disengaging mechanisms or clutches	230
Dividing mechanism, automatic	167
Diving key type of speed-changing mechanism	48
Double back-gears for lathes	44
Drawing press toggle mechanism	72
Drilling machine tripping mechanisms	250

DRIVE — FRICTION

	PAGE
Drive, positive	6
Drop-hammer lifting mechanism	93
Drop-hammer tripping mechanism	257
Eccentric	62
Eccentricity of an eccentric	63
Electromagnetic controller for tripping mechanism	274
Electromagnetic tripping devices	270
Electro-mechanical tripping device for textile machine	256
Elliptical gear and eccentric pinion for quick-return motion	130
Elliptical gearing, arranged for quick-return motion	128
use of, for modifying crank motion	70
Engine speed-limiting device	267
English or multiple system of rope transmission	29
Epicyclic gear and crank combination	86
Epicyclic gear and friction disk combination	56
Epicyclic gearing, action of, under different conditions	204
combined with cone-pulley	44
compound or reverted train	38, 206
for reversing motion	108
use of, for obtaining a rapid reciprocating movement	85
use of, on water turbine governors	217
Epicyclic gear trains	33
Escapements for controlling action of clockwork	141
Evan's friction cones for changing speeds	52
Face or positive motion cam	185
Feeding and reversing movements combined	111
Feeding bullets automatically with pointed ends foremost	290
Feeding mechanism, automatic, for handling separate pieces	281
automatic, for screw blanks	288
with automatic accelerating device	208
Feeding shells automatically with closed ends foremost	289
Feeding shells successively and gaging the diameters	295
Feeding shells successively and in any position	293
Flexible bands, use of, for transmitting motion	30
Floating or differential levers	211
substitute for	216
Fly frame, automatically varying point of reversal	115
mechanism for varying transverse movement of roving	83
Fly frame differential gearing	222
Force-closed mechanism	6
Forging machine, relief mechanisms	264
Frictional ratchet mechanisms	137
Frictional speed-changing devices	49
Friction clutches	232
multiple-disk type	235
ring or plate type	234

FRICTION — GRINDING

	PAGE
Friction clutches, type which expands radially	234
Friction disk and epicyclic gear combination	56
Friction gearing, double-cone and intermediate ring or belt type	52
double-cone and intermediate wheel type	51
factors affecting power transmitted by	25
having concave disks and inclined intermediate wheel	55
multiple-disk type for changing speeds	53
pressure varied according to load	263
transmission by	23
use of, for reversing motion	100
Full-stroke mechanism of adding machine	280
Gear and cone-pulley combinations	43
Gear and rack combination	67
Gear-cone and tumbler-gear mechanism	48
Gear-cones and sliding key for changing speeds	48
Gear-cutting machine, differential mechanism of	225
Geared speed-changing mechanisms	46
Gearing, compound	32
differential, of automobiles	220
elliptical, arranged for quick-return motion	128
epicyclic, action of, under different conditions	204
epicyclic, for obtaining rapid reciprocating motion	85
epicyclic, for reversing motion	108
for high-speed intermittent motion	148, 150
friction, factors affecting power transmitted by	25
friction, pressure varied according to load	263
intermittent	146
mangle or the Napier motion	81
ratchet type	134
toothed, various classes of	26
train of, for transmitting motion	31, 33
transmission by friction	23
transmission by toothed	26
worm, trip for automatically disengaging	249
Gears, calculating speeds	33
for uniformly intermittent motion	147
for variable intermittent motion	148
idler, effect on transmission of motion	32
trains of spur	32
Geneva wheel for intermittent motion	154
Governors, centrifugal and inertia	57
for water turbines, differential	217
Graham dead-beat escapement for clockwork	142
Grasshopper motion	14
Grinding machine, automatic cross-feed mechanisms	139, 144
reversing mechanism	102

	PAGE
Harmonic motion, definition of	64
Header, relief mechanism for bolt and rivet	266
Helical motion	3
Helical or spiral gearing	27
Herringbone gear	27
Hoist, action of differential chain	203
Hoisting mechanism, differential type	227
Hooke's coupling or universal joint	11
Hopper feeding mechanism for screw blanks	288
Humpage's gear for varying speeds	45
Idler gear, effect of, in epicyclic gear train	36
its effect on transmission of motion	32
Impulse face of an escapement pallet	142
Indexing and locking mechanism, combined	171
Indexing mechanism, automatic	167
of screw slotting machine	169
Indexing movement, Geneva wheel for	154
Indicator, pantograph reducing mechanism for	20
straight-line motions for	14
Induction clutch	241
Inertia and centrifugal governors	57
Intermittent bevel gears, locking device for	159
Intermittent gearing	146
designed for uniform rest periods	147
for shafts at right angles	157
rapid acting for moving picture projector	150
with swinging sector	153
Intermittent motion	1
automatic disengaging device	163
automatic variation of	164
constant, from variable motion	161
gearing for high speed	148, 150
gears for variable	148
Geneva wheel for	154
of moving picture projector	150
Intermittent movements	134
automatic reduction of	144
Intermittent rotary motion, two-speed	159
Inverse type of cam	188
Involute and wiper cams	188
Irregular motions	184
Key controlling device of adding machine	279
Lazy tongs or pantograph mechanism	20
Levers, application of	8
bellcrank	8

LEVERS — MOTION

	PAGE
Levers, complete stroke before return movement is possible	280
floating or differential	211
length of arms relative to fulcrum	11
position of, relative to center-lines of motion	10
Lifting mechanism of drop-hammer	93
Lifting toe or wiper cam	188
Link connection between rotating parts	11
Link mechanisms	7
Load-and-fire type of reversing mechanism	101
Load, pressure on friction gearing varied according to	263
prevention of excessive, on driven mechanism	259
Locking and indexing mechanism, combined	171
Locking device for intermittent bevel gearing	159
Loom, two-speed intermittent rotary motion for	159
Machine, factors affecting construction	1
Magazine feeding attachments for separate pieces	281
Magnetic clutch equipped with automatic band brake	240
Mangle gearing or the Napier motion	81
Mechanism, factors affecting construction	1
trains of	30
Miehle press bed motion	75
Milling machine feed mechanism with accelerating device	208
Miter gearing	27
Motion, center-line of	8
classes of	1
constrained	2
continuous	1
curvilinear translation	3
differential	202
for press bed, elliptical gear drive	69
general methods of transmitting	7
helical	3
intermittent	1, 134
irregular	184
lever reducing, for taking indicator cards	9
mechanism for automatically varying reciprocating	83
of crankpin relative to cross-head	61
of Miehle flat bed or cylinder presses	75
of press bed reversed by reciprocating pinions	79
of press bed, the Napier	81
plane	2
quick-return	124
reciprocating	1
rectilinear translation	3
spherical	4
straight-line	12
straight-line for steam engine indicators	14

	PAGE
Motion, straight-line, Peaucellier	17
straight-line, Scott Russell	13
sun-and-planet	38
Motor drives, reversing	122
Motor of revolving cylinder type	65
Moving picture camera claw mechanism	143
Moving picture projector, intermittent motion of	150
Mowing machine, wabble gear for driving cutter-bar	85
Multiple-disk clutches	235
equipped with automatic brake	237
pneumatically-operated design	236
Multiple-disk type of speed-changing mechanism	53
Multiple or English system of rope transmission	29
Napier motion for printing press beds	81
One-cycle type of drive for cold header	72
Over-load, prevention of, by automatically disengaging clutch	260
prevention of, by breakable pins	259
Pallet of an escapement	142
Pantograph mechanisms	19
Pattern chain for operating clutches	246
Pawl, multiple type for ratchet gearing	136
of ratchet gearing	134
rectilinear motion from revolving	91
Peaucellier straight-line motion	17
Pendulum, effect of arc of swing on time	141
Period of a cycle of motions	6
Pins, use of breakable to prevent over-load	259
Piston with traversing and rotating movements	95
Pitch circle of spur gearing	26
Plane motion	2
Planer feed or crank disks	161
Planer reversing mechanism	107
Planetary gearing, action of, under different conditions	204
compound train for varying speeds	38, 206
for reversing motion	108
use of, on water turbine governors	217
Planetary gear trains	33
Plate cam	185
arranged for positive motion	185
Pneumatically-operated multiple-disk clutch	236
Positive driving	6
Positive motion or face cam	185
Power moving picture projector, intermittent motion for	150
Power press clutches	242
Press bed motion, for flat bed or cylinder presses	75

PRESS — RESULTANT

	PAGE
Press bed motion, having elliptical gear drive	69
reversed by reciprocating pinions	79
the Napier	81
Projector, intermittent motion of moving picture	150
Pulley speeds, method of calculating	31
Pump piston with combined rectilinear and rotary movements	95
Punch press clutches	242
Quick-return motions	124
crank and oscillating link	124
derived from elliptical gearing	128
eccentric pinion and elliptical gear type	130
independent crank-operated type	133
modification of Whitworth	127
Whitworth	126
Rack and gear combination	67
Rack and worm drive	74
Rack, double, and shifting gear for reversing motion	75
Racks and pinion arranged for doubling stroke	69
Radian, definition of	5
Rapid starting and stopping clutch and brake mechanism	237
Ratchet gearing	134
arranged for reversal of motion	136
automatic disengagement of	139
double action type	137
methods of varying motion derived from	137
operated by multiple pawl	136
Ratchet mechanism, for releasing sprockets	138
of frictional type	137
which controls a reversing mechanism	117
which reverses automatically	110
Ratio, velocity	5
Reciprocating motion	1
mechanism for automatically varying	83
rapid, from epicyclic gearing	85
Reciprocating slide, withdrawing from working position	90
Recoil or anchor escapement for clockwork	142
Rectilinear and rotary motions, conversion of	60
Rectilinear and rotary movements combined	95
Rectilinear motion, from epicyclic gear and crank combination	86
from revolving pawls	91
mechanism for varying	92
Rectilinear translation	3
Reducing motion, lever, for taking indicator cards	9
pantograph type	19
Relief mechanisms for forging machines	264
Resultant motion of cams, mechanism for obtaining	198

	PAGE
Return cam for follower	187
Reversal of motion, by reciprocating pinions	79
with ratchet gearing	117, 136
Reversing and feeding movements combined	111
Reversing clutches, methods of operating	101
Reversing mechanisms	97
arranged to vary point of reversal automatically	115
automatic control of	112
automatic ratchet type	110
load-and-fire type	101
of epicyclic or planetary gear type	108
of grinding machine	102
of two-speed bevel gear type	99
special methods of controlling point of reversal	105
which reverses after given number of revolutions	117
Reversing motion, by bevel gear and clutch combination	98
by double rack and shifting gear	75
by means of friction disks	100
by means of open and crossed belts	100
by means of spur gears	97
Reversing motor drives	122
Reversing screw, applications of	74
Reverted or compound train of epicyclic gearing	37
Revolution counter for controlling point of reversal	117
Rotary and rectilinear motions, conversion of	60
Rotary and rectilinear movements combined	95
Rotary motion varied by means of cam	196
Safety device, breakable-pin type to prevent over-load	259
for limiting speed of engines	267
for protecting a delicate mechanism	276
which disengages clutch to prevent over-load	260
Safety relief mechanism of forging machines	264
Scotch yoke or slotted cross-head and crank	63
Scott Russell straight-line motion	13
Screw, applications of reversing	74
having differential motion relative to nut	208, 213
use of, for transmitting motion	22
Sellers worm and rack drive	74
Shaper, driving mechanism for crank	124
Skew bevel gearing	27
Sliding key type of speed-changing mechanism	48
Slotted cross-head and crank	63
Speed-changing and controlling mechanisms	39
Speed-changing mechanisms, all-geared	46
frictional	49
multiple-disk type	53
types of mechanical	41